A Collector's Identification and Value Guide

$14.⁹⁵

North American
Indian
Artifacts

4th Edition
By Lar Hothem

BOOKS AMERICANA

ISBN-0-89689-085-6

DEDICATION

TO THE North American Indian artisans of whatever time and place—And to the collectors of today who value what they made.

AUTHOR'S NOTE: Due to the widely changing values of gold and silver, the Jewelry section will be much higher than listed; original information was based on gold at $225 per oz., silver at $6 per oz.

ACKNOWLEDGEMENTS

It is the usual practice for a writer to thank those for without whose help the book could not have been completed. For this project, the writer acknowledges over fifty persons, without whose assistance and encouragement the book would not have gone beyond the early stages of research.

This is not the definitive book on all American Indian collectibles and their values, for such will never be compiled by anyone. It is, however, as comprehensive as possible, including many examples both common and rare.

The book is also authoritative, for many of the contributors are highly knowledgeable and experienced in their respective fields— as will be obvious on even a casual reading. The book, in short, goes far beyond single-individual approach and comprehension.

The persons who provided photographs from private collections are thanked, and their photographs and valuations appear throughout the book. They are, in each case, credited to the sender. The extent of individual contributions, and my thanks, will be evident.

However, there were some who made available photographs that were outstanding in both quantity and quality. They are: John W. Barry, Tom Browner, H. Jackson Clark, Kenneth R. Canfield, Marguerite Kernaghan, Harvey and Rose King, Wayne Parker, Bill Post, and Summers Redick.

Thanks also to Howard Popkie and Robert C. Calvert, for an extended look at some scarce Canadian artifacts. In some cases, collectors and dealers had professionals photograph items, and thanks for that fine work.

A number of institutional or governmental sources were drawn upon for excellent photographs of historic significance. These illustrate a variety of scenes, from contemporary activities to prehistoric ruins. They are:

Florida Division of Tourism
National Photography Collection, Public Archives of Canada
Nebraska State Historical Society, John A. Anderson Collection
South Dakota State Historical Society
Photography Collection, Suzzallo Library, University of
   Washington
U.S. Department of the Interior, National Park Service
Utah State Historical Society, Collection of Smithsonian
   Institution

Thanks are due, very much so, to the various Indian art galleries and dealers that kindly permitted reprinting. This was of descriptions and prices of selected artifacts and artworks from their catalogs and listings. They are:

W.J. Crawford, The Americana Galleries, Phoenix, Arizona
James O. Aplan, Midland, South Dakota
Pierre and Sylvia Bovis, Winona Indian Trading Post, Santa Fe, New Mexico
Kenneth R. Canfield, Plains Indian Art, Kansas City, Missouri
Barry Hardin, Crazy Cow Trading Post, Denison, Texas
Hyde's, Santa Fe, New Mexico
Sam and Nancy Johnson, Caddo Trading Company and Gallery, Murfreesboro, Arkansas
Manitou Gallery, Cheyenne, Wyoming
Armand Ortega, Indian Ruins Trading Post, Sanders, Arizona
R.G. Munn, Whispering Pines Gallery, La Mesa, California

Other specialty listings were used, and are noted and credited throughout the book.

Thanks are due also to auction houses which allowed item descriptions from catalogs and results from bid-sheets. Appreciation to:

Tom King and Tom Porter, Garth's Auctions, Inc., Stratford Road, Delaware, Ohio
Jan Sorgenfrei, Painter Creek Auction Service, Lima, Ohio
Rod Sauvageau, Trade Winds West Auction Gallery, Portland, Oregon

Various private collectors sent thorough descriptions of items, placing a fair market value on some of their prize specimens. Very special thanks, also, to those who went considerably out of their way to provide detailed chapter introductions, namely: Tom Browner (Bannerstones), Dick Weatherford (Baskets), and John Barry (Pottery).

Respects to several gentlemen who contributed literature and all possible help on the Federal level. Robert G. Hart, General Manager, Indian Arts and Crafts Board, U.S. Department of the Interior, Washington, D.C., gave personal help and literature. Also, Charles Dailey, Museum Director, Institute of American Indian Arts (Bureau of Indian Affairs, U.S. Department of the Interior), Santa Fe, New Mexico, for pertinent literature and personal help. Further, to Lloyd New, former Director of the Institute of American Indian Arts, for his excellent summary regarding the state of Indian Art.

Acknowledgement goes to Jean Herzegh, Executive Director of the Indian Arts and Crafts Association, this in two directions. First for literature and reprint permission, and second, for personal correspondence that aided greatly in an area of sensitive coverage.

Thanks further to the firm of Sotheby, Parke, Bernet, Inc., New York City, for superb research materials, covering some of the finest Amerind artworks ever made. Also to Charles E. Hanson, Jr., Director of the Museum of the Fur Trade, Chadron, Nebraska, for valuable suggestions.

Ultimate gratitude to Sue McClurg Hothem, who assisted in suggestions, paperwork and fine moral support throughout. And the same to Adena and Hopewell, for understanding. Deep thanks to Ronald E. Hothem, Attorney-at-Law, San Francisco, for legal counsel in several areas of importance.

Lar Hothem

TODAY, AMERICAN INDIAN ART RIDES AT THE PINNACLE OF APPRECIATION. WORKS WHICH ONLY A DECADE OR TWO AGO WERE VIEWED GENERALLY AS THE CURIOUS OUTPUT OF AMERICA'S ABORIGINAL WAGON TRAIN RAIDERS HAVE SUDDENLY BEEN ACCORDED SUPER-STATUS. THIS PHENOMENAL RISE IN ACCEPTANCE IS MANIFEST IN THE VIRTUAL CRAZE ON THE PART OF THE PUBLIC FOR INDIAN ARTS AND CRAFTS TODAY, NOT ONLY IN TRADITIONAL MODES, BUT IN INNOVATIVE STYLES AS WELL. INDIAN ARTS AND CRAFTS ARE NOW TREATED WITHIN THE SAME ELITIST EXHIBITION AND MARKETING CHANNELS AS THOSE PREVIOUSLY RESERVED FOR THE FINEST ART FROM OTHER SOURCES THROUGHOUT THE WORLD.

From *One With The Earth*, catalog of the Traveling Exhibit; by Lloyd New, Director, Institute of American Indian Arts, Bureau of Indian Affairs, Santa Fe, New Mexico.

INTRODUCTION

Fascination with things American Indian is deeply ingrained in our culture. It began with childhood games, Cowboys and Indians. It is continually reinforced by advertising symbols, company names, movies, television, everyday conversation.

No American needs to ask the meaning of these phrases: "Burying the hatchet"; "Smoke the peacepipe"; "Indian Summer". And how many low-ranking military personnel have complained about "Two many chiefs, not enought Indians"? The American Indian or Amerind presence is everywhere, and a healthy part of our national existence.

This partly explains the present fascination with objects made by Indians. There are today probably well over one million persons who collect Indian goods or are in other ways involved in this vast area.

There are certain characteristics of Amerind collectibles. One is that they are almost always made from natural materials and substances, whether plant, animal or mineral. Another is that all, or almost all, of the work required to complete the object is done by hand, slowly and carefully.

Yet another characteristic is workstyle, with the object being shaped into a form familiar to the Amerind lifeways. It is decorated, if at all, with designs that have their origin in the timeless North American past.

The essence of the Amerind art form — be it utensil, tool, weapon, ornament, whatever — is uniqueness. For all authentic pieces there was, and is, no such "improvement" as assembly-line mass production. And no two objects are ever totally alike, no matter how much they may resemble one another. The pieces are as varied as the individuals that made them; each is a sole creation.

Perhaps still another hallmark of Amerind works, and one that appeals highly to collectors, is the "utility-plus" factor. A great percentage of Amerind objects were made far better than necessary to merely complete a task. Much loving skill and attention to detail were added.

Amerind art and artifacts have long been admired and collected in European countries and elsewhere. Americans, pioneer and recent, have largely failed to understand or appreciate the field. Only within the last few years has there been a broad groundswell of interest and attention, but Americans have now begun to accept good Amerind material as good art.

Native American art, sometimes primitive, sometimes amazingly sophisticated, has gone (in regard to marketability) far beyond the flash and fad stages. It has become a major field to be in, a heritage to be knowledgeable about, **the** collectibles to have. Some preliminary explanations and comments are in order. There are terms used throughout this Guide that are important. "Prehistoric" means before-writing, or the arrival of Europeans to record events. Prehistoric also means cultural items designed by Amerinds alone, without ideological contamination from European sources and generally this means all human-occupied North American time **before** about AD 1500.

"Historic", as used here, means heavy cultural contact with Europeans and Russians, in a time zone broadly ranging from AD 1500 to AD 1900. "Recent", is here considered to be from 1900 to 1970. "Contemporary" indicates years from 1970 to the present. These time-zones are open to debate, but if the meaning is clear they remain sufficient and descriptive.

This book is a **Guide** to American Indian Collectibles and their values. It identifies and describes major collecting areas available today. Representative prices, or close price ranges, are accurately given.

It should be noted that the listed value — whether for item description or photograph — is not an ultimate valuation. It does not usually constitute an offer to sell. It does not represent an appraisal. Instead, it is judged by the possesser to be a fair market value.

To a certain extent, the chapter lengths reflect the quantity of that sort of American Indian material available to the collector. It is to a degree a guide to the amount of material on the market.

For example, for every, say, presentation-grade pipe tomahawk, there are many thousand flint projectile points. For every Plains Indian beaded dress in ultra-fine condition, there are hundreds of other beaded clothing items, more available and less expensive.

Don't be upset by what may seem to be high prices; don't feel that American Indian items are beyond your financial reach. A major and long-term effort has been made, for this book, to secure listings and photographs of some of the top collector pieces in North America. They are here for your study.

These are very good examples, for the most part, of material you will see and have the opportunity to purchase. Bargains can still be picked up at auctions, flea markets and antique shops, providing you know what you are looking at and have some idea of the market value.

And while the Guide should be a general help in acquiring good pieces at reasonable prices, there is yet no substitute for personal knowledge and experience. The more you know about what you decide to collect, the better will be your Amerind collection.

LH

Key to letters preceding price figures: The source
  A) Auction
  C) Collector
  D) Dealer
  G) Gallery

TABLE OF CONTENTS

Consider the value of knowing Indian Collectibles values:

A rancher finds a prehistoric flint artifact which a neighbor tells him is incomplete because it does not have notches. The rancher sells it for $10, which is about what the neighbor tells him it is worth. Later, the rare Paleo-period fluted-base point is sold for $175.

A box of old costume jewelry in an antique shop attracts the attention of a buyer at $12.50. Among the items is a heavy trade-era silver beaver-shaped pendant and a handful of glass trade beads. Once a necklace, the set is now insured at $500.

A man at a Midwestern farm auction pays a few dollars for what the auctioneer called "an old hatchet". It is that and more. The collector who now owns the late-1700's pipe-tomahawk with original handle has twice refused offers of $600 or over.

A "musty old leather thing" is *donated* to a cheritable organization and passes through several hands. The last owner refuses to part with the piece; it is a fine Plains Indian pipebag with exquisite bead and quillwork designs. It is valued, conservatively, at $950, because there was also a genuine two-piece pipe inside.

An old Indian weaving is obtained for a nominal sum at a flea market. A knowledgeable dealer and collector is intrigued; he flies halfway across the country to take a look. He obtains the item, a fine late-phase Chiefs' blanket worth many thousand dollars.

ALLARD AUCTION

Col. Doug Allard, Flathead Indian and well-known auctioneer of Amerind material, presided over the latest auction featuring 1265 fine Indian-related lots. (The Allard catalogs alone have become collector items.) Some 90-plus listings and eight photographs (by Debra J. Allard) are reprinted here, by permission of the Allards.

In-depth coverage is accorded these objects for several reasons. One is the high quality of the items, most being in the advanced-collector category. Another is the great range of artifacts, from many tribes, geographic regions and time-periods. This provides a broad-spectrum look at Amerind works.

Criteria used to select objects for inclusion here included: Types collectors will likely encounter, unusual pieces, or those which due to rarity are not covered elsewhere in this book. All listings included here would of course carry the "A" designation.

My sincere thanks to the Allards for permission to reprint selected auction results from this event. For those wishing further information, the address is: Col. Doug Allard, P.O. Box 460, St. Ignatius, Montana, 59865. Phone is (406) 745-2951.

Kwakiutl mask, 20th Century, carved and painted cedar "Wolf" dance mask with movable lower jaw, 6 X 16 inches. $650

Hopi Kachina, ca. 1900, unusual bird form with elaborate costume in crouching dance position, 8 X 9 inches. $950

Sioux vest, ca. 1900, choice full beaded sinew-sewn child's vest, classic Sioux geometric designs, 11 X 14 inches. $1100

Tlingit spoon, ca. 1900, fine carved Mountain goat and Mountain sheep horn spoon with shell inlay, 1½ X 7 inches. $500

Navajo necklace, ca. 1970, huge and unusual squash blossom with inlaid Indian heads on blossoms and naja, 18 inches long. $950

Sioux painted robe, ca. 1870, very old painted cow-hide with sunburst design, from old South Dakota collection, 60 X 78 inches. $2500

Navajo necklace, ca. 1925, very old all silver squash blossom in the classic old tradition, 15 inches long. $300

Blackfoot knife case, ca. 1910, large hide case with cutout, brass tacks and beaded geometric designs, 5½ X 14 inches. $450

NW Coast cradle, ca. 1975, rare carved wooden baby carrier with birds, fish and humans, signed Charlie Mickey, 34 inches by 3 feet. $500

Navajo rug, ca. 1925, heavy old J.B. Moore floor rug with geometric designs, 48 X 78 inches. $400

Crow mirror bag, ca. 1880, very rare sinew-sewn mirror bag, both sides fully beaded, red stroud straps with brass military buttons, silk-wrapped long buffalo fringe, 47 inches by 5 feet. $2200

Catlinite pipe, 20th Century, red Catlinite "T" bowl in the form of a striking rattlesnake with fangs, 5 X 8½ inches. $300

Yurok purse, 20th Century, carved elk antler container for Yurok "Money" dentallium, geometric designs, 2 X 5 inches. $250

Kiowa dress, ca. 1935, large classic buckskin dress with very elaborate beaded designs and with fringe and tin cone drops. $800

Yurok basket, ca. 1900, superfine round twined basketry bowl with crisp red and black geometric designs, 5 X 6 inches. $900

Navajo bola, ca. 1940, ornate silver bola tie with two carved bear claws, two turquoise stones and silver tips, 3 X 4 inches. $225

Navajo belt, 20th Century, huge silver concho belt with five conchos and six butterflies, each set with single turquoise stone, 4½ X 43 inches. $650

Navajo rug, ca. 1943, huge rug with colorful serrated design, 7 feet by 11 feet 6 inches. $2500

Cheyenne moccasins, ca. 1890, classic full-beaded sinew-sewn moccasins with dusty pink background, geometric beadwork, 4 X 11 inches. $1000

Sioux bag, ca. 1880, old buffalo hide bag sewn with sinew and decorated with ribbon quillwork, 8 X 9 inches $350

Crow saddle, buffalo hide covered sinew-sewn, 11 X 18 inches. $550

Haida powder flask, ca. 1880, rare old carved horn powder flask with brass trim, beautiful, 3 X 8 inches. $700

Potowatamie sash, ca. 1900, fantastic finger-woven beaded sash with braided wool and beaded drops, a true museum piece, 5 X 35 inches. $2200

Navajo rug, ca. 1964, huge Ganado Red rug with geometric designs, 6 ft. 8 in. by 9 ft. 3 inches. $3700

Salish feast dish, 1979, huge carved cedar ceremonial feast bowl in eagle and whale form, signed by the famous Simon Charlie, rare; 15 X 38 inches. $750

Apache basket, ca. 1900, tightly coiled Jicarilla Apache basketry bowl with red and green diamond designs, 5 X 17 inches. $400

Red Star pottery, ca. 1975, carved black miniature pot with bear on each side, signed and dated, 2¼ x 2½ inches. $700

Cheyenne moccasins, ca. 1910, fully beaded sinew-sewn hide moccasins with geometric designs, 4 X 11 inches. $650

Wasco basket, ca. 1860, very rare old figured Wasco "Sally" bag with horse and deer all around, 6 X 8 inches. $1300

Zuni fetish pot, ca. 1940, choice turquoise encrusted fetish pot with choice old animal fetishes attached, rare, 4½ x 7½ inches. $250

Navajo belt, ca. 1935, classic "Old Pawn" Navajo silver concho belt with conchos, six butterflies and a buckle, all set with turquoise stones, 3 X 43 inches. $1200

Haida hook, 20th Century, beautiful carved wooden halibut hook depicting a fish and two animals, 5 X 9 inches. $550

Hupa basket, ca. 1910, huge twined storage basket with lid and with crosses and geometric designs; true museum piece and 12 X 14 inches. $2750

Menomenee bandolier, ca. 1880, very fine old and rare fully beaded shoulder bag with intricate geometric and floral designs and beaded tabs, 9 X 38 inches. $1950

Tlingit ivory, 20th Century, rare carved ivory Shaman's hairpiece with totemic carving and abalone inlay, 1 X 4¼ inches. $600

Indian photograph, ca. 1887, original signed Wm. Natman brown tone photo of an Indian woman in front of tepee, 7 X 9 inches. $200

Nez Perce saddlebags, ca. 1880, classic throwover saddlebags, fully beaded on elk hide with red flannel and pony bead trim; long buffalo fringe, 14 X 120 inches. $3000

Northern Plains pipe, 20th Century, pewter-inlaid black stone "T" bowl with long beaded and tacked "Puzzle" stem, 3 X 5 X 25 inches. $700

Maria pottery, ca. 1965, larger highly polished black bowl signed Maria Poveka (Maria Martinez' Indian name), 4 X 6 inches. $1300

Leekya fetish, ca. 1940, large brown bear fetish with wrap by Leekya Dycee; from the C.G. Wallace collection, 2 X 3 X 5 inches. $300

Pueblo moccasins, ca. 1900, very rare old Pueblo high-top moccasins with hard soles, 3 X 10 X 15 inches. $600

Treaty medal, ca. 1795, rare oval silver Treaty medal with book showing a picture on the cover, 3 X 4 inches. $1800

Pendleton blanket, ca. 1910, antique Pendleton "Cayuse" Indian trade blanket, 58 X 66 inches. $750

Crow club, 20th Century, beautiful brass-tacked "Gunstock" war club with fine beaded drop that looks older than the club, 9 X 34 inches. $1050

Apache basket, ca. 1910, tightly coiled basketry bowl with red and black diamond and line designs, 3 X 11 inches. $1300

Hopi snake, ca. 1935, very rare Hopi carved wooden snake and stand, a Kiva Snake Dance piece, 12 X 19 inches. $400

Peace medal, ca. 1878, round sterling silver Ulysses S. Grant Presidential medal, 3 in. in diameter. $450

Cheyenne drape, ca. 1900, buffalo hide saddle drape with geometric beadwork and long fringe, 13 X 24 inches. $1300

Chippewa outfit, ca. 1920, beaded yoke, mini-skirt, cuffs and leggings, size eight. $900

Indian doll, ca. 1930, Northern Plains male doll with beaded war shirt and leggings, with human hair, 6 X 9 inches. $200

Zuni belt, ca. 1930, rare old Zuni inlay "Knife Wing" dancer concho belt, 3 X 32 inches. $2500

Plateau bag, ca. 1935, rectangular full-beaded bag with eagle and flag on one side and two mountain lions on the other, 9 X 15 inches. $300

Tlingit dagger, ca. 1900, rare totemic carved ivory head and hand-hammered steel blade, 2 X 13 inches. $450

Ute tobacco bag, ca. 1860, classic Ute tobacco bag, sinew-sewn beadwork on yellow ochred antelope hide; hawk bells and long, painted fringe, 5½ X 24 inches. $800

Wasco Sally bag, ca. 1890, very rare polychrome Wasco pictorial Sally bag depicting deer, mountain sheep and birds, 5 X 8 inches. $2500

Cheyenne breastplate, ca. 1870, early bone and brass bead breastplate, completely original, a rare Plains warrior item with great patina, 14 X 18 inches. $2200

Flathead war shirt, ca. 1885, the finest Plateau shirt Col. Allard has seen. Deer-hide with fringe and cutouts and painted medicine sumbols, beaded strips, ermine and human hair along with a photo of Chief Little Martin wearing the shirt in the 1920s, large size. $16,000

Zuni bola, ca. 1940, choice Zuni inlay "Rainbow Man" bola tie with matching tips, 2 X 3½ inches. $1100

Bandolier bag, 19th Century, medicine man Potowatomi or Winnebago bandolier bag, bayeta apron window on reverse shows fine line; museum-mounted and framed, 19 X 38 inches. $1100

Navajo concho, ca. 1950, beautiful old concho belt with eight conchos and nine butterflies, all set with a turquoise stone, 37 inches long. $800

Paiute basket, ca. 1922, beautiful old Washo/Paiute beaded basket made by Ida, document from the Emporium Company, 3¾ X 7¼ inches. $2100

Tsimshian mask, ca. 1989, finely carved and painted Niska woman with labret mask, 8 X 11 inches. $300

Cree pipe bag, ca. 1890, fine Plains Cree hide bag with fringe and floral and geometric sinew-sewn beaded designs, 5 X 26 inches. $1100

Crow necklace, ca. 1890, twelve old buffalo teeth strung on cobalt blue Peking glass trade beads, 26 inches long. $450

Stone vessel, prehistoric, rare greenish-grey stone cup with handle, found on the Wind River reservation in Wyoming in 1915, 3 X 4 X 6 inches. $400

Eskimo ivory carving, kayak containing a man and two seals, 2 X 7 inches. $185

Hupa basket, ca. 1890, very old twined cooking basket with rock-burns in bottom and parallel zig-zag designs, 8 X 13 inches. $600

Sioux club, ca. 1870, very old rawhide-wrapped stone club with horse-tail suspensions, 2 X 31 inches. $400

Apache basket, ca. 1920, choice coiled basketry bowl with framed human figures all around, 3 X 13 inches. $2200

Eskimo mask, ca. 1900, beautifully carved and painted wooden ceremonial face mask, 6½ x 9 inches. $600

Nez Perce dress, ca. 1900, beautiful white buckskin dress with fully beaded yoke in geometric and heart design, medium size. $900

Northwest Coast rattle, ca. 1940, polychrome painted Northwest Coast rattle, face image, with good patina. $500

Haida dish, ca. 1920, carved wooden "Frog" bowl with dentallium and bed inlay, 4 X 5 X 11 inches. $410

Peace medal, ca. 1789, round silver George Washington peace medal attached to old bone and bead choker, medal 3 in. in diameter. $700

Navajo rug, ca. 1940, huge vegetable dye rug with a beautiful soft cornstalk design, size 71 X 108 inches. $2000

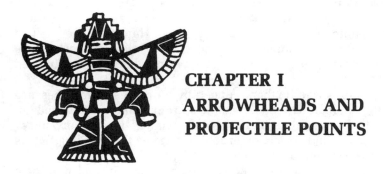

CHAPTER I
ARROWHEADS AND
PROJECTILE POINTS

The small chipped points of ancient times are among the most collectible of Amerind artifacts. They exist in one form or another over all of North America, and many types are still very reasonably priced.

Projectile points — the term means both arrowheads and lanceheads — are often the earliest signs of humans on the land. It has long been agreed that people came from Asia, via the Bering Straits, in excess of 20,000 years ago.

Some of the flint artifacts, including those found by archeologists along the Alaskan Pipeline right-of-way, may be even older. Such chipped tools and weapons may well be the oldest cultural debris in The Americas.

The much-admired fluted-base points are up to 11,000 years old, though related varieties were made until about 5000 or 6000 BC. Points were chipped until the coming of European Whites, the Metal People, when iron and steel points were either traded or made from White-supplied materials.

Until about AD 500, the chief weapon in North America was the Atl-atl, a hand-held wooden lance-thrower, itself a very rare item today. It acted as an extension of the human arm, providing leverage, flinging the lance or javelin further and harder. Many of the existing prehistoric lances had a short and thin foreshaft. This was apparently left in the target animal, and the valuable feather-vaned main shaft was retrieved.

It is not always easy to tell the difference between a lancehead and an arrowhead. One guideline is that most lanceheads **average** about 2 in. (50 mm) in length, and ½ in. (12 mm) between basal notches. Arrowheads tend to be closer 1 in. (25 mm) or slightly longer, and be about ¼ in. (7 mm) between basal notches. Arrowheads are also proportionately thinner and much lighter in weight than the typical Atl-atl point.

1

Projectile points were made by various chipping processes, by controlled blows that flaked off unwanted material. Bone and antler chipping rods and billets were used. Hammerstones helped create the rough blank. Then, percussion flaking worked the material into a preform, similar in size and shape to the finished artifact.

The preform was further reduced by a process called pressure flaking, which added basal notches, retouched and evened all edges. Final steps might include basal grinding, when sharp lower edges were dulled. This was probably done so that binding thongs of sinew were not cut through.

Many different types of material could be chipped, most of them being classed as "crypto-crystalline quartz". This includes the common names, flint, chalcedony, chert, jasper, and so on, many with regional names. Obsidian — natural volcanic glass — was widely used, especially in Western areas.

Other materials were used, like petrified wood (Southwest), agatized coral (Southeast) and many types of quartz (Eastern). Even though brittle, the better grades of material are extremely hard. Many varieties will actually scratch plate glass.

Determinants of point value to both dealer and collector involve over half a dozen factors. Size is important, with a larger point being worth comparatively more than a smaller point, other factors assumed equal. Material is a key element; dull and coarse quartzes are less admired than higher, more nearly pure grades. Color is important, with some collectors preferring bold or subtle hues.

Workstyle means the manner in which any one projectile point was fashioned. Desirable qualities would be the thinness and uniformity of the finished point, plus the number and regularity of pressure-chipping scars. Workstyles range from poor to superb, with an infinite number of in-between grades.

Condition of the point refers to any damage sustained by the piece, no matter when such damage occurred. For example, many points being picked up today show the typical sharp-edged breaks caused by agricultural equipment and construction machinery.

Even minor damage can detract greatly from point value, though each instance is of course judged by itself. Perfect specimens are the most avidly sought and command the higher values.

Point type — there are close to 400 regional main and sub-group point varieties in North America — is a determinate of value, with many collectors willing to pay more for a variety that they admire. One key factor here could be called "intricacy", meaning the delicate and accurate chipping skill evidenced by the point. Examples might be an obsidian fluted Paleo point from the Pacific

Northwest, or the rare Midwestern fractured-base point. The last, by the way, refers to a manufacturing technique, not damage.

The final two value determinants are related. One is the "mirror-image" examination, and simply means how much the point obverse resembles the reverse. Or, are both point sides or faces pretty much the same? If there are startling differences in chipping patterns or one side has areas "bare" of chipping (from the original crypto-crystalline material from which the point was made) this lowers the value. Both faces, in short, should show extensive, similar and good workmanship.

Symmetry, as the writer uses the term, means the degree to which one face, one side of the point resembles the other. Looking at either the left or right side there should be visual "balance".

All the determinants add up to a quality, that can be called esthetics — how pleasing the point is in an artistic sense. While collectors will place different weight on the various determinants, all or most will be considered in regard to collector desirability, hence value.

Fakes are a real problem today. And the person who believes that only the ancients could chip flint well is likely to be surprised at the skill with which modern points are being turned out. There are many ways to tell good (original) points from the bad, but the beginner is advised to purchase only from reputable dealers or collectors with authentic material. And if a price appears too good to be true, it very possibly is.

Most importantly, talk with knowledgeable people. Learn as much as possible about authentic specimens, and study broken points to see how they were made. Before long, modern-made points will begin to stand out.

POINT OR BLADE made of black flint, 3 in. long and 1 ¼ in. wide at shoulders. Serrated edges are still sharp; piece was found in southcentral Tennessee.   C—$35

Photo courtesy of Jim Northcutt, Jr., Corinth, Mississippi.

EASTERN POINTS

Folsom-type fluted point, 1-7/8 in. long, found on New York ocean beach Paleo site. Well-fluted both sides, nearly to tip. All edge treatment extremely well done, with minute chipping. Material, an out-of-state dark flint.　　　　　　　　　　　　　　C—$125

Arrowheads from Connecticut, average 2 in. long.　　D—$3-6 each

Fine white 1 in. **beveled-edge arrowhead,** undoubtedly made in post-AD 500 times, apparently from the tip of an Archaic beveled edge blade. Portion of base missing. Unusual.　　　　　C—$7

Florida **gempoint** made of translucent material called agatized coral. Stemmed point is 1¾ in. long, and ¾ in. wide at sloped shoulders. High colors, fine chipping.　　　　　　　　C—$50

Frame of 24 **arrowheads** and projectile points, from James River, Virginia, area.　　　　　　　　　　　　　　　D—$60

Cahokia gempoint, Illinois, amber and white flint, 1-3/8 in. long. Notched on sides, notched at base center, very delicately chipped. Mississippian period.　　　　　　　　　　　　　C—$45

Set of 3 **Paleo points** from near Hartford, Connecticut.　　D—$50

Stemmed **projectile point,** chipped from white flint, 2½ in long, from Virginia. Wide stem has the base bifurcated, that is, deeply incurvate in base center.　　　　　　　　　　　D—$10

PROJECTILE POINT, Pickwick stemmed variety and probably late Woodland. It is 3 in. long and 1 in. wide; a very fine chipped piece with little basal grinding.　　　　　　　C—$20
Photo courtesy of Jim Northcutt, Jr., Corinth, Mississippi.

BLADE OR PROJECTILE POINT, 2½ in. long and 1¼ in. wide, found in Prentis County, Mississippi. A Benton type point, it has good symmetry.　　　　　　　　　　C—$22
Photo courtesy of Tracy Northcutt, Corinth, Mississippi.

Wide and **shallow-notched point** or blade, Alabama, 2-3/8 in. long, possibly Woodland period. Black flint, low grade.   D—$9

Unusual Paleo **Folsom-type fluted point,** 1-7/8 in. long, but channel-fluted to tip on both sides. Found near Mississippi River, in state of that name. Perfect condition.   C—$125

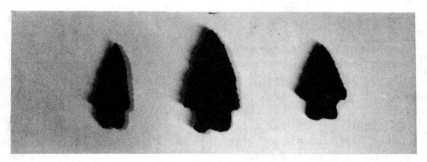

Selection of heavy-duty points or blades, all of glossy black Coshocton (Ohio) flint. Left to right, SERRATED-EDGE POINT, some damage to one base lobe.   C—$12
SERRATED-EDGE BLADE, about 3 in. in length, some damage to base lobe.   C—$18
SERRATED-EDGE POINT or blade, perfect condition, from Illinois.   C—$17
Private collection.

Triangular point, Alabama, made of a gray chert material, and 1¼ in. long. Perfect condition.   D—$4

Common flint **arrowhead,** late prehistoric, and 1 in. long, stemmed, of white low-grade material. Chipping haphazard and uneven, and foreign inclusion makes part much thicker. One notch smaller than the other.   C—$2

Triangular flint **point,** 1¼ in. wide at base. Very thin. Made of black and pink flint, unknown origin. Found in North Carolina and may have been traded there. Base has bottom edges ground, very unusual for the type.   C—$15

Lovely **pentagonal point** or blade, 2 in. long, pink and cream high-quality flint. Corner-notched, ¼ in. of tip missing also one base corner. (Perfect, would have been a $15 point). With damage and as-is, valued less.   C—$10

5

Side-notched Archaic point, gray-brown flint, 1 ¾ in. long, ½ in. wide. Chipping average-good, no major damage. C—$7

Triangular arrowhead, straight base, 1 ¼ in. long, late prehistoric, found in New York state. Point is 5/8 in. wide at straight base. C—$3

Small quartzite **arrowhead,** "sugar" or opaque white type, from near Washington, D.C.; 1-1/8 in. long. Corner notches are wide and shallow. C—$3

Corner-notched point,New Jersey, made of a rough material, collected (according to accompanying card) on an archeological survey as a university project. Point broken near tip. C—$2

Four small sugar quartz **projectile points** or arrowheads from coastal Virginia, average about 1-½ in. in length. No damage, but workmanship about average. D-$1.50 each

Small white flint **Hardin barbed point,** Illinois, 2-¼ in. long and 1-¼ in. wide. G—$15

HARDIN BARBED POINT, found in Adams County, Illinois; Burton Creek area. It is 2 ¾ in. long and 1 ½ in. wide at shoulders. From late Archaic times, approx. 2500 BC. The unique characteristic of this point is that the serrations point forward instead of backward or out to sides.

C—$140

Photo courtesy of Pat Humphrey, Westcentral Illinois.

Quartzite **stemmed point,** from Maine coastal site and probably Archaic period. Point is 1¾ in. long, thick, with short sturdy stem. Rough-chipped due to nature of material.   C—$2

Hopewellian point or blade, 3 in. long, notching fine and medium-depth. Damage to one shoulder tip and one corner of base but very minor. Excellent chipping.   A—$18

Corner-notched serrated-edge point, probably Archaic, 1½ in. long, glossy black flint, from Indiana. Well-notched.   C—$15

Unusual prehistoric salvage work: An **Archaic point** of black flint has typical corner notches and serrated edges, measures about 2 in. long. Obverse shows fine percussion and pressure flaking. Reverse has a long channel, averaging ½ in. wide, running from point base to tip. Without doubt, one of the early Paleo-period fluted points was found much later by an Archaic Indian and reworked to present form. Double-worked.   C—$50

Thin Illinois **side-notched point,** Kramer type, of white flint. Point is 2¾ in. long and 1 in. wide.   G—$12

Small **"birdpoint"** arrowhead, late Woodland or Mississippian period, 7/8 in. long, ½ in. wide, with crisp and well-done basal notches.   C—$4

HOPEWELLIAN PROJECTILE POINTS, showing an interesting range of size and styles. The two specimens on right are both of high grade Flintridge material. Values, from left to right:

C—1st point, $3.00
2nd point, $9.00
3rd point, $20
4th point, $7

Private collection.

Paleo period PROJECTILE POINTS from West Texas surface sites, Edwards Plateau flint. Points are 1 in. to 4 in. in length, of following types:
  Top row: Clovis, Fishtail Yuma, Fishtail Yuma, Yuma, Yuma.
  Middle: Hell Gap, Clovis, Meserve, Plainview, Agate Basin.
  Bottom: Folsom, Folsom, Sandia, Sandia, Sandia.

C—$75-$300 each

Photo courtesy of Wayne Parker, Texas.

Top row, left to right: ASHTABULA-TYPE POINT, dark gray flint.   C—$5
CORNER-NOTCHED POINT of blade, black and cream flint.   C—$9
CORNER-NOTCHED POINT from Indiana Archaic period site, of translucent pinkish material.
Flintridge.   C—$5
Large WHITE CHERT KNIFE, blade from Kansas: stemmed variety, 4¼ in. long.   C—$12
Private collection.

8

STEMMED POINT of blade, well-flaked and thin, of Quitaque flint quarried in the Texas Pan-handle. Found in New Mexico. Piece would be more valuable if not for missing portion on right side above shoulder. Point is 2¾ in. long.　　　　　　　　　　　　　　C—$40

Photo courtesy of Ralph W. White, Oklahoma.

WESTERN POINTS

Arkansas **Dalton-type point,** deeply basal-notched, edges heavily serrated, perfect condition. Point is 1-7/8 in. long, very well proportioned and balanced; basal grinding.　　　　　　　C—$55

Very delicate **Northwest coast arrowhead,** translucent red and orange gem point. Point is 7/8 in. long, notched from bottom, with wide stem. Shoulders drop below stem base. Point almost resembles swallow in flight. Excavated find, state of Washington.
　　　　　　　　　　　　　　　　　　　　　　　　D—$35

Frio point from Texas, 2¼ in. long and ¾ in. wide, of pinkish white material.　　　　　　　　　　　　　　　　　　　　　G—$6

Extra-delicate **Columbia River gem point,** triangular form, reddish translucent chalcedony, square-stemmed; shoulders barbed with tips that extend 1/8 in. below stem. Point is 2-1/16 in. long and perfectly symmetrical; also equally attractive obverse and reverse. Perfect condition.　　　　　　　　　　　　　C—$140

Steuben point, of good gray flint, classic shape. It is 2¾ in. long and 3/8 in. wide.　　　　　　　　　　　　　　G—$10

Oregon arrowhead, chipped from petrified wood, red and yellow striped colors, 1 in. long, stemmed and barbed. Very well chipped.
　　　　　　　　　　　　　　　　　　　　　　　　C—$18

Small slightly damaged **Arkansas Dalton,** white and pink material. Piece is 2 in. long and ¾ in. wide.　　　　　　　G—$9

Small **Epps point** from Missouri, classic type, and made of gray flint. It is 2 in. long and 1 in. wide. G—$8

Agate arrowhead from Columbia River Valley, beautifully colored and translucent material. Reddish color, 1½ in. long. C—$50

SIX FLINT POINTS from a surface site in West Texas, showing long barbs. They are 2 in. to 3 in. long. These are similar to the Calf-Creek points, but have not been named or classified yet in Texas. Archaic period. Five of the points are of Edwards Plateau flint, while middle point, top row, is made of Tecovas jasper. C—$45-$60
Photo courtesy of Wayne parker, Texas.

SMALL SCOTTSBLUFF PALEO POINT, made of brown petrified wood. Material has black streaks and black specs throughout. Artifact has nice form, is of unusual material; it is 2 1/8 in. long, from Oklahoma. C—$40-$50
Photo courtesy of Ralph W. White.

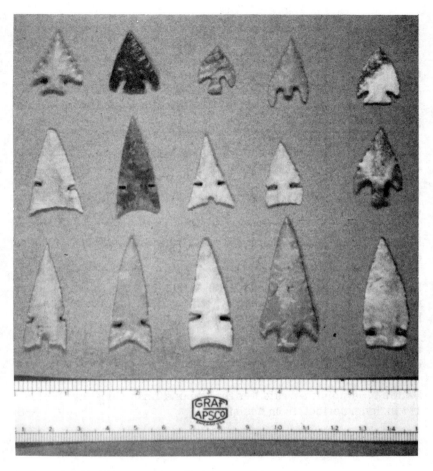

Small ARROWPOINTS from West Texas Surface sites. These are the more common types found in the Panhandle and West Texas. Late prehistoric, they are classified as Scallorn, Harrell, Bonham, Perdiz and Rockwall. C—$20-$70

Photo courtesy of Wayne Parker, Texas.

Red **gem point**, Oregon, 1-1/8 in. long, stemmed, down-swept shoulders reach same distance as stem base. Very balanced.
C—$30

Sandia-type point, heavy-duty and notched on only one side; found by New Mexican rancher in dry cave near arroyo. Point is exactly 2 in. long, rough-made in classic Sandia-II form. C—$110

11

Two nice **Alba-type Caddo points,** white and gray flint, and averaging 1 in. in length.   G—$12

Ornate black **obsidian point,** base deeply indented to "V" shape, high side notches, base ends form curved tangs. Point is 1-7/8 in. long, and just over 1 in. wide at tangs. Very symmetrical and perfect condition.   C—$35

Side-notched **Godar-type point,** from Arkansas, made of pink flint. It is 2¾ in. long and 1½ in. wide.   G—$19

White **Dalton point** from Arkansas, 1¾ in. long and ¾ in. wide, very nice.   G—$20

Birfurcated-base **Archaic period point,** reddish obsidian, 2 in. long, corner-notched. About 1/8 in. of tip gone.   C—$7

Scarce **Hohokam arrowhead,** from Arizona, 2-7/8 in. long, made from a white flint. Very narrow, with 3 deep indentations along lower base sides. Condition perfect, fine chipping.   C—$75

Hohokam point, 1½ in. long, very narrow, edges deeply serrated and undamaged.   C—$55

Dalton-type point, serrated edges, ground base sides and bottom, 1½ in. long, perfect, from Louisiana.   C—$30

Obverse and reverse of a fine DALTON-TYPE POINT, found in Adams County, Illinois. Of high-grade white flint, the point is nearly 3 in. long and perfect condition. Point probably dates to the early Archaic, and lasted thousands of years. Age: 7000 BC to about 3000 BC.

C—$135

Photo courtesy of Pat Humphrey Westcentral Illinois.

FLINT DARL POINTS, average length 2¼ in. These were surface finds in central Texas, and are made of Edwards Plateau flint. The points all have right side bevels, and are from the Archaic period. C—$30
Photo courtesy of Wayne Parker, Texas.

Clovis-type point, 3 in. long, found in Minnesota, made of a regional chert. Fluted both sides. C—$80

Paleo-period flint point, from prehistoric lake (now dried) in Nevada, and 2 in. long, made of a dull chert. Has rounded base, excurvate sides. No damage, but not too artistic. C—$17

Fluted-base Clovis-like point, found in Montana, 2-3/8 in. long. Material a colorful, quality chert. Chipping very distinct, flute-channels deep. Said to have come from a "buffalo-jump" site.

C—$90

Gem point, of black obsidian, found in Nevada. Corner-notched, bifurcated base. Piece is 2-7/8 in. long, translucent, probably Archaic. D—$45

Small **obsidian arrowhead,** ¾ in. long, 3/8 in. wide at base, triangular form with no notches. C—$6

Deep-notch Texas **projectile point,** 2¾ in. long, 1¼ in. wide, and of gray flint. G —$13

Brownish **obsidian point,** from northern California, 2 in. long, side-notched.

C—$15

Evans point from Yell County, Arkansas; length is 3 in. and width is 1¼ in. pink color, double notches.

G—$14

Frame of **arrowheads,** all fine obsidian point from Nevada. They (25) range in length from ½ in. to 2 in.

G—$80

Decorative white flint **Texas "birdpoint"**, serrated edges, small squared notches, base very concave, length 1 in. and very thin. Made of a glossy red flint with superb chipping.

D—$35

Frame of **arrowheads;** frame size 8 in. by 10 in. There are 30 fine obsidian points, with 6 damaged. Range in size from ½ in. long to 2½ in. long.

G—$55

Rare **crystal quartz arrowhead,** Arkansas, ¾ in. long and ¼ in. wide.

G—$35

FRAME OF FINE BIRDPOINTS, gem quality, all from Greene County, Missouri. Some of the forms are drills, the balance arrowheads. Items found by Lynn Denby, Earnest Giboney and Harley Israel.

C—$20-$80

Photo courtesy of Lynn W. Denby, Rogersville, Missouri.

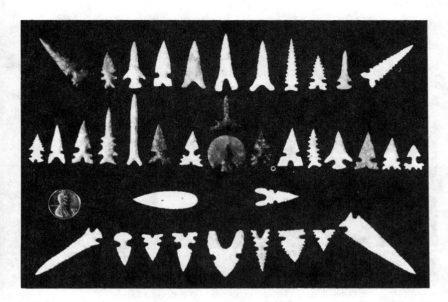

FRAME OF FINE BIRDPOINTS, gem quality, all from Greene County, Missouri. Some forms would be drills, the balance arrowheads. Note the serrated edges on many, and the wide variety of forms. Items found by Lynn Denby, Earnest Giboney and Harley Israel. C—$20-$80
Photo courtesy of Lynn W. Denby, Rogersville, Missouri.

Three **Caddo arrow points,** two of novaculite, one of brown chert. Average length is ¾ in. G—$14, all

Frame of 20 **leaf-shaped arrowheads** from near Twin Falls, Idaho. D—$65

Frame of **arrowheads,** all obsidian, and 21 points. Several styles, and most are perfect. Size range from 1 in. long to 2¼ in. long. G—$95

Clovis-type fluted point, from New Mexico, made of a high-quality translucent agate-flint, gray and green, unusual. Point is 2-7/8 in. long, has two opposite small nicks on sides, probably from being wired to a frame by early collector. Well-fluted both sides, and very attractive piece. D—$285

Beveled-edge shouldered point, from Iowa, 2½ in. long and 1½ in. wide. G—$23

Fluted Clovis-type point, Oregon, obsidian, fluted on only one side and very thin. Perfect, and 3 in. in length. C—$95

Washington state coastal-site **chalcedony point** or blade, 2 ¼ in. long, black obsidian, perfectly symmetrical. Shoulder tips even with flatish base, and is diagonally bottom-notched. Regular chipping with very tiny flakes removed. C—$75

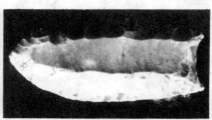

Basic CLOVIS-TYPE PROJECTILE POINT, a Paleo variety often found around Debert in Nova Scotia. In the opinion of a Canadian researcher, this point would be about 11,000 years old; it may have been picked up and modified by later Amerinds, as the edge serrations help make this a unique point. Piece is 2¼ in. long, and less than ¼ in. thick.

C—$115

Photo courtesy of Howard Popkie, Arnprior, Ontario, Canada.

FINE FOLSOM POINT, 2¼ in. long, 7/8 in. wide. Very nicely chipped artifact, as are most Folsoms. From an old Canadian collection. In Canada, Folsom points are generally found on the High Plains of Alberta. C—$90

Photo courtesy of Howard Popkie, Arnprior, Ontario, Canada.

CANADIAN POINTS

Frame of 9 **arrowheads** from central Canada, from 1-1/8 in. to 2½ in. in length. Most are chipped from a gray flint; all in perfect condition. There are 7 notched types and 2 triangular forms, all probably Woodland and later in time. C—$55

Side-notched point, central Canada, gray flint, 2-1/8 in. in length. Archaic period. C—$15

Triangular point, chipped from argillite, from British Columbia, Canada. Piece is 1½ in. long, blackish. C—$6

Small **projectile point**, from Saskatchewan, Canada, Paleo period. Unfluted, has the concave base and good chipping; 2-3/8 in. long. C—$50

Side-notched point, New Brunswick, Canada, made from a white material, and 2 in. long. Edges are lightly serrated. C—$11

CANADIAN PROJECTILE POINT, found at Woodstock, Ontario. Piece is 1¾ in. long, and is a side-notched variety somewhat resembling U.S. Woodland-era points. *C—$8*

Photo courtesy of Howard Popkie, Arnprior, Ontario, Canada.

CANADIAN PROJECTILE POINT, found near Dundas, Ontario. Point is 1½ in. long and is probably an Archaic variety. Made of a green flint. *C—$8*

Photo courtesy of Howard Popkie, Arnprior, Ontario, Canada.

CANADIAN POINT or blade, believed to be Archaic but possibly Paleo era, and picked up near Moose Jaw, Sask. Artifact is 2½ in. long, and made of a brown flint or chert.

C—$9

Photo courtesy of Howard Popkie, Arnprior, Ontario, Canada.

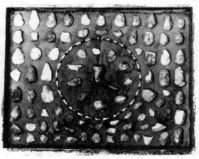

FRAME OF PREHISTORIC POINTS AND BLADES, plus a design of shell beads. All from Ontario, Canada. Longest piece is just over 3 in. Material priced without frame. *C—$400-$600*

Photo courtesy Robert C. Calvert, London, Ontario, Canada.

FRAME OF ARTIFACTS, with small flaked tools and scrapers from prehistoric times, plus clay pipe and fine strand of trade beads. Material priced without frame. *C—$125-150*

Photo courtesy of Robert C. Calvert, London, Ontario, Canada.

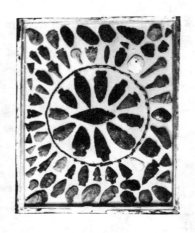

Fine FRAME OF ARTIFACTS, containing prehistoric points and blades, plus French trade
beads. Age of chipped artifacts range from
Paleo to late Woodland and Mississippian
times, and cover some 10,000 years. Material
priced without frame.   C — $500-$650

Photo courtesy Robert C. Calvert, London,
Ontario, Canada.

Suggested reading

Bell (& Perino), *Guide to the Identification of Certain American Indian Projectile Points,* Special Bulletins No. 1-4; Oklahoma Anthropological Society, Oklahoma City, Oklahoma.

Folsom, Franklin, *America's Ancient Treasures,* University of New Mexico Press, Albuquerque, 1983.

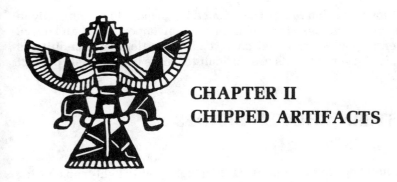

CHAPTER II
CHIPPED ARTIFACTS

Chipping was one, and the first, of the three great prehistoric and early historic tool-shaping methods.

For the first chapter, projectile points were arbitrarily grouped as about 3 in. (75 mm) or under in length. There is some debate in the area, and undoubtedly some of the artifacts listed were actually blades or small knives.

In general, the various other chipped artifacts were made of the same crypto-crystalline materials as were the projectile points. The two requirements seem to have been that the flint or chert chipped well, and had few foreign inclusions, bad spots, to interfere with that chipping.

Some of the value factors for the projectile points are relevant here, like the emphasis on quality material, workstyle, size and condition. There is the added factor of a rare class. There have never been many notches hoes, for example, so an artifact in that category is more highly valued than, say, a crude chopper.

Here, other chipped artifacts are described and listed; there are a number of them, so rather than attempt to introduce and list them all, each sub-group has a brief preface.

Knives or blades are usually medium to large-size chipped tools, apparently used as cutting instruments. They are in many shapes, and no one definition covers them all. If there is a generalization it is that blade edges were more important than the tip; these areas often show minor work-breaks and heavy wear.

Some blades had serrated or saw-tooth edges, while others were sharply angled or beveled. And others had nondescript edge treatment, and many have been multi-purpose knives. The base is usually fairly sturdy, and the distance between notches, or the width of the basal stem, may be an inch (10 cm) or so on average. Other blades do not show specific chipping for hafting, and it is unknown how the handle, if any, was attached.

19

All the valuation factors mentioned for projectile points apply to symmetrical blades. Length is of special importance, and large authentic pieces command much collector attention. Condition is vital, for larger artifacts are difficult to locate in absolutely perfect form.

EASTERN CHIPPED BLADES

Base-notched **translucent blade,** of a high-quality light-transmitting flint, from Florida. Point is 3-3/8 in. long, perfect in all details; notches thin and well-made.   C—$70

Oval-shaped **cache blade,** unfinished, Indiana. Probably Woodland, 5¼ in. long, 3 in. wide, gray flint.   D—$18

Osceola blade, Illinois, made of a reddish and white high-grade flint. Piece is nearly 6 in. long, about 2¼ in. wide; colors form arttistic pattern. Only slight original wear shows on blade sides; base fully ground. No damage.   D—$425

Side-notched blade, probably Archaic, small but deep notches put in about ½ in. from base bottom. Sides are about straight, and then incurvate to tip. Blade is 4½ in. long.   A—$70

Archaic **bifurcated-base blade,** blue-gray flint, 3½ in. in length, 1½ in. wide. Base bottom is indented to same degree as corner notches. Small side serrations.   A—$35

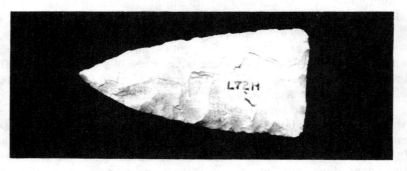

TRIANGULAR BLADE, 3½ in. long and 1½ in. wide at base. This is a very thin piece, 3/16 in. thick. Other artifacts found on the same site include a fluted point and an Atlatl weight. Found in southern Tennessee.   C—$40

Photo courtesy of Jim Northcutt, Jr., Corinth, Mississippi.

PROBLEMATICAL ARTIFACTS, from Prentis County, Mississippi. Largest piece in photos is 1 in. by 2 in. Over 100 have been found on just one village site, and have been associated with Benton points. These seem to have once been blades or points, were broken, and then were smoothed on all sides and faces. These are not water-worn, but abrasion or smoothing was intentional.

C—No value listed.

Photo courtesy Jim Northcutt, Jr., Corinth, Mississippi.

SERRATED EDGE BLADE, 1½ in. wide and 3 in. long, Mississippian period and found in southcentral Tennessee. Base with missing corner has been ground smooth and cutting edges clearly show retouching or resharpening.   C—$15

Photo courtesy Retha D. Northcutt, Corinth, Mississippi.

Large Dovetail or St. Charles blade, damage to one corner of base, otherwise fine condition and just under 5 in. A good specimen for restoration.   A—$150

Dovetail of Carter Cave flint, Kentucky, 5 in. long, and 1¾ in. wide.   G—$70

Large **blade** or knife, uncertain period, may be Archaic. Base-stemmed, with base bottom slightly incurvate. Blade sides are slightly excurvate, serrated edges. Piece is 6¼ in. long.   A—$250

Quartzite **blade,** Pennsylvania, 7 in. long.   D—$45

Serrated blade, found in Ohio near West Lafayette in 1953 on site that produced Archaic and Woodland periods material. Piece is 3-1/8 in. long, wide-stemmed, thin, of red and white flint. Extremely fine chipping, glossy surface, no wear.   C—$70

Five FLINT CORES, the portion remaining after thin flake knives have been knocked off. Highest grade Ohio Flintridge material, very colorful and glossy. Per each.　　　　C—$7

Private collection.

Left to right, rough-chipped FLINT CELT, age unknown. Midwestern; about 6 in. in height.
　　　　C—$10
Rough-chipped FLINT AXE, age unknown, Midwestern; about 7 in. in height. Some collectors feel these may be of Paleo origin, but proof is lacking.　　　　C—$15

Private collection.

Long CHIPPED BLADE, gray color, and 5½ in. in length. Found in Saskatchewan, Canada, and dating about 5000 BC.　　　　C—$30

Photo courtesy of Howard Popkie, Arnprior, Canada.

22

ANGULAR KNIFE, left, 2¼ in. (5.5 cm) by 4½ in. (11.5 cm), Archaic period. Flint is blue-black and condition is perfect.   C—$12

DOVETAIL BLADE, right, 1 3/8 in. (3.5 cm) by 2½ in. (6.0 cm) long, Archaic period and with heavy basal grinding. Blue-black flint with white and gray mottling; Dovetails are increasingly rare finds.   C—$60

Photo courtesy of Mark Hersman, Lucas, Ohio.

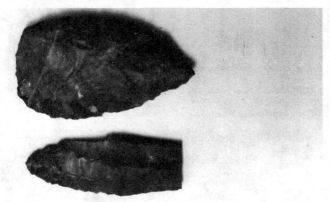

CACHE BLADE, top, 3½ in. (9.0 cm) in length, made of black flint with gray flecks; probably a Woodland-era piece.   C—$15

DOUBLE-FLUTED PALEO POINT, 3 1/8 in. (8.0 cm) long, made of brown-black flint and with lateral grinding. Basal section broken.   C—$15

Photo courtesy of Mark Hersman, Lucas, Ohio.

Afton or **pentagonal blade**, 3¼ in. long, made of Ohio Flintridge multicolored material. Small section missing from one barbed shoulder, hardly noticeable.   D—$24

Hopewellian point or **blade**, Kentucky, 3-7/8 in. long, 2-1/8 in. wide, of a glossy black flint. Perfect.   D—$75

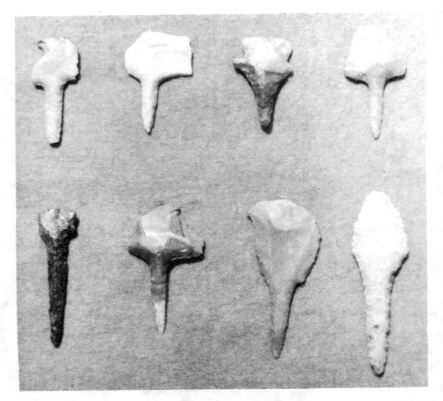

Eight FLINT DRILLS, from different sections of Texas. Archaic and late prehistoric periods. They range in length from 1¼ in. to 3 in. *C—$25-$40 each*

Photo courtesy of Wayne Parker, Texas.

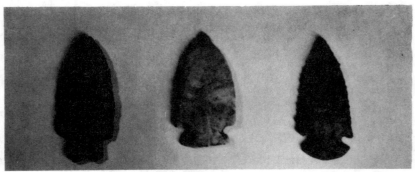

Three Midwestern blades; left, HEAVY-DUTY blade 3¼ in. long, of black Coshocton flint, one minor area of damage in left side, otherwise fine. *C—$25*

LARGE BLADE, probably Woodland and late prehistoric, perfect, edges worn. *C—$25*

Midwestern BEVEL-EDGE BLADE, quality gray flint, serrated edges. One tip of left shoulder missing, minor damage, could be restored. Basal area heavily ground. *C—$55*

Private collection.

Very fine and CLASSIC CLOVIS POINT, made of Edwards Plateau flint. Point is 3½ in. long, and dates from early Paleo times. 10,000 to 15,000 BC. C—$400

Photo courtesy of Wayne Parker collection.

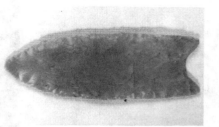

Selection of chipped-flint artijacts, all probably knife blades because of size and configuration. Left to right, top row:

SERRATED-EDGE CORNER-NOTCH, Ohio. C—$8
BLADE marked "Hopewell", Illinois. C—$40
Unusually thin BLADE, Kansas, and piece is almost exactly 4 in. long. C—$15
Bottom row: (left to right)
UNUSUAL BLADE; looks damaged but is not; dip in side almost forms thumb rest. C—$13
SIDE-NOTCH BLADE, Missouri, fine workmanship, good basal treatment. C—$13
SIDE-GROOVE-NOTCHED blade, from Oklahoma, no basal grinding, triangular form. C—$9

Private collection.

Agate Basin type PALEO POINT, found in Adams County, Illinois, in 1975. Piece is 4¼ in. long and 7/8 in. wide, and evidences very fine flaking and good basal grinding. C—$400-$600

Photo courtesy of John P. Grotte, Illinois.

25

PROJECTILE POINT, 1¼ in. wide and 3 in. long, from Tennessee. Point is probably a ·Benton type, and 1000-2000 BC. Perfect condition.   C—$20-$35
Photo courtesy Flint Na Mingo Northcutt, Corinth, Mississippi.

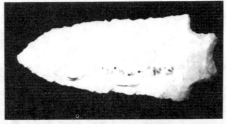

Four blades or points, all from Illinois: left to right:
DOVETAIL (St. Charles) BLADE
                   C—$300.-500.
HARDIN BARB with fine serrated edges
                   C—$225.
PLAINVIEW variant   C—$70
DALTON POINT   C—$100
Photo courtesy of Pat Humphrey, Westcentral Illinois.

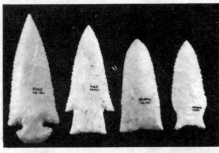

Top: HARDIN BARBED BLADE, Tazwell County, Illinois   C—$350
Bottom left: HARDIN BARBED POINT, Adams County, Illinois   C—$90
Bottom right: HARDIN BARBED BLADE, from Adams County, Illinois   C—$200
Photo courtesy of Pat Humphrey, West-central, Illinois.

PROJECTILE POINTS AND BLADES, with central specimen about 5 in. long. Most appear to be Woodland and Archaic pieces.   C—$35.-55. group
Photo courtesy of Robert C. Calvert, London, Ontario, Canada.

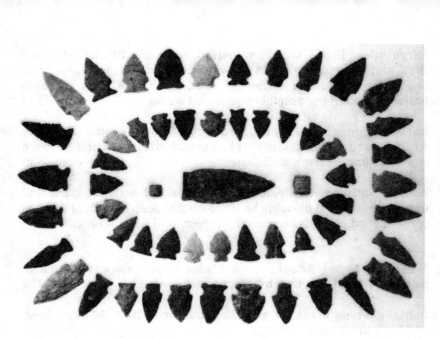

A nice FRAME OF PROJECTILE POINTS, ranging in length from 1 in. to 2¼ in. These range in time from Archaic to Mississippian times, although long point or blade in center may be late Paleo. All found in Pennsylvania; material is flint, rhyolite, jasper, quartz and chalcedony. C—$150 frame

Photo courtesy of Jonas Yoder, Jr., McVeytown, Pennsylvania.

A good FRAME OF POINTS AND BLADES, ranging from 2½ in. to 6 in. in length. Material is rhyolite, jasper and chalcedony; all found in Pennsylvania.   C—$125.

Photo courtesy of Jonas Yoder, Jr., McVeytown, Pennsylvania.

Large **Adena blade,** Woodland period, made of a fine light-colored flint, and 5½ in. long, 2-1/8 in. wide at shoulders; well stemmed. Slight damage to one corner of stem, small nick from one side halfway to point tip, possible equipment strike. A—$110

Barb-shouldered **blade,** of high quality, from Alabama. Probably Archaic, and found on site that has produced such artifacts. Piece is 3½ in. long, perfect condition. C—$30

Archaic **beveled-edge blade,** symmetrical, of a mixed dark and light brown flint in pleasing bands. Notches deep and regular, base well-notched and edges ground. Perfect, and 4½ in. long. A—$225

Fine leaf-shaped **Adena cache blade,** of translucent Flintridge material. About 6 in. long by 3 in. wide. A—$170

Ashtabula-type blade, of a gray, nondescript flint, 4-7/8 in. long, and from Indiana. C—$65

Expanded-notch or **E-notch blade,** 3-1/8 in. long, perfect, from Illinois. Edges worn but overall good lines. C—$55

Grouping of POINTS AND BLADES, wide time dispersion. Left to right:
Late Paleo unfluted-fluted type;   C—$50
Archaic serrated & sidenotched;   C—$35
Adena (?), large blade;   C—$20
Top and bottom, right;   C—$3.50
Private collection.

Alabama **blade,** whitish chert, 5¼ in. long, side-notched. Shaped solely by percussion flaking, no edge retouch. C—$35

Dovetail or St. Charles blade, exceptional piece, large and perfect. Piece is 5¾ in. long, 3 in. wide, no damage anywhere. Basal notches deep, base edges ground. Made of translucent multi-hued Flintridge material; from an old collection. A—$450

Blade, from New Jersey, chipped from black chert and 4 in. long. Leaf-shaped, no edge retouch, average workstyle. C—$11

Archaic **beveled-edge blade,** finely chipped base with deep notches; 5¾ in. long, and surface is nicely patinated to a pale cream. Damage: About ½ in. missing from tip, exposing lighter-colored interior. As is, a superb example of prehistoric flint-knapping. Easily restored. C—$215

Fluted **Clovis-like blade,** Florida, from a black high-grade material. Point is 3-3/8 in. long, deeply fluted both sides, perfect, ground basal edges. C—$125

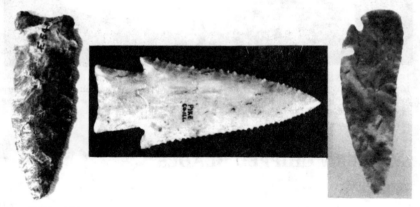

From left to right:

PROJECTILE POINT OR BLADE, 3¼ in. long and 1 in. wide. Very detailed chipping, dark red and white material. Somewhat resembles Paleo points but may be early Archaic. Found in Tishomingo County, Mississippi near the (future) Tennessee-Tombigbee Waterway. C—$30.
Photo courtesy of Jim Northcutt, Jr., Corinth, Mississippi.

Fine HARDIN BARBED POINT or blade, found in Pike County, Illinois. Note the fine and regular serrations on both edges, and the excellent symmetry. C—$225.
Photo courtesy of Pat Humphrey, Westcentral Illinois.

A very fine CORNER-TANG KNIFE of blade, found in Texas County, Oklahoma. It was made from a blue-gray Alibates flint and is larger than average for the type. The blade is 3¾ in. long.
C—$350
Photo courtesy of Ralph W. White, Oklahoma.

29

Large **Turkey-tail blade,** light gray shade of Indiana hornstone flint, found in West Virginia. Blade may have once been part of cache or underground deposit of artifacts, as accompanying card in old-style handwriting states "1 of 13". Blade is 5-1/8 in. long.
C—$125

Tennessee **blade,** triangular, beveled edges, no stem or notches. Piece is 5¼ in. long.
A—$65

Fluted point from lower Michigan, 4-1/8 in. long, made of black Coshocton County (Ohio) flint. Average wear on all sides, base not ground, no damage. Fluting channels extend for approximately 2 in. up both base sides.
D—$250

UNFLUTED CLOVIS-TYPE PALEO POINT, made of a fine quality brown flint; a purple stripe runs from near the base almost to the tip. Piece is 4½ in. long and 1 3/8 in. wide at shoulders. A very colorful point, it was found in Pike County, Illinois.
C—$350
Photo courtesy John P. Grotte, Illinois.

WESTERN CHIPPED BLADES

Corner-notched blade, base excurvate and well-ground, sides deeply serrated, Archaic period. Artifact is 3½ in. long, well balanced, both sides or faces equally good. From Iowa.   A—$95

Shouldered blade from Arkansas, 3½ in. long, blue-white flint.
G—$10

Chipped **obsidian blade,** from Santa Catalina Island, southern California cultural area, and 4-1/8 in. long. Leaf-shaped and un-damaged; unusual locale.
C—$60

Kansas **flint blade**, unusual form, 2-15/16 in. long. Large side notches halfway between tip and base; base bottom deeply indented (bifurcated) which gives blade a tri-notched appearance. Damage to one side near tip, minor.   C—$35

Unusual blade, certainly Paleolithic period, non-fluted piece of a superior flint, origin unknown. Found in Oklahoma in 1972 by a camper. Point is 3-3/8 in. long, and expands from a forked base about 1 in. wide and very thin. Chipping, especially pressure retouch, is regular and excellent. Type not mentioned in any of the standard reference works; may be regional sub-variant.   C—$195

Corner-tang blade from Oklahoma Panhandle region, lower blade slightly excurvate, 4-1/8 in. long, larger than usual for type. Notching is deep, remaining section forms triangular stem, yellowish flint of unknown quarry site.   D—$140

Paleo-period point converted in prehistoric times to a BEVELED-EDGE KNIFE. Blade is made of blue banded Alibates flint, and is from the neo-American period, 900-1300 AD. Blade is 3½ in. long and well-chipped.   *C—$90*
Photo courtesy of Wayne Parker Collection.

BEVELED BLADE, four edges and in diamond shape. It is of a reddish Alibates (?) flint and large for the type. Blade is 6 in. long, while average size is closer to 2½ in. or 3 in. Found in Texas County, Oklahoma. One shoulder has some battering, but minor.   *C—$175*
Photo courtesy of Ralph W. White, Oklahoma.

31

Eden-type blade, 4-1/8 in. long, evidencing parallel flaking, gray flint. Found in a wind-erosion "blowout", Nebraska, in 1951. Perfect condition, flint high grade, well made.   C—$300

Sedalia-type blade, Missouri, squared base, excurvate sides tapering to very sharp tip. Piece is 8-1/8 in. long, widest measurement is 2¼ in. from the tip. Pale white chertish-material, and excellent chipping overall. Perfect condition.   C—$290

Plains-Midwestern (?) **concave-convex sided blade,** resembling a dagger. Piece is 7¼ in. long, 1-3/8 in. wide at squared base. Haft area incurvate; working edges excurvate. This type of flint artifact is not often found intact due to size and brittle nature of flint. Perfect condition.   C—$400

Leaf-shaped blade, Woodland period, of mottled white and dark flint. Not notched or stemmed. Base casually rounded, blade presents an ovate appearance. Piece is 5½ in. long.   A—$110

Wide-shouldered **point or blade,** wide stem, whitish flint, possibly Woodland and resembles Snyder type. Exactly 3 in. long.   C—$27

Chumash **point or blade,** diamond-shaped, 3½ in. long, of a low-grade material. From southern California, site on coast, excavated f i n d .

                                                    D—$14

Pedernales-type blade, from central Texas, with sharply indented base and sharply barbed shoulders, edges finely serrated. Perfect condition, and 3¼ in. long.   C—$110

Four BEVELED-EDGE KNIVES, from Texas, and 4 in. to 6 in. in length. These date from AD 900-1300, and came from a Panhandle Pueblo site. C—$150-$225
Photo courtesy of Wayne Parker, Texas.

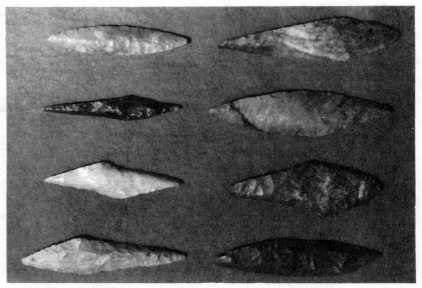

EIGHT BEVELED KNIVES, from South Texas Plains region, and from 3½ to 4½ in. in length. Left column, all of Edwards Plateau flint. Right column, top to bottom: Alibates flint, Alibates flint, Tecovas jasper, Edwards Plateau flint. All were surface finds, from late prehistoric times. C—$150-$225

DOUBLE POINTED AND TRIANGULAR KNIVES, all from Texas. These are 3 in. to 4 in. in length, and from Archaic to late prehistoric times. *C—$75-$150*
Photo courtesy of Wayne Parker, Texas.

Large **obsidian blade,** 9¼ in. long, 2-1/8 in. wide at base near small corner notches. Backside of knife straight-edge, working edge convex and mild wear shows authenticity. Excavated from early Colorado site. D—$220

Late Paleo **lanceolate blade,** chert, Colorado, good form but material not of best quality. Piece is 4-7/8 in. long. A—$27

Large 6 in. **cache blade,** ovate, rough, found in northern Georgia and made of gray Indiana hornstone. Part of a deposit of over 50 blades said to have been found by a fisherman along a river. C—$44

Pink **novaculite blade,** from Arkansas, 3¼ in. long. G—$27

Obsidian blade, excurvate sides with ends nearly identical, duo-tipped, from Washington state. Exactly 4½ in. long. A—$38

Base-notched point or **blade,** Missouri, white flint and 7¾ in. in length. It is 2¼ in. wide at shoulder tips, same measurement at expanded sides near tip. Finely chipped, with flake removal regular and consistent. Perfect.

C—$425

Large **flint blade,** extreme western Midwest, unknown period but probably Archaic because of fine edge retouching and basal grinding and serrated edges. Resembles a cross between Godar and Gravel Kame types; 6-3/8 in. long, notches deep and perfectly matching. Inside of notching heavily ground, bottom of base not.

C—$500

Large **duo-tipped blade,** Oregon, and piece is 9-5/8 in. long. Obsidian of a reddish hue, and surface find from beach area that has produced late Paleo and early Archaic materials. Rather thick, but good chipping.

C—$160

Black **obsidian blade,** Nevada, 4½ in. long, 1 in. wide at mid-length. Concave base, side-notched, and very symmetrical blade. Notches narrow and shallow.

C—$70

Large and **wide blade,** 3½ in. long, 1¾ in. wide, ovate, no notches or stem, well-chipped.

C—$14

Long Missouri **Dalton-type blade,** white flint, smooth edges, 3¼ in. long. One minor chip from blade edge; easily and quickly restored with minimum of detraction from form.

D—$33

Base-notched blade, 3½ in. long, from Oregon. Reddish flint of good quality. Notches ¼ in. deep.

D—$16

Two BASE TANG KNIVES from Central Texas, both of Edwards Plateau flint, 5 in. long and 4½ in. long, respectively. Archaic period.

C—$100. each

Photo courtesy of Wayne Parker, Texas.

PROJECTILE POINTS and blades, all from Dorchester area, Ontario, Canada. Pieces range from 3 in. to 4½ in. in length.   C—$1-$10
Photo courtesy of Robert C. Calvert, London, Ontario, Canada.

CANADIAN CHIPPED BLADES

Obsidian blade found in British Columbia, Canada, 4-7/8 in. long, 1-3/8 in. wide, and leaf-shaped. Perfect.   C—$55

Diamond-shaped blade, of pinkish chert, from Canada's Great Slave Lake region. Believed to be very early, possibly Paleo, edges worn and never resharpened (rechipped). Blade is 3-5/8 in. in length.   C—$8

Large **argillite blade,** made of the black material that can be both carved and chipped. From western Canada, 7½ in. long.   C—$29

Flaked blade, British Columbia, Canada, made of a light chert-like material. Blade is 7¾ in. long and leaf-shaped.   C—$55

Chalcedony blade, 3-3/8 in. long, found in southwestern British Columbia, Canada, and gem quality. Basal notched.   C—$90

Knife **blade,** from Nova Scotia, Canada, 4¼ in. long, made from quartzite. Found on coastal site, middle Archaic period. Rough-chipped but with good overall form.   C—$12

Fluted Paleo point or **blade**, from central Canada near Regina, made of fine-grained quartz. Piece is 4-1/8 in. long, perfect, with flutes extending over 1 in. (25 mm) on both base sides. Good form, but rough due to average-quailty material. C—$55

CHIPPED DRILLS

Drills have been used in North America for at least 10,000 years, and fine specimens have been found on many late-Paleo sites. They range in length from ½ in. to specimens over 4 in., though the longer types are rare.

This particular tool was used to make holes in bone, shell hard-stone, banded slate, wood and rock crystal. Drills were turned with fingers, attached to a rod and twirled between the palms, and secured below the flywheel of the bow-turned drill-set. Because they are long and slender they are fairly fragile, and perfect artifacts of this type command a premium.

Small **drill**, 1¼ in., from Maine. Side-notched, and chipped from a white flint. Perfect condition. C—$10

Large ceremonial **drill**, 4¼ in. long, "T"-shaped top, said to have been a mound recovery in northern Kentucky. Adena or Hopewell periods. Made of a black, glossy flint with thin "lightning" streaks of white. No signs of wear or use. C—$350

Cylindrical **drill** from southern Canada, 2¼ in. long, made from a brown flint. Tip worn from use, but perfect. C—$16

DRILL, chipped from black flint, and 3 in. in length, 1¼ in. wide at notch protrusions. This would be late prehistoric, probably Woodland. Found in Mifflin County, Pennsylvania. C—$70
Photo courtesy of Jonas Yoder, Jr., McVeytown, Pennsylvania.

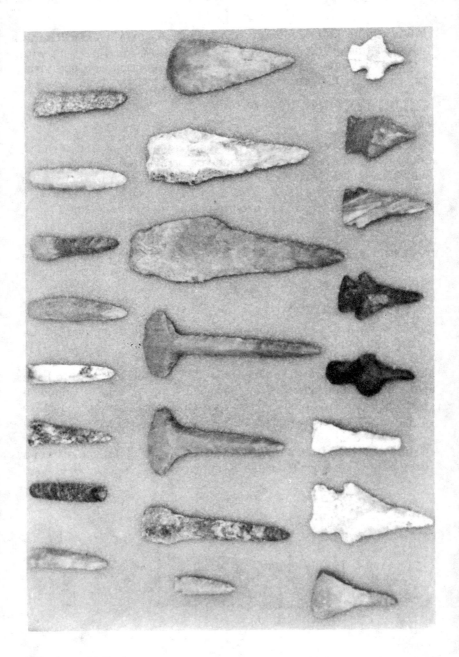

A fine frame of drills, showing a variety of types and sizes.
Photo courtesy of Jim Hovan, Ohio.

Prices vary from $5-$200

Flint **drill**, American southwest, 1½ in. long, of a good flint; perfect condition, base notched.   D—$14

Flint **drill**, 3 in. long, wide base and drill-shaft thin and very well chipped. Pink-white material, glossy.   C—$45

Drill from Missouri, oval base with flaring barbs, and 2-7/8 in. long.   G—$9

Fine flint **drill**, "T"-shaped top, dark flint of good quality, and 3½ in. long. Found in Illinois.   C—$33

Miniature flint **drill**, just under 1 in. long, with notched base. From Oklahoma.   A—$7

Fine **drill** of multicolored Flintridge material, translucent, 3-1/8 in. long. Very fine chipping, no damage.   D—$115

Rounded-top **drill**, 2-3/8 in. long, well chipped.   C—$13

Flint **drill**, made from an earlier Paleo point, with basal flute still extending on both sides of drill base. Rare. Drill is just 3 in. (75 mm) long. Yellow-white material, perfect.   C—$60

Small flint **drill**, cylindrical form, 1½ in. long, tip shows considerable wear.   C—$9

Drill, 2-1/8 in. long, wide-notched base, perfect.   C—$11

FLARED-BIT SPADE, made of brown Mill Creek tabular flint. It is 8-3/8 in. long and 5-3/8 in. wide at bit. Found in Madison County, Illinois, it may be Cahokian, from the Mississippian period.
C—$200

Photo courtesy of John P. Grotte, Illinois.

Drill, Kentucky Carter Cave flint, 1-7/8 in. long, with wide base. Found in central Indiana; possibly Woodland-era.　　　　C—$19

Quartzite **drill,** North Carolina, probably Archaic and 1 ¾ in. long. Roughly notched at base.　　　　D—$5

Early **drill,** found in southern Michigan on site that has produced Aqua-Plano material, about 7-8000 BC. Drill is 3-5/8 in. and with a narrow "T"-shape top, 3/8 in. wide. Exceptionally fine chipping, extremely smooth and glossy surface. Balanced.　　　C—$195

OTHER CHIPPED ARTIFACTS

Scrapers, for hide preparation, and perforators, for piercing materials, and gravers, for scoring bone — all are frequent finds on early Amerind sites. There is, however, not much market activity for such artifacts, and most would fall in the five-dollar range or below. They are, nonetheless, excellent examples of the daily prehistoric lifeway; tools reflect the times.

CHIPPED SPADES

A generally large artifact, spades typically have a smaller often squared, end, and a larger, heavier end with the semblance of a digging blade. Other than traditional value factors, such as size and shape and material, collectors value more highly spade examples with heavy use-polish on the working blade edge. The better the polish the more desired is the object — at least to many Midwestern collectors. Most spades, and hoes, are from this region.

Spade, 8 in. long and 5 in. wide, with outstanding bit polish; fine example.　　　　D—$85

Illinois **spade,** from St. Clair County, Illinois, 11 ¼ in. long and 4 ¼ in. wide.　　　　G—$210

Three very interesting FLARED-BIT SPADES, with large central specimen over 3 in. wide at top, over 5 in. wide at bottom. It is 9 in. long, and all have heavily polished bits. These were part of the largest CACHE of spades ever found. There were 108 specimens; they were found in 1971, in Pointset County, Arkansas.   C—$200-$250

Photo courtesy of Pat Humphrey, Westcentral Illinois.

Spade, from Schuyler County, Illinois, 11½ in. long and 4½ in. wide.   G—$195

Unusual shovel-nose type **spade,** with well-shaped bit and heavy polish. Piece is 8½ in. long, 5½ in. wide.   G—$145

Spade over 7 in. long, from Jefferson County, Missouri.   D—$80

Large and fine flint **spade,** 13 in. long and 5¾ in. wide at curved bit; good polish in blade region. Some small damage to spade base in handle attachment region, minor.   D—$250

Good Arkansas **spade,** 9 in. long and 5¼ in. wide, made from a brown chert. Has polished bit.   G—$130

Very fine **spade,** with extra-heavy polished bit. Piece is 12 in. long and 4-5/8 in. wide; found in Hickman County, Kentucky.   G—$325

Oval-type **spade,** good polish, fine condition, measuring 8¼ in. long and 5½ in. wide.   G—$115

Flint **spade,** very thin and with good polish, 9¼ in. long and 5 in. (12.5 cm) wide.   G—$145

41

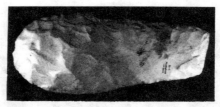

OVAL-BIT SPADE of tabular flint, with markings indicating Muskatine County, Iowa, as the source. It is Mississippian culture, and found rather far north for the type. Heavy use polish on rounded blade. C—$100.-125.

Photo courtesy of Pat Humphrey, Westcentral Illinois.

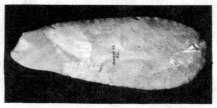

Large FLINT SPADE, made of a brown Mill Creek tabular flint, and is from the Mississippian culture and period. Piece is 11½ in. long and 4¾ in. wide; it was found in Madison County, Illinois. C—$75.-150.

Photo courtesy of John P. Grotte, Illinois.

Polished flint **spade,** from Missouri, not too thin but nice; piece is 7¼ in. long and 4¼ in. wide.   G—$60

Extra-long unnotched flint **spade,** from eastern Missouri, and 14 in. in length. Very thin, fine chipping, good polish.   C—$325

Shovel-nose **spade,** Missouri, 7½ in. long, just under 5 in. in width. Heavily used, some breaks on working edge.   C—$60

CHIPPED HOES

Compared to spades, hoes tend to be smaller, and many varieties have notched bases for a right-angle handle attachment. Bit polish adds to value, as does blade thinness and traditional factors of size, workstyle and quality of material. Late prehistoric, and generally used with the development of agriculture and permanent village sites.

Small **hoe** (?) from eastern Ohio, fine-grade blue-white flint, made from a very large flake. Piece is 4¼ in. wide and 3½ in. high, with no prominant notches. Well pressure-flaked around all four sides and edges.   C—$17

Large notched **hoe**, from Tennessee, 7½ in. long and 5½ in. wide.   G—$595

Square-back **hoe**, from Arkansas, 5½ in. long, 2½ in. wide; made from a pink chert.   G—$45

Fine notched flint **hoe**, from Missouri, 6 in. long and 3-7/8 in. wide, highly polished blade area. Made from a pink and brown glossy flint; thin, good workstyle.   C—$155

Hoe, with polished working edge, 5¼ in. long and 4¼ in. wide. Good quality black flint, notched at base.   C—$85

Fine SPADE OR HOE, 8¾ in. long and 4 in. greatest width. From the Mississippian culture, it is highly polished for nearly half of length. Spade is made of a conglomerate that is pink, gray and yellow in color.   C — $50-$75

Photo courtesy of Jim Northcutt, Jr., Corinth, Mississippi.

SANDSTONE SPADE or agricultural implement, 8½ in. long and 4½ in. wide. Piece was rough-flaked into form; found in Mifflin County, Pennsylvania. This may be a Woodland-era object.   C—$28

Photo courtesy of Jonas Yoder, Jr., McVeytown, Pennsylvania.

TWO POLISHED HOES, each 3¼ in. by 7½ in. in size. Example on left contains a visible seashell fossil at the top right and in center of back side.   C—$55-$75

Photo courtesy of Bob Brand Collection, Pennsburg, Pennsylvania.

Brown flint hoe, not notched, but upper portions are narrowed, 5-1/8 in. long, 3¼ in. wide, Midwestern.   C—$65

Ornate white flint hoe, strangely notched with two shallow notches at top sides, one at top center. Piece is 5½ in. long, well made, with use-polish on bit.   C—$200

OTHER CHIPPED TOOLS

Flint spud, (sharp, narrow spade) classic shape and with wide flaring bit, much polish. From Union County, Illinois, it is 9 in. long and 4 in. wide.   G—$395

Flaked celt (ungrooved axe) Arkansas, 3½ in. long, good shape.   G—$24

Duo-bladed flint **axe**, 6 in. long, blades semicircular with nice curves, flint unremarkable. Percussion chipping average; large notches in sides, no blade polish, unknown period. C—$25

Cache of 15 **digging tools**, average length 3½ in. all made of white and gray flint. D—$55

Unusual **eccentric flint** chipped in the form of a half moon. Piece is 1 in. long and ½ in. wide, authentic. G—$12

Fine polished flint **spud**, from Johnson County, Illinois. Made of white flint, 8 in. long, and 3½ in. wide. It has the flared bit and polished for entire length. G—$495

Flaked **celt**, from Missouri; 5 in. long and 3 in. wide, made from brown flint. G—$25

Flint **celt**, white flint, very good lines; 5 in. long, 2-1/8 in. wide, no damage. Polish over the entire surface that has largely obliterated original chipping scars. C—$195

Suggested Reading

Whiteford, Andrew H.; *North American Indian Arts*, Western Publishing Company, Inc., New York, 1970.

Indian woman and dog, with axe and firewood; picture taken in state of Washington, date unknown.

Photographer unknown; courtesy Photography Collection, Suzzallo Library, University of Washington.

CHAPTER III
ARTIFACTS OF
ORGANIC MATERIALS

Artifacts made from mammal and shellfish parts were widely common in prehistoric times. Relatively few of the objects survive to the present. Such organic materials, like wood artifacts, have largely disappeared due to the combined actions of time, moisture and bacteria.

Antler, from deer and elk, was a much-used raw material for tools and weapons. Flaking rods of antler helped make the incredible numbers of chipped objects, and deer tines were often used for projectile points. Antler, due to the hardness and availability, was used in much of North America, including all of the Continental U.S. states.

Horn, usually from the so-called buffalo (the American bison), was made into ladles, spoons, and ceremonial objects. In the northern reaches of the Rockies, horn also came from mountain goats and bighorn sheep. Horn strips were sometimes used to reinforce bows, and the material was made into knife handles and charms and decorations.

Ivory has been widely used in the Alaskan region (see later Chapter) and northern Canada. Ivory artifacts form a scarce class, especially for prehistoric items in the adjoining U.S. states. Among animals that provided ivory are the walrus and narwhale, a mammal with a single twisted tusk and which may have inspired the unicorn legend.

To a limited degree ivory also came from the twin tusks of long-dead mastodon and mammoths, preserved in permafrost. Smaller objects made from the teeth of other sea creatures are sometimes referred to as ivory.

Antler, Horn and Ivory Artifacts

Plains Indian **horn spoon**, unusual carved handle, cow horn, and 10 in. long. Probably 19th Century.   G—$60

HORN SPOON, 8-1/16 in. long, with sinew sewn beaded handle in colors white, green, yellow and blue. Material is cow horn, and piece is ca. 1910.   D—$220
Photo courtesy of Crazy Crow Trading Post, Denison, TX.

Buffalo horns from old headdress, Taos Pueblo, Ca. 1800's.
                                                                        D—$75

Elk horn point, from southern Oregon, 3¼ in. long, thinly notched at base. Narrow, may be an arrowpoint.   C—$25

Horn spoon, large 11 in. in length, with curved handle done in quill-work. Probably recent, but good piece.   C—$60

Plains Indian spoon or ladle, of bison horn, 12 in. long no damage, some painted designs on handle portion.   D—$60

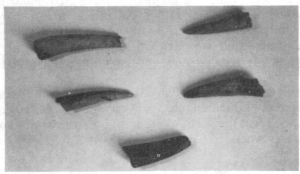

Five DEER-ANTLER ARROWHEADS, with base of large ends hollowed out to receive the arrow shaft. From late prehistoric site, poss. Ft. Ancient. Longest point is just over 1 in.   C—$7
Private collection.

Deer-antler arrowpoint, Kentucky rock shelter, 2¼ in. long; base hollowed out for arrow shaft. C—$6

Wide-bowled **horn spoon,** or ladle, 7 in. long, 4 in. wide at shallow bowl. Northwest Coast, probably historic and late 1800's. C—$85

Nez Perce deep **horn ladle or dipper,** 8¾ in. long, of bent and shaped horn. No decoration, but good lines. C—$75

Elkhorn scraper, 13 in. long with right-angle curve; has a snub-nose scraper of quartz still in position. Held by rawhide bindings and pitch. Horn polished by much use; condition good. D—$180

Six DEER-ANTLER TOOLS, from Archaic site in Kentucky near Ohio River. Excavated from rock shelter, longest piece is just over 4 in. It is believed these are flint-chipping tools; all six sections. in good condition. C—$12
Private collection.

Incised ivory bar, western Canada, 3½ in. long, about ¼ in. thick. Both sides have a series of zigzag lines, in parallel rows of 3. Possibly a gaming token or marker; actual use unknown. Golden brown with slight age cracks. C—$125

Hand-carved Sioux **horn spoon.** D—$40

Freshwater pearls, evidently **necklace beads,** probably Hopewellian, approximately 70 drilled pearls, none in good condition. C—$70

Set of 7 **elk teeth,** drilled at bases for suspension. C—$21

Antler Atl-atl hook, rare piece, removed from North Carolina rock shelter. Piece is 6¾ in. long, averages 1 in. in diameter, material in medium-good condition. Notched at end to receive lance base.
C—$125

Ivory pendant, northern California; may have been made from walrus ivory, but uncertain. Drill hole at one end; 2¾ in. in length. Oval shape. C—$90

Plains Indian horn spoon; 11 in. overall length; and has beaded handle. Pre-1900. G—$160

Antler pick, from prehistoric period, probably 4000 years old. Tip shows polish from long use, but rest of material is chalk-like. Piece is 13 in. long; may once have had wood handle. C—$30

Adz with wooden handle and **elk horn blade.** Piece is 12 in. long, good condition. G—$160

Elk horn hide scraper, ivoryized from much use, good condition.
G—$135

BONE ARTIFACTS

Bone items were made from the skeletal material of many animals, from raccoons to whales. They were less common in the American southwest, but other regions had a wide variety of such artifacts. These ranged from turkey wing-bone flutes to deer-bone awls to elk-horn hoes. Flint and obsidian blades shaped the bone.

Bone hoe, made from bison shoulder blade, with original handle.
D—$145

Bone awl, from New York, 4-5/8 in. long, made of splintered deer bone. From late prehistoric site. C—$18

Tennessee **bone whistle,** 3-1/8 in. long. Has incised lines in spiral design around sides. D—$50

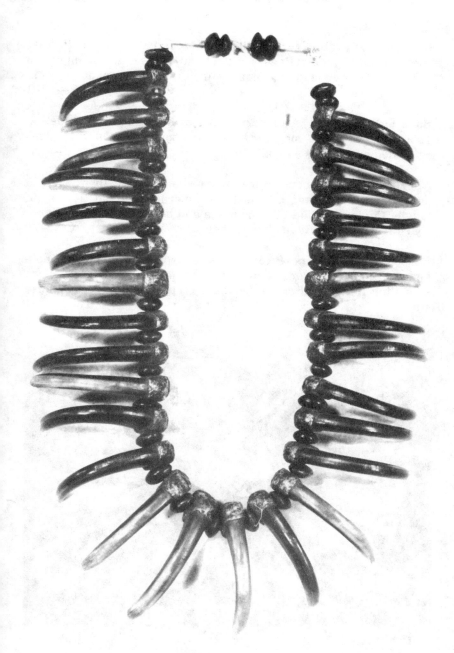

BEAR CLAW NECKLACE, with longest claw 5 in. long. Inside of claws is painted with vermillion; the necklace was made from the now-extinct prairie grizzly. Piece is Northern Plains and ca. 1870.   G—$1600

Photo and item courtesy Fenn Galleries, Ltd., Santa Fe, New Mexico.

Bone comb, probably Iroquois, with rounded comb teeth that resemble outstretched fingers of the hand. Piece is 4½ in. high; two effigies on top, resembling facing animals, species unknown.

C—$210

Bone hide scraper, Mesa Verde area of Colorado, and made ca. 1900. Piece is 7½ in. long, perhaps bison bone, with working edges smoothed by use; has quartzite blade. C—$75

Necklace elements, consisting of 8 bone beads, each about 1 in. (25 mm) long, and 3 bear canine teeth, averaging about 2½ in. in length. Canines drilled at rear; fangs and beads in good condition. Age unknown; from Wyoming dry cave. C—$120

Raccoon **penis-bone perforator,** from Georgia, 3-1/8 in. long. Knobbed at one end, smaller end has been sharpened by abrasion. Piece in outline forms part of an "S" curve. Found on late prehistoric site. C—$11

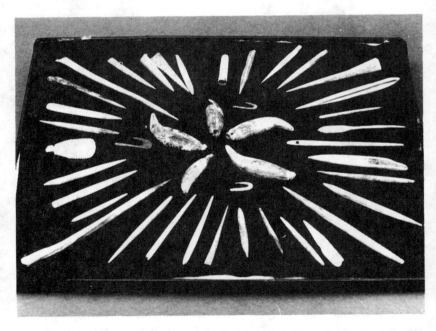

COLLECTION: *Various types of bone artifacts. Such include needles, awls, hair pins, fish hooks, perforators and a single bone pendant. Note the five large bear canine teeth, all either drilled or notched for suspension. All from Tennessee.* C—Not listed.
Photo courtesy Joseph D. Love, Chattanooga, Tennessee.

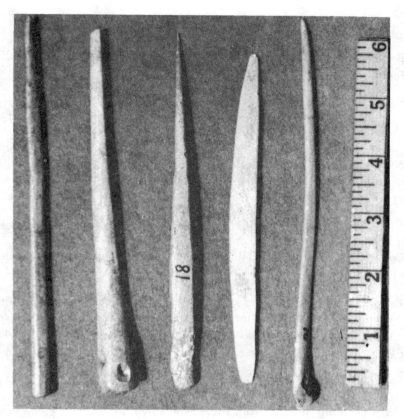

Five long BONE AWLS, from Texas sites, and late prehistoric era. These were excavated from a Panhandle Pueblo site along with 2-notch and 3-notch Harrell points. Awls are 6 in. to 7 in. in length.
C—$25-$35

Photo courtesy of Wayne Parker, Texas.

Hupa **ceremonial ladle**, 11 in. long, carved from bone; handle decorated with central cutouts and expanded serrations just above bowl. Used for important feast occasions. C—$170

Bone flaking tool, broken and reglued. Piece is 5½ in. long and 1½ in. wide. G—$12

Bone whistle, emits a single-pitch tone, 7 in. in length. Made from deer or antelope bone. Piece collected in California, early 1900's.
D—$60

Elk-bone perforator, 3-7/8 in. in length, one tip ground to sharp point. Shows much use; surface very smooth. C—$9

Deer bone awl from Mimbres, New Mexico.   D—$15

Bone fish hook, from Alabama coastal site, 1¼ in. long, fine condition.   D—$9

Polished **bone awl** from Missouri, 3 in. long, and ¼ in. in diameter.
                                                                G—$13

Decorated **bone hairpin**, 7½ in. long, nearly pointed at tip, expanded at base end. Designs of crossed and dotted lines for about half distance from base to tip. Highly polished overall; has a yellow-brown color.   C—$85

Excavated **bone awls** or quill flatterners.   G—$5 each

Bone fish-shaped wand, Tlinget, 15½ in. long, recent and still used in ceremonies.   C—$45

Bone harpoon tip, Oregon river valley, 4 in. long, double barbs on each side; socketed base for insertion into long wooden shaft. Base has knobs or protrusions for securing line that was fastened to the tip.   D—$75

Split bone awl, Missouri, 3¾ in long.   G—$11

Polished **bone needle**, from Dickerson Cave, Kentucky. Piece is 4 in. long and ¼ in. in diameter.   G—$16

Bone fish-killer club, made of marine animal bone, 19¼ in. long. Plain, heavy, 2-7/8 in. in diameter at striking end. Handle end has circular extension like a baseball bat for non-slip hold. Weathered a bleached pale gray, but good condition.   D—$215

Polished **bone needle** from Kentucky, 4½ in. long and ½ in. in diameter.   G—$17

Woodlands region **bone comb** or hair decoration, historic Indian, probably Iroquois. About 2½ in. wide at base, part of human figure effigy on comb back. Figure would have stood about 5 in. high, but head broken off. Several teeth missing from comb but a fine example.   D—$160

Bone **fish hook**, 1½ in. long, very thin, of deer bone. Highly polished; line end has groove near top.   C—$12

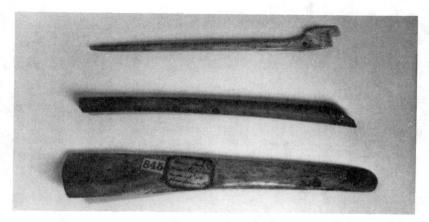

Long POLISHED-BONE HAIRPIN, 5-7/8 in. long, light incised lines along shank sides.   *C—$35*
Portion of BONE FLUTE or whistle, said to have been recovered from Kentucky mound.   *C—$40*
BONE SPATULA or hide-working tool, tapers to sharp founded blade at end, shows heavy polish in lower regions. Old label states it was recovered from a mound at Henderson, Kentucky.
C—$20
Private collection.

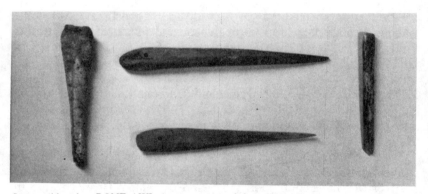

Long wild turkey BONE AWL, in two sections left and right, each about 3 in. long and polished from much use.
Center, two fine BONE AWLS or needles, all from West Virginia rock shelter, longest about 5 in. long. The small holes are modern-drilled, by an earlier collector, who secured pieces together with cord. All four tines.   *G—$28*

Private Collection.

Blackfoot **bone scraper,** 12 in. long.   Piece has original metal scraper blade. This is 19th Century.   G—$100

Polished **bone bead,** probably part of a necklace, 1 in. long and ½ in. wide; well-drilled.   Faint circular incised lines on surface, now almost obliterated.   C—$6

End-drilled pieces of polished bone, probably **necklace segments** or miniature pendants. Probably deer bone, from Colorado rock shelter. Bone pieces are nearly matching in size, averaging 2-1/8 in. long. There are 14 in all. D—$70

Long **bone needle**, from Todd County, Arkansas; it is 5 in. long and ¼ in. in diameter. Good polish and with a perforated eye. G—$28

Bone pendant, Louisiana, about 2 in. wide and 3½ in. long, end-drilled with a single hole. Rectangular form, age unknown, incised with series of x-like marks on one side. C—$55

SHELL ARTIFACTS

Shell, the exo-skeletons of a multitude of fresh and salt water species, had a long and extensive period of usage for artifacts. Amerinds used shell, with some minor changes, for spoons, containers and hoes. Other shell portions became pendants and bracelets.

Tiny shell segments of larger shells became the disc and tubular beads of early and historic times. The well-known "wampam" beads served as a medium of exchange even to the first Colonists in New England.

Shell—like some high grades of flint, copper and other desired materials—is an example of far-flung trade in prehistoric times. Gulf of Mexico conch shell was used by Ohio's Gravel Kame Indians 4000 years ago. Pacific abalone shell was traded into the Southwest at the close of the BC years. Other bivalve halves were even, by the legendary Hohokam, treated with pitch and saguaro cactus acid to become the first etchings in the world.

Two **shell rings** and two **shell pendants**, from Arizona, average diameter 1 in. G—$12 for the four

Fort Ancient, late prehistoric, **shell effigy gorget** illustrating the human face with weeping-eye motif. Specimen is 4-1/8 in. high and 3-1/8 in wide, with some parts missing at lower shell fringes or "chin" area. C—$225

Complete **shell dipper or spoon** from a shell-mound site in Kentucky. Dipper is mussel-shell, 5 in. long by 3¼ in. wide. One long side has been notched in early times.   C—$35

STRAND OF ASSORTED BEADS, made of bone and shell, with largest bead ¾ in. in diameter. These are probably prehistoric.   C—$35-$45 Photo courtesy of Robert C. Calvert, London, Ontario, Canada.

Marine **shell gorget,** Mississippian culture, found in Georgia. Piece is 5 in. high, inscribed with "eagle warrior" motif, lines not all clear. Depiction is faded and shell not in good condition.   C—$260

Necklace of prehistoric **graduated-size shell beads,** disc-shaped, about 21 in. long. Largest discs in center measure 5/8 in. There are approximately 140 beads in the strand.   C—$170

Shell bead strand, tube type, length 26 in. Material is from Arkansas.   G—$60

Shell necklace with drilled cougar fang pendant, probably Mississippian, late prehistoric. There are 17 freshwater mussel beads, pendant drilled very much off-center, all in fair condition. Beads average ¾ in. in length; pendant is 1-1/8 in. long.   C—$60

Large Arkansas **shell beads,** dics and barrel types, and length is 20 in.   C—$50

Shell beads and pendant, which is carved in the form of an animal; strand is 17 in. long.   G—$40

Mississippian period **engraved shell gorget,** 4 in. by 4¾ in. Central motif depicts man dancing or flying. Excellent condition, some surface flaking due to age.   C—$395

Shell fish hook, made of abalone shell, coastal California. Piece is 1½ in. long, nice curve, good condition, notched for string, excavated find.   C—$14

COLLECTION: A fine assemblage of shell artifacts in central frames, with flint points. Surrounding artifacts include stone celts, axes, flint blades, gorgets, discoidals, plummets and a spatulate form. All pieces are from Tennessee.   C—Not listed.

Photo courtesy of Joseph D. Love, Chattanooga, Tennessee.

String of early Indian **shell heishi,** restrung to be worn.   G—$35

Strand of documented **Spiro Mound shell beads,** disc and barrel types, 37 in. in length.   G—$59

Decorated **abalone shell pendant,** 4-1/8 in. long, about 2 in. average width. Single drill-hole at one end; scalloped cut-outs at other end; from California.   C—$80

Strand of shell beads, graduated sizes and well shaped beads, with 40 in. length.   G—$170

Polished **shell pendant,** one side with heavy polish, drilled with three holes. It is 1¾ in. long and 1½ in. wide, from Virginia.

G—$12

Graduated **strand of shell beads,** well shaped and 19 in. in length; from Tennessee. G—$50

Shell hoe, Virginia, 4 in. long 2½ in. wide. Made from shell of a freshwater mussel. Single hole in thick central portion for handle. Shell somewhat deteriorated. C—$19

Effigy shell head of alligator; strange piece excavated in Arkansas; it is undrilled and 2 in. long. G—$23

Northern California **tube shell beads,** made by pump-drilling abalone shell. G—$150

Conch shell plummet, from Florida, double grooved at the top. Piece is 4¼ in. long, slender, about 1 in. in diameter at center. Lower end tapers to near-point. Discolored with age. C—$53

Otter hide necklace with large **sea shell ornament,** possibly a personal amulet. G—$60

Grooved shell bead, perforated at each end to be worn as a pendant. From Tennessee, it is 3¾ in. long. G—$18

String of **marine shell beads,** approximately 50, recovered from site in Tennessee. Beads average ¾ in. long and 3/8 in. in diameter. Well preserved necklace. C—$70

Outstanding strand of **shell heishi beads,** prehistoric, very well made; 31 in. in length, and from Arizona. G—$75

Shell ornaments in the shape of birds, from California. Two have holes; the third is undrilled. Average size, 1¼ in. by 1½ in. G—$28 set

Perforated shell disc, with hole in the center; 2 in. in diameter. G—$12

Suggested Reading

Miles, Charles, *Indian & Eskimo Artifacts of North America,* Bonanza Books, New York, 1963

Doorway in ruins showing curtain made of reeds. Aztec Ruins National Monument, New Mexico. Photo courtesy U.S. Department of the Interior, National Park Service.

CHAPTER IV
AXE FORMS

Indian axes are a touchmark of prehistoric occupation of the land. Most were made of some type of hardstone which worked well and provided a durable cutting edge and a pounding surface. The first well-made hardstone axes, as opposed to chipped flint, were made about 6000 years ago. Then Amerinds discovered how to shape stone by pounding, grinding and polishing.

Pecking and abrasion are the second of the three great tool-making methods. A stone a bit larger than the axe-to-be was selected. This was struck rapidly and repeatedly with a smaller hammerstone, each blow powdering and removing bits of stone.

Grooves were pecked and ground, except for celts. The axe was then polished, perhaps with sand and leather. Sometimes the entire axe head was so-treated; more often, the lower blade and groove area only were polished.

The groove of course was for the handle, and helped secure the axe while in use. This matter of the groove appears to follow a logical sequence, with the oldest axes being full-grooved, or entirely circled with the handle channel.

Later axes were either three-quarter grooved or half-grooved, depending on period and region. And the most recent axe form, used until the arrival of Whites, was the celt. This was essentially a long and narrow grooveless axe, and was mounted in a hole of socket of a rather thick-ended handle.

Some areas did not follow this exact progression, and the full-grooved axe was used by some later peoples. Whatever the type, the axe heads are scattered over most of North America. There is an interesting theory that a prime use for axes in prehistoric times wasn't for battle, or even for felling trees, though such woodwork was certainly done. Instead, axes were an aid in obtaining sufficient firewood for heat, light and food preparation.

The collecting of axes is a major field. Prices can range from several dollars for a battered, low-grade specimen to $1500 for a fine trophy-grade ceremonial axe.

The rare monolithic (one-stone) axes are late prehistoric copies of the celtiform axe — complete with handle. There's really no top price limit to axes of this type. But the average price for the average axe is probably in the $60 to $125 range.

For the dozens of thousands of collectible axes, a number of guidelines are used to judge axe quality. Material is important, with a compact, close-grained stone most desirable. According to several knowledgeable axe collectors, size and condition are the two key factors, followed by shape or type. Large size is preferred to smaller sizes, because these have more "visual impact" and do in fact represent more workmanship by the prehistoric creator.

As with **all** early Amerind works, condition — the presence and amount of damage or absence of same — is vital. (A particular perfect axe might be worth $200 to a collector; half the same axe, nothing.) Some axe types are considered extra-good, because they have additional, often regional, "extras".

Examples might be the Michigan barbed axes, with the end-projecting groove ridges, or the fluted Wisconsin varieties. These have various arrangements of shallow channels, usually at an angle to the actual axe groove. The purpose of such varieties is not known; it may have been only decorative.

Still other axe value determinants are overall workstyle and balance and symmetry along several examination planes. The blade edge or bit ought to be regular and without heavy use-damage. Groove ridges, if present, should be even and similar. Polish adds to value, and the more the better.

Fakes exist in all axe categories, but abound in two. One is the low-cost axe, made of a softer stone (brown and gray sandstone seem to be popular) with the axe made first, then the groove pecked in. Widely sold in the $25 to $50 range, they are fine examples of nothing.

A tougher area is the well-made trophy-grade hardstone axe-head, complete with a few just-still-visible peck marks. Consult with advanced collectors before laying out any large sum, and if the piece is at all questionable, pass it by.

FULL-GROOVE AXES

Full-groove axe, Minnesota, 8¼ in. long, about 5 in. wide. Unusual in that groove is very near the center of axe, not closer to pounding poll. Little polish, a very utilitarian form, fine condition.   C—$90

Superb **axe** from Richland County, Ohio, 7¾ in. long and 3¾ in. wide. Fine condition.   G—$200

Miniature Ohio **grooved axe**, highly polished, 3 in. long and 2 in. wide; material is a dark green color.   G—$25

Full-grooved axe, Michigan, and blade tapers to about half of extreme width, 4¼ in. at grooved ridges. Piece is 6½ in. long, made of a white or gray stone. Some original wear on blade edge, but only average.   C—$130

Full-groove axe, 5 in. long and 2-5/8 in. wide, and a dark brown color. From Iowa.   G—$35

Full-groove axe, Arizona, 6 in. long, of a black basaltic rock. Groove is near rounded poll, with long, polished blade and excurvate blade edge.   D—$155

FULL GROOVE AXE, 4 in. by 6¾ in., and very heavy. Semi-polished, with some nicks, this piece is from Michigan.   C—$75

Photo courtesy Bob Brand Collection, Pennsburg, Pennsylvania.

FULL GROOVE AXE, 4¾ in. by 8¼ in. Unpolished, but a good example of a Pennsylvania axe. From the Delaware River area.

C—$85

Photo courtesy Bob Brand Collection, Pennsburg, Pennsylvania.

Full-groove axe, Missouri, 6¼ in. long, about 4 in. wide. Some damage to lower blade region, probably prehistoric breakage, disfigures piece.   C—$35

Miniature **full-groove axe,** Illinois, 3-1/8 in. long, and well-polished over all surface. Shallow groove.   C—$65

Large **full-groove axe,** from Illinois, perhaps ceremonial. Piece is 14½ in. long, 8 in. wide and was a surface find on Archaic site. Well-polished in groove and lower blade regions; peck-marks remain on other surfaces.   C—$495

Raised groove dark gray **axe,** found while excavating for the railroad building in St. Louis. Some damage to bit; piece is 7¼ in. long and 4 in. wide.   G—$140

Full-groove axe, probably middle Archaic, with pronounced ridge around groove, upper and lower areas. Axe is 10¼ in. long, of dark compact stone; high polish, especially on blade.   C—$325

Small black **full-groove axe,** 4-3/8 in. high and 2¾ in. wide. Groove is shallow but very regular, good overall polish to piece. Blade edge shows mild battering.   C—$42

FULL GROOVE AXE, 4 in. by 7¼ in. and very heavy. Somewhat crude, but an unusual type; semi-polished, and with several nicks.

C—$200

Photo courtesy Bob Brand Collection, Pennsburg, Pennsylvania.

FULL-GROOVED AXE, 4¼ in. long. Archaic, excellent condition. Edge has very mild battering, but piece has overall high polish.   C—$50

Private collection.

FULL-GROOVED ROUND-TOP AXE, 3 in. by 7¼ in. This piece is from New Jersey, unpolished, and with slight nick in the top.   C—$75

Photo courtesy Bob Brand Collection, Pennsburg, Pennsylvania.

LIGHTLY GROOVED AXE, full-grooved type, 7 in. long. Almost round, it has an extreme diameter of 2½ in. Found in Mifflin County, Pennsylvania; cutting edge or bit is only 7/8 in. long, and is polished.   C—$70

Photo courtesy Jonas Yoder, Jr., McVeytown, Pennsylvania.

Note: A **full-groove axe**, the midwestern trophy-grade axe, is not represented here. Sometimes these are also **three-fourth groove**. This axe is made of colorful high-grade hardstone, is between 4 in. and 6 in. long, with ridged groove. No dealer had one in stock, and none have been offered at auction recently. The "going rate" for classic specimens is said to be in the $750 to $3000 range. One knowledgeable collector stated that probably no more than three hundred authentic pieces exist.

THREE-FOURTH GROOVE AXES
(also called "three-quarter groove")

Black and white granite **three-quarter groove axe**, Brown County, Illinois; 7 in. long, 4 in. wide. An exceptional axe.   G—$250

Three-quarter groove axe, from Southwestern cliff dweller site, and with wide, shallow groove near large and rounded poll. Stone head is 6¼ in. long, of black material, with very small cutting edge, 1-7/8 in. long, curved. Fine condition.   D—$110

Very large **three-quarter groove axe**, Southeastern U.S., possibly ceremonial size. Axe head is 13¼ in. long, and 7 in. wide below groove. Good condition; not polished.   A—$160

THREE-FOURTH GROOVE AXE, 4 in. by 6 in. Piece is in very good condition, with a small nick on the back; semi-polished.   C—$135
Photo courtesy Bob Brand Collection, Pennsburg, Pennsylvania.

66

Large **three-quarter groove axe,** 9 in. long, 5½ in. wide, nearly 4 in. thick. Overall high polish.   A—$175

Miniature axe, three-quarter groove, exactly 3 in. long, about 5/8 in. thick. Well-made piece.   C—$65

Large **three-quarter groove axe,** Missouri, 6 in. long and 4½ in. wide.   G—$125

Three-quarter groove axe, about 6 in. long, about 3 in. wide, made of a dark, dense material. High polish in lower blade region.
A—$85

Hardstone **three-quarter groove axe,** Missouri, 4 in. long and 3 in. wide.   G—$50

Hohokam **three-quarter groove axe,** Arizona, 9½ in. long, with typical wide and shallow groove. A little over 3 in. wide; stone head tapers to a small, rounded blade edge.   D—$100

Three-quarter groove axe, Western U.S., 5-3/8 in. long. Narrow groove is rather deep; perfect condition. High polish in groove and all of blade area. Edge good.   C—$115

Exceptional **three-quarter groove axe,** with slight basal flute, from Jersey County, Illinois. Piece is 7 in. long and 3½ in. wide. Material is dark green and white in color.   G—$180

Fine Southwestern U.S. **axe,** three-quarter groove, perfect condition. Has made-up (recent) handle for display, but axe-head is original and fine.   A—$95

Outstanding **Hohokam axe,** three-quarter groove, 8 in. long and 3 in. wide. Bit is highly polished.   G—$170

THREE-FOURTH GROOVE AXE, 3¼ in. by 6½ in. with the Keokuk groove. From Pike County, Illinois, this is a good piece, semi-polished. It was formerly in the E. W. Payne Collection.

C—$160

Photo courtesy Bob Brand Collection, Pennsburg, Pennsylvania.

Very fine THREE-QUARTER GROOVED AXE, Archaic period, made of a brown fine-grained stone. It is 8½ in. long and 4½ in. wide; weight is 7 pounds. This axe has exceptionally fine lines, and was found in Illinois.

C—$250.-$600.

Photo courtesy John P. Grotte, Illinois.

THREE-FOURTH GROOVE AXE, 3½ in. by 8 in., from Pike County, Illinois. Material is a greenish-black; piece is semi-polished, fine condition.   C—$160
Photo courtesy Bob Brand Collection, Pennsburg, Pennsylvania.

Fine THREE-QUARTER GROOVED AXE, of a granite-like fine grained brown stone. Axe is 8½ in. long, 4¼ in. wide and 2-5/8 in. thick. It weighs 6 pounds and was found in Adams County, Illinois; this axe is very finely made.   C—$250.-$600.
Photo courtesy John P. Grotte, Illinois.

HALF-GROOVE AXES

Half-groove axe, 4¼ in. long and 2¾ in. wide, good groove but blade is canted off to one side, giving lopsided appearance. Made of a close-grained sandstone-like material.　　　　　C—$32

Half-groove Keokuk-type axe, rectangular outline, 3¾ in. long. Made of a dark compact stone; groove and blade area well polished. Crisp, clean lines on this specimen.　　　　　D—$75

Half-groove axe from Missouri, well-shaped and polish over entire surface. Edges, front and rear, undamaged. Axe is 7 in. long, 3¼ in. wide. No damage, fine specimen.　　　　　C—$240

Unremarkable **half-groove axe,** 4 in. long and 2¾ in. wide. Lacks polish; poll area is battered, blade average.　　　　　C—$17

Half-groove Keokuk-type axe, made of a highly polished granite-like stone, black and tan color. Axe is 4¼ in. high. From Iowa. Blade edge forms very pleasing excurvate contour.　　　　　D—$90

CELTS (ungrooved axes)

Large **celt,** from northern Louisiana, 7¼ in. long, 3¼ in. wide, well polished. Made of a green and black material, no damage, good lines.　　　　　D—$75

Large polished **celt.** From Shelby County, Illinois. Piece is 7 in. long and 3¼ in. wide.　　　　　G—$150

Fine gray stone **celt,** 5 in. long and 2¼ in. wide. No damage.
　　　　　G—$32

Rectangular **Hopewellian celt,** central Ohio, 6 in. long, 2¾ in. wide at blade, both sides flatish. No damage, and made from a yellow and tan stone. Good lines.　　　　　C—$70

COLLECTION: Excellent grouping of stone and slate artifacts, all from Tennessee. Pictured are axe and celt forms, Atl-atl weights, gorgets, pendants, and cones. C—Not listed.

Photo courtesy Joseph D. Love, Chattanooga, Tennessee.

Miniature celt, 2 in. long and 1 in. wide. G—$14

Fine speckled granite-like **celt** 10 in. long, about 4 in. wide. Polished cutting edge; celt is cylindrical in shape, and even poll area is well polished. C—$95

Arkansas **Caddoan celt,** dark gray stone; 5 in. long and 1¾ in wide. G—$24

Hardstone **celt,** average form, late prehistoric, from Illinois. Piece is 5½ in. long, 2¾ in. wide, about 2 in. thick. Several minor plow scars, otherwise good condition. D—$23

Granite **celt,** squared-base type, 5-7/8 in. long, 2¾ in. wide. Good polish in lower blade area; two minor plow marks that disfigure blade side. C—$16

Celt from Virginia, 5¼ in. long and 2¼ in. wqide. Stone is a light gray color. G—$14

Hopewellian **rectangular celt**, from Illinois, 9¼ in. long, 3¾ in. wide near bit, and evidencing almost perfect balance. All lines pleasing; entire surface area polished to a uniform medium-high gloss. No damage; piece looks as if it has never been used. Granitic stone approaches coal-black. C—$210

Dark greenstone **celt**, outstanding polish, good condition. It is 4¼ in. long and 2¼ in. wide. G—$50

Miniature celt, 1-3/8 in. long, from Iowa, found during tilling of garden. Proportionate to full-size specimens. C—$23

Miniature celt, 2¼ in. long, slightly flared blade corners, found in Missouri. Black and white hardstone. C—$55

Fine polished **miniature flare-bit celt,** from Oklahoma. It is 2½ in. long and 1½ in. wide. G—$23

Dark green **celt** from eastern Texas, polished bit, 5 in. long and 2¼ in. wide. G— $26

CELTIFORM TOOLS, all from Canada, and averaging 5 in. in length. Piece in center may be unfinished; all in fine condition. C—$10-$30
Photo courtesy Robert C. Calvert, London, Ontario, Canada.

Adz blades, all late prehistoric, Adena culture, Midwestern. Top: Lower portion of larger ADENA ADZ, salvaged in rear section, 3¼ in. long, colorful material. C—$18
Black ADENA ADZ, edge shows heavy wear, good form. C—$16
Small brown stone ADENA ADZ, exactly to scale of much larger specimens, 3¼ in. long.
C—$23
ADENA ADZ blade, almost identical to black specimen at left; edge is sharp. C—$16
Private collection.

Three fine Midwestern celts. L to R: Fine Late prehistoric HOPEWELLIAN CELT, nicely tapered. Polish on lower blade, 5-3/8 in. long. C—$35
Slender TAPERED CELT, prob. late prehistoric, made of a brownish quartz. Unusual material and good lines to piece. C—$40
Large HOPEWELLIAN CELT, nearly round at center, heavily polished over entire surface. Brown material, black inclusions, granite-like stone. C—$45
Private collection.

Small selection of late prehistoric artifacts, longest (bot. 1.) 3½ in.
(Top row, L to R: Small CELT.) C—$15
Rectangular HOPEWELLIAN CELT, perfect form and highly polished overall. C—$30
SLATE CELT, probably Adena, good edge and well-rounded. C—$17
Celt or CHISEL, well-polished overall, two small damaged areas appear as light-colored spots. C—$15
CHISEL, well-tapered but no polish. May be fragment from larger specimen. C—$7
Private collection.

Unusual THREE-QUARTERS GROOVED AXE, from Franklin County, Ohio, and 6-7/8 in. long, 3-5/8 in. wide. Made of grayish quartzite material. Axe has narrow ridge running from front of groove to lower blade, then up rear portion to flatish area behind groove. Also, blade size is small for axe of this size.

C—$130

Private collection.

Fine THREE-QUARTERS GROOVED AXE, 7½ in. long, 3¼ in. wide below notch. Very good condition, some polish, Franklin County, Ohio. Archaic period; axe is made of a compact brownish material.

C—$150

Private collection.

Chipped flint artifacts with polished blade areas. L to R:
FLINT CELT about 5 in. long, blade region highly polished.   C—$35
FLINT CELT or chisel, lower blade region nicely polished, good edge.   C—$15
FLINT CHISEL, highly polished blade area, small working edge   C—$22
Private collection.

Banded slate celt, 6¾ in. long, from Illinois, and exactly 3 in. at greatest width. Cylindrical form, black bands on green background. One agricultural equipment mark toward top of rounded poll, not deep. C—$50

Granite **celt,** rectangular form, 4 in. long and 2¼ in. wide. High polish overall, and speckled black and white material. No damage; perfect proportions. From Missouri. C—$48

From left to right:
CELTS AND GOUGES, *average-good condition, made of slate and hardstone. All from Canada.*
C—$5-$25 each

Large CELTS, *possibly Woodland period, one 10 in. long, other 8¾ in. Blade lengths are 2½ in. both from Canada.* *Left (longest)* *C—$30*
Right C—$30

Photo courtesy Robert C. Calvert, London, Ontario, Canada.

CELTIFORM TOOLS, *hardstone and slate, 4½ in. to 6 in. long. All from Canada, and evidencing varied degrees of workstyle and condition.* *C—$5-$30*
Photo courtesy Robert C. Calvert, London, Ontario, Canada.

AXE VARIETIES

Lightly **grooved celt,** Indiana, with the tapering characteristics of the celt and very light axe-like full grooving. Piece is about 6 in. long, and groove was pecked in at no great depth. Celt head is lightly polished overall except for groove. D—$45

Porphyry **Michigan barbed axe,** very colorful material. Outstanding specimen that has been pictured in archeological publications. It is 7¼ in. long and 3¾ in. wide. G—$800

Very good **flared-bit celt** or spatulate form, nearly 6 in. long and 2½ in. wide at blade-edge tips. Well-contoured and is made of a dark, compact material. D—$95

Black **stone monolithic axe,** 15¾ in. long, and 6¼ in. high at celtiform head height. Copy is one-piece stone of complete celt-axe with handle. Piece has exceptional polish over-all. Very rare; probably no more than a few hundred complete specimens exist. Late prehistoric. (Private collection): C—$4500

Unusual DUO-BLADED CELT, from collection in New Jersey. Material is a light green very compact material almost resembling soapstone. Both edges fine condition, overall polish. Piece is 6¼ in. long, about 3½ in. wide. D—$30 Private collection.

DOUBLE-GROOVE AXE, fully grooved, 3 in. by 5 in. This is a very rare axe form; it is blackish in color with tanish speckles, and in perfect condition. C—$400+ Photo courtesy Bob Brand Collection, Pennsburg, Pennsylvania.

Flare-bit celt, fine condition, polish on blade. Piece is 7½ in. long and 3¼ in. wide. G—$75

Wisconsin fluted axe, three-quarter groove, with fluting running parallel to groove and lower blade regions. Fluting is very shallow but regular. Axe is 6½ in. long. C—$300

Notched celt, from Indiana, 3½ in. long, and with pecked notches on side edges. Faces polished; interesting specimen and not common. D—$25

Top "SLAVE-KILLER" CEREMONIAL AXE, 15 in. long. Item was traded for at the mouth of the Columbia River in 1840 by Joseph Moore, Mate of the ship Salem Queen.

Bottom "SLAVE-KILLER" CEREMONIAL AXE, 15 in. long. This piece was found about 1833 on the Oregon coast.
C—Museum quality; No value listed.
S. W. Kernaghan photo; Marguerite Kernaghan Collection.

MONOLITHIC AXE, 9½ in. high and 20 in. long. Mississippian period, and a ceremonial item. This specimen was found by Colonel Masion east of Tazewell, Tennessee, in the early 1900's.
C—Museum quality; no value listed.
S. W. Kernaghan photo; Marguerite Kernaghan Collection.

Hardstone spud-type celt, with extended blade corners. Dark granite, from Missouri. Spud is 13 in. long, 3¼ in. across at blade corners. Highly polished all over, especially in blade region. Probably ceremonial; no use marks whatsoever. C—$900

Extremely fine **Michigan barbed-ridge axe,** with groove extensions at both ends, top and bottom. Material is a gray speckled granite, and piece is 8½ in. long, average width for piece. Perfect condition. Axe poll is almost pointed. Fine polish. D—$650

Celtiform spud or **flare-bit celt,** found in eastern Minnesota. About 8 in. long, 3½ in. wide at blade corners. Each face has 3 shallow grooves, for unknown reasons. Not a common specimen. D—$350

Wisconsin fluted axe, three-quarter groove type, 6½ in. long, with single central flute on each blade side. From this, other grooves radiate. Rounded poll also has two grooves on sides, which follow contour of the top. Unusual, interesting example of multiple fluting.

D—$700

Large flare-bit celt, blade sides and edge highly polished, body of piece retains some peckmarks. It is 11¼ in. long, and 4-1/8 in. across at blade edges.

C—$375

Missouri **flare-bit celt,** 6½ in. long and 2½ in. wide.

G—$55

Double-groove axe, from northern Missouri, unusual. Piece is 5¾ in. long, about 2½ in. wide, lower groove a bit deeper than upper groove. Green, compact stone.

C—$135

HUMP-BACKED AXE OR ADZ, 6½ in. long and 2 in. wide and thick at central ridge. Blade is at wider end, and piece is in excellent condition; not a common artifact. Material is a green hardstone.
C — $75-$125

Photo courtesy Robert C. Calvert, London, Ontario, Canada.

Double-groove axe, Iowa, black granitic stone and 6½ in. long, 2-7/8 in. wide. Distinct double groove, and lower blade is in perfect condition. Little polish.

C—$125

Long-poll celt, Lower Mississippi Valley, 6¼ in. long, 1-3/8 in. wide. Fine example and undamaged; unusually slender for type.

D—$85

Half-groove axe, Iowa, 3½ in. long and 3¼ in. wide. Well-polished, fine color, perfect condition except for tiny chip from cutting edge, depression polished. C—$80

Hardstone adz, 4-7/8 in. long, 1-7/8 in. wide at curved cutting edge. Flat bottom, very minor damage to rounded end. D—$50

Three-quarter groove axe, from Arizona, 9 in. long and 3¼ in. wide at groove area. Good polish in groove and on lower blade. Fine overall form. D—$140

One of the most notable and best-preserved of prehistoric cliff dwellings in the Southwest, with many stones left just as the Indians had placed them. Mesa Verde National Park, Colorado.

Photo courtesy U.S. Department of the Interior, National Park Service.

–Portion of the Keet Seel ruins, among the most important of cliff dwellings in the American Southwest. Navajo National Monument, Arizona.

Photo courtesy of U.S. Department of the Interior, National Park Service.

CHAPTER V
STONE COLLECTIBLES

"Stone" here means hardstone, natural rocks commonly used in prehistoric times to make artifacts. This chapter deals with a variety of classes, among them the curious discoidals, food grinders and pulverizers, and the mundane hammerstones. There are effigies, utensils and many others.

For each grouping, a slightly different set of measures determine collector interest and help set fair market values. All of these artifacts are relatively simple in design, except for effigy figures.

Portrayals of human, and animal, figures from early times have always been premium collector items. In all this stone-collectible area, the one aspect to be examined is the nebulous term, "first appearance".

Assuming the article is genuine — and no listing or photograph of a questionable piece has been put in this book — there are some questions to be considered. Is the artifact pleasing? Why? Does it bother, confuse, you? Again why? Is it larger or smaller than usual for the type — and is it too large or too small for your taste? Does it, as-is, give a feeling of completeness, of well-accomplished form?

Granted, this is looking at early Indian items as art — but that is what is being done these days. Again, the value-range can be jolting. A plain oval pestle, little more than a natural cobble with some wear-marks, can have literally no market value. A long ceremonial-grade pestle, say from the Northwest U.S. region and evidencing supreme care in the making can easily be in the $300 to $500 class.

There is still some diversity of opinion as to what discoidals ("discs" to collectors) are. It is agreed that they are found in the Mississippi watershed area and are late prehistoric. Numerous historic-period reports state they were rolled along the ground and were used as targets for arrows and thrown darts in a game called "Chunkey".

However, the workmanship displayed for many fine examples suggests they were more than utilitarian in nature, at least the better specimens. And there is a definite lack of damage which would have resulted from such violent use. A superb specimen sold a few years ago for $1000, but the average disc price would be nearer $40 to $50.

Plummets are still another enigma; few are listed here, as they were commonly made of materials other than hardstone. Plummets are shaped like elongated eggs, with a hole or groove at the smaller end. Most meticulously made, well proportioned and polished.

For a long time, it was thought they were fishing or net sinkers. New thought is that they were **bolas** weights, and were secured by short thongs in sets of 3 to 5. In use, they were whirled and thrown, to bring down waterfowl or small game.

The following information on spatulates was written by Tom Browner of Davenport, Iowa, who has contributed greatly to the prehistoric section of the book; used with permission.

SPATULATES

"Spatulates, commonly known as spuds, probably began around AD 500, having evolved from the Woodland culture's flared-bit celts. Like celts, many spatulates show halfting lines where they were attached to wooden handles. Spatulates continued to evolve until the end of the Mississippian period, about AD 1700.

"It is uncertain where spatulates began; however, the Mississippi River Valley north of St. Louis is an educated guess. This assumption is based on the large numbers of spuds found in the region and the fact that Cahokia seems to be the divisional point between Northern and Southern traditions.

"The "heart area" of the Northern Tradition seems to be Illinois, Missouri, Indiana and Ohio. Northern Tradition spatulates are made of fine-grained granites and occasionally slate. The earlier types tend to have thicker bodies like celts, oval cross-sections and rounded bits. As time progressed, the polls became thinner and more rounded. The bits became more elongated and convex. To the North, the polls became shorter; likewise, the further South the longer the polls tend to be.

"Southern Spatulates tend to have rounded and long polls. The material of choice tends to be green-stone or slates. The bits flatten and become almost square in classic types, with tally marks or grooves being common. The Southern Tradition heartland is southern Illinois, Missouri, Kentucky, Tennessee, Georgia, and Alabama. Cohokia, near St. Louis, Missouri, seems to be the area where the two traditions met.''

Unfortunately, because of space limitations, this section can only give a sampling of the rich and varied field of hardstone Indian collectibles.

SPATULATES OR SPUDS

Granite **spud**, 10 in. long and 1¼ in. wide, made of well-polished material, good overall form. This piece was broken and restored.

A—$135

Elongated **spud**, 13¼ in. long and 1-7/8 in. wide, with good material, blackish fine-grained hardstone. Beautiful form, evenly flared bit, high polish; one slight plow-scar along poll side but barely visible. Rare item in size and shape.

C—$1350

Granite **spud**, 10 in. long and 2 in. wide at bit. Bit or blade area has softly rounded corners instead of sharp shoulders.

A—$70

Granite **spud**, 8 in. long and 3 in. wide, well polished and good form. Fine condition.

A—$225

NORTHERN TRADITION SPATULATE, 9 in. long and 3 in. wide at flared bit. This specimen is one of the finest of the type. Note the lighter hafting band 3½ in. from the bit tip. Rounded bit and oblong poll show it to be from about AD 900. Material is a gray, polished granite; this piece is from Fulton County, Illinois.

C—$900

Courtesy Ferrel Anderson, photographer; Thomas Browner Collection: Davenport, Iowa.

Banded slate **spud,** 7½ in. long and 1-3/8 in. wide, made of a finely banded green and black material. Good shape and overall polish, no damage. C—$475

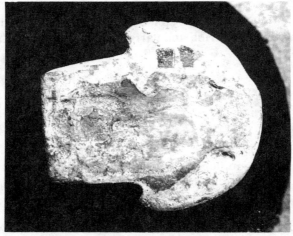

LATE SOUTHERN-TYPE SPATULATE or spud form, 5¾ in. by 5-1/8 in. A large specimen of a rare type, it lacks the drilled hole common in many pieces. Exfoliation of the surface and large size identify this as authentic. There are generally no genuine artifacts of this type on the market. Specimen is made of red and tan limonite, and is from Woodruff County, Arkansas.
C—$150.-$400.

Courtesy Ferrel Anderson, photographer; Thomas Browner Collection: Davenport, Iowa.

DISCOIDALS

Double-cupped discoidal, 3¼ in. wide, 1-3/8 in. high, light tan granitic material and overall high polish. Midwestern piece.
C—$130

Tennessee discoidal, uncupped and of a black material. It is 2¼ in. in diameter and 1¼ in. high. G—$75

Pink and black **quartz discoidal,** 3½ in. in diameter and 1½ in. high, slightly cupped each side. Piece is from Illinois. G—$195

Miniature discoidal, 1¼ in. in diameter, 3/8 in. thick, very shallowly cupped, medium-good polish. Rare. C—$50

Quartz discoidal, cups on each side (double or duo-cupped), and has a golden color. Piece is 2¼ in. in diameter and ¾ in. thick.
G—$135

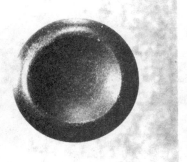

DOUBLE-CUP LATE WOODLAND DISCOIDAL, 2¾ in. in diameter. This specimen is notable for its deep cups, perfect symmetry and polish; even the cups are polished, which is unusual for most discoidals. The piece is from Des Moines County, Iowa, and is made of rhyolite.

C—$275

Courtesy Ferrel Anderson, photographer; Thomas Browner Collection: Davenport, Iowa.

DOUBLE-CUP WOODLAND DISCOIDAL, 4¼ in. in diameter, 2 in. thick. Made of black granite, this is an Ohio piece. The specimen has good size, shape and deep cups. It also lacks color and sharply delineated cup rims; not quite unique enough to command the top discoidal prices of $200-$300. Perfect condition.

C—$325

Courtesy Ferrel Anderson, photographer; Thomas Browner Collection: Davenport, Iowa.

COLLECTION: Nice grouping of discoidals and game-stones, all from Tennessee. Note especially the very large double-cupped disc. These artifacts often display superior workstyles.

Photo courtesy Joseph D. Love, Chattanooga, Tennessee.

85

Tan and brown striped DISCOIDAL, Jersey Bluff or Cahokia type. It is 3½ in. in diameter and 2 in. high, and from Woodland times.
C—$195

Photo courtesy John P. Grotte, Illinois.

Jersey Bluff type DISCOIDAL, 2-5/8 in. in diameter and 1½ in. high. Made of a dark green material, from Adams County, Illinois, and highly polished. Prob. from Woodland period.
C—$215

Photo courtesy John P. Grotte, Illinois.

Hardstone discoidal, made of a light-colored close-grained stone. Cupped on both sides, perfectly round, smooth finish. A bit over 4 in. in diameter, and 1-3/8 in. thick at outer rim. Hole at center where the bottom of cups meet. C—$325

Pink **hardstone discoidal,** with deep cups, 2¼ in. in diameter and 1¼ in. thick. G—$210

Quartz discoidal, duo-cupped, nearly 6 in. in diameter and 2-1/8 in. in thickness. Polished to a high gloss overall, no damage or imperfection in stone. Piece glitters with quartzite inclusion when strong light strikes it; very pleasing piece. C—$600

CAHOKIA TYPE DISCOIDAL, 3 in. in diameter. This is a classic Cahokia discoidal with deep cups and prominent rims. When competing local collectors attempt to obtain a limited number of classic artifacts, the prices go up. This piece is made of gray granite and is from Pike County, Illinois. C—$325
Courtesy Ferrel Anderson, photographer; Thomas Browner Collection: Davenport, Iowa.

STONE DISCOIDAL, Jersey Bluff type (has somewhat flattened portion around both outside rims) and made of an attractive yellow, green, black and pink granite. Discoidal was found in Adams County, Illinois, and is 3¾ in. in diameter, 2¼ in. high. It displays exceptionally fine workmanship.   C—$700

Photo courtesy John P. Grotte, Illinois.

DISCOIDAL, Jersey Bluff or Cahokia type, found in Humphrey County, Tennessee. It is 2-3/8 in. in diameter and 1¼ in. high. From Mississippian times, it is made of a colorful reddish purple and gray quartz.   C—$325

Photo courtesy John P. Grotte, Illinois.

Discoidal of pottery, only 1½ in. in diameter, and with decorations of incised lines scratched into surface.   C—$10

Discoidal from Tennessee, double-dish (duo-cupped) form, perfectly scooped and "dimple" in center of cup on each side. Piece is 3¾ in. in diameter, made from fine orange-red stone.   C—$360

Double-cupped discoidal, Indiana, 2-7/8 in. in diameter and 1¼ in. thick.   D—$90

Biscuit-type discoidal, 2-1/8 in. in diameter, made of black and reddish hardstone. Perfect, and polished.   C—$95

Quartzite **double-cupped discoidal,** 2½ in. in diameter and of a dark green steatite. Outside rim has a single meandering line incised around it.   C—$140

Sandstone **discoidal,** battered around outside rim, 2¼ in. in diameter.   C—$20

Barrel-type discoidal, 2¾ in. in diameter, 2-1/8 in. thick. Average good condition; not much polish.   D—$32

CAHOKIA TYPE DISCOIDAL, 2¾ in. in diameter, and made of a red quartzite. This is a nice intact and colorful specimen, with traceable history. It is from Pike County, Illinois. C—$145

Courtesy Ferrel Anderson, photographer; Thomas Browner Collection: Davenport, Iowa.

Cahokia-type white quartz DISCOIDAL, with outer rim nearly joining central cups on both sides. Found in Madison County, Illinois, this would be a Mississippian period artifact. It is 2-5/8 in. in diameter, and 1¼ in. high.

C—$315

Photo courtesy John P. Grotte, Illinois.

BISCUIT-TYPE DISCOIDAL, 3¼ in. in diameter. Material is a brown and tan claystone. The piece is from Menard County, Illinois, and very colorful and nicely polished. C—$175

Courtesy Ferrel Anderson, photographer; Thomas Browner Collection: Davenport, Iowa.

BISCUIT-TYPE DISCOIDAL, 2-7/8 in. in diameter and made of black diorite. The specimen shows high polish, center pecking and very shallow cupping; it was found on an early Woodland site on the bluffs near Quincy, Illinois. C—$200

Courtesy Ferrel Anderson, photographer; Thomas Browner Collection: Davenport, Iowa.

SALT RIVER TYPE DISCOIDAL, 4½ in. in diameter and 2¼ in. thick, and a large and colorful specimen. Salt River discoidals vary from other types in that the circumference is not oval, but comes to a fine edge like a "V". They are found in the Mississippi River area above St. Louis, Missouri. This piece is made of red quartzite and came from the LaSalle-Peru area of Illinois.   C—$450

Courtesy Ferrel Anderson, photographer; Thomas Browner Collection: Davenport, Iowa.

DOUBLE-CUP DISCOIDAL, sometimes called a "dimple" cup, from the Mississippian era. The disc is 4¾ in. in diameter and is a classic piece. Note the well-defined edges and dimple. Large size, polish and symmetry make this an outstanding artifact. Made of brown granite, this comes from Ohio County, Kentucky.
            C—$425

Courtesy Ferrel Anderson, photographer; Thomas Browner Collection: Davenport, Iowa.

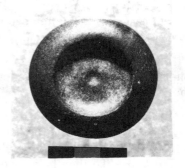

MORTARS & PESTLES (Eastern U.S.)
MANOS & METATES (Western U.S.)

Round boulder **mortar,** from California beach site. It is 9 in. across, and the pounding hole in center is about 4½ in. across. Exterior surface of mortar is fairly smooth.   C—$28

Pear-shaped pestle, probably Archaic, 3 in. high, found in Alabama. Made of a dull-colored hardstone.   C—$14

Missouri **mano** or hand-held corn-grinding stone, 2 in. high and 3 in. wide.   G—$8

Bell-type pestle, 6½ in. high and 3-5/8 in. wide at basal diameter. Top expands slightly while central section is about 2 in. in diameter. Piece is made of a yellow-tan material and there is high polish on the central shaft.   C—$115

Stone pestle, Oregon, 8 in. high. Cylindrical form, and tapering from top to base. Base has an extended band 2 in. high; top has similar but smaller band. Central portion of cylinder forms a handgrip.   C—$110

Roller-type pestle, Vermont, 11½ in. long, about 2 in. in diameter. Some polish around circumference, and polished at both ends, rounded in same areas.   C—$55

Stone mortar from North Carolina, oblong and about 10 in. long. Top depression for holding seeds averages ¾ in. in depth. Center shows extensive wear.   C—$22

Pole-shaped mano, New Mexico, 9½ in. long. Chip on one end, otherwise fine condition.   G—$27

Large round **mortar and pestle,** latter over 14 in. in diameter, 7¾ in. high. Pestle about 10 in. high. (May not have been an original set, but looks like they belong together). Central California origin.   C—$90

Metate or grinding slab for the mano; seed-grinder is 19 in. long, large for the type. Made from a loose-grained stone, upper working surface ground down from long use. Northwestern Nevada.

                                                                      C—$45

Flat **stone metate** from Texas, near Mexican border, about 7 in. long. Grinding stone has 3 protrusions on bottom in triangular pattern, like short legs.   C—$50

Mano or hand-stone for grinding grain or seeds, oblong, 7 in. in length. Underside flat; may have been used with both hands. Probably prehistoric Hohokam, Arizona, and made from a slate-gray porous volcanic rock.   C—$14

Bird-faced **paint mortar,** Oregon, perhaps depicting a hawk. Piece is 7 in. high, 4 in. in diameter, and in battered but good condition. Made from a rough-grained river boulder. Effigy has indented eyes, projecting beak.   C—$125

Long decorative and cylindrical **stone pestle,** probably Yurok, and 16½ in. in length. Piece is 3¼ in. in diameter at base. Extended ring rear bottom and near top. Fine and highly polished stone.

C—$320

WOODWORKING TOOLS

Grooved **stone gouge,** New York, 8¼ in. long, 2-1/8 in. wide at rounded cutting bit. Groove on underside runs from bit to poll end. (Such length is unusual, as many are only partially grooved). Light tan stone, high polish.   D—$95

Black **hardstone chisel,** 4-3/8 in. long, and 1 in. wide, tapered to straight blade at one end, rounded at other. No damage, some heavy use-marks on bit or blade edge.   C—$50

Three-quarter groove adz, from Georgia near Florida line; 9 in. long. Well-finished overall, some use-marks; this is not a particularly common type of artifact.   C—$140

Hardstone gouge, New Jersey, 6-1/8 in. long, deeply scooped concave groove on underside running half the length of piece. It is 1½ in. wide at the cutting edge.   D—$55

Hump-backed adz, from Indiana, 6¾ in. long, with protruding ridge on topside, evidently to aid hafting. Believed to be a woodworking tool. Made of a gray-black material, and piece is about 2 in. wide. Nice polish, no damage. C—$120

OTHER STONE ARTIFACTS

Sandstone **shaft smoother,** 4 in. long. The flat stone has a straight groove along the top, about ½ in. across and 3/8 in. deep. From South Dakota. C—$15

Stone adz handle, from southwestern Washington. It is 11¾ in. long, with a down-curved handle grip. Unusual, but without the once-attached adz head. Well-made piece; well-worn. C—$135

Rare piece from northern Alabama; **hardstone bowl,** 9-5/16 in. in diameter, nearly 3 in. high. Polished inside and out. Pink, close-grained stone, but not Catlinite. Probably a ceremonial item; possibly Mississippian period in origin. C—$480

From left to right:

RARE STONE OBJECT, fully drilled and 2 in. long. Stone still retains painted brown bands, marking this item as probably used in historic times. Exact purpose of item unknown, but may be a medicine man's healing stone. It somewhat resembles ball bannerstones. C—$175
Photo courtesy Robert C. Calvert, London, Ontario, Canada.

UNKNOWN STONE OBJECT, probably prehistoric, found near London, Ontario. Piece is 4½ in. long and has a hole ½ in. deep at one end, with incised marks along end sides. Unfinished pipe? Effigy form? C—$35
Photo courtesy Robert C. Calvert, London, Ontario, Canada.

UNUSUAL STONE OBJECT, purpose unknown, 4 in. long. Item may be a preform, but appears to be a complete artifact. Made of a compact green stone, and found near Komoka, Ontario. C—$85
Photo courtesy Robert C. Calvert, London, Ontario, Canada.

Hematite CONE, 1-5/8 in. in diameter and ¾ in. high. It is from Adams County, Illinois, of a colorful red hematite. This piece is flatbased.
C—$135
Photo courtesy John P. Grotte, Illinois.

Hematite CONE, measuring 1-7/16 in. in diameter and 7/8 in. high. It has a small concave dimple on the flat bottom center. Piece is from the river bottoms of Adams County, Illinois, and prob. dates from Woodland times. The surface of this cone is partially exfoliated or in the process of flaking.
C—$150
Photo courtesy John P. Grotte, Illinois.

Left, concretion cup CONTAINER, may have been for paint, about 2 in. in diameter, center worn smooth.
C—$14
Right, notched pebble NET-SINKER, though exact use of these artifacts is not known. Frequently found near streams in the Midwest.
C—$5
Bottom, small concretion cup CONTAINER, dark brown stone. Outside has also been nicely rounded, central depression is absolutely circular.
C—$15
Private collection.

L to R: DRILLED PEBBLE, unknown use. Good drilling, but rest of stone rough, medium polish only.
C—$8
DO-NUT STONE, California, 3⅓ in. across, very fine central hole. High polish overall. May have been a club head.
C—$75
Unusual SLATE CUTTING TOOL, or for chopping tasks; has characteristics both of notched celts and three-quarter grooved axes. Good edge, probably Archaic period. Midwest.
C—$24
Private collection.

"Donut stone", California, 3½ in. in diameter, and with central hole 1 in. across. Made of a compact hardstone, no damage, highly polished piece. May have been a clubhead. C—$95

Historic **Sioux food pulverizer**; stone head 4 in. high, flat bottom, used for tenderizing meat, crushing seeds and making pemmican. An all-purpose tool, with plain wrap-around leather covered handle 14 in. long. D—$75

Small **stone bowl**, from Oregon, 2¼ in. high, about 5 in. in diameter, of smooth brown stone. Edges chipped in a number of places. A—$50

Sandstone spool, very late prehistoric (Woodland), and from Ohio. Piece is 3-1/8 in. long, and has incised wavy lines on central part of cylinder, which is concave. It is thought that sandstone spools were used with pigment to ceremonially decorate the body. C—$500

Clear rock crystal pebble pendant or bead, smoothed almost flat on one side, left naturally rounded on the other. Hole had been drilled in one end, but had broken through. Very small hole 1/16 in. had been drilled in opposite end. Period unknown; picked up on Midwestern site that has produced Archaic and Woodland artifacts. C—$29

Sandstone awl-sharpener, 3 in. long, with several thin grooves on upper surface. Believed to be "needle tracks". C—$10

Left TEAR-DROP PLUMMET, 4-3/8 in. long and 1-1/8 in. wide. Made of pink and black mottled granite, this item is from the Los Angeles area of California. C—$150

Middle TEAR-DROP PLUMMET, 4-7/8 in. long, made of a black and red mottled granite. It is from the Sacramento area of California. C—$250

Right DRILLED PLUMMET, 4-3/8 in. long and 1 in. in extreme diameter. Made of a yellow and brown granite, this too is from the Sacramento, California area. C—$150

Courtesy Ferrel Anderson, photographer; Thomas Browner Collection: Davenport Iowa.

PLUMMET of hardstone, drilled and grooved at one end. It is 3 in. in length, and 1½ in. in diameter. Object almost resembles an effigy form, perhaps of a manatee, but resemblance is probably accidental. Found in Fairfield County, Ohio.　　　　　　　　　C—$30
Photo courtesy Bob Champion, Ohio.

Grouping of PLUMMETS, all three quite different. L. to r.:
Polished HARDSTONE PLUMMET, 2-3/8 in. long, glossy surface.　　　　　C—$25
Small egg-shaped HEMATITE PLUMMET, very shallowly grooved near top.　C—$25
Fine-grained SANDSTONE PLUMMET, grooved near top for attachment.　　C—$20
Private collection.

Ceremonial club, from British Columbia, Canada. Piece is 16 in. long, and with human head at base of handle. Blade has a blunt cutting edge; weight is just over 4 pounds, and made of a compact dark gray stone.　　　　　　　　　C—$700

Hardstone pendant, 2¾ in. long, 1-3/8 in. wide, made of a fine-grained salt and pepper colored hardstone. Single hole drilled in smaller end, from both sides. Surface is highly polished. Perfect condition, from Illinois.　　　　　　　　　C—$340

Plain **stone club,** of the "fish-killer" type, **miniature** form, only 7½ in. long and 7/8 in. in diameter. Quite unusual, and has small hole drilled in handle end.　　　　　　　　　C—$250

Steatite or soapstone bowl, 12 in. by 16 in. and about 5 in. deep. Exterior walls about 1½ in. thick. Recovered from central California, and in undamaged condition except for extreme wear on upper edges. A rare item.　　　　　　　　　C—$495

Cupstone, about 12 in. long and 4 in. wide, with 2 depressions in top about the size of a silver dollar. Common on Archaic sites in Midwest, purpose uncertain.　　　　　　　　　C—$8

Plummet, from Archaic site, 2¾ in. long, 1 in. in diameter. Made of pink sandstone, top grooved. Perfect.　　　　　　　　　C—$19

Plummet, granite, 1½ in. long and 5/8 in. in diameter. Very shallow groove about in middle.　　　　　　　　　C—$22

Drilled stone tube, 3-7/8 in. long, flat on bottom, highly polished surface. Piece has a central hole about ½ in. in diameter. Stone mottled green and white, one small scratch across top.   C—$120

Sandstone scooped bowl, Massachusetts, 9 in. in diameter and about 3 in. high. Rounded base, and vessel is rather roughly made, time period unknown; much damage to rim area.   C—$65

Hammerstone, ungrooved, 3½ in. high, well polished over-all. Both ends evidence some battering. This was a tool used to make other tools.   C—$2

Fully grooved hardstone maul or club head, 4½ in. high and over 2 in. thick. Groove about ¼ in. deep; this could be considered a heavy-duty hammer-stone.   D—$36

Left DRILLED COFFIN PLUMMET, 3-7/8 in. long, made of green and black granite. This piece is from California.   C—$125

Middle EXPANDED-TOP PLUMMET, 3¾ in. long and 1½ in. in diameter. It is made of a pink and black mottled granite and is from California.   C—$175

Right DRILLED PLUMMET, 3¾ in. long, and material is a green granite. This piece is also from California, the Sacramento area.
     C—$150

Courtesy Ferrel Anderson, photographer; Thomas Browner Collection: Davenport, Iowa.

Left, PLUMMET, ungrooved and undrilled specimen. Item is 2-7/8 in. long, made of gray granite, well-polished.   C—$30

Center, PLUMMET, grooved type with knobbed top. Made of well-polished hematite, plummet is 2¾ in. high.   C—$45

Right PLUMMET, a classic grooved type. Made of hematite, it is 3¾ in. high and 1¼ in. thick.
     C—$70

Courtesy Ferrel Anderson, photographer; Thomas Browner Collection: Davenport, Iowa.

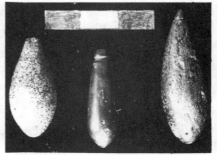

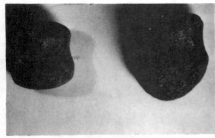

Small THREE-QUARTER GROOVED HAMMER-STONE, measuring 2 in. by 2 in., good groove and well-polished in that region. Midwestern Archaic.   C—$20

Right, larger THREE-QUARTER GROOVED HAMMERSTONE, with one poll tapered. Very little polish, but good form.   C—$25

Private collection.

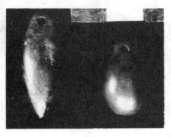

Left, PLUMMET, coffin-shape and 3-1/8 in. long. Material is hematite, and plummet is from Lincoln County, Missouri.   C—$100

Right, PLUMMET, extended-top drilled type. It is 2 in. high and 1¼ in. wide, made of claystone.
                                                 C—$90

Courtesy Ferrel Anderson, photographer; Thomas Browner Collection: Davenport, Iowa.

L to R: FULL-GROOVED HAMMERSTONE about 2½ in. high. Good groove, no damage, compact dark stone.   C—$25

FULL-GROOVED HAMMERSTONE, may be a miniature less than 1 in. high. Unusual, Mid-western.   C—$20

Wide FULL-GROOVED HAMMERSTONE, from Midwestern Archaic site, nearly 2 in. wide, good intact grooving, some battering on polls.
                                                 C—$21

Private collection.

Three-quarter groove hammerstone, 1¾ in. high and 1¼ in. wide. Well polished, perfect condition, from Pennsylvania. Groove area has very smooth finish.   C—$25

Kneeling figure, sandstone, undoubtedly Mississippian, from Georgia mound. An old excavated find, it depicts a clothed woman; figure is 15½ in. high, and weight is over 15 pounds. Well-detailed, especially face. (Private collection):   C—$3500

Pelican-stone charm, effigy figure, California. It somewhat resembles the neck, head and beak of that bird. Piece is 4-7/8 in. high, with extended base.   C—$360

Hardstone drilled object, purpose unknown, 2½ in. high and 1½ in. wide at flattish base. Smaller, rounded top was drilled from both ends and shows much wear. Unpolished.   C—$55

Bell photo of three Sioux Indians dressed for the Sun Dance, probably in Black Hills. Two of the men are wearing large "sun disc" pendants.

Photo courtesy South Dakota State Historical Society.

An 1891 photo taken by Gravill of Deadwood, with original caption: "Home of Mrs. American Horse. Visiting women at Mrs. A's home in hostile camp". Note the proliferation of White-made goods throughout the encampment. Interestingly, one of the more valued things in nearly treeless regions were the long lodge poles used for the tipis.

Photo courtesy of South Dakota State Historical Society.

CHAPTER VI
BANNERSTONES
AND RELATED OBJECTS

The introduction to this chapter was written by Thomas E. Browner, officer of the Central States Archaeological Societies, Inc., and a man thoroughly knowledgeable in the field; used with permission.

"Bannerstones are a loose category of Archaic artifacts. In outline, bannerstones or banners are symmetrical, usually winged artifacts possessing a drilled center hole or notches. Large numbers of blending forms in a great variety of stones lead to difficulties in classifications as well as value.

"Beginning in the Southeast portion of the United States, bannerstones over a period of centuries migrated North and Westward. Evolving with territorial expansion into more eccentric forms and utilizing finer grades of stone, some of the banners are top collectors pieces today.

"As Atl-atl weights, bannerstones were simple tubular forms. Later, the advanced types were too large and thin to take the pressures of hard everyday use. Theories of social status emblems and tribal or religious significance have been placed on the later types.

"As in any commerce, a tangible object must be matched with an intangible concept called value for it to change ownership. Artifacts like bannerstones are one-of-a-kind. Each is different, and therefore values as absolutes do not exist. An artifact is only worth what an individual collector is willing to pay for it. Such a value must be viewed as an extension of the collector's personality, thus reflecting his personal taste, interest and income.

"One collector alone can set the price for a particular class of artifacts by purchasing all that are presented at a higher than normal market value. However, this is unusual as market value is normally determined by the demand of larger groups of collectors, all bidding for a limited number of genuine artifacts.

"In 1912, Warren K. Moorehead stated, "the farther away from the source of supply the more valuable the material — shell, copper, hematite". Of course, he was referring to the economic importance to the Indians. It is interesting to note that the finished artifact today is worth the most in its region of origin. Local artifacts, being the most prized by local collectors, command premium prices.

"Besides demand and location of origin, artifacts generally follow a broad range based, in order of importance, on these factors:

1. Rarity of type
2. Perfection
3. Workmanship
4. Material
5. Size
6. Color
7. Pedigree

"These are self-explanatory, with the possible exception of pedigree. By pedigree is meant a traceable history, beginning with a list of previous owners and ending with photographs in various publications and books. It is a line of ancestry.

"Unfortunately, fakes and fakers do exist. A pedigree does not guarantee genuineness, but it does increase the collector's chances. Many of the fraudulent specimens being produced today are so realistic that they almost defy detection.

"Therefore, only purchase what you know about, and then only from reputable dealers and collectors. Never buy if you have any doubts about a piece. Ask to take the artifact on approval for a reasonable time. This will allow you the opportunity to trace the history and secure other opinions.

"There are no experts, only collectors like yourself with more knowledge and experience. Anyone can be fooled. Unfortunately, one of the byproducts of this situation is that the unknown, the slightly out-of-type, and the unusual are characteristically branded as frauds. The final forms are much treasured and therefore do not tend to change hands as often.

"In choosing a bannerstone, a collector must check the planes, drillings, patination, manufacturing techniques, etc. Many old pieces were scrubbed to bring out the ancient color. The Indians salvaged many specimens. Thus a double crescent banner could end up as a butterfly type. Therefore, even genuine specimens may not be without recent fault or ancient change of profile.

"Are the planes normal for the type? Is the patination even, including edges and salvaged sides? Are the drillings tapered? Has the surface defoliated? Are there any so-called "worm marks"? Once authenticity has been established, merit as to value must be made on the basis of type, perfection, size, color and so forth.

"Unusual range highs and lows may be caused by some of the following factors. Obvious bleaching, scrubbing, or the use of oil, shellac or other caustic agents may lower the value of an artifact by as much as 50%. On the other hand, a good pedigree could increase the asking price by 20%. Buying an artifact in its home locality might cost an extra 30%.

"The finest artifacts of a type could demand a price two or three times the going range high. Prices are generally higher at shows than in homes. However, travel expenses and the reluctance of collectors to sell cherished pieces often makes the dealer's price the only price available.

"Unlike some other collectibles, there are a very limited number of genuine, intact Indian artifacts. Many of these have gone into the vaults of museums and schools and civic organizations and are not readily available for study. In many cases the pride of ownership, more than the object's true value, is a prime objective of the collector.

"Finally, common artifacts remain common.

"The increase in the number of collectors has driven the prices of better grade specimens higher each year. Therefore, buy for the long range appreciation of your investment by selecting the best of what is offered to you. Rare specimens will only become more valuable with time."

(T.E.B.)

Bannerstones

Slate banner, butterfly type, not drilled in center, but nicely grooved to either side, perfect. Wings are 4¼ in. wide from tip to tip. From Michigan.   C—$600

Geniculate bannerstone, banded slate, some minute original damage in hole region. It is 3¼ in. long, 2 in. high, of very colorful blue-black material. Illinois.   C—$450

Pick banner, worked so that bands converge near center, adding to attractiveness. Some battering to slate near one end of central drill hole, unimportant to overall appearance. Somewhat crescentic form, and 3-7/8 in. long. A—$200

Double crescent banner, 5 in. wide, 3-1/8 in. high, some damage to 3 of the 4 arms or wings. Central portions, including hole, are fine. Retains good polish; ideal for restoration. C—$600

Fine **geniculate banner** of banded slate, size about 3 in. by 3 in., pristine condition and a scarce Archaic form. All corners well-rounded, oblong hole, and extension comes to a rounded tip.

A—$470

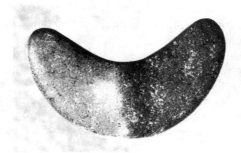

CRESCENT BANNER, hardstone, 3¾ in. by 2½ in. and illustrated in INDIAN AND ESKIMO ARTIFACTS OF NORTH AMERICA. Material is a brown, finegrained granite. C—$600
Courtesy Ferrel Anderson, photographer; Thomas Browner Collection; Davenport, Iowa.

Large **winged banner,** of banded slate, remaining portions measuring 5 in. by 3 in. Lower wing edges broken in prehistoric times, and piece was salvaged by grinding down broken areas to balance the appearance. Salvaged regions not quite as well done as original edged. A—$265

Winged banner, banded slate, of a type sometimes called "butterfly". Piece is 3-1/8 in. wide and 1-5/8 in. high. Finished on exterior; cane-drilled hole not quite completed. C—$200

Pick banner, curved and 4¼ in. long, 1 in. wide, with the slate a banded black, and gray background. D—$195

Chlorite pick banner, hardstone, 2-3/8 in. long 1¼ in. wide at center. Completely drilled and color an amber-yellow, hard to describe. Very minor surface scratches here and there, original, with polish extending into the scratches, which are really only faint lines. C—$700

Tubular banner, Kentucky, rounded top and sides, flat bottom, drilled for entire length, which is 2¾ in. Material a dark gray unbanded slate.   A—$155

Winged banner, Wisconsin, hardstone and made from a material resembling granite. Piece is 3¾ in. wide and 2-1/8 in. long. Undrilled, but highly polished specimen.   C—$245

Fluted ball banner, Ohio, 1-7/8 in. long and 1-1/8 in. wide. Very colorful green slate with red and black bands. Some very slight original damage around one end of drill-hole.   C—$90

End-view of a fine HOURGLASS-TYPE BANNERSTONE. Made of a colorful rose quartz, piece was reed-drilled approximately half way through center. Length is 2-3/8 in. and width is 1-1/8 in.; artifact was found in Adams County, Illinois.   *C—$400*

Photo courtesy John P. Grotte, Illinois.

HOURGLASS BANNERSTONE, from Fulton County, Illinois. It is 1-15/16 in. long and 1¾ in. wide, made of a fine grade of quartz. Drilling is slightly broken out at one end, color is not evenly distributed, nor vivid. It is yet a good, acceptable artifact; if everything were perfect, it could be worth closer to $1000.   *C—$600*

Courtesy Ferrel Anderson, photographer; Thomas Browner Collection; Davenport, Iowa.

From left to right:

Unfinished BUTTERFLY BANNERSTONE, from Chenango County, New York. It is 6 in. wide and 2¾ in. long. Not completed because the drilling missed and bypassed. Shape only fair, and a wing chip breaks the outline. Made of a green and black banded slate.　　　　C—$300-$550

Courtesy Ferrel Anderson, photographer; Thomas Browner Collection: Davenport, Iowa.

BUTTERFLY BANNERSTONE, brown and black banded slate, 4½ in. wide and 2 in. long. Two minor edge nicks do no major harm to this banner. Note also the light "worm trail" from left to right on specimen, moving down at about 45-degree angle. Such markings are within the natural material.　　　　C—$225-$400

Courtesy Ferrel Anderson, photographer; Thomas Browner Collection: Davenport, Iowa.

FLUTED-BALL BANNERSTONE, 2 in. by 1-7/8 in., and from Van Buren County, Michigan. Material is green and light-green banded slate. Plow scar is noticable but does not detract greatly from value as it does not break the contour of the piece.　　　　C—$250

Courtesy Ferrel Anderson, photographer; Thomas Browner Collection: Davenport, Iowa.

BALL BANNERSTONE, 1-5/8 in. by 1½ in. from Bureau County, Illinois, piece is made of green and black banded slate. Note high degree of polish on this well-banded banner.　　　　C—$250

Courtesy Ferrel Anderson, photographer; Thomas Browner Collection: Davenport, Iowa.

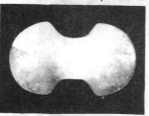

From left to right:

QUARTZ BUTTERFLY BANNERSTONE, 3 in. wide and 1-5/8 in. long. It is from Cedar County, Missouri, made of white quartz with reddish tinges. Perfect in every detail, it lacks only color and more size to command the highest prices. Edges are nicely rounded and wings are proportionate to the size of the barrel.　　　　C—$800-$1200

Courtesy Ferrel Anderson, photographer; Thomas Browner Collection: Davenport, Iowa.

UNDRILLED FETISH KNOBBED LUNATE BANNERSTONE, made of brick-colored hematite. It is 2-7/8 in. wide and 1-5/8 in. long. This specimen is rather crude in form, but does represent a one-of-a-kind object. It is from Hudson County, Tennessee.　　　　C—$150

Courtesy Ferrel Anderson, photographer; Thomas Browner Collection: Davenport, Iowa.

From left to right:

DOUBLE-BITTED AXE BANNERSTONE, from Pope County, Indiana. It is 5½ in. wide and 3¾ in. long, and made from green and black banded slate. Exceptional shape; note the even color and the centered eye (in banding). Both size and color help make this specimen one of the finest of the type.

C—$900-$1500

Courtesy Ferrel Anderson, photographer; Thomas Browner Collection: Davenport, Iowa.

BUTTERFLY BANNERSTONE, 5 in. wide and 1-7/8 in. long, from Miami County, Ohio. Material is a green and black banded slate. An earlier collector scrubbed the piece with steel wool to bring out the colors, but destroyed the surface patina. This should never be done.

C—(without scrubbing) $300-$400

C—(after scrubbing) $125-$175

Courtesy Ferrel Anderson, photographer; Thomas Browner Collection: Davenport, Iowa.

SALVAGED DOUBLE-CRESCENT BANNERSTONE, 4-3/8 in. long and 1½ in. wide. Piece is from Kent County, Illinois. Current appearance of this banded-slate artifact is that of a butterfly or double-bitted axe banner form; crescentic extensions were ground off in prehistoric times.

C—$400-$600

Courtesy Ferrel Anderson, photographer; Thomas Browner Collection: Davenport, Iowa.

WISCONSIN WINGED BANNERSTONE, from Clark County, Missouri. It measures 3¾ in. by 2 in. and is made of a black and white porphyry. This specimen was expertly restored in one corner; in 1956 it was purchased for $300. The exceptional color and workmanship make this artifact a rare collector's item.

C—$700-$1000

Courtesy Ferrel Anderson, photographer; Thomas Browner Collection: Davenport, Iowa.

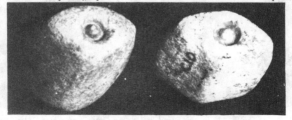

UNFINISHED BANNERSTONES, each measuring 2 in. by 2 in. These clearly show the drilling (hollow cane type), with central "islands" protruding about ¼ in. Both are Archaic and found in northeast Mississippi. The C10 piece is made of quartz material.

C—$60, each

Photo courtesy Jim Northcutt, Jr., Corinth, Mississippi.

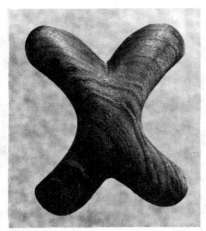

SALVAGED DOUBLE-CRESCENT BANNER-STONE, 3-7/8 in. wide and 3-1/8 in. long. Material is a green and black banded slate. One prong was broken in ancient times, and the other three ground down to create a symmetrical piece. *C—$450-$700*

Courtesy Ferrel Anderson, photographer; Thomas Browner Collection: Davenport, Iowa.

RECTANGULAR BARRELED BANNERSTONE, 4-1/8 in. by 2¾ in. The symmetry and raised barrel are the major features of this artifact. Material is a pink and black granite. It is from Preble County, Ohio. Most bannerstones offered for sale can be considered in the more common classes. *C—$600-$1000*

Courtesy Ferrel Anderson, photographer; Thomas Browner Collection: Davenport, Iowa.

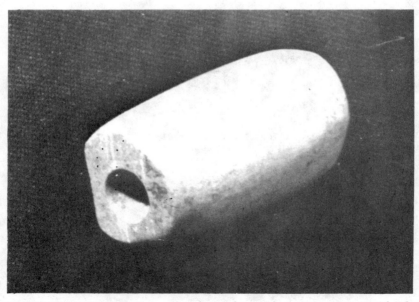

TUBE TYPE BANNERSTONE, 1¼ in. wide and 2½ in. long, made of a green stone material. Hole measures ½ in. at both ends; tube has a flat bottom. Archaic, it was found near the Hatchie River in Alcorn County, Mississippi. *C—$300*

Photo courtesy Jim Northcutt, Jr., Corinth, Mississippi.

106

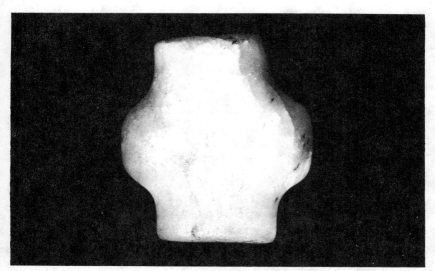

BIFACE BOTTLE BANNERSTONE. 2½ in. by 2 in. It is a fine white quartz with small black inclusions. Though small, it is well-documented since the beginning of the 1900's; most collectors will pay more for a traceable artifact. From southern Indiana. *C—$900-$1000*

Courtesy Ferrel Anderson, photographer; Thomas Browner Collection: Davenport, Iowa.

HOURGLASS BANNERSTONE, from Adams County, Illinois and made of green quartzite. It is 2 in. long and 1-15/16 in. wide, and might be considered a common specimen. Browner: "Size is small and shape only fair; with most of its history lost, it is reduced to an orphaned piece of common art". *C—$400-$500*

Courtesy Ferrel Anderson, photographer; Thomas Browner Collection: Davenport, Iowa.

TRIANGULAR DUAL BANNERSTONE, from Hancock County, Illinois. It is 4¼ in. long and 2-7/8 in. wide, made of mottled granite. This is both a rare piece and somewhat controversial, in that only a portion of its history has been traceable. So . . . if you collect, you must catalog and trace and record all findings. This means authentic specimens are fully documented.

C—$1500-$2000

Courtesy Ferrel Anderson, photographer; Thomas Browner Collection: Davenport, Iowa.

PEBBLE BANNERSTONE, from Boone County, Missouri. It is 2½ in. wide and 1½ in. long, made of a tan sandstone. Bannerstones began like this, a simple perforated pebble around 4000 B.C. This specimen was only shaped slightly by flattening the circumference. Many banners are believed to have been Atl-atl weights. *C—$80*

Courtesy Ferrel Anderson, photographer; Thomas Browner Collection: Davenport, Iowa.

UNDRILLED WISCONSIN WINGED BANNERSTONE, 2½ in. by 1¾ in. From Illinois, it is made of mottled granite. The specimen is a bit thick and lacks good polish. *C—$80*

Courtesy Ferrel Anderson, photographer; Thomas Browner Collection: Davenport, Iowa.

SINGLE-FACE BOTTLE BANNERSTONE, from Lincoln County, Missouri, and 3 in. long. Note the flared lips forming mini-rectangles at both ends. Topside is gracefully rounded, bottomside is flat. The material is red quartzite.

C—$1000-$1500

Courtesy Ferrel Anderson, photographer; Thomas Browner Collection: Davenport, Iowa.

SADDLE-FACE BANNERSTONE, from Dubois County, Indiana. It is 2½ in. by 2 in., and made of a green quartzite. Softer inclusions have leached out giving a rough finish; plow damage has changed the specimen's outline.

C—$100

Courtesy Ferrel Anderson, photographer; Thomas Browner Collection: Davenport, Iowa.

HOURGLASS BANNERSTONE. 3 in. long and 2¼ in. wide, and from Randolph County, Illinois. Has the classic shape. At some early time, a person scratched the initial "W" on it; this fault would be penalized to some degree by different collectors. Made of reddish-brown slate; material could be better for the artifact type.

C—$450-$700

Courtesy Ferrel Anderson, photographer; Thomas Browner Collection: Davenport, Iowa.

From left to right:

Drilled center BANDED SLATE BANNERSTONE, Archaic times, and 4½ in. in length. Found near Pembroke, Ontario, Canada.   C—$300

Photo courtesy Howard Popkie, Arnprior, Canada.

KNOBBED LUNATE BANNERSTONE, from Delaware County, Ohio. It is 5-7/8 in. long and 2 in. wide. Piece is made of green and black banded slate.   C—$600-$900

Courtesy Ferrel Anderson, photographer; Thomas Browner Collection: Davenport, Iowa.

WINGED BANNERSTONE, 4½ in. long; from near Pond Mills, near London, Ontario. While not shown in photo, piece is fully drilled.   C—$200-$250

Photo courtesy Robert C. Calvert, London, Ontario, Canada.

Rare **notched-ovate banner,** Midwestern Archaic, banded slate, 5-3/8 in. long, 3¼ in. wide. Some restoration to two of the curved tips. Notched in center of convex edges. C—$700

Winged bannerstone, 4-1/8 in. between tips. About 1 in. of one wing has been carefully restored. Reddish slate with black bands, colorful. C—$375

Pick banner, a hardstone similar to diorite, smooth-grained, good polish. Piece is 4-7/8 in. long and slightly pointed on one end, slightly flattened on other. No damage; unusual. C—$600

Duo-tipped slate pick, from Canada, 5¼ in. long and 7/8 in. wide. Material is a dark gray slate, not banded. Piece is well-shaped but undrilled. C—$110

Fine **panel banner** of very attractive, thinly-banded slate, good condition. Edges have regular tally notches. As is common for the form, one end of the banner is slightly larger than the other. Central hole runs lengthwise; piece is 3½ in. long. A—$250

Hardstone banner, 2-3/8 in. wide, 1-7/8 in. long, Midwestern origin, made of chlorite (?), well-drilled, no damage. Small but perfect; highly polished buff-colored surface. C—$550

Quartz bannerstone, 1-7/8 in. wide and 2¾ in. long. Made of a well polished translucent quartzite having black inclusions. Perfect condition, but undrilled; drill-hole was just started, never completed. C—$200

Cresentic pick banner, 3½ in. long, with central hole ½ in. in diameter. Very symmetrical, nicely polished, made of dark, close-banded slate. From an old collection. A—$155

Lunate banner, about 5 in. across at the tips, which lack the typical notches or grooves. One arm is slightly shorter than the other and projects at a different angle than does its twin. No restoration and unusual in an unbroken or damaged condition. A—$210

ATL-ATL WEIGHTS

There is considerable evidence from the association of grave goods that at least some bannerstones served as Atl-atl weights. It is easy to imagine some of the heavier and more compact forms employed in this manner, more difficult in the case of the large, thin-winged types.

Banners, already described, can be quickly (and incompletely) summarized. They are artifacts with a single large round or ovate central hole, and with symmetrical protrusions on both sides of that hole. Only a form like the atypical geniculate family alters this "rule"; even then, set on edge, the symmetry is regained.

There is a whole other great collecting field, that of the Atl-atl weights. These generally lack a large central hole and tend to be flat or concave on the bottom. As a broad class, they are long, narrow, and may have squared or rounded sides and top. Many forms have grooves or drill-holes for attachment.

It is believed weights were both functional and ornamental. Functional, because the weight would have given some added impetus to the lance-throw. They also would have served as a counter-balance when the flint or obsidian-tipped lance was in place.

Ornamental, because many varieties are extremely well made, small works of fine proportions and high polish and static grace. Some were effigy forms, adding perhaps luck and magic to the hunter's foray.

Atl-atl weights were used over the entire Continental U.S., plus into Canada and Mexico. It is believed the weights were used from early Archaic times until around AD 500, giving the Atl-atl/lance weapons system perhaps 8000 and more years of dominance. Early weights were somewhat plain and crude, little more than flattened rocks that could easily be glued or fastened to the wooden lance-thrower.

What is, and what is not, a weight will no doubt be as hotly debated in the future as it is today. New thought is that any prehistoric Amerind artifact that is long, thick and flat-bottomed—and served no other obvious function—may well have been a weight. The writer leaves it at that.

Because many of the weights are highly collectible, and these may include some slate and hardstone gorget and boatstone forms, the fakers have been at work. Some of the fraudulent specimens go back to the early years of the century and are now beginning to look old.

There are so many classes of weights that it is difficult to give guidelines on what to watch out for. Drill-holes for weights should be conical, from the tapered flint drills, and not of uniform diameter. Note that drilling, good drilling, adds much to the value of a piece

One of the more difficult fakes to deal with is the authentic-improved piece, an old artifact that has been recently drilled to increase the value. In most cases, this will be obvious; after all, a semi-skilled person is working on an object that is thousands of years old. The marks of steel tools are not the same as those made by prehistoric implements.

Generally, the patina, the microscopically thin surface layer, is disturbed. If in doubt, do not collect the piece.

Stone **Atl-atl weight,** Klamath River area of Oregon, 3 in. long, 1-5/8 in. high, speckled white stone. Flat bottom, piece nicely grooved front to back and across the center. Surface well-polished.
D—$195

Boatstone, Arkansas, 3¾ in. long, 1¼ in. wide. Bottom side, flat on edges, and deeply hollowed out or scooped. Good workstyle, high polish overall, perfect condition.
D—$230

Shaped shell **Atl-atl weights,** set of 9, from northern Kentucky. Each has a basic triangular shape, corners rounded; each is drilled with central hole about 5/8 in. in diameter. Placed together and approximating original positions, set is about 4 in. long and 1¼ in. wide. Segments evidence polish, and each is carefully made.
C—$210

Hardstone **Atl-atl weight,** state of Washington, 3-3/8 in. long. Bottom is flat, top has two longitudinal grooves, and is highly polished. Made of a compact tan stone.
C—$165

Sandstone weight, from Scioto River Valley, Ohio. It is 3½ in. long and 1-5/8 in. wide, about 3/8 in. thick. Perfect, and an early specimen. Unremarkable.
C—$13

Drilled and scooped banded-slate **boatstone,** Indiana, 3-7/8 in. long, 1-1/8 in. wide. Flattish base has been scooped to a depth of nearly ½ in. Some battering on the ends, but shallow and polished over.
C—$125-200

Dark-colored slate **bar amulet,** 4½ in. long and 1-5/8 in. wide. From Michigan.   D—$200

Bar-type grooved Atl-atl weight, 4 in. long, 7/8 in. wide, and made of a blackish slate. Bottom flat, top rounded, with two thin grooves about 3/8 in. from each end. Unusual and a well-finished piece.
C—$195

Layer-slate weight, from New York, 2¾ in. long, 1 in. wide, with rounded top. Rough finish.   C—$40

Grooved weight, 3-1/8 in. long, 7/8 in. wide, and of a light-colored slate. Bottomside flat, top rounded, wide groove across the center. Semi-polished, good condition.   D—$90

STONE ATL-ATL WEIGHT, excavated from a cave shelter in Arkansas. Found in the same occupational zone as Gary points, and from the Archaic period. Weight is 2½ in. long.
C—$75

Photo courtesy Wayne Parker, Texas.

Note: There are other forms that are almost certainly weights, although currently called by other names. These are covered in other chapters consistent with nomenclature. Such artifacts include some late Archaic Glacial Kame gorgets and some Woodland (Adena) bi-holed forms, which are in fact often undrilled.

Suggested Reading

Knoblock, Byron W., *Bannerstones of the North American Indian;* Privately published, La Grange, Illinois, 1939

The archeological societies quarterly journals are excellent sources. See last Chapter.

CHAPTER VII

BANDED SLATE ORNAMENTS AND OBJECTS

In a vast region ranging from the Mississippi watershed area East to the Atlantic Coast and from North of the Great Lakes South nearly to the Gulf, slate was a favorite material in prehistoric times. Much of this slate was of glacial origin, and the slate was traded far into non-glaciated areas. The slate was compact and colorful, and it worked well.

The beauty of banded slate certainly attracted prehistoric crafts-people, just as the finished artifacts attract collectors today. Very simple methods were used to turn out some very well-designed and executed objects. The peck-and-abrasion method was employed, basically the same used for making hardstone tools.

When the final form was approached, the piece was ground against loose-grained stone, and some very delicate work could be done in this fashion. And last, the surface was polished and any drilling put in.

For slate artifacts, determinants of present-day value include size of the artifact and the condition. The greater the damage, the greater the loss of value. Collectors seek symmetrical slate, and the pattern, regularity and boldness of the bands count for much.

Especially admired are pieces where the slate has been worked so the bands are either in harmony with the artifact's lines, or emphasize a key part of the artifact. An example is a panel banner with the slate bands all at the same angle on the top surface. Another is when bands converge to emphasize the eye region of a birdstone.

Slate surfaces should be highly polished and have no serious scratches, either from prehistoric use or today's agrriculture equipment. (A surprising amount of breakage and damage occurs when unknowing people acquire fine artifacts and treat them as mere stones.) In the general slate categories of pendants and gorgets, drilling is important. Pendants generally have one hole, gorgets two or more. Both tend to be long and flat, with a varied width.

All holes should be artistically placed and the same space from sides for pendants, the same space from sides and ends for most gorgets. While some collectors admire very thin slate pieces for the workmanship involved, others seek thick slate for the weight and contoured three-dimensional artistry.

Fakes exist. In the more valued classes, like birdstones, several knowledgeable people have stated there are probably more fraudulent than genuine pieces. There **are** lucky occurrences. One man bought a box of junk at a farm sale for the bag of nails he saw at the top. After getting it home, he discovered something else on the bottom. His cost was a dollar. His prize was a hardstone, perfect-condition birdstone, worth in excess of one thousand dollars.

Another man bought two birdstones from a pawnshop owner, because they looked good and were priced at only $300 each. With the average "bird" selling in the $1,500 range, they were a bargain providing they were authentic. They were neither.

For the average slate pendant, gorget, birdstone or effigy, the prices listed here are about market, but many examples can be obtained for far less. A good slate artifact collection can be put together, made up of under $100 pieces, but it is still buyer beware. Know your seller or get a written guarantee that the piece can be returned for a refund if it proves to be questionable.

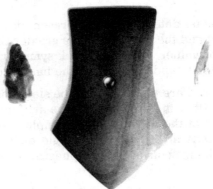

Hopewellian PROJECTILE POINTS of Flintridge material, translucent and very colorful.
C—$10 each

Very unusual Hopewellian SHIELD-SHAPE PENDANT, of fine banded slate, piece is 1/8 in. short of 5 in. Topside is slightly convex; underside is very slightly concave. Very symmetrical and an outstanding type specimen.
C—$2500

Private collection.

SLATE PENDANTS

One-holed slate pieces, if they are in fact completed by drilling, are termed pendants. It is believed they were worn around the neck like a large medallion. As prehistoric decorative items, great care seems to have been used in making many of them, though their relative thinness — 1/8 in. to 3/8 in. — makes them rather fragile.

L to R: POINTED-END PENDANT, perhaps salvaged from larger artifact in early times, 2-1/8 in. long.   C—$20

Large and good ANCHOR-TYPE PENDANT, made of a high grade yellowish slate. Perfect condition, from Ohio, about 5 in. long.   C—$225

Fine RECTANGULAR PENDANT, made of a smooth-grained hardstone; may have been salvaged from larger gorget in early times.   C—$45

Private collection.

Anchor-type **slate pendant,** 5 in. long and 1½ in. wide at expanded lower base. One anchor prong is a bit smaller than the other.

A—$120

Biconcave pendant, made in gorget form, but centrally drilled with single hole instead of usual two holes. Exactly 4 in. long and 1-7/8 in. wide at ends; from Missouri. Material is a green slate with green bands.   C—$150

Rectangular banded slate pendant, 2 in. wide by 5 in. long. Single large hole drilled from both sides, about 1¾ in. from one end. Very nice black bands against a reddish slate.   C—$225

Anchor-shaped pendant, 4¼ in. long and 1½ in. wide, with minor damage.   G—$100

Trapazoidal slate pendant, 5 in. long, 2 in. wide at base, and 1¼ in. wide at top, with single suspension hole. Perfect condition, good polish, very symmetrical. A—$210

Two small Midwestern slate PENDANTS; example on right is 3-1/8 in. long. Highly polished surface. C—$30

Left, completed but undrilled small PENDANT, Midwest, banded slate with white "Lightning" inclusion. C—$12

Private collection.

Adena bell-shaped pendant, large central hole in upper portion, and with tally marks (regular incised lines) at pendant top; piece about 4 in. long. A—$150

Slate pendant, 3½ in. long and 1½ in. wide at base. Nicely balanced pendant; partly restored. A—$30

Slate shovel-shaped pendant, 4½ in. long and 1¾ in. wide; very good lines to this piece. A—$80

SLATE GORGETS

These artifacts typically have two holes, but variations have three or more. As with pendants, hardstone examples exist, but they are rare and high-priced. Most gorgets are long and thin. They are believed to have been ornaments, although how they were worn is a matter of individual belief. Some gorgets that average about 1½ in. in width, are thick and drilled, may have been Atl-atl weights. The gorget class pulls together some rather dissimilar types.

Elongated **two-hole expanded center gorget,** very well drilled, Midwestern Woodland period, and 5½ in. in length. D—$90

Hardstone two-hole gorget, very well drilled, and from Illinois. It is 4-1/8 in. long, just under 2 in. wide and only 5/16 in. thick. Highly polished, holes symmetrical and equidistant from ends and sides. Granite-like stone with black, white and yellowish colors. C—$600

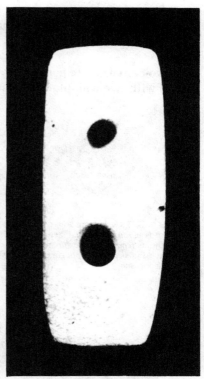

Unusual BAR GORGET, 2-9/16 in. long, and 1 in. wide. It is a humped-back type, made of galena and is covered with a thick white patina. Both obverse and reverse are shown. It evidences conical drilling and may be from the Adena culture, Woodland period. Found in Adams County, Illinois.

C—$85-$115

Photo courtesy John P. Grotte, Illinois.

Fine Hopewellian **reel-shaped gorget,** angular and very well balanced. Size, 4½ in. long and 3 in. wide, of attractive banded slate. Surface has a high polish; in perfect condition and from an old collection.   A—$325

Two-hole rectangular gorget, 1¾ in. by 3¼ in., clay-colored slate. One plow-mark across face, not deep.   C—$50

Nice **sandal-sole gorget,** a rare form, Glacial or Gravel-Kame period of late Archaic. Bottom wider than top, which is 2 in.; piece is just over 6 in. in length. Good banded slate, and drilled in diagnostic pattern of 3 in-line holes, the last about ½ in. from top.
A—$400

Large slate **expanded-center gorget,** 6¼ in. long, 1¾ in. wide in center, very good overall form. A—$300

Concavo-convex slate gorget, 4¼ in. long, and 2¼ in. wide at ends. Drilled with two well-placed holes. A—$275

STONE GORGET, 3¼ in. long 2 in. wide and ½ in. thick; it is made from a red stone material. Other artifacts from the same site indicate this may be a Mississippian type gorget. It was found in Tennessee. C—$75-$100 Photo courtesy Jim Northcutt, Jr., Corinth, Mississippi.

SLATE GORGET, 3½ in. long and 2-1/8 in. wide at center. Very well drilled with two holes; slate highly polished, and in good form. Item came from near Brantford, Ontario. C—$125-150 Photo courtesy Robert C. Calvert, London, Ontario, Canada.

SLATE OBJECT, drilled, 5¼ in. long and 1½ in. wide, ¼ in. thick. Piece is damaged at top end. C—$15-$20

Photo courtesy Robert C. Calvert, London, Ontario, Canada.

Humped slate gorget, 4¼ in. long and 1¾ in. wide, drilled with two holes. Piece has good lines. A—$175

Adena expanded-center gorget, holes equidistant from ends, drilled in Adena style from bottomside only. About 4 in. long, in perfect condition. A—$110

Fine elliptical gorget, 5 in. long, about 3 in. wide at center. Woodland era; two holes equidistant from rounded ends. C—$450

120

Very large **slate gorget,** a rare 3-hole sandal-sole type. It is 7 ¼ in. long and 2 ¾ in. wide at lower "instep" region. Symmetrical and well-finished. A—$320

Cross-shaped **slate gorget,** two holes, 3 in. long and 1 ¾ in. wide. Projecting arm ends have a concave outline. Perfect condition.

A—$225

Key-hole type gorget, dark banded slate, central hole high up and near top which is irregular to a small degree. Sides and bottom with nicely rounded contours. Average size. A—$140

Adena **oval-shaped gorget,** 4 in. long and 2 ¼ in. wide; well-drilled from a dark slate. Bands barely visible. D—$135

SLATE GORGET, 2 ¾ in. long and 2 in. wide, ¼ in. thick. Found in Brant County, Ontario; made of well-banded slate and is nicely drilled. C—$75-$100

Photo courtesy Robert C. Calvert, London, Ontario, Canada.

BLACK SLATE BIRDSTONE, not drilled, and found Point Peely, Ontario, Canada. It is 5 ¼ in. long and appears completely finished except for basal holes. Slight scrapes on one side, some damage to left side of head, minor. Very good lines to birdstone. C—$1000-$1400

Photo courtesy Robert C. Calvert, London, Ontario, Canada.

SLATE BIRDSTONES

Birdstones are from the late Archaic period, and are top-of-the-line for slate collectors. Most "birds" have a head and beak, a flat-bottomed body, and a tail region. Many are drilled wilth two holes, front and rear on the bottom, forming "L"-shaped holes. Obviously, they were attached to something, but no one has yet proved what that might be.

All that can be said today is that birdstones do resemble a bird setting a nest. Strangely, wings are never depicted in any way. Birdstones are found in a 500-mile range of Lake Erie, and many examples come from New York state and the Canadian provinces. A great many have been found in Ohio, Indiana, Illinois and Michigan.

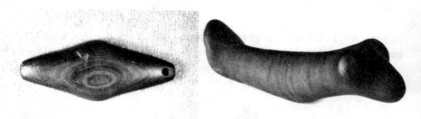

From left to right:

EXPANDED-CENTER TYPE GORGET, 4¼ in. long. Of banded slate, piece is drilled at both ends, but only one hole at one end is visible. Unusual drilling.   C—$225-$350
Courtesy Billy Hillen, Ohio.

SLATE BIRDSTONE, unusual form, and 6¼ in. in length. Found near Onondaga, Ontario, near the Grand River. Like other birdstones, this is probably from late Archaic times. The specimen is not drilled.   C—$1200-$1800
Photo courtesy Robert C. Calvert, London, Ontario, Canada.

Banded **slate birdstone,** 5¾ in. long, 1½ in. wide. Classic Glacial Kame elongated type, forward-slanted head and long beak.

A—$1200

Slate birdstone, 4 in. long and 1½ in. wide, good shape, perfect condition.   A —$900

Slate birdstone head, broken from body. Head is 1½ in. long; break area salvaged by grinding and base of neck has a slight groove around it, as if for thong attachment.   C—$135

Slate birdstone, 4 in. long and 1½ in. wide, good lines. The piece has been restored.   A — $185

SLATE BIRDSTONE, from near London, Ontario, Canada. Of banded material, piece is 4-3/8 in. long. Birdstone has well-drilled base and is tally-marked on sides of neck, body and tail. Very small damaged area on left side, original. Incised mouths on birdstones are not common.
C—$1200-$1800

Photo courtesy Robert C. Calvert, London, Ontario, Canada.

Birdstone head, "popeye" type of green and black material. It is 1¼ in. long, and was salvaged in prehistoric times. The break is ground so that head sits firmly and erect.   C—$180

Elongated **banded slate birdstone,** classic style, 5-7/8 in. and 1½ in. wide at flared tail. Very graceful design and well-drilled. C—$1350

Slate birdstone, 4 in. long and 1¼ in. wide; a small-base type.
A—$140

Quartzite birdstone, 4½ in. long and 2¼ in. wide. Piece has been restored.   A—$135

Porphyry birdstone, popeye type, 4¼ in. long and 2-1/8 in. wide, 2¾ in. high. Made of a mottled black and yellow material.
C—$4000

SLATE BIRDSTONE, from Victoria County, Ontario, Canada. This is a fine popeyed specimen, and measures 4-1/8 in. in length. Piece is drilled on bottom ridges and is in perfect condition.
C—$2500-$3800

Photo courtesy Robert C. Calvert, London, Ontario, Canada.

PRE-FORM BIRDSTONE, made of a green, mottled hardstone and 3½ in. long and 1¾ in. high. Found near Komoka, Ontario, London District, Canada. This piece evidences slight polishing. **C—$50-$100**

Photo courtesy Robert C. Calvert, London, Ontario, Canada.

BIRDSTONE, from near Sault St. Marie, Ontario, Canada. Piece is 3½ in. long and 2 in. high at head and tail. Hardstone material, undrilled, and is probably an unfinished specimen. Good form. **C—$400-$700**

Photo courtesy Robert C. Calvert, London, Ontario, Canada.

EFFIGY SLATES

While no one really knows how birdstones were used, neither is it known what effigy slates represent. They most resemble "lizards", or salamanders, but many forms are either so highly stylized that not much more can be said. Some forms resemble animals like swimming beavers or otters; others look like a snake that has swallowed a large meal.

Effigies are rarely drilled. They have a flat bottom, a head region, jutting shoulders and generally taper into a tail region. Some were crudely made while others are superb specimens of the slate-workers' art.

In the opinion of the writer, these are Atl-atl weights from the middle Archaic time-frame. The market value of better specimens is beginning to approach that of average-grade birdstones.

PAINT PALETTE, 10½ in. in diameter, made of slate. Design is a repeated bird motif; this piece was found near Memphis, Tennessee, in 1837 and is late prehistoric, Mississippian era.

C—$800

S. W. Kernaghan photo; Marguerite Kernaghan Collection.

Banded slate effigy stone, Midwestern area, 5 in. long. Head squared off, shoulders very high, short neck region. Body and tail tapered very nicely; overall, well-made and polished piece.

A—$525

Slate effigy stone, nicely tapered and with abrupt expansion near head region. Piece is 4-1/8 in. long, of a dark-colored and banded slate.

C—$485

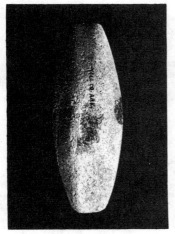

BOATSTONE: FLAT, UNCUPPED PRIMARY FORM. (Browner:) "Boatstones are an Archaic cultural manifestation. Like bannerstones, they seem to have begun in the Southeastern states. From simple uncupped bars used as Atl-atl weights they evolved into intricately shaped and deeply cupped artifacts of unknown use. Boatstones continued into Mississippian times and some of the forms are incised and show rare symmetry and workmanship."

This piece is 3¾ in. long and is made from a brown sandstone. It is from Yell County, Arkansas.   C—$90-$150

Courtesy Ferrel Anderson, photographer; Thomas Browner Collection: Davenport, Iowa.

125

Slate effigy figure, 5 in. long and 1½ in. wide. Piece has a wide, elongated body, small head and broad tail. More than a salamander, it resembles the profile of a beaver.   A—$100

Slate lizard effigy, 4 in. long and 1½ in. wide, very rounded features including head, shoulders and short tail. Perfect condition, well-polished.   A—$225

Slate beaver effigy, 4 in. long and 1½ in. wide. Rather an abstract depiction, rare form, fine condition.   A—$245

CEREMONIAL PICK made of slate, and 13¾ in. in length. It is well-polished and in good condition, from Brant County, Ontario. An unusual artifact type.   C—$200-$300
Photo courtesy Robert C. Calvert, London, Ontario, Canada.

Slate effigy or lizard, 5 in. long and 1½ in. wide.Piece has squared-off head and tail ends, very narrow and jutting shoulders. No damage. An exceptionally well-made and attractive piece.
A—$650

Slate effigy form, 4 in. long, 1¾ in. wide at shoulders. Blunt head, straight taper from shoulders to tail. Perfect condtion.
A—$145

DRILLED SLATE BOATSTONE, top & bottom views. This boatstone is of the rounded type and is a near-perfect example of the type. In size, color and workmanship it would have few equals. Note the excellent cupping, typical of the type. This piece is 4½ in. long and 1¼ in. wide at center. Made of a green and black banded slate, it is from the Grand Rapids, Michigan area.
C—$500-$800
Courtesy Ferrel Anderson, photographer; Thomas Browner Collection; Davenport, Iowa.

*Casa Blanca (the white house) is one of the more spectacular cliff dwelling ruins in the Southwest.
Canyon de Chelly National Monument, Arizona.*

Photo courtesy U.S. Department of the Interior, National Park Service.

OTHER BANDED SLATE ARTIFACTS

Slate tube, 3¼ in. long and 1¾ in. wide, drilled for entire length with one large hole. **A—$60**

Banded slate phallus, depicting male penis glans, 3-5/16 in. high, resting on enlarged flat base. Realistic and colorful material, black bands on reddish background. Unknown time period. Surface find in western Ohio. **C—$325**

Slate bar amulet, 7¾ in. long and ¾ in. wide, with raised section, ridge-like, in center. Beautiful flowing lines, and high-quality slate. **A—$420**

BOATSTONE; DEEP CUP TYPE. (Browner:) "This example represents the end of boatstone evolution. This specimen is notable in both its deep cup and its extremely thin walls. Minor chips at one edge detracts a bit, but does not harm overall value. Boatstones are usually made of banded slate. However, quartz, granite, sandstone, limestone and steatite were also used."
This piece is 2¾ in. long and 1-7/8 in. wide. Made of brown sandstone, it is from Independence County, Arkansas. *C—$325-$450*
Courtesy Ferrel Anderson, photographer; Thomas Browner Collection: Davenport, Iowa.

Banded slate spud, (unusual flared-bit celtiform axe), 10¼ in. long, 3-1/8 in. wide at blade tips. Dark green slate with reddish bands. **D—$400**

Banded slate tube or tubular pipe, 7¼ in. long, ¾ in. wide. Good lines; piece has been restored. **A—$115**

Slate bar-weight, notched in center, 3¾ in. long, 1 in. wide.

A—$35

Slate pestle, bell-type, 6 in. high and 4 in. in basal diameter.

A—$50

Slate pestle, long roller type, 19½ in. in length and 2½ in. in diameter.
A—$75

Slate axe, 8½ in. high and 4¾ in. wide.
A—$140

Slate pendant, 3¼ in. long and 1¾ in. wide, thin and rectangular, one-hole at end. Piece interesting because one face is cross-hatched with incised lines.
C—$130

Slate lizard effigy, 4-7/8 in. long, bulbous-body type, rounded "tail", tally-marks around shoulder ridge. Perfect condition, very nice banding.
C—$700

Fine SLATE TUBE, 3-5/8 in. long, of green slate with bold black bands. Perfect condition; completely drilled and straight, from small or larger end. Old markings, "Forest, Hardin Co.". An Ohio piece, probably Archaic period. C—$160
Private collection.

A hogan or dwelling at Standing Cow Ruins, Canyon de Chelly National Monument, Arizona. Photo courtesy of U.S. Department of the Interior, National Park Service.

The excavated ruins of a prehistoric pueblo which flourished between A.D. 1000 and A.D. 1400. These are outstanding examples of large late-prehistoric pueblos of the Verde Valley. Tuzigoot National Monument, Arizona.

Photo courtesy of U.S. Department of the Interior, National Park Service.

Spineback gorget, 4-3/8 in. long, with single protruding knob between two drill-holes. Fine banding in specimen and highly polished surface.   C—$700

Animal-head effigy, 1-7/8 in. long, unknown species, picked up on Illinois Archaic site.   C—$140

Suggested Reading

Townsend, Earl C. Jr., *Birdstones of the North American Indian;* Privately published, Indianapolis, Indiana, 1959

The famous hogan, the earth-covered dwelling of the Navajo Indians. Note the one woman grinding material with a mano and stone metate, also the Navajo blanket to the right of hogan doorway. Dwellings like these were common into the early 1900's; photo ca. 1930.

Photo courtesy of Utah State Historical Society, Collection of Smithsonian Institution.

Sioux ration camp in Nebraska. Meat, probably beef or bison meat, dries on racks out of reach of camp dogs. Indians gathered periodically to receive U.S. government food supplies.

Photo courtesy of John A. Adderson Collection, Nebraska State Historical Society.

CHAPTER VIII
ARTIFACTS OF COPPER
AND HEMATITE

Copper and hematite, both found in natural deposits, were much-used to make artifacts in prehistoric North America. They were, however, quite dissimilar and were worked in entirely different ways.

Copper was mined, dug from near the land surface, for thousands of years in the Lake Superior region, and copper artifacts are still being found today. Copper was formed by hammering the malleable material into new and useful shapes. This process — treating the metal almost like a plastic stone — was the third great tool-making method used in prehistoric North America.

Despite extensive copper use, and beginning with the Old Copper Culture (5000 BC) in Northcentral U.S., Amerinds above the Mexican-U.S. border did not melt of smelt copper. It was cold-worked. There is some evidence that Woodland and later-period groups heated the metal, but only so it could be pounded into thinner sheets and more varied forms. The small late-prehistoric cast bells (lost-wax process) of the Southwest have not been proven to have been made in the region.

The use of copper for tools, weapons, ornaments and ceremonial items spans more than 7000 years and the material was widely traded in early times. Among the groups which made important use of copper were the middle Archaic peoples centered in what is to-day Wisconsin, the Glacial Kame peoples of 1500 BC, the Hopewell groups of pre-BC and post-AD years, Southeastern Amerinds of Mississippian times, and Northwest Coastal groups well into historic times. Other Amerinds valued copper and made artifacts from it.

Much copper was made into routine tools, but much was also reserved for specialty items and artistic creations. These range from beads to headdress ornaments and from finger rings and bracelets to panpipe whistle sets.

Collectors look for size in a copper piece, good condition, and an even color. Weight, an indication of solid copper, is a factor. Appearance is important. Rare artifacts, like a matched pair of earspools in good condition, would be especially desirable, also any copper with artistic forms or human figures.

There are some fraudulent prehistoric copper pieces around, but the early copper is difficult to fake convincingly. The forms — awls, points, celts — are easy enough to pound into shape. But two factors limit reproductions. One is corrosion or chemical erosion of the artifact itself.

Depending on whether the artifact was under water or beneath the earth, various mineral salts leach away copper parts, giving a characteristic pitted surface. Also, a colorful patina appears on the surface, this often a shade of dark green or brown. It is not easy to put the two together in a way that matches the appearance of an authentic specimen.

COPPER ARTIFACTS

Socketed copper blade, hafted by a wide base that has been pounded around to form an almost closed socket; overall length, 5 in. Lightly patinated and good condition.   C—$115

Flat-stemmed copper blade, 5½ in. long, with stem the same thickness as blade, 3/16 in. All parts in good condition.   C—$165

Copper rattail-hafted blade, blade-back straight, blade edge excurvate. Piece is 4 in. long, beautiful green patina. Said to have been found in shallow waters of a lake. Some corrosion on thin parts of blade but metal not weakened.   C—$120

Socketed copper blade, 6 in. long, about 2 in. wide at midlength. Center of back portion of socket base also has a small hole for a handle peg. Light patina, good condition.   C—$160

Copper celt, flared bit, fine shape. Piece is 3¾ in. long and 3 in. wide, with much patina.   G—$125

Copper chisel, Wisconsin, and 5¼ in. long, 1-3/8 in. wide, 3/8 in. thick. Base shows some hammerstone battering. Very unusual, good condition.   D—$120

Copper beads from Midwestern late prehistoric site. Nine beads of similar small size, ¼ in. in diameter. Unusual.　　　　　C—$45

Copper Adena bracelet, Woodland period, contains about 300 degrees of arc, tapered tips. About 3/8 in. thick at center. Scarce artifact from an admired culture.　　　　　C—$295

Curved **copper semi-lunar knife,** Wisconsin. It is 4½ in. long, has two upright tangs formerly secured to wooden handle, now gone. Blade averages ¼ in. thick.　　　　　C—$195

Copper rattail point, unusual in that it is also tanged and with shallow notches at sides of point. Piece 3 in. long. Tangs both slightly bent. Nice patina overall.　　　　　C—$80

Conical **copper point,** 2½ in. long; patinated.　　　　　D—$35

Copper chisel, northern Michigan, 1 in. wide at center, 4-7/8 in. long. Medium corrosion, convex blade edge, flat poll, good lines.
　　　　　D—$220

Duo-tipped **copper awl,** Michigan, 8-1/8 in. long, 3/8 in. in diameter in center. Has medium corrosion, overall good condition.　　C—$245

Copper celt, Minnesota, 7 in. long, 2¾ in. wide at bit, 1½ in. wide at squared poll top. Nice patina and good lines.　　　　　C—$300

Copper fish-hook, Wisconsin, 1½ in. long. Made of a thin roll of beaten copper, twisted and pounded into shape.　　　　　C—$25

Copper needle, Minnesota, 3-1/8 in. long, bent and badly corroded.
　　　　　C—$10

Copper celt, New York state, 3¾ in. long and ½ in. thick. Green patina, very regular lines.　　　　　C—$150

Copper celt, 4-3/8 in. and 2-1/8 in. wide. Found in 1969 in Wisconsin.　　　　　C—$275

Copper fish-hook, 1¼ in. long made from rolled and pounded copper strip. Good condition.　　　　　C—$19

Tapered-stem blade, 3½ in. long, lightly corroded. It is not known whether this form was knife or spear as blade edges are similar and excurvate. D—$65

Historic period copper needle, from Apache site near Cajote, New Mexico, and ca. 1850. D—$20

Contemporary **Northwest Coast chief's copper**, made and signed by Lelooska. A—$600

HEMATITE ARTIFACTS

Hematite, an iron ore, is colored steel gray to black and from dull to brilliant red. It has a double distinction, for it was used for both artifacts and paint in prehistoric times. Many cultures, including the Red Ochre peoples, valued powdered hematite or ochre in rituals. Occasionally paint cups are found with ochre traces still in them.

This hard material, from examination of unfinished pieces, was made into artifacts by the familiar peck-and-abrasion method. Hematite was widely used for both tools and strange artifacts that seem to have had no utility, like the Woodland-era cones that resemble tiny mounds.

Hematite was preferred for certain artifacts, like the plummets and some small adz-blades. And almost any artifact made of hardstone is likely to have a counterpart, somewhere, in hematite. Some of the artifacts for certain reasons become exfoliated. That is, the surface peels and flakes away, becoming uneven.

Collectors look for good shape and pleasing lines. Size is of some importance, but hematite artifacts tend to be rather small due to weight. A high polish is admired, plus few or no rough areas remaining from the original nodule of ore.

At present fakes are not a serious problem, partly because hematite is a difficult material to work due to its hardness. Apparently, artifacts made today would not be a paying proposition.

Hematite cone, ¾ in. high and 1½ in. in diameter. A—$35

Red Hematite celt, 1-5/8 in. long and 1-5/8 in. wide, with polish on bit. G—$30

Hematite plummet, 3-1/8 in. long, drilled at small end, classic teardrop shape. Polished overall, black color.   D—$95

Hematite celt, Missouri, 3½ in. long.   G—$20

Hematite plummet, 2-7/8 in. long, one end rounded and grooved, other end pointed. Slender and well-polished.   C—$90

Hematite cone, 1¼ in. high and 1¼ in. in basal diameter.

A—$25

Hematite pendant, 3¼ in. long and 1½ in. wide at bottom. Well-made, with single large drill-hole at top center, rust-red color, highly polished.   C—$195

Hematite plummet, 2 in. high and 1 in. in diameter.   A—$35

HEMATITE ARTIFACTS: counter-clockwise, from top—
Fine small FULL GROOVE AXE, Warren County, Missouri.   *C—$105*
DISCOIDAL, from Calhoun County, Illinois.   *C—$85*
Small ADZ BLADE, Adams County, Illinois.   *C—$30*
PLUMMET, with small groove at top.   *C—$100*
Photo courtesy Pat Humphrey, Westcentral Illinois.

Hematite gorget, rectangular form, two drill holes; piece is 3½ in. long, with highly polished surface, no damage.   C—$275

Hematite discoidal, 2½ in. in diameter and 1½ in. high. Very good color in this extremely well-made piece.   G—$265

Hematite plummet, extra-large size. It is 3¼ in. high and 1 in. in diameter.   A—$135

Hematite birdstone, 2¼ in. long and 1½ in. high.   A—$795

Hematite plummet, 1¾ in. high and ¾ in. in diameter.   A—$35

Hematite celt, 3¾ in. long and 1¾ in. wide.   A—$55

Artifacts made from other natural materials

Cannel coal gorget, 6½ in. long and 2¼ in. wide. Three-hole sandal-sole type, fine condition.   A—$450

Sheet-mica cut-out, ca. AD 500, Hopewellian and Midwestern. Piece depicts the canine tooth of a bear and is 1-3/8 in. long. Base has a small drill-hole. Material probably imported from the Carolinas via early trade. A scarce piece, in that mica layer-flakes easily.   C—$125

Cannel coal disc, 2¼ in. in diameter, 1/8 in. in thickness, probably late prehistoric. Use unknown.   C—$7

Thin, curved **mica strips,** each with minute holes at one end. Seven pieces, each measuring 1-1/8 in. long and resembling eagle or hawk claws. Rare decorative ornaments and from southern Ohio.
    C—$25 each

Cannel coal pendant, 2¼ in. long and about 1 in. wide, drilled at smaller end.   D—$30

Meteoritic iron chisel, collected in state of Washington, and remaining section 3¼ in. long. Lower blade in good condition but back portion of piece broken in early times. Rare piece.   C—$150

Jadeite blade, probably for woodworking adz, from West Coast of Canada, and 4-3/8 in. long. Has typical concave adz blade and good condition. Rare material and probably very early.   C—$550

Galena (lead ore) pendant, 2¼ in. long, ¾ in. wide, and pale white color. Undrilled, so may also have been intended as a small gorget.
    C—$26

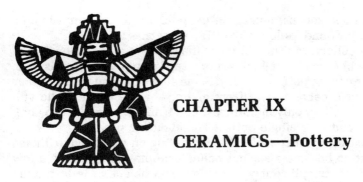

CHAPTER IX

CERAMICS—Pottery

(Considerable writing and material was contributed to this chapter by John W. Barry, P.O. Box 583, Davis, Ca. 95616, who is especially knowledgeable in the contemporary Pueblo pottery field. He contributed the entire pre-listings sections, also selections from his Indian Rock Arts catalog and suggestions for further reading. Used with permission.)

INTRODUCTION

Reflections of native American art through the ceramic media equal and often surpass artistic expression through weavings, jewelry, and canvas. Traditional ceramics usually are executed with natural materials and methods employed for several centuries.

Recognizing that there are contemporary styles using contemporary materials and methods to create ceramic Indian art, the skill, creativity and inspiration of the artist are inherent in every piece of Pueblo pottery. These people have an apparent need, coupled with a natural artistry, to express beauty.

It is a natural sequence of events that there is an increasing awareness of this art form as we take shelter from the complexities of our society, examing values and searching for natural esthetics.

There are several excellent books on American Indian pottery. For those interested, a list of references is included at the end of this article. The purpose of this chapter is to provide an overview of this art form.

Within the scope of our discussion, ceramics is defined as items crafted from clay by Native Americans. This includes numerous types, styles, colors, designs and shapes to include beakers, vases, bowls, bottles, scoops, mugs, plates, pitchers, animal and human figurines, jars and ladles, and effigy vessels.

Pottery collectors differ in what they collect as do collectors of any other art form. Some collections represent either prehistoric, historic or contemporary pottery. Some single out one pueblo; other may collect a certain style from one or several areas while still others may collect only miniatures, non-traditional pottery, or pottery produced by a single potter. The choice is great.

I suggest that you consider concentrating on a particular theme if you plan to become a serious collector; otherwise, choose a few pieces which compliment your decor. The objective is to pursue this art form in a manner which provides you the most enjoyment.

HISTORIC DEVELOPMENT AND CLASSIFICATION

Archeologists and anthropologists (Martin et al 1947) estimate that pottery made its debut in North America 2500 years ago. Fine ceramics were made by the Hohokam people of the Southwest 200 BC, and by the Mogollon culture around the opening of the Christian era (Tanner 1968). Later Indian immigrants may have brought pottery types to North America, as suggested by similarities to some Asian types.

But pottery had already been established in the New World. Pottery is of immense importance to the archeologist in classifying, dating, correlating cultures, and providing valuable clues to their rise and fall.

Pottery is a sensitive indicator of changes within a culture. It shows the influences and mixing of other cultures, and when found in site with burials or ceremonial chambers it provides the archeologist opportunities to understand the user's life styles. A two-name system is used by archeologists to describe distinctive pottery classes, such as Mesa Verde Black-on-White.

Prehistoric pottery. Classifying prehistoric pottery, particulary those pieces found east of the Mississippi River, is best accomplished by geographic area as there was simultaneous development in various geographical areas. For those interested in more of an in-depth study of the pottery produced by various cultures, books such as Martin, Quimbly and Colliers' book, *Indians Before Columbus,* should be reviewed.

Historic pottery. Historic pottery, chronologically, is pottery produced after the arrival of Coronado to the area of New Mexico in

1540. Some define historic pottery as that produced after 1600 AD, while others use 1700 AD.

Pueblo V: 1700 to Present. Pottery was produced by many of the Pueblos during the early part of the period, at the Pueblos of Acoma, Cochiti, Walpi, Sichomovi, Hano, Skungopovi, Shipaulovi, Mishongonovi, Isleta, Jemez, Laguna, Nambe', Picuris, Sandia, San Ildefonso, San Juan, Santa Ana, Santo Domingo, Zia, Taos, Pojoaque, Tesuque, and Zuni.

Pottery from this period reflects the most advanced of all pottery produced in North America. There were great varieties of types, styles, decoration, colors and designs. This and the contemporary expressions which are an extension of the Historic Period provide the most commonly collected and desirable pottery for the collector.

By 1900 AD pottery seemed destined to extinction. Except for ceremonial and very limited utilitarian use, native pottery was not in general use or needed by the Indian. The reason was the ready availability of cooking and eating ware from the Anglo Culture.

The 20th century has seen a dramatic revival of pottery and the emergence of new types and styles. Thanks to the efforts and encouragement of the traders, museums, and numerous interested individuals, pottery continues and even flourishes in parts of the Southwest. Pottery is now being made for market by all the inhabited pueblos of the Southwest.

Traditional pottery is now being made by the Cherokee and Catawba. Other pottery forms and styles are appearing on the market from tribes throughout the United States. For the most part, however, they are non-traditional in design or manufacture.

CONTEMPORARY POTTERY

Visiting a potter at her home is a rewarding experience. Most potters are more than willing to visit and explain the process of making pottery. They usually have pots in various stages of production and depending upon your timing you may see a group of pots being removed from their primitive type firing pit. The potter will show you the clay, polishing stone, and pots awaiting delivery to customers.

It is advisable to make an appointment before your visit. Winter is the best time to visit and make your purchases. At that time you will not be competing with other tourists and various public shows and markets, which require a large inventory. Potters also will keep their better pieces for these shows. Some reservations require that you check in with the reservation officials or Pueblo governor's office before visiting potters within their boundaries.

Most Indian pottery produced today is made by Southwestern pueblos and rancheria people of Arizona. The Southwest pueblos which produce significant amounts of pottery include the Pueblos of Santa Clara, San Ildefonso, Zia, Cochiti, Jemez, Zuni, Acoma, and the Hopi (First Mesa). There is somewhat limited production at San Juan, Tesuque, Santo Domingo, San Lorenzo (Picuris), Taos, Laguna, Pojoaque, Isleta, Sandia, San Felipe, Santa Ana and Nambe.

The rancherias, including Maricopa, Yuma, Pima, and Papago, have either ceased making pottery or produce relatively small amounts. Generally the latter has not shared the popularity of Pueblo wares. The Navajo make a traditional working ware primarily for their own use; **however,** some Navajo pottery is sold to the public. Through Federal programs designed to provide employment to the Utes and Sioux, non-traditional kiln-fired ceramics with Indian motif are produced in limited quantities for the tourist market. With the popularity of Indian pottery more of the non-traditional types will undoubtedly appear on the market.

POTTERS — A PROFILE

There are many excellent ceramic artists today producing a great variety of pottery. Their excellence equals and may even surpass the accomplishments of well known Indian potters. They are producing traditional styles and patterns. Others are creating contemporary ceramics which express an unlimited imagination of style, media, and shape, such as the carved pots made by Joseph Lonewolf.

Young potters such as Laura Gachupin of Jemez Pueblo and Thelma Talachy of Pojoaque Pueblo are making outstanding examples of contemporary pottery with a balance of traditional designs and contemporary styles. Virginia Ebelacker at Santa Clara Pueblo specializes in traditional black storage jars. Her award-winning pieces are sought-after by museums and collectors.

Seferina Ortiz of Cochiti uses traditional methods to produce story tellers, figurines, and pots with lizards. Like the other potters she learned from her mother and finds a ready collector market for her pots. Minnie Vigil of Santa Clars is a prolific potter who produces an outstanding variety of styles and colors. These potters have two traits in common — they are outstanding artists and are willing to share their enthusiasm of the art with you.

METHOD OF PRODUCTION

There were five basic methods used by North American Indians to make pottery. None employed a potters wheel or anything resembling a wheel.

1. **Coil method.** Rolls of clay are built upon a clay base in a spiral manner. The sides of the pot are developed by successive coils and the sides are smoothed by a piece of gourd, shell, or smooth stone. The Hopi and Rio Grande Pueblos use this method today.

2. **Coil method with Paddle and Anvil.** This method is similar to the coil method except that coils are rarely applied spirally. A paddle and anvil are used to thin and compress the seams. The rancheria and prehistoric people of the Middle and Lower Gila River district of Arizona used this technique.

3. **Paddle and Anvil Method.** No coils are used but the paddle and anvil were used as described above. Some northern plains Indians used this method.

4. **Modeling Method.** Eskimos probably used this method which consisted simply of modeling clay into the desired form by hand.

5. **Molded in Basket Method.** In this method a layer of clay was molded to the interior of the basket. During the firing process the basket is lost, producing a pot with indentations of the basket on the exterior. This is probably one of the first metods used to produce pottery in the Southwest.

There are two types of firing processes commonly referred to as oxidation and reduction. In the oxidation process the fire, having access to air, burns hot and clean. In the reduction process the fire is cooler and fueled with animal manure to produce carbon.

Red ware and lighter colored pots are produced by the oxidation method while the popular black pots from Santa Clara and San Ildefonso are fired by the reduction process. Firing usually lasts for about three hours and may reach temperatures up to 1500 degrees F.

A skillful potter can produce a small simple pot in about two hours, exclusive of drying and firing, which may take at least another 15 hours. Large pots require several weeks to complete, depending upon the amount of decoration and polishing.

Present day Pueblo pottery is made essentially in the same manner as prehistoric pottery. Women usually are the potters, although assistance is often provided by son and husband in decorating the pottery. In recent years several men have become known as outstanding ceramic artists, such as Tony Da, Carlos Dunlop and Joseph Lonewolf.

Maria Martinez's husband Julian was probably the first modern day male potter. He decorated many of Maria's pots. Pottery making is usually learned from mother or grandmother.

The type and source of clay, which dictates the color and use of the final product, varies widely among the pueblos. Clay collected from the Rio Grande Pueblo area usually turn red or orange when fired, while those west and north turn white to gray. Proper selection and preparation of the clay are essential to making a quality pot.

The pulverized clay is mixed with water and cured for several days. The clay must be uniformly moist. A base is formed free hand and coils of clay are used to build the side. Vessel walls are thinned usually by a gourd rind and the outer sides are polished with a smoothed river pebble. After the pot is allowed to dry it is decorated with vegetal or mineral paints. The process, although simply presented, requires skill, patience and experience.

SELECTING A PIECE OF POTTERY

Your initial reaction to a piece of pottery should guide your ultimate selection. If the piece is esthetically pleasing initially, in all probability it will remain so if it satisfies other secondary characteristics. Disregard price if possible, particularly if you are looking for collector pieces. A collector piece is one made by a famous potter, is usually unique and probably demands a high price.

First look for cracks. Cracks do occur during the firing and cooling process. Some are readily detectable while others are very inconspicuous. Be sure to examine the pottery interior. Prehistoric pottery usually has chips and cracks. Although these effect the price, they are not particularly objectionable because of the rarity of prehistoric pottery.

It is best to avoid any pot which has a crack or chip as it will always be of lesser value. Experienced collectors have their own method of testing for soundness. One common test is to tap the rim of the pot with your fingernail, as you would to evaluate a crystal wine glass. There should be a resonant sound and not a thud. Many pieces of pottery such as miniatures and figurines are not suitable to this test. Symmetry or overall evenness is important and the pot should sit tall, not lopsided.

Polished pottery such as Santa Clara Pueblo blackware should be smooth and even-textured. Polishing inside the bowl and on the bottom represents additional effort of the potter, usually not encountered in most pottery. The design should be symmetrical, lines relatively even, and designs balanced. Condition dictates prices of contemporary, historic, and prehistoric pottery. Note that when handling a pot always place one hand on the bottom.

Generally each pueblo or pottery-producing reservation has a style and technique which is culturally acceptable. What might be acceptable or even necessary to one may be entirely unacceptable to another.

An example would be black firemarks on Taos pottery which reflects higher firing temperatures necessary for utilitarian purposes. These would be unacceptable to fine Santa Clara redware. Round bottom Navajo pots also serve a purpose for open-fire cooking while decorative San Ildefonso pots with a round bottom would be unacceptable as a decorator or collector item.

One cannot generalize about color. Many potters are experimenting with various color, media and combinations. If you are a traditionalist, look for color, particularly in polychrome pieces, which represent the traditional style. Most pots are painted before firing which fixes the color. If the paint will rub off, reconsider your purchase.

Inexpensive pots from a few pueblos are painted after firing. These represent a style and it is your decision whether or not they have a place in your collection. These are not to be confused with some of the outstanding oil and acrylic painted pots from Zia made by Madinas which have appeared in recent years and are in demand by collectors.

Look for small pits on the surface. Some pots from Acoma and other pueblos have impurities and tempering materials essential to strengthening and bonding. Occasionally pitting may develop after firing. This is no reflection upon the skill of the potter; depending upon the severity, it may affect the pots' appeal and value.

Some of the traditional type pots from the pueblos of Zia, Taos, Picuris, Acoma and Santo Domingo are utilitarian while most pots from other pueblos are strictly decorative. Your dealer or the potter will discuss this with you.

Properly seasoned pots from Taos and Picuris are excellent for oven use. Although some Indians may use their native pottery for special purposes, cost usually dictates that the pot be displayed as a piece of art. There is a wide choice and the informed buyer will make fewer mistakes in his selection. If you are inexperienced, buy from a knowledgeable dealer or a recognized potter.

THE FUTURE

The future of all Indian arts and crafts is dependent upon the attitude, motivations and changing culture of the Indians. Pottery is no exception, although there are several fulltime potters making a living as ceramic artists. They are motivated by economic benefits as well as by a need for recognition of their accomplishments. As long as there is an appreciation of pottery it will continue to be produced.

Quality pottery by recognized potters will continue to appreciate in value. Historic and prehistoric pottery will become part of institutional collections and this will result in less pottery being available to private collectors. Styles will continue to change with the imagination of the artists. This creativity is essential to the future vitality of this art.

(J.W.B.)

EASTERN AND MISSISSIPPI WATERSHED PREHISTORIC POTTERY

Large **pottery bowl,** from Arkansas, 7 in. high and 7¼ in. in diameter. No restoration or cracks; piece has cross-hatched rim design. G—$160

Mississippi culture **ceramic bowl,** 8 in. wide and 3½ in. high; rim has coiled baked clay resembling 3-strand rope twist. One major break has been skillfully restored. Except for rim decoration, a plain but well-made piece. D—$150

Round-bodied **Iroquois vessel,** 5 in. high, 5½ in. wide at mid-body. Reinforced upper rim decorated with incised lines. Gray-white in color, pot is in good condition. C—$295

BROKEN SECTION OF POTTERY VESSEL, found near Calabogie, Ontario, Canada. A Canadian archeologist has identified the section as "Black-necked" type, typical of the late Huron-Petun people of southern Ontario. Age: AD 1450—AD 1550.　　　　C—$10

Photo courtesy Howard Popkie, Arnprior, Ontario, Canada.

Low **ceramic bowl,** Mississippi culture and from Louisiana, painted lines decorate the straight sides. Bowl is 8½ in. in diameter, 3½ in. high. One section of the bowl bottom has been restored.　　C—$150

Caddoan effigy bowl, 3 in. high and 8 in. wide. Piece has three raised head-like nodes on an outstanding polished and engraved friendship bowl. Lines filled with red pigment.　　G—$825

Mississippi culture **ceramic vessel,** Tennessee, circular and with knobs on the rim. Piece is 9 in. in diameter and 4 in. high, with a reinforced rim. No decorations.　　C—$260

Grayware bowl, fine condition and 5 in. high and 7 in. in diameter. From Arkansas.　　G—$35

Flare-top ceramic vessel, Louisiana, 13 in. high and 8½ in. in diameter. It has cord-marked decoration on the surface, is a brown-gray color. Round body and rim. No restorations.　　D—$295

Ceramic effigy vessel, from southeastern Missouri and 8½ in. high. Human figure depicts kneeling man; some red paint remains on exterior. Vessel damaged and restored in base area, also in several sections of the rim. Figure is fine.   D—$450

Southern Cult pottery bottle, rare, 8½ in. high and 7 in. in diameter. Four human hands go around the bottle, in raised relief. No restoration, but some very minor rim and body damage.

G—$700

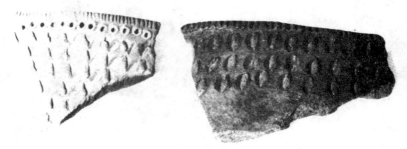

TWO POTTERY SHARDS, found near Pickwick Dam, Tennessee. They are rare for the area because of the thumbnail impression in darker piece and forefinger and thumbnail impression on the other. These are probably Mississippian in origin. The larger sherd is 5 in. long.   C—$3
Photo courtesy Jim Northcutt, Jr., Corinth, Mississippi.

Quapaw ceramic "teapot", 8 in. high and 9¼ in. in diameter. Painted red, white and brown; in fine condition.   G—$1100

Pottery bowl, from Woodland site in Pennsylvania, thick shell-tempered piece 6 in. in diameter, the same in height. No decoration and no handles. Very early vessel, probably BC period.   C—$160

POTTERY SHARDS, four of which have been cord-or bark-impressed. The largest shard is 2½ in. across; all were found at the same site in southcentral Tennessee. These are interesting in that each has a hole drilled near an edge, purpose unknown.   C—$4 each
Photo courtesy Jim Northcutt, Jr., Corinth, Mississippi.

Fine ceramic **frog effigy vessel,** 4 in. high and 7 in. long. Superb workstyle, finely detailed, and with a rattle head; no restoration.

G—$700

Caddoan **ceramic vessel,** from Arkansas, late prehistoric times. It stands 9 in. high and rounded base is 9½ in. in diameter. Deeply incised with swirling-circle pattern. Well-done, no damage and no restoration.

C—$800

Turkey effigy rattle bowl, 10 in. in diameter and 6½ in. high. From Mississippian mound-builder period.

G—$400

Caddoan water bottle, 9¼ in. high and 6½ in. width. No designs, but piece has a fine slick black finish and fine balance, only very minor repair.

G—$320

Group of six **Caddoan miniature bottles,** averaging 2 in. in height. Some fine engraved examples, and sold as a group only.

G—$275

CERAMIC VESSEL, 4½ in. high and 8 in. in diameter, plainware. Gray color, and found in Canada. Vessel is ca. AD 700—1100.　　　　　　*C—$80*

Photo courtesy Howard Popkie, Arnprior, Canada.

Square-bodies **Iroquois vessel,** New York, 7 in. high and 5½ in. wide at top. Top rim is decorated with incised ladder-like markings, while body has parallel lines. Gray-black color and no restoration. D—$300

Mississippi culture **water bottle,** from Missouri, with some minor restoration. Piece is 7 in. high and 7 in. in diameter, with a pedestal base. G—$65

Mint condition **water bottle,** from Arkansas, 7 in. high and 6 in. in diameter. Good shape. G—$60

Perforated disc base water bottle, found in Arkansas and 8 in. high and 6-5/8 in. in diameter. Perfectly balanced and with some restoration to rim and base. G—$200

SHELL-TEMPERED POT, from Hardin County, Tennessee, and probably from the Mississippian culture. Pot is 5 in. high and 5¾ in. across at top opening; circumference is 22 in. It was fully packed with a different soil from that in which it was placed; in the bottom was the ankle bone of a deer, also shown. C—$400

Photo courtesy Jim Northcutt, Jr., and Sr.; Corinth, Mississippi.

Bird effigy vessel, 5 in. long, from Florida and ca. AD 500. Well-executed and originally had painted features, now gone. An unusual piece and in fine condition.　　　　　　　　　C— $550

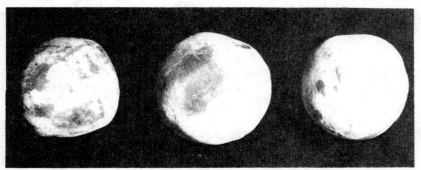

POTTERY BALLS, found with 16 others on the bank of the Tennessee River near Savannah, Tennessee. Each shows evidence of having been in a fire. Use uncertain; may have been heated and used as we use charcoal, or dropped in a vessel for heating and cooking. Each is about the size of a golf ball. Mississippian culture.　　　　　　　*C—$3 each*

Photo courtesy Jim Northcutt, Jr., Corinth, Mississippi.

WESTERN PREHISTORIC CERAMIC VESSELS

Anasazi/Pueblo III vessel, 12½ in. in diameter, exterior and interior decorated with geometric squares and alternating bands of white and red. Small portion of bowl rim has been expertly restored. Quite impressive piece.　　　　　　　　C—$795

Mimbres geometric design bowl, with usual kill-hole. Piece is 10 in. in diameter and 5 in. high. Restored.　　　　　　　　G—$550

Anasazi handled mug, Colorado, with geometric motif painted on sides. Ceramic piece stands 4½ in. high, and is in perfect condition.　　　　　　　　C—$300

Early **seed pot,** or storage vessel, from Colorado, and painted with varied motifs and Pueblo I or II period. It is 12½ in. high and 18½ in. in diameter. Unusual item, and in fine condition, no restoration.　　　　　　　　C—$900

Mimbres ceramic bowl, 11¾ in. in diameter, with checker-board design in black and white on interior. Has small kill-hole in bottom, otherwise perfect condition.　　　　　　　　D—$600

Coal mine Mesa corrugated jar, 11 in. in diameter and 14½ in. high. Some rim damage. G—$325

Handled ceramic pitcher, Anasazi, but looks almost modern. Piece is 10½ in. high, with expanded base. Bottom has circular streaks, top has lightning pattern. Some restoration to handle, but not major. D—$500

Mimbres vessel, 9 in. in diameter and 3 in. high, red on white concentric rim bands with inner concentric bands. Star in center, and kill-hole. G—$700

Anasazi corrugated ceramic jar, 9 in. in height, some original damage to base but could be restored. C—$260

Salado ceramic jar, 7½ in. in diameter and 5 in. high. Geometric designs, excellent condition, and ca. AD 1200-AD 1450. G—$600

BLACK-ON-WHITE BOWL, 3½ in. high and 6 in. in diameter. This type is called a "seed pot" by collectors. It has a small crack on the rim but is in excellent condition. Anasazi culture, from San Juan County. Colorado. near Mesa Verde. Circa AD 1100—1300. C—$400

Photo courtesy Claude Britt, Jr., Many Farms, Arizona.

DECORATED EFFIGY VESSEL, 6½ in. by 7 in., black-on-white. It is slightly restored, but a rare and valuable piece. Anasazi culture, Mesa Verde area, San Juan County, Colorado. The vessel is AD 1100—1300. C—$1000

Photo courtesy Claude Britt, Jr., Many Farms, Arizona.

Chaco Canyon black on white **pitcher,** 4½ in. high and 4 in. in diameter. G—$290

Zuni ceramic bowl, prehistoric, with stylized horned toad (?) motif painted around interior. Piece is circular, 13¼ in. in diameter, and some damage to rim area. C—$565

Anasazi ceramic bowl, 13 in. in diameter, about 4 in. high. Semicircular designs painted inside, except for bottom. Rim is damaged in several places. D—$395

Jeddito pottery bowl, 8 in. in diameter and 3 in. high. Geometric painting inside and out, and in mint condition. This piece is ca. AD 1400. G—$425

Southwestern Indian large **ceramic spoon or scoop,** probably Hohokam, 9¼ in. long, and shallow. Decorative interior lines of yellow and brown. Handle cracked in places. C—$185

MESA VERDE LADLE or dipper, 10 in. long and with bowl 4½ in. in diameter. Anasazi culture, from Mancos, San Juan County, Colorado. The handle is restored; otherwise in fine condition; this piece would be worth $300—$400, if not restored and perfect. Circa AD 1150. C—$225
Photo courtesy Claude Britt, Jr., Many Farms, Arizona.

Fine **Casa Grande effigy bowl,** 4½ in. high and 7½ in. in diameter. Has bird-like head, and four legs which were broken off and smoothed.   G—$440

Black on white bowl, 6 in. in diameter and 5 in. high. The piece has a stylized human effigy figure on the bottom, interior. Large chip missing from the rim.   G—$500

Hohokam pottery vessel, 11½ in. in diameter, undecorated, good condition; top opening 7 in. in diameter. Base is fire-darkened and heat-cracked.   C—$245

Four Mile Ruin bowl, 9 in. in diameter and 4 in. high. Polychrome, with geometric design. Painted inside and out; this is a restored piece.   G—$700

Black on white **pitcher,** 3½ in. high and 4½ in. at base. Geometric designs, Tularosa type, good condition.   G—$295

Salado ceramic, 7 in. in diameter and 5 in. high. Geometric designs, and ca. AD 1200-1450.   G—$475

Mimbres bowl, 6 in. in diameter. Has a well-executed rabbit design, only usual minor deterioration. Ca. AD 1250.   G—$1100

Casa Grande bowl, unusual square shape, mint condition. Piece is 2½ in. high and 4¼ in. in diameter. Note: It had a miniature axe, a polished stone pendant and miniature bowl and shell ring all inside bowl when it was found. All included.   G—$450

Zuni food bowl, 12 in. in diameter and 4 in. high. Painted geometric designs inside and out, and one small area of restoration on the bottom.   G—$1150

Casa Grande culture **effigy ceramic,** 6 in. high and 5 in. wide. Human male, superb detail, excellent condition, and from New Mexico.   G—$500

Mimbres bowl, 9 in. in diameter and 3½ in. high. Design is concentric rim bands with inner-spaced geometrics; with kill-hole.
                                                                    C—$800

MESA VERDE MUG, 5 in. by 4½ in., and decorated with black mineral paint on a white background. Anasazi culture, from Yellow jacket, Colorado, and ca. AD 1100—1300. C—$400
Photo courtesy Claude Britt, Jr., Many Farms, Arizona.

Anasazi/Pueblo-III ceramic bowl, 14 in. in diameter, interior painted with swirls and zigzag lines, exterior similar. No damage, no restoration. G—$800

Chaco Canyon type black on white **pitcher,** 5½ in. high and 4 in. in basal diameter. Geometric design, and good condition. G—300

Diegueno olla or storage vessel, Southwestern California, 13 in. high and 8 in. wide, mouth 4 in. wide. Restoration to rim and part of bottom. C—$325

Anasazi black on white **mug,** 5½ in. high and 6 in. in diameter. Has a rope-twist pottery handle, in excellent condition. Piece is ca. AD 950. G—$375

Mogollon polished brownware, 9 in. in diameter and same measure high. Piece has heavy restoration and is ca. AD 400-600.

G—$265

Black on orange **ceramic bowl,** Bedehochi type. Zone geometric design, and 6½ in. in diameter, 3 in. high. G—$385

SAN ILDEFONSO JAR, 3½ in. high and 4½ in. in diameter. This Pueblo is the home of the famous potter Maria Martinez. Although Ildefonso pottery is quite heavy, not thin like the Zia and Acoma, prices of well-finished pieces are rather high. C—$185
Photo courtesy Harvey and Rose King, Muskogee, Oklahoma.

HISTORIC CERAMICS

Hopi pottery vessel, mint condition, 4-7/8 in. high and 5½ in. in diameter. Unsigned, and ca. 1920. G—$300

Zia ceramic pot, 4½ in. high, 6 in. in diameter, with brown slip. Red and black painted bird designs; cracked and repaired, but with good appearance. Zia Pueblo, ca. 1940. Marked S. P. Medina.

G—$225

Acoma ceramic vessel, 4½ in. in diameter, stylized animal depicted, nice finish and good design. C—$150

Hopi vase, Sikyatki revival style, and ca. 1935. G—$225

San Ildefonso polychrome plate, 10 in. in diameter, 2 in. high. Ca. 1920. G—$295

Miniature Acoma pot, with loop handle. Piece is 2½ in. high and 3½ in. wide. Has good paint and age. G—$295

Zuni fetish bowl, depicting frog and water bugs. It is 9 in. across and 4 in. high, in good condition. Ca. 1930. G—$45

Santa Clara bowl, with incised serpent design. Piece is 6½ in. in diameter and 5½ in. high. Ca. 1940, and signed, Helen. G—$500

Santa Clara wedding vase, 7 in. in diameter and 8½ in. high. Good condition; ca. 1920. G—$200

San Ildefonso ceramic, 12 in. in diameter and 11½ in. high; black on black water jar. It has minor rim chips and is ca. 1910.

G—$165

Acoma head pot, 9 in. high and 12 in. across. It has geometric designs, is in excellent condition, very thin-walled. Ca. 1920.

G—$375

Small basket-type **miniature Acoma pot,** 2½ in. high and 4 in. in diameter, and ca. 1930. G—$625

Hopi ceramic bowl, reddish slip, 4 in. high and 8½ in. in diameter. Excellent condition, with red and black painted design. Ca. 1930.

G—$40

Historic **San Ildefonso bowl,** 11 in. across and 5 in. high. Polychrome bowl painted inside and out, geometric design. There is chip damage around lower exterior. G—$650

Hopi jar, 4½ in. high and 6 in. in diameter. Not signed, but well done and ca. 1920's. G—$160

Mojave pitcher, 5 in. high, and diamond painted design. Ca. 1940.

G—$90

Tesuque rain god, 7 in. high, with figure sitting with hands over eyes and bowl in lap. Ca. 1920. G—$135

CONTEMPORARY AND/OR SIGNED SOUTH—WESTERN POTTERY

Small, well-made **Santo Domingo pottery vessel,** bird effigy, 2 in. high and 4 in. long. G—$75

Miniature Acoma pot, with lightning designs. A—$35

Acoma bowl, whiteware with brown flowers painted design, 3 in. high and 4½ in. in width. Piece has large coiled handles. G—$75

ACOMA UNPAINTED COOKING BOWL, 6½ in. high and 8½ in. in diameter. This bowl was made undecorated, for the maker's personal kitchen use only. Ca. 1963. C—$150-$225
Photo courtesy Harvey and Rose King, Muskogee, Oklahoma.

Tesuque **pottery effigy figure.** A—$35

Santa Clara pottery vessel, 3½ in. high and 7½ in. in diameter, red and white, and in mint condition. G—$110

Acoma pottery vessel, 8 in. high and 9 in. in diameter, very thin and extremely fine shape. G—$550

Santo Domingo pot, 11 in. across and 10 in. high, excellent condition, and with geometric checkerboard design. G—$575

ZUNI POLYCHROME POT. 9½ in. high and 11 in. in diameter. These are no longer being made; ca. 1960.
C—$1200
William Sosa photo; Marguerite Kernaghan Collection.

Hopi contemporary pot, 5 in. high and 6½ in. in diameter, with stylized bird design. Signed, Emily Komalestewa. G—$260

Santo Domingo pot, made by Santana Melchor. A—$85

Miniature Acoma pot, made by B. Cerno. A—$50

SAN JUAN BOWL. 3½ in. high and 7½ in. in diameter. Polychrome and ca. 1972.
C—$250
Photo courtesy Harvey and Rose King, Muskogee, Oklahoma.

SANTA CLARA PAINTED POLYCHROME BOWL, 3¾ in. high and 5 in. in diameter, with painted snake design. Ca. 1973.   *C—$275*
Photo courtesy Harvey and Rose King, Muskogee, Oklahoma.

Santa Clara pot, made by Jo Ann.   A—$75

Ceramic plate, perfect condition and with feather design, by Maria and Popovi Da.   G—$3500

Hopi contemporary pot, 8½ in. in diameter and 8 in. high; designed with fine-lined center band with geometric neck. Signed, Ruby Shroulate.   G—$250

Hopi bowl, 3 in. high and 7 in. in diameter, very nice. Signed, Viola Hawato.   G—$225

Santa Clara ceramic, 5½ in. in diameter, 4 in. high. Small black on black piece, with painted knife design. Signed, Minnie.   G—$220

Hopi pot, 7 in. in diameter and 6 in. high, showing fine geometric design. Signed, Rondina Huma.   G—$290

Hopi bowl, 3 in. high and 7¾ in. in diameter. Signed, Viola Howato, First Mesa, 1968.   G—$700

Santa Clara seed jar, 6 in. across and 5 in. high. Design is an incised bear paw. Signed, Minnie.   G—$250

San Ildefonso pot, made by Blue Corn. A—$425

Miniature Santa Clara pot, made by Little Snow. A—$50

Hopi cylinder-shape jar, 9 in. high and 5½ in. in diameter. Beautiful firing marks and design. Signed, by Sadi Adams, Flower-woman. G—$290

Ceramic miniature, 2 in. high and 4 in. in diameter. Black on black design. Signed, Blue Corn. G—$385

Acoma pot, 9 in. in diameter and 8½ in. high. Fine line work, with geometric wide band. Signed, R.S. G—$230

Ceramic bowl, 6 in. high and 8 in. in diameter, good design and black on black. By Maria and Santana. G—$1500

Miniature Acoma pot, by B. Cerno. A—$50

Acoma pot, 8½ in. across and 7 in. high, zone fine-line design. Signed, Ruby Shroulate. G—$260

San Ildefonso pot, made by Florence Naranjo. A—$70

HOPI POLYCHROME BOWL, 3 in. high and 6 in. in diameter, and ca. 1975.
C—$125-$200
Photo courtesy Harvey and Rose King, Muskogee, Oklahoma.

HOPI POLYCHROME BOWL, 5 in. high and 7½ in. in diameter. Ca. 1972.   C—$200-$300
Photo courtesy Harvey and Rose King, Muskogee, Oklahoma.

SAN JUAN CARVED POLYCHROME BOWL, 3½ in. high and 5 in. in diameter. Ca. 1972.
C—$200-$275
Photo courtesy Harvey and Rose King, Muskogee, Oklahoma.

ZIA JAR, 7 in. in height and diameter. (HK: "Zia pottery has long been recognized as among the best pottery of the Southwest. This is due to precision firing, which produces a 'ring' when tapped, like our fine cut glass. GOOD Zia pottery will hold water, the only Pueblo pottery that will. The roadrunner, New Mexico's State Bird, is the typical decoration of the Zia. Their pottery is still being used in the kitchen of the Zia household.") Ca. 1973. C—$375-$500

Photo courtesy Harvey and Rose King, Muskogee, Oklahoma.

HOPI BOWL, 3¾ in. high and 11 in. in diameter. Ca. 1973. C—$200-$300

Photo courtesy Harvey and Rose King, Muskogee, Oklahoma.

164

San Ildefonso Ceramic bowl, 5 in. high and 8 in. diameter. Piece is black on black, feather design. By Blue Corn.   G—$1800

San Ildefonso pot, made by Lida.   A—$125

Acoma pot, 9 in. across and 7½ in. high. Band of fine-line work around center, geometric design on neck. Signed R. Shroulate.
                                                                              G—$225

ACOMA BOWL. 6½ in. high and 8 in. wide. Black and white prehistoric pattern. Ca. 1972.
                                                                C—$250-$325
Photo courtesy Harvey and Rose King. Muskogee. Oklahoma.

The following information is a special section on the pottery and artwork of the various Southwestern Pueblos. Those that currently produce contemporary (post-1950) ceramic wares are represented. The writer — for this 2nd Edition — wishes to thank John W. Barry for special permission to use this material. Examples have been selected at random.

Mr. Barry operates INDIAN ROCK GALLERY (PO Box 583, Davis, California 95617-0583) and is especially knowledgeable in the field of contemporary Pueblo ceramics. His primary business is contemporary Pueblo pottery and he authored the important recent book, *American Indian Pottery,* which is listed following this section.

CONTEMPORARY PUEBLO POTTERY

Acoma Pueblo jar-bowl black on cream with deer design, by Lucy M. Lewis, 5¾ in. dia., 1977.   G—$900

Acoma Pueblo wedding vase, polychrome with stylized bird, by Marie Z. Chino, 8½ in. high, ca. 1970.   G—$1200

Acoma Pueblo olla, brown and tan on cream, by Juanita Keene, 10 in. dia., 1979.   G—$650

Acoma Pueblo jar, polychrome with stylized birds, by Ethel Shields, 9 in. high, ca. 1960.   G—$500

Acoma Pueblo jar, fine-line design, black on white, 3½ in. high, ca. 1950.   G—$125

Acoma Pueblo miniature, turtle, polychrome turtle shell on white, Ca. 1977.   G—$15

Acoma Pueblo corrugated seed jar, white, by Stella Shutiva, 10 in. dia., 1979.   G—$1200

TESQUE MINIATURE WEDDING VASE, 4 in. high and 4½ in. in diameter. Tesque pottery is not fired, but sun-dried and painted with gaudy showcard paints. Many were made as tourist curios. Ca.1975   C—$15

Photo courtesy Harvey and Rose King. Muskogee. Oklahoma.

ZIA BOWL. 2½ in. high and 5¾ in. in diameter. Note the roadrunner motif Ca. 1970.
C—$100
Photo courtesy Harvey and Rose King, Muskogee, Oklahoma.

Acoma Pueblo canteen, polychrome, with Mimbres lizard design, by Emma Lewis, 5 in. dia., ca. 1975.   C—$325

Cochiti Pueblo Storyteller, polychrome, by Dorothy Truiillo, 7 in. high, 1979.   G—$395

Cochiti Pueblo owl, by Seferina Ortiz, 3 in. high, 1979.   G—$75

Cchiti Pueblo Storyteller, polychrome, signed "Felipa", 4 in. high.   G—$250

Hopi bowl, brown-black on buff, by James Huma, 4 in. dia., ca. 1970.   G—$195

Hopi jar, four-color on cream, by Frogwoman, 8 in. high, ca. 1978.   G—$750

Hopi jar-bowl, red and black on tan, by Dextra Nampeyo, 5½ in. dia., 1978.   G—$850

Hopi jar, black and red on orange-tan, by Verla Dewakuku, 7¾ in. dia., ca. 1970.   G—$400

Hopi jar-bowl, black on tan, 2-5/8 in. high, ca. 1977.   G—$65

ACOMA WEDDING JAR OR VASE, 6¾ in. high and 5¾ in. wide. The Acomas are noted for producing a fine quality, extremely thin lightweight pottery. Well-fired, it has a "ring" but pieces do not hold water long-term. Ca. 1973. C—$175

Photo courtesy Harvey and Rose King, Muskogee, Oklahoma.

Hopi seed jar, black on cream, 1¾ in. high, ca. 1977.   G — $75

Hopi jar, black on red, 5½ in. dia., ca. 1965.   G — $200

Isleta Pueblo bell, polychrome, by Stella Teller, 4 in. dia., ca. 1975.   G — $60

Jemez Pueblo "Kiva" bowl, pale lemon color, by Juanita Fraqua, 6½ in. dia., 1978.   G—$375

Jemez Pueblo owl, polychrome, by Maxine Toya, 3 in. high, 1978.   G—$200

Jemez Pueblo wedding vase, maize design, by Laura Gachupin, 10½ in. high, 1979.   G — $700

Jemez Pueblo miniature jar, black on red, 2 in. high, 1979. G — $40

JEMEZ BOWL, 7½ in. high and 8½ in. diameter. Some of the pottery was sun-baked for the tourist trade. Ca. 1970   C—$40.-$50.

Photo courtesy Harvey and Rose King, Muskogee, Oklahoma.

SANTO DOMINGO JAR OR BOWL, 4 in. in height and diameter. This piece is ca. 1973.   C—$75

Photo courtesy Harvey and Rose King, Muskogee, Oklahoma.

Jemez Pueblo bowl, poster paints, 2 in. high, ca. 1970.   C—$15

Jemez Pueblo jar, polychrome, by Bertha Gachupin, 4 in. dia., 1978.
G—$75

Nambe/Pojoaque Pueblo vase, polychrome, by Virginia Gutierrez, 7½ in. high, 1980.   G — $185

Pecos Pueblo bowl, modern, with swastika interior design 5 in. dia., 1979.   G—$125

Pojoaque Pueblo textured vase, polychrome, by Joe and Thelma Talachy, 1½ in. high, 1979.   G — $75

San Ildefonso Pueblo bowl, plain black polish, by Maria Poveka, 5 in. dia., 1979.   G—$850

San Ildefonso Pueblo jar, by Carlos Dunlap, 4½ in. high, 1979.
G—$275

San Ildefonso Pueblo bowl, polychrome, by Blue Corn, 5-3/8 in. dia., some spalling, 1974.   G—$750

San Ildefonso Pueblo vase, feather design, by Albert and Josephine Vigil, 5 in. high, 1977.   G—$375

San Juan Pueblo bowl, by Rosita de Herrera, 6 in. dia., 1976.
G—$395

Santa Clara Pueblo bowl, incised bird figure, by Art and Martha Cody (Haungooah), 2 in. high, 1975.   G — $750

Santa Clara Pueblo lidded jar, polished black-ware with bear paw imprint, by Anita Suazo, 7 in. high.   G—$950

Santa Clara Pueblo plate, Eagle dancer design, by Goldenrod, 2-5/8 in. dia., 1980.   G — $425

Santa Clara Pueblo jar, black-ware with melon design, by Anita Suazo, 3 in. high, 1979.   G — $120

CHEROKEE JAR. 5¾ in. high and 5½ in. in diameter. C—$125
Photo courtesy Harvey and Rose King. Muskogee. Oklahoma.

Santa Clara Pueblo carved vase, black-ware, by Mary Singer, 12½ in. high, 1979. G — $1200

Santo Domingo Pueblo pitcher, rare shape, double-lipped, by Santana Melchor, 11 in dia., ca. 1960. G—$700

Santo Domingo Pueblo jar, polychrome, with stylized bird, by Robert Tenorio, 9 in. high, 1979. G—$400

Santo Domingo Pueblo bowl with handle, polychrome, by Robert Tenorio, 4 in. high, 1977. G—$250

Taos Pueblo Mud-head figurine, by Alma L. Concha, 5½ in. high, ca. 1975. G—$200

Tesuque Pueblo "Rain god" figurine, tourist item, 6 in. high, ca. 1970. G—$100

Ysleta-Tigua Pueblo wedding vase, polychrome, by Lucy F. Rodela, 12 in. high, 1979. G—$150

WATER-SERPENT (Avanyu) POT, 13 in. high and 11 in. diameter. Santa Clara Pueblo, by Belen Tapia.   *C—$2200*
Photo courtesy William Scoble. The Ansel Adams Gallery, Yosemite National Park, California.

Zia Pueblo olla, polychrome with pattern triple-replicated, by Sofia Medina, 12 in. high, ca. 1969.   G—$775

Zia Pueblo olla, polychrome, stylized red bird outlines in black, by Helen Gachupin, 8½ in. dia., 1979.   G — $275

Zia Pueblo jar, polychrome, by Eusebia Shije, 5 in. dia., ca. 1969.
G — $175

Zia Pueblo bowl, acrylic painted dancing figure, by J. D. Medina, 10½ in. dia., l1979.   G—$2500

Large SAN ILDEFONSO POT, 9½ in. high and 7½ in. in diameter. black on black feather design. Pot was made and signed by Maria and Popovi Da. and received by present owner as a gift from Popovi Da in 1962.   C — $7000

Small SAN ILDEFONSO POT. (near Santa Fe. New Mexico). 2½ in. by 3½ in. Black on black design. made and signed by Maria and Santana. ca. 1958.   C—$350

Marguerite Kernaghan Collection; William A. Sosa. photo.

Zuni Pueblo jar, polychrome, by Jennie Laate, 4-1/8 in. high, 1979.
G—$275

Zuni Pueblo olla, animal designs, polychrome, 9½ in. high, ca. 1960.   G — $950

Pottery basket with twisted handles, 4½ in. by 5 in., and fine collector piece. Ca. 1965, black on black matte. By Lucaria Tofoya, Santa Clara Pueblo. Signed.   G—$125

Carved pottery bowl, 5¼ in. high, the same in diameter. Color, red on tan in carved area, good collector piece. By Helen Tapia, Santa Clara Pubelo. Signed.   G — $210

Pottery dish, 5 in. in diameter, black on black and with feather design. By Ramona Tapia, Santa Clara Pueblo.   G—$100

Pottery dish, 1¾ in. high and 6¼ in. in diameter. Piece has design on rim and inside of clouds, raindrops, kiva steps and mountains. By Minnie Vigil, Santa Clara Pueblo. Signed.   G — $280

ACOMA BOWL, 7½ in. high and 8½ in. in diameter. This piece was done in the black and white prehistoric pattern. Ca. 1972.   C—$150

Photo courtesy Harvey and Rose King, Muskogee, Oklahoma.

Miniature storage jar, 2¼ in. high and 2¾ in. in diameter, red, tan, and black with feather design. By Minnie Vigil, Santa Clara Pueblo.
G—$135

Pottery bowl, 4 in. high and 4½ in. in diameter. Piece is red, white and black, with traditional flower design. By Santa Melchor, Santo Domingo Pueblo. Signed.   G—$450

Pottery bowl, 4¼ in. in diameter and 3¼ in. high, black, red and pale red. Piece has flower and bird design. By Robert Tenerio, Santo Domingo Pueblo. Signed.   G—$200

Wedding vase, 7 in. high and 4¾ in. in diameter. Piece has traditional Zia bird design. Sofia Medina, Zia Pueblo. Signed.   G—$350

Pottery bowl, 4½ in. in diameter, with bird design. Red, brown on white colors. By Dominguita H. Pino, Zia Pueblo. Signed.   G—$200

Pottery bowl, 5¼ in. in diameter. Outstanding traditional piece, red, brown and white. By Eusebia Shije, Zia Pueblo. Signed.
G—$250

Suggested Reading

Maxwell Museum of Anthropology, *Seven Families in Pueblo Pottery*; University of New Mexico Press, Albuquerque, New Mexico, 1974

Hyde Hazel, *Maria Making Pottery*: The Sunstone Press, Santa Fe, New Mexico, 1973

Tanner, Clara Lee, *Prehistoric Southwestern Craft Arts*; University of Arizona Press, Tucson, Arizona, 1976

Bunzel, Ruth J., *The Pueblo Potter, A Study of Creative Imagination in Primitive Art*; Dover Publications, New York, NY., 1972 edition.

Arizona Highways, (Special Edition) *Southwestern Pottery Today*; Arizona Highway Department, Phoenix, Arizona, May 1974

Lambert, Margaret F., *Pueblo Indian Pottery*; Musuem of New Mexico Press, Popular Series Pamphlet No. 5, Santa Fe, New Mexico, 1966

Toulouse, Betty. *Pueblo Pottery of the New Mexico Indians.* Museum of New Mexico Press. 1977.

Martin, Paul S., George I. Quimby and Donald Collier. *Indians Before Columbus.* The University of Chicago Press, Chicago and London. 1947.

Harlow, Francis H. *Modern Pueblo Pottery.* Northland Press. Flagstaff, Arizona, 1977.

Barry, John W., *American Indian Pottery,* Books Americana, Florence, Alabama, 1984.

THE PAPAGO POTTER: Edward S. Curtis, photographer.
Photo courtesy National Photography Collection, Neg. # C-30076, Public Archives of Canada.

CHAPTER X
HISTORIC TRADE—
ERA COLLECTIBLES

The field of trade-era objects has two aspects. One is that the objects were made, for the most part, by Europeans for trade with the Indians. And, though whites did indeed use some of these items (axes, kettles and the like) themselves, the artifacts have been identified with Amerinds ever since.

In short — and for the only such chapter in this book — these are Indian collectibles not actually made by Indians.

Before, during and after the great fur trade of the 1700's and early 1800's, axes and other edged tools were popular. After the utilitarian objects were obtained, apparently the decorative items were sought. Trade silver and glass beads were much in demand, partially because they were well-made and attractive, but also because they were made of materials unknown to the Native Americans.

BASIC TRADE AXE FORMS

Most trade axes were of wrought (hand-forged) iron, made in the American Colonies, Canada and Europe. The iron head had a round or oval hafting "eye", a long, often back-slung blade, and an inletted steel cutting edge. Inferior specimens sometimes lacked this last feature, being traded to unsuspecting recipients, making the axe both brittle and nearly useless. Trade axes were used throughout the 1700's and most of the 1800's, until factory-made examples became widely available.

Similar axe and tomahawk heads are being made today for the frontier afficionados, and can be mistaken for old and valuable pieces. A certain amount of pitting and scabbing should be on genuine specimens, and the lap-weld around the eye and flowing into the flat blade is usually visible. Value is much less if the steel cutting edge is missing.

Condition is important; a small, intact specimen is more to be desired than a larger piece with much serious rusting and large chips missing from the blade. To paraphrase a knowledgeable Midwestern collector, one should look for a good piece in good condition, at a good price.

A legible and traceable marker's stamp, town or state of origin, or a date will add to specimen value. All three make a very desirable, and rarely obtainable, combination. (Information in this paragraph, by the way, also pertains to the pipe-tomahawks.) Many axeheads have been surface-finds, and will show the signs of having been weathered for many years.

TRADE-ERA AXE HEADS

Trade-iron axe head, round hafting eye, 6¾ in. long. Some corrosion, but average; from northern Illinois trading-post site, ca. 1830.

G—$160

Metal trade axe, 5½ in. long and 2 in. wide, nice shape. It has a hole in the back portion, and possibly used as a pipe.   G—$140

Small squared **belt axe,** 4¼ in. high, and with oblong haft receptacle or eye. Cutting edge good, condition good. Probably late 1800's and found on an historic Indian site in Iowa.   C—$95

Historic iron TRADE AXE, about 8 in. long. Iron is somewhat battered and corroded around the upper haft portion, the eye.   D—$90

Photo—Lar Hothem.

IRON AXE HEAD, 8¼ in. long and 4-3/8 in. wide. Heavy blade is typical of belt axes of this type. The eye is rounded, showing evidence of flattening. The entire head is uniformly pitted and shows a fine brown patina. No doubt it was highly prized as tool and weapon. Touchmark has not yet been identified; piece is ca. late 1700's/early 1800's.   C—$145-$200

Photo courtesy Sheridan P. Barnard, Franklin, Massachusetts.

Metal **trade axe,** good size, 7¾ in. long and 3½ in. wide, and ca. 1700.   G—$165

Trade iron **axe head,** no haft or handle, 8 in. long and blade 5-3/8 in. wide at cutting bit. Nicely hand-forged, light age pitting, and a solid piece.   D—$175

Badly corroded trade **axe head,** from northern Ohio, 6¼ in. high. Undamaged, but heavy rust has eaten out portions of the lower blade and portions of the eye-strap.   C—$55

(The following five listings, of metal axe and pipe-heads only, are courtesy of Bob Coddington, Illinois. Note that these are 1970 figures. In the writer's opinion, values would now be triple or more.)

THREE TRADE-ERA IRON AXES, with middle specimen about 6 in. long. Top and middle pieces have damaged blade edge; bottom piece, market "ARIT" is heavily worn.

AXES: Top   D—$30
Middle   D—$100
Bottom   D—$100

Lar Hothem photo.

Tomahawk head of iron, with surface rust, recovered by means of a metal detector on site of old Ottawa or Huron village along bank of Thames River in Ontario, Canada. This piece was part of a cache of trade tomahawk heads in an old iron pot with a mixture of mud and beads. While rusted, this item must have been in new condition when cached, as it has the appearance of having never been used. It has the steel insert on leading edge of blade. The location where this piece was recovered was not far from the site of "The Battle of the Thames" (1813) where the American General Harrison defeated the Shawnee Chief, Tecumseh and General Proctor of the British Army, in the War of 1812. It was in this engagement that Tecumseh lost his life. This piece is the "modern" type squaw hatchet.   (1970) C—$95

Iron pipe-tomahawk head. British-type bowl of either American or English manufacture.   (1970) C—$225

IRON PIPE TOMAHAWK with 27 in. ash stem. A horse design is stamped on both sides of the blade. A human skull bone is tied to the stem-handle. Ca. 1870.   *G—$1000*
Photo and item courtesy Fenn Galleries, Ltd., Santa Fe, New Mexico.

Belt hatchet head, ca. 1780, found on Chippewa National Forest site, Old Leech Lake Indian Reservation, while digging a well. Steel insert in leading edge of blade. This type of squaw axe was popular as a trade commodity and was widely distributed by the Hudson Bay and X.Y. companies.   (1970) C—$200

Spontoon-type tomahawk head, of the squaw hatchet variety, of Trois Rivieves, or Chautiere, Quebec (Canada) manufacture. Piece is heavily rusted. Obtained from Six Nations (Iroquois) Reserve at Brantford, Ontario, and a very early French type. Ca. 1750.
                                        (1970) C—$280

Squaw hatchet head, of early trade variety. Recovered by Peter Cloud, a Chippewa Indian, on Squaw Point of Leech Lake, Minnesota, while plowing garden on site of Chief Flatmouth's old Pillager Chippewa village. From its condition this piece was evidently discarded as being worn out, and of no further use. Ca. 1780.   (1970) C — $75

HAFTED TRADE-ERA HEADS (complete)

(Information courtesy Bob Coddington, Illinois)
So-called **squaw hatchet** with very unusual haft, elaborately decorated with carvings of diamonds, stars, etc. Top of handle has thirteen carved five-point stars encased in "Vs" at each end. Ring in end of haft. This piece could possibly have belonged to a frontiersman (White) during the American Revolution, or a friendly Indian ally of the original Thirteen Colonies.   (1970) C—$350

Iron **squaw hatchet,** haft decorated with brass braid tassel, probably from tunic facings, or epaulet of British or French uniform tunic. Ca. 1760-1780.   (1970) C—$375

Squaw hatchet of iron, haft decorated with trade tacks and five large white bead sets, typical trade items. Ca. 1780.
                                                                      (1970) C—$265

PIPE-TOMAHAWKS

Better specimens of the pipe-axe/tomahawk (best not to use the terms "pipe-'hawk" or "hawk" around serious collectors) are considered a high-art form. Ranging from plain to fancy to presentation-grade — these with the original handle — they grace a limited number of collections.

Still, the writer is aware of several instances where good pipe-tomahawks were purchased at farm auctions for nominal sums, at two to ten percent of actual value. In the world of Amerind collectibles, such things happen.

It may not be possible to totally fake a complete pipe-tomahawk (considered by collectors to be pipes, not weapons) head and handle. Beyond the factors of metal-working re. the head, there is the problem of properly shaping and aging the wood handle-stem. More likely, and to beware of, is an oldish handle hafted to a good but mediocre head.

Usually the fit is not close, the wood is not a seasoned hardwood, and the whole is not a unit. The two sections just do not belong together. If the haft is supposed to be original, or at least of comparable age, both head and handle should evidence a believable amount of wear.

And conversely, an ornate handle will usually not accompany a very plain pipe-tomahawk head. Also don't be too impressed with the assertion that the piece belonged to famous Chief So-and-So, for this usually cannot be documented.

IRON PIPE AXE, haft 19½ in. long, blade 7-5/8 in. high. It has a heavy forged blade of flaring design, while pipe bowl is crudely made and shows some repair. The maple haft appears to have been a later addition and shows multi-beaded cuffs and a horse hair suspension. The piece is typical of the Midwest-Great Lakes region; it is ca. early to mid 1800's. Note beaded strips on handle.

C—$1000-$1500

Photo courtesy Sheridan P. Barnard, Franklin, Massachusetts.

Pipe-tomahawk, ca. 1780. Head is 7¼ in. high; blade has 1-7/8 in. cutting edge. Original or at least very old handle, 15¾ in. long. Fine condition.

C—$950

STEEL PIPE AXE, haft 20½ in. long and blade 7¾ in. high, 2-3/8 in. wide. The undecorated, drilled and cylindrical wooden handle has a flared steel blade of fine manufacture. The blade is attached with a flanged, engraved pipe bowl of cylindrical shape. Handle is a later addition to the head. This is a Plains region pipe, ca. late 1800's.   C—$1000-$1500

Photo courtesy Sheridan P. Barnard, Franklin, Massachusetts.

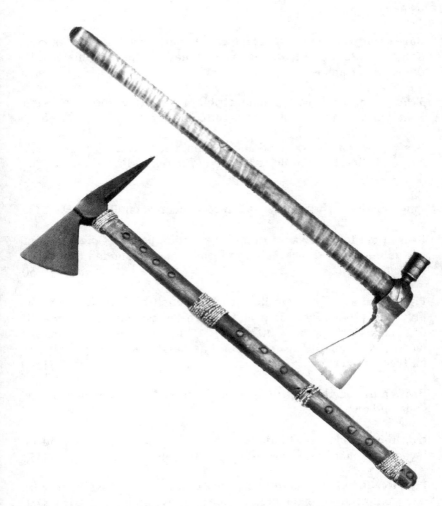

IRON SPIKE AXE, with haft 18 in. long, and blade 7½ in. high. The axe head has a long, straight spike of square cross-section, eye is wedge-shaped; flared blade shows definite notches on the edge. Haft is ovoid in cross-section, decorated with brass tacks; suspensions of hairpipe and beads appear to be a later addition to the axe. Style attributed to Western Great lakes East to New England. Piece is mid-1700's to early 1800's.   C—$1000-$1500

Photo courtesy Sheridan P. Barnard, Franklin, Massachusetts.

Pipe-tomahawk, ca. 1780. Head is 7¼ in. high; blade has 1-7/8 in. cutting edge. Original or at least very old handle, 15¾ in. long. Fine condition.   C—$800

Spontoon-type pipe tomahawk head, no haft. Piece is 9½ in. long and 3½ in. wide. Spontoon-types have a spear-like blade instead of a curved blade.   G—$325

Rare spontoon-head pipe-tomahawk, no haft. Piece is 10¾ in. long, and seems to be all iron. Reported to have come from historic Indian site in Kansas.   C—$400

Trade tomahawk with hammer poll, 10 in. long and 3 in. wide. Found in New York, and ca. mid-18th Century.   G—$145

Brass pipe tomahawk, good and original head, with a later (but still old) undrilled handle. Stem-handle is file-burned and beaded.
                                                                   D—$530

Pipe tomahawk, head only, and in good, sound condition.   D—$325

Brass pipe tomahawk, of later Reservation period. Original stem, but value reduced when an uninformed person sanded the wood.
                                                                   D—$350

Pipe-tomahawk, presentation-grade. French or British and probably late 1700's. Piece is from western Pennsylvania, and head is 6½ in. high. Length, with handle, 17 in.; handle may be maple wood. Good condition, and blade has pewter inserts in shape of half moon and stars.   C—$1500

Brass pipe-tomahawk with original handle. A genuine piece of fine style and quality.   G—$825

Iron tomahawk, cast blade with heart cut-out; handle is lead inlayed with bands and crosses. Ca. 1880-1890.   D—$350

Pipe-tomahawk, authentic early wooden handle, brass head with only minor battering damage at pipe poll. Attractive.   D—$750

Good **brass pipe-tomahawk,** guaranteed genuine and in excellent condition. Nice patina on brass, file-burned handle, partially beaded.   G—$600

Pipe tomahawk with old handle, iron head in good condition, has the steel insert. Plain but solid piece.　　　　　D—$575

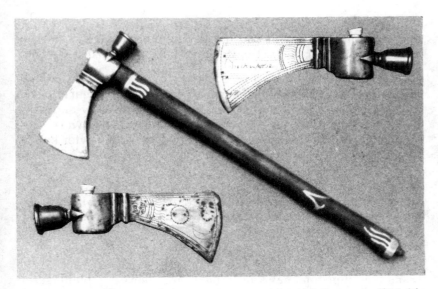

Cheek-cah-kose (Little Crane) presentation grade pipe tomahawk. Little Crane was a Chief of the Pottawattomie, with a village at the headwaters of the Tippecanoe River in northern Indiana. Three views: Left and right sides of head; and full view. Head is of engraved pewter, with a brass screw-out bowl. The blade is hallmarked (DV) over a coronet. Presentation pieces of this quality are rare. Ca. 1767.　　　　　C—$2500

Photo courtesy Bob Coddington, Illinois.

Pipe tomahawk, ca. 1790. Brass pipe tomahawk with original wood haft. Heavily worn. Leading edge formerly held dovetailed steel bit. Floral motif on bowl and blade. Length of haft 19½ in. and head is 5½ in.　　　　　G—$550

(The following listings in trade-iron section are courtesy Bob Coddington, Illinois. Values are 1970, and in the writer's opinion, are currently less than half fair market prices.)

Typical early **trade iron pipe-tomahawk,** with curl at base of haft very plain, ca. 1790.　　　　　(1970) C—$375

Massive British Broad-Arrow marked **iron pipe-tomahawk,** with superb inlays of pewter or silver on haft. Type presented to chiefs by British government for loyalty and friendship.   (1970) C—$600

Iron pipe-tomahawk with unusual flaring pipe bowl, slim narrow blade, with pewter-inlayed haft. Ca. 1780-1800. (1970)   C—$600

Pewter pipe-axe elaborately engraved with bleeding heart, leaves and scrimshaw on one side of blade. Large turtle, bow and what appears to be initials "L. H." and profuse engraving. Bowl is deeply and elaborately engraved. Handle is inlayed with pewter bands.
(1970) C—$650

Iron pipe-axe, small short handle with "wi ix" burned in haft. Example of the early French type, strap tomahawk, very old. Ca. 1695-1710, and heavily rusted.   (1970) C—$335

Trade-type pipe-tomahawk of wrought iron, severely plain, scroll type mouthpiece, probably of British manufacture. Strap type with steel insert on leading edge of blade. Ca. 1770-1800.
(1970) C—$325

Excellent **French-type pewter pipe-tomahawk** of presentation quality with Trois Rivieves, Quebec (Canada) markings. Type presented to Canadian chiefs for loyalty. Ca. 1750, and with pewter inlays.   (1970) C—$600

Very fine presentation **pewter pipe-axe** with inscription dated 1797. Half-moon and star cut-out, acorn-shape pipe bowl. A wolf is engraved with leaves and star on one side of the blade. Handle has nice pewter inlays. From a Canadian collection.   (1970) C—$650

Brass pick-type spoontoon tomahawk, "J.H." over sword. The pick is four-sided. Piece has a beautiful handle inlayed with silver and bone, overall an exquisite work of art. Ca. 1760.   (1970) C—$550

TRADE SILVER ORNAMENTS

Even before a man named Paul Revere invented a rolling press to flatten silver bars to a predetermined thinness, trade silver artifacts were very popular items. In addition to the flat pendants and brooches, crosses and gorgets of myriad forms, there were solid-cast and hollow-cast effigies.

Such forms ranged from turtles to beavers to the esoteric and much-admired "kissing otters", touching noses and swimming, seen from above. Hudson Bay Company contributed countless fine specimens, most of which went into the Northern reaches of the United States, the top fur-producing regions.

Trade silver copies are being made today from a metal called nickel silver, a combination of copper, nickel and zinc. It is cheaper and more durable than pure silver. Such copies are very good and they sell for a fraction of genuine trade silver.

Unfortunately, most are not marked as reproductions. Amerind trade silver may have a blackish tarnish and may be somewhat corroded. It should show some signs of one and a half to two centuries of age.

TRADE SILVER BROOCH, 2 in. in diameter, and with elliptical and circular cutouts, scalloped rim, and touchmarked "DE". Sheet silver, and perfect condition.   C — Above $250
Photo courtesy Bob Coddington, Illinois.

Double-bar cross, trade silver of typical thin sheet metal, 4½ in. high. The top has a small silver ring for suspension; piece was probably worn as a pendant. Good condition.   C—$200

Trade silver pendant, 1-7/8 in. wide, 2¼ in. high, single suspension hole at top. Piece has star cut-outs and floral designs. Touchmarked by maker; probably Canadian. From the Great Lakes area.
C—$160

Double-bar cross, trade silver of typical thin sheet metal, 4½ in. high. The top has a small silver ring for suspension; piece was probably worn as a pendant. Good condition.   C—$150

Trade silver pendent, 1-7/8 in. wide, 2¼ in. high, single suspension hole at top. Piece has star cut-outs and floral designs. Touchmarked by maker; probably Canadian. From the Great Lakes area.   C—$145

From left to right:
TRADE SILVER CROSS PENDANT, 1¼ in. high, drilled for suspension. Piece has incised lines on face.   *C — $150*
Photo courtesy Bob Coddington, Illinois.

TRADE SILVER CROSS, 7/8 in. in length. Piece has inscribed lines on face, with touchmark "DS" This was purchased with the original string of trade beads, not shown; price was for the entire necklace.   *C — $225*
Photo courtesy Bob Coddington, Illinois.

Small TRADE SILVER CROSS PENDANT, 1 in. high, and with circular loop for cord.   *C — $125*
Photo courtesy Bob Coddington, Illinois.

From left to right:

TRADE SILVER MOSONIC EMBLEM, 1¼ in. high. Pin that held brooch is visible in center.   *C — $85*
Photo courtesy Bob Coddington, Illinois.

TRADE SILVER BROOCH, circular form and with cross-shaped cutouts; piece is ¾ in. in diameter, of sheet silver.   *C — $125*
Photo courtesy Bob Coddington, Illinois.

Hatchet-shaped TRADE SILVER BROOCH, 1¼ in. high.   *C — $100*
Photo courtesy Bob Coddington, Illinois.

Trade silver brooch, with both suspension hole and back-pin. Piece is somewhat corroded, said to be an excavated find in Upper Michigan. About 2 in. high. Has a council-fire cut-out design.

C—$115

Trade silver finger ring, plain, but not common. It is 13/16 in. in exterior diameter. Fair condition. C—$95

Small **trade silver brooch,** has pin on back for attachment; 2-1/8 in. high, with rounded triangular shape. It has masonic-symbol cut-out decorations. Touchmarked by maker. C—$120

Large circular **trade silver brooch,** scalloped edge, 3-1/8 in. in diameter, with touchmark of 1728 Canadian silversmith. Has pin at cut-out center; extremely good workmanship and condition, no corrosion. C—$445

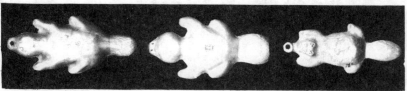

From left to right:

TRADE SILVER BEAVER PENDANT, solid-cast silver, 1½ in. long. Touchmarked on rounded back. C—$250

Photo courtesy Bob Coddington, Illinois.

TRADE SILVER BEAVER, 1-3/8 in. long, hollow-cast silver. Touchmarked "B" on back. C—$260

Photo courtesy Bob Coddington, Illinois.

TRADE SILVER BEAVER PENDANT, solid-cast silver, 1½ in. long. C—$240

Photo courtesy Bob Coddington, Illinois.

From left to right:

TRADE SILVER BEAVER PENDANT, solid-cast silver, 1¼ in. long. C—Above $250

Photo courtesy Bob Coddington, Illinois.

TRADE SILVER TURTLE PENDANT, ¾ in. long, and solid-cast silver. C—Above $200

Photo courtesy Bob Coddington, Illinois.

TRADE SILVER TURTLE IMAGE, ¾ in. long and hollow-cast silver. Touchmarked on back. C—Above $200

Photo courtesy Bob Coddington, Illinois.

Trade silver headband, 6 in. in diameter, sheet silver, with heart and diamonds cut-outs. Perfect condition, slight pitting only, touchmarked. C—$950

Trade silver cross, 3¼ in. long, holed for suspension and with decorative tool impressions. Thick-cast, touchmarked. C—$140

Trade silver buttons, high-domed and backed. Very decorative and well-made. C—$18

Plains Indians in Montana, date unknown. Note the fine baby carrier woman carries between tipis, and dramatic feather headdress worn by standing man.

Photographer, Roland Reed; courtesv Photography Collection, Suzzallo Library, University of Washington.

Three Nez Perce men, with tipis to side and background. Note the fine necklaces and blankets; photo taken at Colville, Washington, ca. 1904.

Photographer, Dr. E. H. Latham; courtesy Photography Collection, Suzzallo Library, University of Washington.

Trade silver cross, double-bar type, 4¾ in. high. Piece is touch-marked. C—$200

Trade silver beaver, 5½ in. long and solid-cast silver. Fine condition, professionally tested (not German silver) and weight is one pound. Touchmarked. C—$950

Trade silver beaver pendant, 2¾ in. long, solid-cast, touchmarked. Canadian or U.S. Colonies. Ca. 1780. C—$300

Trade silver beavers, each 1¾ in. long, hollow-cast. Set of three, each is touchmarked and perfect condition. C—$500

Trade silver cross, double-bar type, sheet silver, 5½ in. high. Excellent condition and touchmarked. C—$250

Trade silver armbands, pair, sheet silver and 4¼ in. in diameter. Edges scrolled, otherwise plain. Fair condition. C—$325, pair

GLASS TRADE BEADS

The early trade-glass beads were usually medium to large in size. These are far different from the countless tiny "seed" beads that were worked into designs on bark or fabric or leather. The "major" trade beads were worn in strands of a dozen to many hundred.

Such glass beads were largely made in Europe, especially the old glass-manufacturing towns of Italy. And the crafts people there made some wonderful products. Solid-colored, faceted, round, oblong, multi-colored — all found their way to North America. There was also a heavy traffic into Africa, and many beads sold today as "American Indian" have actually come from Africa.

Glass beads are being reproduced, of course, so it is best to first check the seller's credentials. Good beads may show extensive wear around the hole-ends. Some may be chipped, with such edges not sharp. Single beads to the advanced collector may be worth from a few cents to $25 or $30 and more depending or rarity.

Fine strand of **old trade beads,** found on a site near the Red River in Texas. They are at least late 1600's, and may have been traded by the Spanish. Strand is 20 in. long, graduated from small size to larger, and with heavy patina.   G—$85

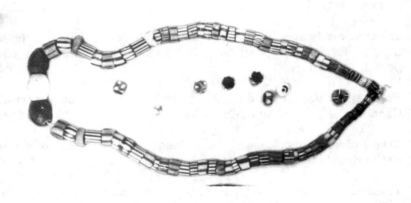

Large strand of Western U.S. TRADE BEADS, large blue beads to either side of central large white bead; said to have been screened from a historic Indian site.   *C—$95*
Private collection.

Cranberry red glass beads, 24 in. long strand.   G—$60

Strand of **mille fiore trade beads**.   A—$30

Blue glass beads, strand, with smaller striped beads interspersed, and length of 26 in.   G—$65

Trade beads, strand 34 in. long, white milk glass in tube shape, with six shell spacers. Excavated in Oklahoma.   G—$65

Strand of **cobalt blue globular beads** 28 in. long.   G—$75

Strand of old **glass trade beads**, 20 in. long. Colors are pale red, yellow, blue and black.   G—$35

Hudson Bay **white beads** with Cornaline d'Aleppo red beads, and a length of 26 in.   G—$80

Extremely long strand of **white milkglass trade beads**, tube shaped with average bead length of 1 in. (25 mm). Strand is 90 in. in length.   G—$105

Red "whiteheart" beads, with one section of blue beads, strand 27 in. long.   G—$75

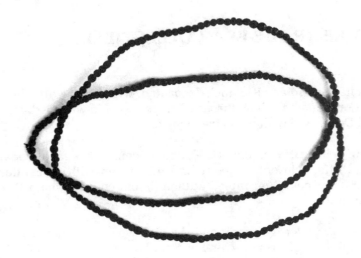

FRENCH TRADE BEADS, with 248 beads in the two strands. Beads average 1/8 in. in diameter, and came from a Brant County site in Ontario. Such beads were used before 1650. Beads are red, blue, white and amber.   C—$75-$115

Photo courtesy Robert C. Calvert, London, Ontario, Canada.

Pale red **round trade beads,** strand length 24 in. and ca. late 1800's.   G—$70

Tile beads, various colors, strand 28 in. long.   G—$72

Strand of pale **blue and white trade beads,** 20 in. in length. Beads have a heavy patina and are from site on the Tennessee River.
G—$115

Strand of faceted **Russian blue beads,** 33 in. long.   G—$105

Strand of small **red glass beads,** 22 in. long; excavated in north-west Oklahoma.   G—$60

Strand of **trade beads,** green glass beads with 13 amber glass beads, and 24 in. long.   G—$70

Strand of deep **cobalt-blue beads,** 24 in. long. They are round and all the same size; a beautiful strand.   G—$90

Fine old **trade bead necklace,** with two large dentilium shells, large blue chevron beads and red "whiteheart" beads. Strand is 22 in. long.   G—$105

OTHER TRADE-ERA COLLECTIBLES

Winchester **Indian rifle,** tack-decorated, with history attached via tag. Condition only fair; throat of stock rawhide-wrapped, may be split. Decorated with brass trade tacks.   A—$420

Indian Police rifle, caliber 45/70, and a Remington-Keene repeating rifle. Difficult to obtain today and a problem with fakes, due to premium prices. Guaranteed authentic and collected on a Dakota Reservation.   G—$1295

Old musket, average condition for metal, wood stock not good. Last decorated with brass tacks in Plains Indian style.   D—$450

Indian musket, old Barnett trade piece. Stock has minor repair that does not affect value; overall fair-good condition.   D—$1850

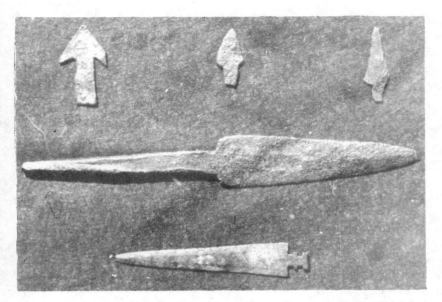

Metal TRADE-ERA PROJECTILE POINTS and large blade. Top three are Indian-made frm barrel hoops. The long blade or spear was Indian-made from a file. Bottom point was a Comanchero trade item, with four basal notches. All from the historic period, 100 to 300 years old. Artifacts are from 1 in. to 7½ in. in length. C — $10-$40, each

Photo courtesy Wayne Parker, Texas.

Cut-down trade musket, old and with brass tack decorations. From a Montana collection. D—$225

Northwest trade gun, by Barnett. The earliest of the Barnett's marked 1805 and in original flintlock. Possibly saw service at the start of the Northwest Company or the American Fur Company, etc. Absolutely genuine; circle fox visible on stock. G—$2500

Metal arrowpoint, 4½ in. long. A good old piece, and Cree type from South Dakota. G—$28

Iron arrow point, Tesuque Pueblo, 18th or 19th Century. D—$35

Brass arrowhead, from historic Indian site in New Jersey. Probably salvaged from White-made brass kettle or utensil. Piece is 1½ in. long and triangular-shaped with small stem. C—$15

Taos Pueblo arrow, wooden shaft with blood-line and metal point. Sinew wrapped, good condition, 24 in. long. G—$65

Old **converted musket,** with old brass tacks showing Indian use, authentic. G—$395

Rare **1866 Winchester carbine,** with all wood carved in various Northwest Coast designs. A—$2200

Barnett trade musket in original percussion, late trade period. Once covered with brass tacks on wooden portions, many now removed. D—$1900

Spear or lance point, fine hand-forged early piece. Excellent condition. D—$100

Old brass trade pail, as traded or issued to the Indians. These were once common on reservations, but now are scarce. D—$135

Gun barrel hide scraper, made from the barrel of a trade musket; hide-wrapped. D—$140

Strike-a-light, hand-forged, and an excavated find. D—$60

Iron-tipped arrows, Sioux and old. D—$22, each

TRADE-ERA CLAY PIPES. human face or effigy variety. Such pipe bowls were made in molds, pressed into shape. The clay is kaolin, a white, yellow or gray material found in deposits in New England area and some Southeastern states. C—$10, each

Private collection.

PICTORIAL NAVAJO WEAVING, contemporary, 1' 6" x 4', showing the reservation as you might see it today. D -- $3,500

Photo and Item courtesy Jackson David Co. /Tah-Atin Trading Co.; Durango, Colorado.

NAVAJO YEI RUG from Lukachukai, Arizona, on Navajo reservation, 22 1/2" x 33 1/2 " Acquired in 1973. C -- $600

M.J. Kernaghan photo; Marguerite Kernaghan Collection.

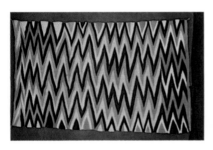

NAVAJO WEAVING, 3' 6" x 5' 6", very rare wedge-weave (or pulled wrap), ca. 1880. D -- $ 18,000

Photo and Item courtesy Jackson David Co. /Tah-Atin Trading Co.; Durango, Colorado.

NAVAJO STORM PATTERN WEAVING, 3' x 5', contemporary. Weaving has all handspun wool, and a combination of natural colors and aniline red dye. D -- $2,000

Photo and Item courtesy Jackson David Co. /Tah-Atin Trading Co.; Durango, Colorado.

TEEC NOS POS WEAVING, contemporary, 2' 4" x 4', very fine tapestry weave featuring a unique optical type of pattern. Blue Ribbon winner, New Mexico State Fair, 1977.
D -- $15,000

Photo and Item courtesy Jackson David Co. /Tah-Atin Trading Co.; Durango, Colorado.

BURNTWATER/WIDE RUINS WEAVING, 2' 6" x 4', contemporary piece, with all hand-spun wool, and vegetal dyes.
D -- $1,900

Photo and Item courtesy Jackson David Co. /Tah-Atin Trading Co.; Durango, Colorado.

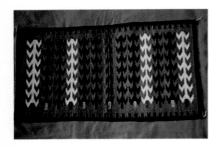

NAVAJO PICTORIAL RUG with corn pattern, 34" x 61". Purchased at Tsegi Canyon Trading Post in 1960.   C -- $1,600

M.J. Kernaghan photo; Marguerite Kernaghan Collection.

TWO GREY HILLS WEAVING, 2' 6" x 4' 6", contemporary, fine weave, and all natural wools.   D -- $7,000

Photo and Item courtesy Jackson David Co. /Tah-Atin Trading Co.; Durango, Colorado.

Above: *GERMANTOWN WEAVING*, 3' x 6'
6", and a fairly rare collector item. Weaving is
ca. 1890.   C -- $10,000

*Photo and Item courtesy Jackson David Co.
/Tah-Atin Trading Co.; Durango, Colorado..*

Left: *INCISED SANTA CLARA POT,* by
Golden Rod, potter. (background is rug C - 59)
Pot is 3 1/2" high, and was Blue Ribbon win-
ner at the 1977 Santa Fe Market.   D -- $1,800

*Photo and Item courtesy Jackson David Co.
/Tah-Atin Trading Co.; Durango, Colorado..*

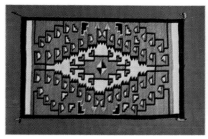

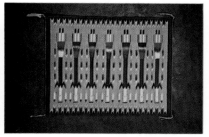

Above: *NAVAJO YEI WEAVING,* 2' x 3', and
contemporary. This piece has all handspun
wool and vegetal dyes.   D -- $1,500

*Photo and Item courtesy Jackson David Co.
/Tah-Atin Trading Co.; Durango, Colorado.*

Above left: *TWO GREY HILLS RUG,* 36" x
63 1/2". Two Grey Hills area is west of the
highway from Gallup to Farmington, New
Mexico, on the Navajo reservation. Rug was
purchased in 1973.   C -- $1,800

*M.L. Kernaghan photo; Marguerite
Kernaghan Collection.*

Left: *CHILD'S WEARING BLANKET,*
Navajo weaving, 2' 6" x 4' 6". This is a very
rare raveled Bayeta combined with homespun
wool, ca. 1860.   D -- $20,000

*Photo and Item courtesy Jackson David Co.
/Tah-Atin Trading Co.; Durango, Colorado.*

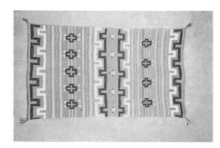

BEADED DECORATIVE SASH, fringed, 1/2" wide and 45" long. Over a dozen different colored beads were used, and nearly 4,000 are in the sash. Good condition.   C -- $55

Private collection.

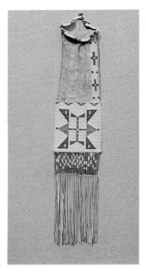

SIOUX PIPE BAG, 33" long and 7" wide. It is ornamented with seed beads and porcupine quills, and is early 1900's.   C -- $850

M.L. Kernaghan photo; Marguerite Kernaghan Collection.

BEADED BAG, 4" long. Rounded beaded pouch with flap, thong drawstring and carrystring. Yellow cross in center and encircling blue triangle on white field. Sioux (?), from Northern Plains, and pre-1900.   G -- $300

Photo courtesy Kenneth R. Canfield, Plains Indian Art , Kansas City, Missouri.

PIPE BAG, 33" long. Piece has a red, green, blue and purple beaded pattern over a solid white field. Bottom panel consists of painted purple and orange rectangles over a field of lavender quillwork. The three beaded symbols may be symbolic feathers. Sioux, Northern Plains area, ca. 1890.   C -- $950

Photo courtesy Kenneth R. Canfield, Plains Indian Art , Kansas City, Missouri.

POSSIBLE BAG, 17" high and 23" wide. This hide container was called a possible bag because it could hold "any possible thing". Front panel of solid blue beading, interlined with narrow bands of red and yellow quillwork. It has red-dyed horsehair and tin-cone suspensions. Sioux or Cheyenne, Northern Plains, ca 1890.   G -- $1,200

Photo courtesy Kenneth R. Canfield, Plains Indian Art , Kansas City, Missouri.

WOODLAND-INDIAN BEADED POUCH, 5" high and 4 1/2" across. Iroquois, from northern Ohio, historic. Piece has red trade ribbon strap, floral design in beadwork, very good condition.   C -- $200

Photo courtesy Larry Conrad, Lancaster, Ohio.

Left: BANDOLIER OR SHOULDER BAG, 14 1/2" x 21". This is the earlier type, a true bag, with the strap forming an endless pattern. Bag opening is across, below the back velvet section. Chippewa, ca. 1900-25.   C -- $700 - $800

Photo courtesy Harvey and Rose King, Muskogee, Oklahoma.

Center: BANDOLIER OR SHOULDER BAG, 13" x 14". Worn as clothing item rather than used as bag; there is a 3" wide full-depth pocket in the bag or apron. Finely beaded, Chippewa, ca. 1900-25.   C -- $700 - $900

Photo courtesy Harvey and Rose King, Muskogee, Oklahoma.

Right: BANDOLIER OR SHOULDER BAG, 17 1/2" x 17 1/2". This is not a true bag, but a flat "apron" type with no openings. Worn by males as decorations; piece is exquisitely and solidly beaded on entire surface. Chippewa, ca. 1900-25.   C -- $700 - $900

Photo courtesy Harvey and Rose King, Muskogee, Oklahoma.

Above: *ASSORTED MOCCASINS*, adult sizes, all Plains Indian. Conditions excellent.
G -- $225 - $350

Photo courtesy Kenneth R. Canfield, Plains Indian Art , Kansas City, Missouri.

Below: *MOCCASINS,* 11" long. Soft buckskin uppers dyed light green and yellow, with beaded bands and tabs. Contemporary informants often explained heel fringes such as these were intended to drag in the dust, obscuring footprints, and confusing the enemy. Kiowa, Southern Plains area, ca. 1880.
G -- $500

Photo courtesy Kenneth R. Canfield, Plains Indian Art , Kansas City, Missouri.

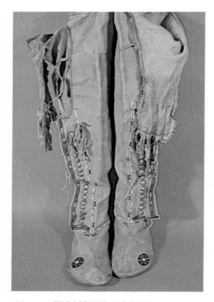

Above: *WOMEN'S BOOTS*, 24" long. Yellow-painted buckskin is accented with red and green paint; rows of German silver conchos, framed by bands of multicolored beadwork. Kiowa (?), Southern Plains in origin, ca. 1880.
G -- $850

Photo courtesy Kenneth R. Canfield, Plains Indian Art , Kansas City, Missouri.

Below: *SALISH BAG,* 9" wide and 12 1/2" in length, Northwest Coast area. Made of twisted cedarbark fibers, shredded by beating over the edge of a paddle with a wooden chopper and twisted into twine. An old piece. C -- $275

M.L. Kernaghan photo; Marguerite Kernaghan Collection.

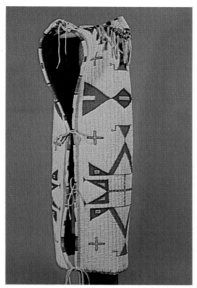

Above: *UMBILICAL FETISH*, 4 1/2" long. Buckskin fetish beaded in red, dark blue and light blue on a green background, with thong attachments. Sioux, Northern Plains area, pre-1890.   G -- $375

Photo courtesy Kenneth R. Canfield, Plains Indian Art , Kansas City, Missouri.

Above: *CRADLE*, 32" high, fully beaded, hide cradle bundle. Beaded on back and decorated with multicolored geometric patterns on a white field. Brass trade beads on the top flap. Item is lined with red calico. Perfect condition. Sioux, Northern Plains region, pre-1900.
G -- $3,600

Photo courtesy Kenneth R. Canfield, Plains Indian Art , Kansas City, Missouri.

Above: *CHILD'S DOLL*, 10" high. Beaded buckskin doll ornamented with hair, paint and calico. Northern Plains attribution, ca. 1885. G -- $475

Photo courtesy Kenneth R. Canfield, Plains Indian Art , Kansas City, Missouri.

Above: *IROQUOISE FALSE FACE MASK*, 8 1/2" x 10 1/2". This is a ceremonial dance mask worn to cure humankind of certain afflictions, and, when put outdoors, it splits destructive winds. If begun in the morning it is painted red but if started in the afternoon, the mask is painted black. This is the Protruding Tongue mask made by Ti'nyun'gwus.
C -- $195

M.L. Kernaghan photo; Marguerite Kernaghan Collection.

EASTERN LOOM BASKET, so-called from the days when such types held weaving aids. Later examples were hung for odds and ends. Basket is 9" both high and wide.   C -- $60 - $85

Left: *MICMAC QUILLED BIRCH BARK CONTAINER*, with bark lining. Piece is 2 1/4" high and 3" in diameter. Quillwork has come apart in some sections, but container is still in good shape, ca. early 1900's.   C -- $35 - 50

Center: *LADIES BASKETRY PURSE*, or handing basket, 4 1/4" high and 4 3/4" in diameter. Probably a Southeastern work, decorations in brown and purple pine needles, excellent condition. Recent or contemporary.   C -- $25 - $35

Right: *BEADED NAPKIN HOLDER*, 2" wide and of slightly different designs, butterflies and flowers. Beading done on rolled birch bark. Northeastern U.S.; there are over 3000 beads in each holder.   C -- $25

Private collection.

THREE CHEROKEE BASKETS

Large, 19" high, made by Lizzie Youngbird on the Qualla reservation near Cherokee, North Carolina. Made of dyed river cane, walnut and bloodroot.   C -- $350

Medium-size, 13" x 14", made by Eva Wolfe on Qualla reservation. Basket was made of white oak splits dyed with walnut root. Both of these baskets were acquired in 1961.   C -- $200

Small purse-basket is made of natural river cane on the Qualla reservation.   C -- No value listed

M.L. Kernaghan photo; Marguerite Kernaghan Collection.

CONTEMPORARY LIDDED BASKET, by Faye Stouff; she and husband Emil are the last of the Chetimacha Indians near Jeanerette, Louisiana, to weave baskets. Made of coiled pine needles with raffia interweave. It took 3 days to make this item, which is 7" in diameter.   C -- $55 - $75

Private collection.

LIDDED SWEETGRASS BASKET, 2 1/2" high and 4 3/4" in diameter. Great lakes area and eastward; well made, fine condition.   C -- $20 -$30

Private collection.

THREE TRADITIONAL NAVAJO SILVER PIECES, done by Wilson Begay, son of Luke Begay, using Nevada blue turquoise. Narrowest piece is 1" wide, widest piece is 1 1/2" wide.

Large Bracelet, D -- $1,500
Small Bracelet, D -- $850
Ring, D -- $425

Photo and Items courtesy Jackson David Co./Tah-Atin Trading Co.; Durango, Colorado.

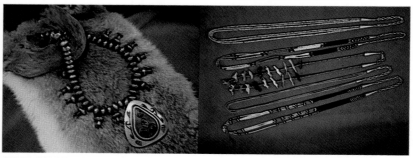

HOPI SILVER-INLAY NECKLACE, by Phillip Sekaquaptewa. 25 karats of Lander Blue Spider-web turquoise. First Prize, 1973 Swaia Annual Indian Market, Santa Fe.
D -- Highest Quality -- *not priced*

Photo courtesy G. Khalsa, Golden Temple Emporium, Cambridge Massachusetts.

SANTO DOMINGO HEISHI, excellent examples of many materials, including a fine fetish necklace in center.   C -- Unlisted

Photo courtesy G. Khalsa, Golden Temple Emporium, Cambridge Massachusetts.

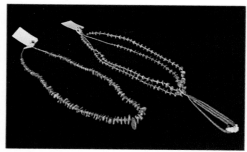

DEAD PAWN CHUNK NECKLACES, two, each about 20" in length, ca. 1953.
D -- $700 each

Photo and Item courtesy Jackson David Co. /Tah-Atin Trading Co.; Durango, Colorado.

POTTERY SHRED NECKLACE, a unique piece combining sections of prehistoric pottery and silver squash blossoms.   G -- $50

William M. Ciesla photograph; courtesy John W. Barry, Indian Rock Arts, Davis California.

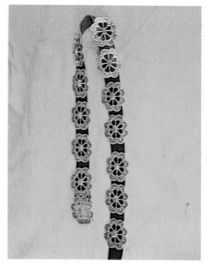

CHOKER AND EARRINGS, contemporary, by Navajo silver and goldsmith Jimmie King, Jr.. Set is 14 ct. gold and inlayed with turquoise.   D -- $7,000

Photo and Item courtesy Jackson David Co. /Tah-Atin Trading Co.; Durango, Colorado.

SANDCAST CONCHA BELT, by Navajo silversmith Wilson Begay.

D -- $2,900

Photo and Item courtesy Jackson David Co. /Tah-Atin Trading Co.; Durango, Colorado.

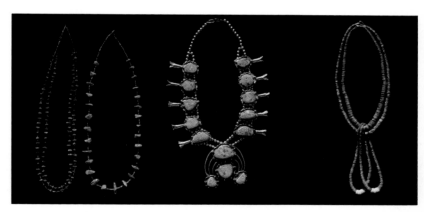

Left: *TURQUOISE NECKLACES*, both of Santa Domingo Turquoise (natural unstablized) nuggets with olive shell heishe. Length is 12 1/2" for each, ca. 1970.   C -- $350

S.W. Kernaghan photo; Marguerite Kernaghan Collection.

Center: *MAN'S SQUASH BLOSSOM NECKLACE*, 17" long when clasped 6" wide at naja. This is an extra large piece and weighs 1 lb. 3 oz.. Stone is a natural old Morenci (Arizona) fine turquoise.
C -- $2,250

S.W.. Kernaghan photo; Marguerite Kernaghan Collection.

Right: *SANTA DOMINGO NATURAL (unstablized) TURQUOISE HEISHE*, 15" long, clasped, including jaclas.   C -- $525

S.W.. Kernaghan photo; Marguerite Kernaghan Collection.

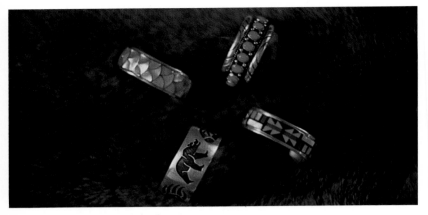

FOUR FINE BRACELETS by three silver-smithing tribes.
Bottom left: Hopi, 3-legged bear by lawrence Saufkie.   C -- unlisted
Top Left: Zuni, green snail-shell bracelet by Orlinda Natewa.   C -- unlisted
Top Right: Navajo, Kingman turquoise, by Emma Carviso.   C -- unlisted
Bottom right: Zuni, fine multistone inlay bracelet by Viola Eriacho.   C -- unlisted

Photo courtesy G. Khalsa, Golden Temple Emporium, Cambridge, Massachusetts.

Left: *SILVER PENDANT*, 1 3/8" high. Piece has very nice silverwork; stone has discolorations. A fairly old example.   C -- $45

Private collection.

Center: *ZUNI SILVER AND TURQUOISE BRACELETS*, with light blue turquoise bracelet 2 5/8" across. Green turquoise bracelet is 2 1/2" across.   Blue turquoise bracelet, C -- $125
    Green turquoise bracelet, C -- $175

Photo courtesy Larry Conrad, Lancaster, Ohio.

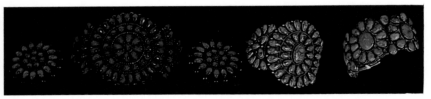

Left: *BRACELET AND EARRINGS*, Zuni cluster style. Bracelet is of natural turquoise, matching stones. The earrings are of natural turquoise, made by Zunis, but purchased from Popovi Da at San Ildefonso Pueblo in 1962.   Bracelet only, C -- $600

M.L. Kernaghan photo; Marguerite Kernaghan Collection.

Right: *CLUSTER BRACELETS*, dead pawn bracelet on right, above 2 1/2" in width. Contemporary cluster bracelet on left with Nevada Blue Sider-web stones.
    Dead pawn cluster, D -- $1,000
    Spiderweb cluster, D -- $1,500

Photo and Items courtesy Jackson David Co./Tah-Atin Trading Co.; Durango, Colorado.

SANTA CLARA PUEBLO BLACK WARE, showing the great diversity of shapes.
R. Keck photo, Dugway Proving Ground, U.S. Army photograph, 1974.

POLYCHROME PUEBLO POTTERY; left to right: Santa Domingo, San Juan, Hopi, Zia, and Santa Clara.
R. Keck photo, Dugway Proving Ground, U.S. Army photograph, 1974.

WATER SERPENT BOWL, by Fidel Onquan Archuleta, and signed.   D -- $200

Photo courtesy John W. Barry, Indian Rock Arts, Davis, California.

POTTERY BOWL, 5" in diameter, with the feather design. By Ronald Suazo, signed.
G -- $150

Photo courtesy John W. Barry, Indian Rock Arts, Davis, California.

BLACK ON MATTE BOWL, 4 3/4" in diameter, with traditional matte design. By Marie and Julian Martinez.   G -- $2,000

Photo courtesy John W. Barry, Indian Rock Arts, Davis, California.

CARVED BOWL, 3 1/2" in diameter, with feather design. By Stella Chavarria, and signed.   G -- $395

Photo courtesy John W. Barry, Indian Rock Arts, Davis, California.

POTTERY BOWLS, 5" high, 4 1/2" in diameter, with an excellent bird design. By Eusebia Shije.   G -- $250

Photo courtesy John W. Barry, Indian Rock Arts, Davis, California.

ZIA POLYCHROME POT, 8 1/2" x 10". Pot is ca. 1925.   C -- $1,200

S.W. Kernaghan photo: Marguerite Kernaghan Collection.

POLYCHROME HOPI POT, contemporary, made in 1977. This pot was made and signed by Rondina Huma.   C -- $400

S.W. Kernaghan photo: Marguerite Kernaghan Collection.

TWO HOPI BOWLS; small bowl is 5 1/2" in diameter and 3" high, while large bowl is 10 1/2" in diameter and 7 1/4" high. Both first Mesa, ca. 1974.

Small bowl, C -- $40 and up
Large bowl, C -- $175 and up

Photo courtesy Harvey and Rose King, Muskogee, Oklahoma.

CARVED BOWL, 8 3/4" in diameter, and an outstanding piece. By Richard Ebelacker, and signed.   G -- $1.200

William M. Ciesla photograph; courtesy John W. Barry, Indian Rock Arts, Davis, California.

ACOMA BOWL, 9" in high, with small owl effigy and miniature jar. Acoma Mesa, ca. 1974.

Large bowl, C -- $100 and up
Owl effigy, C -- $25
Miniature jar, C -- $15

Photo courtesy Harvey and Rose King, Muskogee, Oklahoma.

POLYCHROME BOWL, carved, 5 1/2" x 3 1/4" from San Juan, ca. 1974.

C -- $100 and up

Photo courtesy Harvey and Rose King, Muskogee, Oklahoma.

STORAGE JAR, an outstanding collector piece with detailed design. By Blue Corn, signed, ca. 1974.   G -- $3,500

William M. Ciesla photograph; courtesy John W. Barry, Indian Rock Arts, Davis, California.

CARVED BOWL, 5 1/4" high, the same in diameter. Famous potter. By Belen Tapia, signed.   G -- $375

Photo courtesy John W. Barry, Indian Rock Arts, Davis, California.

VASE WITH HANDLES, 9 1/2" high, 6" in diameter. By Faustina, signed.   G -- $600

Photo courtesy John W. Barry, Indian Rock Arts, Davis, California.

MIRACOPA BOWL, 5 1/2" across and 3 1/2" high, ca. 1974.   G -- $125

Photo courtesy Harvey and Rose King, Muskogee, Oklahoma.

STORY TELLER WEDDING VASE, in pleasing, traditional design. By S. Teller.

G -- $100

Photo courtesy John W. Barry, Indian Rock Arts, Davis, California.

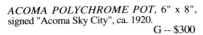

ACOMA POLYCHROME POT, 6" x 8", signed "Acoma Sky City", ca. 1920.

G -- $300

M.L. Kernaghan photo: Marguerite Kernaghan Collection.

WEDDING VASE, 8" high and a fine collector's piece. By Minie Vigil.   G -- $750

William M. Ciesla photograph; courtesy John W. Barry, Indian Rock Arts, Davis, California.

RAIN GOD FIGURINE, 6" high. Traditional piece and difficult to obtain. From Tesuque Pueblo, potter unknown.   G -- $100

Photo courtesy John W. Barry, Indian Rock Arts, Davis, California.

TAOS PUEBLO, 9" high and 6 1/4" across, ca. 1974.   C -- $200

Photo courtesy Harvey and Rose King, Muskogee, Oklahoma.

KIVA BOWL, 6" high and 7 1/2" in diameter, a fine collector's piece. By Laura Gachupin, signed.   G -- $750

William M. Ciesla photograph; courtesy John W. Barry, Indian Rock Arts, Davis, California.

OWL EFFIGY JAR, contemporary Cherokee, made by Mrs. Anna B. Mitchell, Oklahoma. Large size, the piece was made entirely using the ancient coil method, ca. 1977.   C -- $250

Photo courtesy Harvey and Rose King, Muskogee, Oklahoma.

FOUR SLATE PIECES, PREHISTORIC, of different kinds of banded slate. Right to left; a rectangular two-hole gorget form 6" long, and with one large and one small end; a bell-shape pendant 4 1/2" long of very good work-style; a keyhole-type pendant 5" long, very symmetrical; a Bi-concave gorget, undrilled, and 5" long.

Two-hole gorget, D -- $375
Bell pendant, D -- $325
Keyhole pendant, D -- $400
Bi-concave gorget, D -- $300

Photo courtesy Summers Redick, Worthington, Ohio.

TWO FINE PIPES, larger specimen is 2 7/8" high, from Kentucky. Slightly smaller piece is 2 5/8" high, from Ohio. Large pipe has cross-hatch decorative lines, and smaller pipe evidences fine polish.

Ohio pipe, D -- $500
Kentucky pipe, D -- $600

Photo courtesy Summers Redick, Worthington, Ohio.

NEAR-CEREMONIAL CLASS STONE PESTLE, probably Northwest Coast region, prehistoric, of a highly polished dense black material. Piece is 6 3/4" long and 3 1/2" across at base (larger) end.   D -- $550

Photo courtesy Summers Redick, Worthington, Ohio.

THREE STONE DISCOIDALS. Left; perforated-center disc, 3 1/8" in diameter, possibly from Ohio. Center; large disc, 4 3/8" in diameter, from Illinois. Right; very unusual flint disc, 2 1/4" in diameter from Tennessee.

Smaller disc, D -- $200
Medium-size disc, D -- $450
Large disc, D -- $500

Photo courtesy Summers Redick, Worthington, Ohio.

QUARTZ CONE, 2" in diameter at bottom. A well-made piece probably from the Woodland era.   D -- $200

HARDSTONE CONE, prehistoric and Woodland, 2 1/4" in basal diameter. Center of base is scooped or hollowed, basal edges are tally-notched. Overall high polish, and in fine condition.   D -- $275 - $350

Private collection.

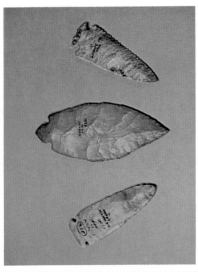

FINE FLINT BLADES, of exceptional size and workstyle. They are left to right, a beveled-edge type. Turkeytail, and a side-notched blade. The bevel is 4 1/2" long, the Turkeytail 6" and the side-notch 4 3/8" in length.

Bevel, D -- $300
Turkeytail, D -- $375
Side-notch, D -- $250

Photo courtesy Summers Redick, Worthington, Ohio.

SELECTION OF GUILFORD-TYPE POINTS, averaging 2 3/4" long. Of various types of chert and flint, all are from the North Carolina region.   D -- $12 each

Photo courtesy Summers Redick, Worthington, Ohio.

DOVETAIL BLADE, over 4" long, of translucent Flintridge material, white and rust-red. Very slight damage to tip, but fine form and superb chipping.   D -- $250

Photo courtesy Mike Miller, Lancaster, Ohio.

Left: POLISHED FLINT SPADE, 10" long and 4 1/4" wide. In position photographed, top side is excurvate, bottom side flattish. Piece shows good use-polish.   D -- $350

Photo courtesy Summers Redick, Worthington, Ohio.

Selection of *POINTS AND BLADES*, with long, dark knife 4 1/4" long. All were chipped in Archaic and Woodland times, and are Midwestern specimens. C -- $60 - $90

Private collection.

PIPE-TOMAHAWK, 16 3/4" long and head 6 1/4" high, cutting edge 2" long. Tecumseh-type, with original cane handle suggestive of use in Kentucky canebrake country, ca. 1790.
C -- $850

Photo courtesy Larry Conrad, Lancaster, Ohio.

COOPER AWL OR CHISEL, from Michigan, 9 1/8" long and 1/2" in diameter at center. This piece is in fine condition and shows good form. D -- $350

Photo courtesy Summers Redick, Worthington, Ohio.

FLINT CORES, from which small knives were struck. Examples are high-quality Flintridge materials. The cores are only valued as artifacts.   C -- $5 - $8

Private collection.

LARGE COPPER CELT, from Michigan, 6 7/8".   D -- $350

Photo courtesy Summers Redick, Worthington, Ohio.

MINIATURE CELT, 2 1/4" long, made of a yellow-brown close-grained stone.   D -- $35

Private collection.

HEMATITE AXE, three-quarter groove type, 4 1/8" long.   D -- $500

Photo courtesy Summers Redick, Worthington, Ohio.

GRANITE AXE HEAD, 6 5/8" long extremely well-made piece.   D -- $450

Photo courtesy Summers Redick, Worthington, Ohio.

TWO FLINT CELTS or adzes, one 8 1/4" long, other 9 1/4" long. Of cream-brown flint, both are highly polished.   D -- $300

Photo courtesy Summers Redick, Worthington, Ohio.

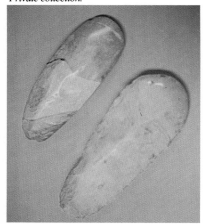

TLINGIT BASKET, 5 1/2" high, damaged, ca. 1900.　　　　　　　　C -- $200

Courtesy John W. Barry, California.

HAT CREEK BASKET, 12" in diameter, ca 1910.　　　　　　　　C -- $750

Courtesy John W. Barry, California.

PIT RIVER BASKET, 8 1/2" in diameter, ca. 1910.　　　　　　　C -- $700

Courtesy John W. Barry, California.

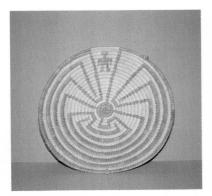

PAPAGO BASKET, 14 1/2" in diameter, ca. 1970.　　　　　　　C -- $225

Courtesy John W. Barry, California.

YAVAPAI BURDEN BASKET, 12" high, ca. 1920.　　　　　　　C -- $900

Courtesy John W. Barry, California.

CRYSTAL RUG, by Lula Laughing, 1976.
C -- $935

Courtesy John W. Barry, California.

BLACKFOOT GAUNTLETS, by Alice Walter, ca. 1943.
C -- $525

Courtesy John W. Barry, California.

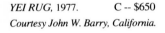
YEI RUG, 1977.   C -- $650

Courtesy John W. Barry, California.

PAIUTE WATER JUG, basketry, 9" in diameter, ca. 1970.   C -- $200

Courtesy John W. Barry, California.

YUROK HAT, 6 1/2" in diameter, ca. 1910.
C -- $400

Courtesy John W. Barry, California.

PAPAGO BASKET, 7 1/2" high, ca. 1974.
C -- $350

PAPAGO BASKET, 13" high, by Ruth Martinez. This basket won the Blue Ribbon at the Gallup Ceremonial, 1974.   C -- $2,000

Courtesy John W. Barry, California.

PAPAGO BASKET TRAY, 10" x 13 1/2", lizard design, ca. 1970.   C -- $250

NOOTKA BASKET, Canadian, 6" x 9 x 12", ca. 1950.   C -- $300

Courtesy John W. Barry, California.

POTTERY Zia Pueblo, 4" to 9" high, ca. 1970.   C -- $150 - $500

Courtesy John W. Barry, California.

ISLETA PUEBLO POTTERY, left, 3" high, ca. 1910; right, 2 1/2" high, ca. 1910.
Left, C -- $125
Right, C -- $125

Courtesy John W. Barry, California.

WEDDING VASE POT, 10 1/2" high, by Laura Gachupin, Jemex Pueblo, ca. 1979.   C -- $1,000

Courtesy John W. Barry, California.

POTTERY, 3 1/2" high, Santa Domingo Pueblo, by Robert Tenorio, ca. 1979.
C -- $150

Courtesy John W. Barry, California.

SANTA DOMINGO POT, 8 3/4" high, by Robert Tenorio, ca. 1979.   C -- $650

Courtesy John W. Barry, California.

TAOS PUEBLO POTTERY, 4" high, by Almo Concha, ca. 1977.   C -- $250

Courtesy John W. Barry, California.

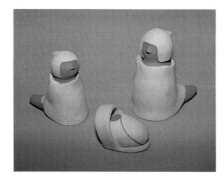

TESUQUE NATIVITY SET, 4" high, by Manuel Vigil, ca. 1974.   C -- $1,000

Courtesy John W. Barry, California.

CERAMIC NATIVITY SET, Jemez Pueblo, ten pieces, 4" high, by Marie Romero, ca. 1978.   C -- $1,200

Courtesy John W. Barry, California.

POTTERY CORN-GRINDING SET, 4" high, Jemez Pueblo, by Marie Romero, ca. 1979.   C -- $390

Courtesy John W. Barry, California.

BASKET, Alaskan Eskimo, 5 1/2" in diameter, of baleen and ivory, ca. 1960.

C -- $2,000

Courtesy John W. Barry, California.

BASKET, Alaskan Eskimo, 12" x 14", ca. 1960.

C -- $350

Courtesy John W. Barry, California.

SAN JUAN POTTERY
Left, 4 1/2" high, ca. 1950   C -- $200
Right, 4 1/2" high, ca. 1978   C -- $395

Courtesy John W. Barry, California.

HUPA BASKET, 5" in diameter, fine piece, ca. 1910.   C -- $400

Courtesy John W. Barry, California.

ACOMA PUEBLO POTTERY, left, 9" high, ca. 1979; center, 13" diameter, ca. 1920; right, 5 1/2" high, ca. 1950.

C -- $495; $1,800; $160

Courtesy John W. Barry, California.

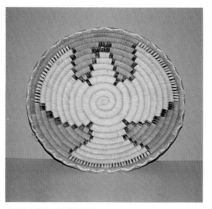

PAPAGO BASKET, 15 1/2" in diameter, ca. 1970.   C -- $225

Courtesy John W. Barry, California.

PAPAGO BASKET, 16" in diameter, ca. 1970.   C -- $225

Courtesy John W. Barry, California.

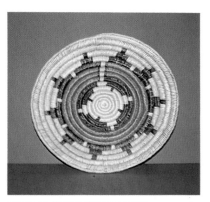

NAVAJO WEDDING BASKET, 15 1/2" in diameter, ca. 1970.   C -- $300

Courtesy John W. Barry, California.

NAVAJO WEDDING BASKET, 13 3/4" in diameter, ca. 1970.   C -- $250

Courtesy John W. Barry, California.

HOPI BASKETRY PLAQUE, 10 1/2" in diameter, fine.   C -- $450

Courtesy John W. Barry, California.

POTTERY PLATE, 11 1/2" in diameter, by
Virginia Ebelacker, Santa Clara Pueblo. Piece
has bear paws in turquoise, ca. 1979.
C -- $3,000

Courtesy John W. Barry, California.

HOPI BOWL, 7" in diameter, by Vina
Harvey, ca. 1970. C -- $250

Courtesy John W. Barry, California.

SAN ILDEFONSO PUEBLO POT, 12"
in diameter, by Carmilita Dunlap, ca.
1977. C -- $1,500

Courtesy John W. Barry, California.

POTTERY, 11" in diameter, by Vange
Tafoya, Jemez Pueblo, ca. 1978. C -- $400

Courtesy John W. Barry, California.

ACOMA POT, 8 1/2" high, damaged, ca.
1960. C -- $150

Courtesy John W. Barry, California.

SANTA CLARA POT, 5 1/2" high. By Minnie
Vigil, ca. 1978. C -- $500

Courtesy John W. Barry, California.

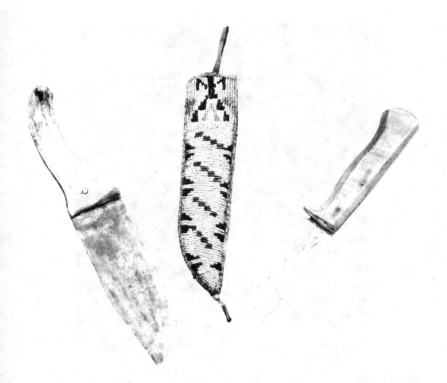

TWO STEEL-BLADED KNIVES, with beaded sheath fitting blade to right. Left, a single-edge blade fashioned from a discarded saw blade; blade riveted to a section of antler forming a handle. Piece is Northern Plains Flathead, Montana. Ca. mid to late 1800's.

Right, typical "butcher" type trade knife, with steel blade marked "Bozum", a wooden split handle and riveted brass hardware. The piece is Montana Sioux, and ca. mid to late 1800's.

C—$390 each

Photo courtesy Sheridan P. Barnard, Franklin, Massachusetts.

Sioux steel-tipped arrow. G—$25

Apache arrow, 25 in. long. Wooden shaft with metal point, sinew wrapped, good condition. G—$57

Three **metal lance heads,** different sizes and types. Average length is 5½ in. Sold as group of three. G—$100

Trade-iron lance head, from Iowa. Piece is 9 in. long, and maximum thickness about 3/8 in. Head is triangular and in good condition. Iron is slightly pitted. C—$195

Copper trade token, from New Mexican trading post ruins. D—$3.00

TRADE-ERA CLAY PIPES, some plain and some with effigy faces. Condition is average-good for most pipes were mold-made from a high-quality clay called kaolin. Ca. 1800.

D—$10 for three

Lar Hothem photo.

Russell **Green River trade knife,** 9½ in. long. Has an antler handle and old leather sheath. 　　　　　　　　　　　　　　　　G—$100

Skinning knife in old case, blade trade-steel and possibly made from an old file. Plains Indian, but sheath plain and deteriorated. 　　　　　　　　　　　　　　　　D—$105

Drilled Germanic coin pendant, found in central Ohio. Site has produced gunflints and brass points that were Indian-made from salvaged metal. Reverse of coins read, "12 Einen Reichs Thaler, A. 1771". Hole made with hot needle or awl, as there is minute silver-melt on both sides of small hole. 　　　　　　　　　　C—$35

Hand-forged strike-a-light, good old excavated item. (Such pieces were the steel in flint and steel kits for fire-making.) 　　G—$52

TRADE-ERA CLAY PIPES. plain variety. and common over Eastern U. S. historic sites.
C—$5.00 each.
Private collection.

Historic Midwestern **gunflint,** ¾ in. long, native-chipped from Ohio flint, probably late 1700's. Found on Muskingum River site that has produced objects from that era. Uncommon.   G—$7

Steel **strike-a-light,** good condition.   D—$35

Trade iron hoe, 5¾ in. high and 5-7/8 in. wide, with circular hafting hole partially forming hoe top. Some corrosion along rounded sides, but cutting edge very good.   C—$75

Iron fish-spear head, from Columbia River region, perhaps used during annual salmon run. Head is 7 in. long and 4½ in. wide. Each tine has a single barb. Apparently a trade piece.   C—$100

George Washington peace medal, the facing bust that has considerable mention in the peace medal book. Silver plated and guaranteed genuine.   G—$650

Rectangular soapstone bullet mold, picked up near a South Dakota historic Indian site, with two cavities for round bullets. Probably early 1800's. Both halves are present; piece is 3½ in. long, 2-1/8 in. wide.   C—$95

GEORGE WASHINGTON PEACE MEDAL, 2½ in. in diameter. Item is made of pewter and dated
1789. This medal was not made by the U.S. government but by a fur trade company. This medal
was much-coveted by the Indians.   G—$850

Photo and item courtesy Fenn Galleries, Ltd., Santa Fe, New Mexico.

Spark-striker, "knuckle-duster" type made from an old steel file, and with ends upturned in an artistic fashion. Piece is 3¾ in. long, fine condition. C—$50

Suggested Reading

Kuck, Robert, *Tomahawks Illustrated*, Brookside Enterprises, New Knoxville, Ohio 45871

Peterson, Harold, *American Indian Tomahawks*, Museum of the American Indian, Heye Foundation, 1971

Prucha, Francis P., *Indian Peace Medals In American History*, University of Nebraska Press

The Museum of the Fur Trade Quarterly, Rte. 2/Box 18, Chadron, Nebraska 69337; Charles E. Hanson, Jr., Editor/Director.

Indian woman, and child in suspension-type wooden cradle. She is rocking the cradle with cord and foot. Note reed or fibre matting, basket, and woven tapestry in background. Picture taken at Neah Bay, Washington, ca. 1890.

Photographer, Samuel Gay Morse; courtesy Photography Collection, Suzzallo Library, University of Washington.

CHAPTER XI
BASKETS

(The writer wishes to thank Dick Weatherford, Columbus, Ohio, for the introduction to this chapter on basketry, and for the books in the Suggested Reading section of it. Used with permission.)

Like most of the great Aboriginal Art in existence today, the baskets of the Indians of North America were intended primarily for everyday use. The decorations applied and woven in, the curious shapes, whimsical lids, and hanging feathers and beads may look useless, but they all attest to the Indians' talent for making what is useful also pleasing to the eye and touch.

Baskets in collections today are, for the most part, only the very latest representations of the craft. Baskets, trays, woven mats and clothing, reed and stick toys and jewelry existed in prehistoric times all over the world, as surely as did the more durable arrowheads, spearpoints, pipes, pottery and other ceremonial rock and wood art.

But because textiles are more susceptible to disintegration with age and use, the vast majority of baskets, trays, mats and burial sacks by which we judge the art as practiced by the Indians of North America have been made in the past 200 years, and most of those since 1880.

Collectors of baskets may judge the commercial value of an item by different standards. For some, age alone determines value. That is, any basket in any condition over, say, 150 years old is automatically rare and expensive. Others are more interested in the aesthetic properties: shape, coloring and patina, the use made of the fiber — how tightly the basket is coiled or woven — how carefully the shape and size of the coils and other elements are matched, and how well the decorative fiber matches the structure fiber.

Still others collect only baskets whose condition is as near to new as possible. And, finially, there are those who collect for size only, or for decorative motifs, or for tribal area and type. All of these reasons for collecting baskets, but not all of them determine commercial or market value per se.

For example, age alone is not a sufficient reason for a basket being valuable, especially if the basket, although quite old, is crudely made or heavily damaged or aesthetically unpleasing. Size also does not determine value, since a very large basket may bring a smaller price than a very small, finely woven and decorated piece.

Value is itself a relative term, and monetary value is only one factor to be considered in making up a collection. Sentimental association is as real to the collector as cash value, but sentimental value more often than not cannot be expressed to others and usually cannot be marketed.

For the serious collector, then, who wishes to gather some baskets, regardless of their sentimental value or particular age, for the purposes of show, personal enjoyment, and, possibly, investment, there are some things to consider before buying.

The first rule of collecting anything is that the condition of each piece must be excellent. Baskets — like books, stained glass windows, arrowheads, beaded vests, Navajo rugs and other collectibles — must be in fine condition in order to bring and retain high prices. Baskets with broken edges, repairs, re-dying or painting over, missing parts, holes, etc., are simply not as valuable as perfect pieces, and they never will be, even if they are restored.

Having slightly damaged baskets in a collection does not necessarily diminish the value of the collection, but it doesn't help much either. Of course, some baskets are so rare as to put the lie to the absoluteness of the condition rule, but the exceptions are very few indeed.

Next to condition, the aesthetic qualities of a basket determine value. These qualities are difficult to explain in this short space, and they won't mean much to the collector who has not seen and studied a number of baskets. But aesthetic qualities include the fineness of the weaving and/or coiling, the regularity of the design and the degree to which it enhances the shape of the basket itself — as opposed to detracting from its shape by being too large or small or complex or simple to be comfortably accomodated on the piece.

One of the most pleasing qualities of North American Indian basketry is its sensory appeal. Good baskets feel and look and even smell natural; they are well-shaped and well-made. The genius of them is that they incorporate art in the utilitarian object, that they make what is useful also pleasing to touch and see. That quality is difficult to assess and describe. It is easier to see and appreciate sensorily, and that is one reason why many examples of baskets are pictured in this book.

Collectors who read this will note that I have not touched on such considerations as materials and tribal groups as determinants of market value. I agree that what a basket is made of and who made it have something to do with the value of it. But these values are more relative to the collector's own tastes, and they are first subject to the standards of condition and aesthetic quality mentioned above.

Certainly, a finely made Tlingit or Washoe basket brings more on the market than a small, plain, rather crude Pomo basket. But beginning collectors will not be able to make successful determinations of value without some more study. I suggest it is not wise to study, or even to buy, simply for tribal area or material.

One must see many types of baskets themselves, as well as pictures of them, in order to get a clear idea of their shapes, designs, and materials. Most larger state, city, and university museums have some baskets to see and compare. And the collector will want to frequent the auctions, antique shows and shops, Indian gallery showrooms and the like before making any selections.

I strongly suggest that the collector also read about baskets, how they are and were made, materials and methods of construction, designs, shapes, age, etc. The collector who relies purely upon rumor and the seller's word is very likely to be unhappy about some purchases.

It is always best to know, to be able to judge independently and with some authority the baskets one is likely to pay a good deal of money for. See Suggested Reading for a few selected major reference works for the collector. These will, in addition to this book, provide necessary information.

(D.W.)

The basket listings in this section have been set up in alphabetical form rather than the usual regional/chronological sequence. This has been done so that baskets by known Indian groups can be easily located.

While not all basket-making Indian groups are represented, these are some of the baskets likely to be encountered. Historic and recent baskets are included, plus many contemporary examples. A wide selection has purposefully been included here.

Apache shallow-bowl basket, with designs in stars and crosses. It is 14 in. in diameter, and condition is fair.   D—$950

Indian woman, in state of Washington, seated before rough-plank dwelling squatting on rough mat. Note small-mesh fishnet in background and fiber strands in hands, perhaps for basketry work. Ca. 1900-1905. Photographer, Norman Edson, courtesy Photography Collection, Suzzallo Library, University of Washington.

Apache shallow-bowl basket, 18 in. in diameter, and in excellent condition. Designs of dogs, men and horses; two major breaks on rim which do not detract from value.   C—$1100

Apache burden basket, 11½ in. high, typical construction with hard leather or rawhide bottom, plain, average condition and showing much wear. ca. 1920's.   D—$425

Apache burden basket, contemporary, and 6½ in. across and 5 in. high. Geometric pattern, with tin cones hanging from buckskin straps.   G—$75

Apache burden basket, contemporary, 8 in. across and 6 in. high. Geometric pattern; tin cones on buckskin straps.   G—$150

Apache burden basket, contemporary, 12 in. across and 10½ in. high. With negative pattern, excellent conditon, and tin cone danglers.   G—$385

BURDEN BASKET: White River Apache, Arizona. Used as a utility basket by Indian women, carried on the back and supported by a strap from the person's forehead. Excellent condition; 18 in. wide and 10 in. high; ca. 1940.
          G—$320

Photo courtesy W. J. Crawford, The Americana Galleries, Phoenix, Arizona.

Apache grain barrel basket, 11 in. high and 10 in. in diameter. Geometric designs with eight human figures. Rim of basket shows some wear and repair, but generally in nice condition. Ca. before 1900.   G—$475

Apache grain or seed container basket, 17 in. high. Has geometric designs in black, on tan background. Extra-fine overall condition. Ca. early 1900's.   C—$1295

Apache plaque basket, geometric design. Piece is 16 in. in diameter and 5 in. high. Nice stitch, good condition.   G—$875

Apache plaque basket, 22 in. in diameter and 6 in. high. Design: Twenty dog and men figures. One bad spot 3 in. from rim, and condition fair.   G—$1550

Apache miniature basket, 5½ in. across and 1 in. high. Good condition, with radiating-star design.   G—$225

Apache storage basket, with black chain-link and human figure decorative motif on side. Basket is 14½ in. in diameter.   C—$575

Apache basketry tray, 10½ in. in diameter, and very old. Ca. late-1880's or 90's.   C—$210

Apache wedding basket, 13 in. in diameter, and ca. 1880.   D—$55

Apache water-bottle basket, (or "tus"), with coating of pine to make it waterproof. Collected about 1935 and 17 in. in height. Good condition and not common.   C—$800

Apache water-bottle basket, with one of two horsehair handles remaining. Pitch missing in small sections. Piece is 13½ in. in height, and not well preserved. Old.   C—$175

Apache water-bottle basket, with pine-pitch covering. Contemporary. Has leather carrying straps; it is 5 in. across and 9 in. high.   G—$90

Mescalero Apache lidded basket, 7 in. wide and 5 in. high. Good condition, and ca. 1900.   G—$275

Western Apache basket, 12 in. across and 2 in. high, with a moderate stitch. Whirlwind design in bottom and geometric design on exterior.   G—$235

Athabascan birchbark basket, and Washo basket, both one auction lot. Athabascan is 2¾ in. by 4 in., Washo is 1½ in. by 3½ in.   A—$35

Bannock/Shoshone berry basket, 8 in. by 8½ in.   A—$75

Bannock basket, 8½ in. by 13 in.   A—$65

Bannock/Paiute gathering basket.   A—$35

Bella-Bella basket-covered jar.   A—$28

Bella-Coola cedar-bark basket, state of Washington, and 12¼ in. high. Decorated with enter-twined cedar root strips, and of some age.   C—$55

Chehalis basket, 4½ in. by 9½ in.   A—$27

Chehalis basket, 4¼ in. by 6¼ in. Has woven designs of geometrics and crosses; in mint condition.   A—$195

Chemehuevi basket, 11½ in. across and 2 in. high, with a design of two geometric concentric bands. Piece has a moderate stitch; good condition.   G—$475

two geometric concentric bands. Piece has a moderate stitch; good condition. G—$460

Chippewa birchbark basket, 4½ in. high and 9-5/8 in. in diameter. Designs done in sweetgrass and quill. A—$52

Coushatta swampcane basket, collected in Louisiana in the 1950's. Size, 4-3/8 in. in diameter. C—$55

CONTEMPORARY BASKETS. Left, Passamaquoddy lidded basket, 6¾ in. in diameter. Wood splint and sweetgrass. *D—$35*
Right. PENOBSCOT LIDDED BASKET, 3½ in. in diameter. *D—$25*
Photo courtesy American Indian World, Ltd., Denver, Colorado.

Coushatta basket tray, 6 in. in diameter, and with two unusual handles. Made of coiled pine needles, small floral designs, slight damage to bottom. D—$35

Cowlitz lidded basket, 3 in. by 4¼ in. A—$100

Cowlitz basket, 10¾ in. by 14¼ in. A—$325

Fraser River basketry trays, two sold as one lot. A—$25

Fraser River basket, 7¼ in. by 9 in. by 7 in. A—$115

Hat Creek basket-covered wine bottle, 10 in. high. It has lightning design in redbud weave. Good condition. G—$150

Hat Creek basket, 3½ in. by 6¼ in. A—$250

Havasupai basketry bowl, 7 in. across and 4 in. high. It has red analine dye swastika pattern, good condition.   G—$435

Havasupai basket, coiled fiber, 11¾ in. in diameter. Designs a series of small, connected triangles.   C—$215

Havasupai basketry plaque or plate, 12 in. in diameter. It has orange and black geometric "crepe paper" design.   G—$325

Hoopa basketry hat, 3¾ in. high by 7¼ in. across, of close-twined weave. Fine condition. (Hupa.)   C—$275

Hopi coiled-bowl basket, 9¼ in. in diamter, faded floral designs. Basket overall in good condition.   C—$155

Hopi coiled-bowl basked, 7 in. in diameter, with geometric designs on sides. Average good condition, bottom somewhat deteriorated.
                        D—$105

Hopi coiled-bowl basket, Second Mesa, 4 in. high and 4 in. in diameter.   A—$30

Hopi wicker-bowl basket, 9 in. in diameter, excellent condition. Geometric designs on side.   C—$175

Hopi corn-sifter basket, recent, with sturdy hoop around top. Wicker form is 15 in. in diameter, decorated with spiral designs radiating out from center.   C—$125

Hopi miniature plaque, Second Mesa, contemporary. Has Polychrome star design, and is 4 in. across.   G—$65

Hopi miniature bowl, 1½ in. across and 1½ in. high. Second Mesa contemporary, with geometric design.   G—$68

Hopi miniature coil plaque, 3¼ in. in diameter.   D—$18

Hopi miniature coil plaque, 2½ in. in diameter.   D—$15

Hopi coiled plaque, old. Second Mesa, ca. 1930. Piece is 14½ in. across.   D—$200

Hopi coiled tray, 14½ in. in diameter, Third Mesa.   A—$65

WISHHAM BASKET WORKER: Edward S. Curtis, photographer.
Photo courtesy of National Photography Collection, Neg. # C-30251, Public Archives of Canada.

Hopi basketry tray, 11 in. in diameter, Second Mesa. Has mythical figure as central design. C—$160

Hopi wickerwork tray, 17¼ in. in diameter; very regular designs in black. C—$210

Hupa cooking basket, 3-1/8 in. by 5¼ in. A—$69

Hupa covered basket, 8 in. in diameter, with geometric designs in tan and cream colors. Some damage to one portion of bottom, not major. D—$115

Hupa basketry hat, 6-5/8 in. in diameter. A—$125

Hupa basketry hat, 7 in. in diameter and 4 in. high. Made using half-stitch; piece has two geometric and concentric bands.
G—$195

Hupa basketry mush bowl, 3½ in. high and 6 in. in diameter. Tan and light brown colors, nice design, perfect condition. Ca. 1900.
G—$175

Karok basketry cradleboard, sit-down style. Piece is finely woven basketry, with sun shade in yellow quillwork. G—$295

Karok basketry mush bowl, reverse pattern. It is 5½ in. across and 3½ in. high. Good condition. G—$105

Karok oval-shape basket with inverted bottom. Half-twist polychrome design, measuring 10 in. long by 7 in. wide and 5 in. high. Good condition. G—$175

Klamath basket, 3½ in. by 6½ in. A—$25

Klamath trinket basket, 3 in. high, 4 in. in diameter. Simple design in brown colors, excellent condition. G—$90

Klamath gambling tray, 14 in. in diameter. Good condition, and ca. 1900. G—$375

Klikitat basket, 4 in. by 4½ in. A—$115

Klikitat gathering basket, with undulating and raised rim top. Basket is 11¼ in. high, medium-good condition. C—$175

Klikitat miniature basket. A—$35

Klikitat baskets, both miniature, sold as one lot. A—$70

Two small LIDDED BASKETS. On left, larger basket is 6 in. in diameter, of reed and sweetgrass, fine condition. This is a recent Eastern U. S. item. D—$25
Smaller basket, woven from thin reed splints, is about 4 in. in diameter, also recent. D—$17

Photo — Lar Hothem.

Klikitat basketry trunk with lid, 14½ in. across, 15 in. high and 26½ in. long. It has polychrome geometric design, in nice condition.

G—$795

Kuskokwim River basket, with yarn trim. Piece is 5½ in. by 6½ in.

A—$40

Lilooet basket, 12½ in. by 16 in. and 14 in. high.   A—$195

Lilooet basket, 8¼ in. by 10¼ in. and 12½ in. high.   A—$40

Maidu basketry bowl, 6 in. across and 3 in. high. In traditional Maidu pattern, average weave, good condition. Piece is ca. 1910.

G—$250

Maidu miniature basket, 1¼ in. high, 1¾ in. in diameter. Very tight and regular weave, perfect condition.   C—$150

Maidu basketry tray, 8½ in. in diameter.   A—$75

Makah lidded basket, 4 in. across and 2 in. high. Geometric banded design in polychrome.   G—$75

Makah basket, 7 in. in diameter, with zigzag designs on side. Slight fraying at one portion of rim. Tight weave.   D—$80

Makah basketry covered bottle, 12 in. high, good condition.

G—$165

Makah basketry covered bottle, 12½ in. high, weaving with figure design.   A—$100

Makah basketry covered bottle, one-half pint whiskey, and 6½ in. high.   G—$120

Makah/Nootka basketry-covered bottle, 12¼ in. high.   A—$120

Makah jewel basket.   A—$28

Makah/Nootka miniature baskets, two, sold as one lot.   A—$25

Makah basketed net float and small **basketry covered bottle,** sold as one lot.   A—$75

Makah twisted-twine basket, 5 in. in diameter. C—$45

Mandan basket, wood splint, rare item and quite old. Piece is circular and 8¼ in. high. C—$295

Mission basket, very large, 18½ in. in diameter and 10 in. high. Minor rim damage, and ca. 1900. G—$660

Mission basket, from California, 20 in. across and 12 in. high. Has a six-point negative star in bottom. G—$170

Mission basket, bowl-shape, 6 in. in diameter and 2 in. high. Geometric design with star pattern on bottom. Average weave and condition. G—$145

Mission plaque, made of varigated juncus grass, average weave. It is 15 in. across by 2½ in. high. G—$230

Mission basketry tray, made by the California Mission Indians, and 12 in. across and 2½ in. high. Mint condition. G—$530

Miwok basket, 12 in. high and 7 in. in diameter. Good condition, and ca. 1900. G—$425

Modoc hat, 6 in. by 11½ in. A—$140

Modoc hat, 7 in. in diameter. A—$100

Modoc basketry cap, diamond decorations, 6¼ in. in average diameter, and about 5 in. high. C—$200

Mohawk sweetgrass gift baskets, two, sold as one lot. A—$30

Navajo wedding basket, 15 in. in diameter, tight weave, ca. 1860. D—$57

Navajo wedding basket, 13¼ in. in diameter. A—$195

Nootka basket, tan with black and brown designs depicting early seafaring scenes. Lidded, piece is 9 in. high, 15 in. in diameter. Perfect condition. C—$1325

Nootka basket, old, 2-5/8 in. by 4-1/8 in. A—$75

Indian woman weaving a basket. Note completed basket, two partially finished, and supply of spare weaving materials. Picture taken in state of Washington, ca. 1897-1899.

Photographer, Anders B. Wilse; courtesy Photography Collection, Suzzallo Library, University of Washington.

Nootka whaler's hat, 10½ in. by 10½ in.   A—$325

Ojibwa wicker basket made of peeled willow, and collected in Minnesota. About 8 in. high. Not recent, but not of great age. C—$65

Splint collecting basket, Indian group unknown, New England area. Piece is 8 in. by 9 in. by 5 in. high. Wood well-woven, good condition.   C—$95

Maine Indian birch-bark container, possibly a blueberry collecting basket. Piece is 9¼ in. wide and 14 in. long, with average wear. Old, and not common.   C—$100

Penobscot white ash basket, ribbed and handled, 13 in. long and 7 in. wide. Recent.   C—$70

Passamaquoddy "curlicue" basket, made of ultra-thin strips of brown ash. Round and 5 in. high. This type of "what-not" basket often had a cover; if so, it is now missing.   C—$18

Passamaquoddy basket, Maine, splint-woven of brown ash. It stands 18¾ in. high, carved wood handles on opposite sides of top. Style is the familiar commercial fish-scale basket. Tightly woven, and contemporary.   C—$90

Paiute coiled-bowl basket, with beaded exterior. Piece is 4¾ in. in diameter. A few beads missing, but an exceptional work.
                                                                                                    C—$275

Paiute lidded basket, 5 in. high and 6½ in. across. Has polychrome geometric design.   G—$255

Paiute basketry covered bottle, 10 in. high. Good condition, and ca. 1900.   G—$150

Southern Paiute basketry hat.   A—$95

Paiute hat, 8½ in. across and 5½ in. high. It has two geometric concentric bands.   G—$220

Paiute seed jar, with in-and-out weave for design, a single concentric band. Piece is 8 in. high and 5½ in. in diameter.
                                                                                                    G—$105

Paiute basketry water jar, with pine pitch on outside. Has horse hair handles, and is 7½ in. high and 5½ in. across. Nice condition.
                                                                                                    G—$135

Panamint basket, 10½ in. across and 5 in. high. Design is two geometric concentric bands with rim ticking; there are 15 stitches to the inch, five coils to the inch.   G—$750

Panamint basket, 10½ in. across, 4 in. high. Has reversing diamond pattern, with unusual start on bottom. Fair condition, with some rim damage. G—$435

Papago basket, 13 in. in diameter, 4½ in. high. Faint geometric designs on sides. C—$140

 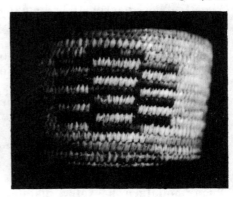

From left to right:

PITCH BASKET, White Mountain Apache, Arizona. The basket is woven by the Indian women, then pitch is applied to make the basket water-tight. It is 19 in. high and 17 in. wide, and ca. 1930. G—$910

Photo courtesy W. J. Crawford, The Americana Galleries, Phoenix, Arizona.

PAPAGO BASKET, Good typical form with brown design against golden yellow background. Piece is 3¾ in. high and 6 in. in diameter. D—$75

Photo courtesy Crazy Crow Trading Post, Denison, Texas.

Papago lidded basket, 5 in. in diameter and 3½ in. high. Of bleached yucca and devil's claw, it has large butterflies on side and coyote tracks on lid. G—$150

Papago miniature basket, 1 in. high, 1½ in. in diameter, brown with white simple designs. C—$75

Papago oval basketry tray, 12 in. wide, 15 in. long and 3½ in. deep. Loose weave typical of Papago, and with brown design. Good condition. G—$125

Papago plaque, old, and 15 in. in diameter, 3½ in. high. Design is concentric squares from center. G—$235

Papago waste paper basket, contemporary, 10 in. in diameter and 12 in. high. Design of dogs and men. G—$170

Pima basketry bowl, 16 in. in diameter and 5 in. high. Has salt and pepper design, and in fair condition. G—$400

Pima coiled-bowl basket, 6½ in. high, with geometric designs. In poor condition, has extensive damage. C—$40

Pima shallow-bowl basket, 17½ in. in diameter, with star design. Extra-good condition. D—$325

Pima fretwork basket, 16 in. in diameter. In nice condition and old, early 1900's or before. G—$315

Pima grain barrel, 12½ in. high and 11 in. in diameter. Has large open mouth and geometric design. Good condition. G—$665

Pima lidded horsehair miniature basket, 1 in. in diameter and 1 in. high. Has a geometric design element. G—$52

Pima coiled plaque, 11 in. in diameter, with "maze" design on bottom. Average good condition. C—$275

Pima miniature basketry plaque, 2-3/8 in. in diameter. Very uniformly woven, and geometric design. Good condition. C—$55

Pitt River basket, 8 in. across and 7½ in. high. Has geometric design interspaced with snow flakes. G—$315

Pitt River basket, 10 in. in diameter. In good condition, and ca. 1900. G—$165

Pomo basket, 6 in. in diameter. D—$125

Pomo basket, beaded, coil manufacture, and 9¼ in. in diameter. Two sizes of shell beads used to set off basic stepped-pyramid design. C—$275

Pomo beaded boat-shape basket, 4½ in. long, 3½ in. wide and 1½ in. high. Has green beaded background with red bead for geometric pattern. Fully beaded. G—$545

Pomo feathered basket, from California, about 12 in. in diameter. Decorated with blue, green and white feathers. Condition good. A—$235

Salish (Coastal) miniature baskets, two, sold as one lot. A—$25

Salish (Coastal) basket, 5 in. by 7½ in.   A—$20

Satsop basket, twined, 7½ in. by 12 in.   A—$185

Seminole coiled basket, with coils of sweetgrass. Basket is 4 in. high, 6½ in. in diameter, and plain. Has flat cover, undecorated. Collected in the 1950's.   C—$60

Shasta miniature basket.   A—$40

Shasta basket, 3¼ in. by 5½ in.   A—$90

Shasta basket, 3 in. high and 6½ in. in diameter. Geometric designs, exceptionally good condition.   C—$125

Shoshone burden basket, 10 in. by 12½ in.   A—$100

Shoshone basket, 5 in. high, 5½ in. in diameter, plain utility container, good condition.   C—$68

Siletz burden basket, 9 in. by 18 in.   A — $55

Skokomish berry basket, 6¾ in. by 8½ in.   A—$145

Skokomish basket, 5 in. by 7 in.   A—$45

Thompson River lidded basket, British Columbia, Canada, 4 in. by 4 in.   A—$115

Thompson River basketry trunk, with lid. Piece has imbricated diamond and cross designs. Dimensions are 15 in. across and 27 in. long and 15 in. high. Fair condition.   G—$1025

THOMPSON RIVER BASKET. 9 in. high and 12½ in. in top diameter. Bottom is oblong and shape moves to round at top. Basket has tan and black imbricated designs against dark tan background, with some white in outline. Very good condition. C—$175-$200
Photo courtesy R. M. Weatherford, Columbus, Ohio.

Tlingit basket, 6 in. in diameter and 4½ in. high. Geometric design, medium stitch, excellent condition. G—$530

Tlingit basket with butterfly designs, 4 in. by 6¾ in. A—$100

Tlingit basketry tray, 5¾ in. in diameter and 1¾ in. high. A—$57

Tlingit basket, 5 in. in diameter and 6 in. high. Good condition and ca. 1880. G—$525

Tlingit lidded basket 4½ in. by 6½ in. A—$535

Tlingit basket, 5½ in. high and 6 in. across. Design of two concentric geometric bands; slight damage to piece. G—$340

Tlingit basket, measuring 2½ in. by 3-1/8 in. A—$35

Tsimshian lidded basket, 4¾ in. by 7 in. A—$45

Tulare basket, California, small base and flaring top, 9 in. high and 16½ in. in top diameter. Lightning decorations on exterior sides. Fair condition. C—$960

Tulare basket, very large, 21 in. in diameter and 11 in. high. Pattern is two bands of polychrome rattlesnake designs. Condition excellent. G—$2200

Tulare basket, 7½ in. in diameter and 3½ in. high. Piece has serrated step pattern, polychrome, and squaw stitch. Condition good. G—$215

Tulare basket with rattlesnake designs. A—$145

Washo basket, oval shape, 2¾ in. by 6¼ in. and 4-7/8 in. high. A—$175

Washo basket, 7¼ in. in diameter, with banded exterior design. Has close weave, and is in good condition. C—$160

Washo basket, 7 in. in diameter and 4 in. high, with geometric design. G—$125

Washo basket, 10½ in. in diameter and 5½ in. high. Single-rod construction; design is a serrated concentric band.   G—$190

Yavapai olla, a fine example of the storage basket.   A—$180

Yokuts burden basket.   A—$125

Yurok basketry mortar skirt or grain-catching hopper.   A—$160

Yurok miniature tobacco basket, 2½ in. by 2¾ in.   A—$60

YUROK BASKET, 9½ in. in diameter and 7 in. high. Design is diamonds and rectangles. Piece is in good condition and probably early 1900's.
C—$185
Photo courtesy R. M. Weatherford, Columbus, Ohio.

WOOD-SPLINT BASKET, recent, about 12 in. high and 15 in. in diameter. This could either be a Great Lakes area piece, but is more likely Cherokee-made ca. 1950. Note characteric way each handle end is worked back through the wood, which is typical of Cherokee work. Collected in Ohio; bottom is square and top opening is round. Perfect condition. C—$100-$125
Private collection.

CANADIAN INDIAN BASKETS

It should be noted that some of the baskets already listed are also Canadian in origin. The names sometimes represent a basket making region rather than a specific Indian group. Among such baskets are Frazer RIver and Thompson River in British Columbia in Western Canada.

Plaited wood-strip basket, 14 in. in diameter and 8½ in. high. From Vancouver Island; work is good and serviceable. Probably a gathering basket for roots or shore seafoods. No decoration, fair condition.   C—$78

Ash-splint basket, alternating dark and light brown colors, 16½ in. high, 11½ in. wide at rounded shoulders. Collected in Southeastern Canada. Basket design is from square at the bottom to round opening at top, with nice merge. Ca. 1900.   C—$100

Small nondescript basket, wood splint, from Central Canada, and 3-7/8 in. in diameter. Original colors of separate plaint were red and black, now faded. No cover. Good condition.   C—$27

Historic-period basket, from Canada just above the Montana border. Piece is 7½ in. in diameter, and from an old collection. Material is a kind of reed, species unidentified. No decorative work. Basket is in good condition.   C—$140

MISCELLANEOUS BASKETS

Northwest Coast basketry hat, 13½ in. in lower diameter, flat crown, and 9 in. high. For rain protection, this basketry hat has a very tight weave. Unusual.   C—$525

Miniature sweetgrass basket, Eastern Woodlands, 3 in. in diameter, with cover.   D—$20

Miniature sweetgrass basket, Eastern Woodlands, 2 in. in diameter, with cover.   D—$18

Northern California basketry mortar skirt, 9½ in. high. It is 14 in. across the open top, and 4 in. across open bottom. Whole is shaped like a funnel, and the shield kept the pounded meal from flying from the mortar and being lost or mixed with grit. Historic; with diamond and lightning design.
                                                                    C—$675

Basketry head ring, used between top of head and carrying pot for steady transport of water vessel, etc. About 4½ in. in diameter, open center, about 1 in. thick. From Southwestern U.S., and old.
                                                                    C—$75

Southwestern prehistoric basket, 8½ in. in diameter, 4¾ in. high, gray-brown color. Basket has a medium-tight weave, no remaining decoration. Found during excavation of a dry cave in New Mexico. Reed used, but is now very brittle.   C—$300

Cone-shaped California burden basket, 17 in. high; would have been used with the forehead strap or tumpline. Tribe unknown. A plain piece, showing average and acceptable wear.   C—$1200

Southwestern Oregon basketry cooking pot, circular, with extremely tight weave. Stepped pyramid designs, reinforced rim. Used with water, meat and roots; hot rocks were dropped in to boil the water and cook the food. Item is 11 in. high, 13½ in. diameter. Historic; damage to bottom.   C—$300

Suggested Reading

James, George W., *Indian Basketry*; San Francisco, 1902 (reprinted)

Mason, Otis T., *Aboriginal American Basketry: Studies In A Textile Art Without Machinery*; published in the Annual Report of the U.S. National Museum for 1902, and by Doubleday, Page, New York 1904 (3 Volumes)

Miles, Charles, and Bovis, Pierre; *American Indian and Eskimo Basketry: A Key To Identification*, San Francisco, 1969 (reprinted)

MAKAH LIDDED BASKET, Northwest Coast, 4-5/8 in. high, ca. 1940.   C—$200
John Barry photo.

MAKAH LIDDED BASKET, fair condition, 2¼ in. high, ca. 1940.   C—$75
John Barry photo.

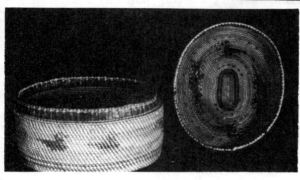

MAKAH LIDDED BAS-KET, Northwest Coast, 2½ in. high, fair condittion, ca. 1930.   C—$125
John Barry photo.

MAKAH LIDDED BAS-KET, Northwest Coast, ca. 1940.   C—$150
John Barry photo.

MAIDU BASKET, 7 in.
width, 6 coils per inch,
13 stitches per inch,
Northern California.
Coiled, dark material
redbud, ca. 1890.
C—$1000

Courtesy LaPerriere
Collection, California.

MAIDU BASKET, coiled bowl, 4 in. high, ca.
1910. C—$900
Bob LaPerriere photo.

MAIDU BASKETS, both 3½ in. diameters,
Northern California. Miniatures, coiled, dark
material redbud, early 1900's. Top specimen
with stain.

Top, C—$200
Bottom, C—$300

Courtesy LaPerriere Collection, California.

MAIDU BASKETRY PLATE, 14 in. diameter,
from Northern California. Coiled, ca. 1900.
C—$2500
Courtesy LaPerriere Collection, California.

Left: HOOPA BASKET, Northern California, 10 in. diameter, ca. 1910. C—$700

John Barry photo.

HUPA-YUROK BASKETRY HAT, from Northern California, 7½ in. top diameter. Twined, early 1900's.   C — $170-$200
Courtesy LaPerriere Collection, California.

HOOPA-YUROK BASKET, 7½ in. high, ca. 1910.   C — $300
Bob LaPerriere photo.

HOOPA BASKETRY HAT, 4 in. high, ca. 1910.
C—$500
Bob LaPerriere photo.

HOOPA BASKET, 4 in. high, ca. 1910.
C—$400
Bob LaPerriere photo.

226

Left: APACHE BASKET, 21 in. high, ca. 1910.
C—$5500
Photo courtesy John Barry.

Right: HAVASUPAI PLAQUE, Arizona, 11¼ in. diameter. Materials willow and devil's claw, 15 coils per inch, 13 stitches per inch. Coiled, representation of two women, men and dogs. By Karen Martinez, 1974.
C—$500

Courtesy LaPerriere Collection, California.

Left: WESTERN APACHE BASKET, 10 in. diameter, from Arizona, ca. 1930. Coiled, 5 coils per inch, 14 stitches per inch. C—$500
$175

Courtesy LaPerriere Collection, California.

Right: APACHE BASKET, 10 in. diameter, ca. 1910. C—$550

John Barry photo.

Far Left: LUMMI BASKETRY BOTTLE, from Bellingham, Washington, fine condition, ca. 1930. *C—$400*

John Barry photo.

Left: LUMMI BASKETRY BOTTLE, from Bellingham, Washington. Item 11½ in. high, ca. 1930. *C—$350*

Bob LaPerriere photo.

Below: WASHO SINGLE-ROD COIL BASKET, Northern California, 6 in. top diameter. Coiled, 6 coils per inch, 10 stitches per inch, uncertain age. *C—$300*

Courtesy LaPerriere Collection, California.

Left: LIDDED BASKET, Yurok-Hupa-Karok group, Northern California, 6¾ inch top diameter. Twined, ca. 1910. *C—$750*

Courtesy LaPerriere Collection, California.

Right: WASHO BASKET, 6 in. wide diameter, 4 in. high, Northern California. Coiled, plain black fern design (Mt. Brake), 7 coils per inch, 15 stitches per inch, ca. 1890. *C—$800*

Courtesy LaPerriere Collection, California.

228

KLAMATH BASKET, Southern Oregon, 6 in. top diameter. Twined, soft and flexible, early 1900's.   C—$300
Courtesy LaPerriere Collection, California.

KLAMATH BASKET, Northern California, 4 in. high, ca. 1910. C—$375
Bob LaPerriere photo.

KLAMATH BASKET, Southern Oregon, 5 in. top diameter. Twined, with yellow porcupine-quill decorations, early 1900's.   C—$200
Courtesy LaPerriere Collection, California.

MODOC BOWL BASKET, 8¼ in. diameter, Northern California, ca. 1910.   C—$400
Bob LaPerriere photo.

MODOC BASKET, Northern California, 8½ x 10 in. top measurements, unusual shape. Ca. 1890, twined, with dark of swamp tule and light of white or bear grass.   C—$500
Courtesy LaPerriere Collection, California.

Left: PAPAGO BASKET,
10 in. diameter at top,
Southern Arizona. Coiled,
6 stitches per inch, con-
temporary.   C—$200
Courtesy LaPerriere Col-
lection, California.

Right: PAPAGO BASKET, 6¾ in. top
diameter, Southern Arizona. Coiled, 8
stitches per inch, zoomorphic designs,
1930's or earlier.   C—$200
Courtesy LaPerriere Collection,
California.

Left: PAPAGO BASKET, 6½ in. top diameter, 4 coils per inch, 8 stitches per inch.
Coiled, Southern Arizona, mid-1900's.
                          C—$150
Courtesy LaPerriere Collection, California.

Right: TLINGIT BAS-
KETED BOTTLE,
(prob. Tlingit),
Southern Alaska, 3
inch bottle height plug
2½ in. wooden totem.
Twined, inkwell, carv-
ed stopper with paint.
Ca. 1910.
        C—$800
Left: TLINGIT
BASKET, 6 in. high,
Southern Alaska.
Twined, early 1900.
This specimen with
tear damage.
Torn condition
        C—$300
if perfect condition
        C—$400

Left: HOPI BASKETRY PLAQUE, 11 in. diameter, Northeastern Arizona. Coiled, pre-1940; From Second Mesa, this is the old type, thick, with more subtle colors.   C—$300

Courtesy LaPerriere Collection, California.

Right: YUROK BASKET, by Geneva M. Maltz, Northern California, 2 in. high, ca. 1974.
C—$150

John Barry photo.

Right: EASTERN MONO COOKING BASKET, Northern California, 14 in. top diameter. Coiled, 12 stitches per inch, 7 coils per inch. Black zig-zag design, ca. 1900.   C—$2000
Courtesy LaPerriere Collection, California.

Far Left: PIT RIVER BURDEN BASKET, small size, 7 in. high. Twined, Shasta area of Northern California, uncertain age.   C—$350
Courtesy LaPerriere Collection, California.

Left: BASKET, prob. Shastan Group, Northern California, 17 in. in height and top diameter. Large burden basket, some-what crude, some rim repairs, possibly early 1900's.
C—$2500
Courtesy LaPerriere Collection, California.

231

Left: HAT CREEK BASKET, *Shasta area of Northern California, 6½ in. wide. Twined, about early 1900's.* C—$350
Courtesy LaPerriere Collection, California.

Above: SALISH BASKET, *British Columbia or Washington state, 8 inch top diameter. Imbricated design, coiled, 4 coils per inch. Ca. 1910.* C—$250

Left: NOOTKA-MAKAH BASKETRY BOTTLE, *from Vancouver, Washington state. Twined, 11½ in. high, early 1900's.*
C—$500

Below: NAVAJO WEDDING BASKET, *usually not made by Navajos. Northeastern Arizona, 9 in. diameter. Coiled, and contemporary.* C—$150
Courtesy LaPerriere Collection, California.

Left: KILIKAT BASKET, age uncertain, from British Columbia or Washington state. Top diameter 5¼ in., 3 in. high. Coiled, 6 stitches per inch.   C—$150

Courtesy LaPerriere Collection, California.

Right: POMO BASKET, age uncertain, Northern California, 2 in. top diameter. Coiled, 10 coils per inch, 23 stitches per inch. With war-canoe design.   C—$500

Courtesy LaPerriere Collection, California.

Left: SHOSHONE BASKET, Southeastern California. From East of Sierras, prob. Inyo County. Coiled, lightening design, 14 stitches per inch. Stabilized, pre-1900.
      C—$1800
Courtesy LaPerriere Collection, California.

Right: ESKIMO BASKET, 13 in. high, Alaska, ca. 1960.
      C—$400

John Barry photo.

Below: TULARE (YOKUT) BASKET, 4¼ in. top diameter, Northern California. Coiled, in snake pattern, 13 stitches per inch.   C—$300

Courtesy LaPerriere Collection, California.

233

A young Ute warrior and his dog, with bow and iron-tipped arrows. Note the attractive necklace and full-length leggings. Picture taken in the Uintah Valley, on the eastern slope of the Wasatch Mountain, in Utah. Photo by John K. Hillers, 1873-1874.

Photo courtesy Utah State Historical Society, Collection of Smithsonian Institution.

CHAPTER XII
BEADWORK AND
QUILLWORK

American Indians are widely recognized to have done the world's finest decorative work with beads and quills. Quills were used in the Eastern Woodland regions and the Rocky Mountains and parts of Canada. The Plains Indians and many other groups favored beads. Quills and beads were sometimes used on the same item.

Porcupine quills were processed and dyed before use; the beads were ready-made trade goods. While generalizations regarding Amerind objects are somewhat difficult, there are basic design differences. In the Eastern Third of the country, bead or quillwork designs were often floral patterns, rounded designs. Western areas had more geometric patterns, angular designs.

The Indian appreciation for things of beauty meant that even everyday objects were sometimes decorated. Ceremonial items, like the fine pipe bags, were often heavily beaded in pleasing color combinations. In this chapter are some collecting areas in which bead or quillwork are especially important.

Value factors include the item decorated, with a complete work (example, bandolier bag) more admired than a part of an original piece (example, pipe bag panel). The complexity of the design counts considerably, involving both the design and the quantity of beads. A typical beadwork design employs many thousand small beads.

Fully beaded items, such as fetishes, are generally higher priced than a partially beaded object of the same size and type. The percentage of beads missing or quills lost or damaged is of great importance in arriving at a value.

The condition of the leather or trade cloth to which beads or quills are secured is to be regarded; a supple, quality leather is much better than poorly tanned and cracked leather. Indian-tanned leather is generally desired over commercial leather.

PIPE BAGS—FULLY OR PARTIALLY BEADED

Sioux pipe bag, old and of fine quality, large size and good condition. G—$545

Cheyenne pipe bag, 22½ in. long with very nice beaded exterior over soft leather. Fringed and beaded tassles add another 7 in. to length. Good condition. D—$725

Sioux pipe bag, 7 in. wide and 35 in. long, including fringe. Quillwork is fifty percent missing but beadwork is excellent and in geometric design with various colors of beads on white background. G—$800

Cheyenne pipe bag, partially beaded, fully fringed. A—$295

Cree pipe bag, done on fine Indian-tanned leather. No quillwork, usual for this type; beaded panel at bottom is 6 in. by 6 in. One side shows floral design and other side shows tea cup and flowers beaded on white background. Old, and in nearly perfect condition.
G—$545

Sioux (?) pipe bag, quillwork and beadwork missing a considerable percentage of units. D—$375

Sioux pipe bag, 12 in. long with fringe extra. The beaded panel at bottom is 4 in. by 7 in. and in excellent condition. Probably pre-1890. G—$275

Sioux pipe bags, private collection, per each: C—$550-650

Sioux pipe bag with full drop that is nicely quilled. D—$775

Cheyenne pipe bag, well beaded and quilled, good condition.
D—$550

Sioux pipe bag, rebuilt. Old beadwork panels with new buckskin top, quillwork and fringe. Good designs and colors. G—$445

Sioux pipe bag, beaded, and with unusual parfleche bottom.
A—$395

QUILLED BREASTPLATE with American flag motif, 21 in. long. Piece is ca. 1885.   *G—$885*
Photo and item courtesy Fenn Galleries, Ltd., Santa Fe, New Mexico.

Plains Indian pipe bag, fringed and quilled, good condition.
D—$575

Cheyenne pipe bag, old and of very large size for a Cheyenne. Typical designs with fringed, quilled, drop. Piece has slight damage. G—$700

Cree pipe bag. No quillwork as is common on this style bag, but beaded panel on both sides and in stylized flowers. Vari-colored beads on white background. Piece is 7 in. wide and 28 in. long including fringe. Almost perfect condition. G—$650

ARAPHOE PIPE BAG, standard size, with fringed bottom. Lower sections very well beaded in red, white, black and buff colors. Excellent condition, and ca. 1890. D—$775
Photo courtesy Crazy Crow Trading Post, Denison, Texas.

Sioux BEADED PIPE BAG, 36 in. long, good design, well beaded, and ca. 1870-80. D—$795
Photo courtesy Winona Trading Post, Santa Fe—Pierre & Sylvia Bovis.

QUILLWORK

(Additional quillwork listings are in the **Clothing** chapter)

Plains Indian hair roach, nicely quilled, with horsehair.   D—$195

Quilled coat, hide with floral quilled designs on front and back. Beautiful early piece with about twenty percent of quillwork gone but in excellent condition. Colors are bright.   G—$1195

Cheyenne armbands, beaded and quilled.   A—$85

Sioux quilled armbands, trimmed with ermine fur. Quilled danglers, and pair 12 in. in circumference. Good condition, and ca. 1900.   G—$125

Hair ties, pair, nicely quilled.   D—$75

Hair ties, quilled pair, with brightly colored fluffs and tin cone danglers.   G—$42

Sioux quilled cuffs with American flag designs, good quality and condition. Pre-1900 items.   G—$375

Dance wand, Plains Indian with wooden handle and quilled head, 14 in. long. Recent.   C—$35

QUILLED BIRCH BARK BOX, 5 in. on a side and 2¼ in. high. Flower designs done in dyed and natural quills (dyed, red and green); dried grass edging, with sides done in natural quills. Collected at Wisconsin Dells, Wisconsin. This is a Chippewa box, from the early 1900's.

C—$295

Photo courtesy Bill Post Collection.

PAPAGO COIL BASKET, 5¼ in. high and 8¼ in. in diameter at top. Has chocolate brown zigzag design on light tan background, with dark center on bottom just over 1 in. in diameter. Very good condition.   C—$100-$145

Photo courtesy R. M. Weatherford, Columbus, Ohio.

QUILLED HORSE MANE HAIR PIECE, 14 in. long. The quills and hair are dyed red; tin cone jangles hang on the quilled leather. Ca. 1870.   G—$750

Photo and item courtesy Fenn Galleries, Ltd., Santa Fe, New Mexico.

Quilled cradle, Arapahoe. Top fully quilled in natural and purple quills. Quilled strips down side to cloth base; replaced boards but was done correctly. A beautiful example, and ca. 1870.   G—$2500

Hair drop, very old, with trade beads and quillwork.   D—$145

Quilled pouch, 7 in. circular size. Front fully quilled, with quills dyed red, green and orange. Collected in 1930's from Big Sorrell Horse, a Blackfoot Indian in Montana. Piece is excellent, early and rare.   G—$725

Quilled basket, Eastern Woodlands, 3-1/8 in. in diameter, with fitted, original cover. Interior is birchbark, the whole covered with dyed porcupine quills, brown background. Probably early 1900's. Good condition.   C—$100

BEADED AWL CASES

Awl case, fine fully beaded example. Cheyenne, with white, green and blue beadwork. Old horsehair dangles with tin cones. Piece is 8 in. long and ca. 1900.   G—$205

Awl case, Sioux, fully beaded, with beaded drops; extra-fine condition, and old.   D—$125

Awl case, Apache, beaded in geometric designs with tiny seed beads. Larger beads and tin-cone dangles; 14 in. long and in good condition.   D—$235

Awl case, 12 in. long, with circular design done in blue, yellow and red beads. Sound condition and pre-1900 item.   G—$110

Awl case, nicely beaded Plains Indian piece.   A—$65

Awl case, with bone awl. Wooden top, and fully beaded; 9 in. long plus fringe.   G—$150

This 1891 photo by Grabill was captioned simply "Tent and child". Note top area of tipi darkened by smoke from cooking and heating fires, and blanket closure for tipi entrance. To left a child's play tipi has been constructed from sticks and an old woven blanket.

Photo courtesy South Dakota State Historical Society.

BEADED CARRIERS—VARIOUS TYPES

Beaded bag, probably Nez Perce, 9 in. wide and 12½ in. long; all frontal beading intact. Simple star-like designs, two small and one large. Leather is dry but could be treated.   C—$295

Beaded bag, 8 in. by 9 in. and a beautiful item. Bag has a blue backgroud with roses and leaves design, with many early cut-glass beads. Excellent condition.   G—$120

Beaded pouch, Sioux, and similar to a strike-a-light bag.   G—$85

Beaded bag, Plains Indian, 6 in. by 8¼ in. Well-beaded on one side; good condition.   D—$275

Beaded bag, Woodland Indian style and 6 in. by 6 in. Beadwork is done on black velvet as was usual; floral design with all beadwork intact. Top rim of bag shows some wear.   G—$105

Bandolier bag, Chippewa, a large bag with typical floral designs on velvet. Good condition.   G—$885

Paint bag, a rare Sioux item. It is 12½ in. long, nearly full-beaded and with beaded fringes. A pouch-type container, it still has interior traces of ochre or powdered hematite. Beads are red, yellow and green.   C—$650

BEADED DOCTOR'S BAG, 13 in. long. Item is from the Northern Plains and ca. 1890.
G—$650

Photo and item courtesy Fenn Galleries, Ltd., Santa Fe, New Mexico.

Bandolier bag, Menominee, 38 in. long and 11 in. wide. Fully beaded and in very good condition. Ca. 1880.   G—$885

Horseshoe-shaped pouch, classic Sioux, fully beaded and fringed. Piece is ca. 1885.   C—$650

Leather bag, Woodlands Indian and beaded front in typical floral pattern. Possibly Ottawa in origin, it is 6¼ in. high. The pouch is fully fringed on all sides except top, which is closed by a beaded flap.   C—$385

Wall bag, Sioux (?), fully beaded and with tin cone jangles. Nice condition, and piece is 12 in. long, ca. 1910.   G—$145

Belt pouch, with beaded eagle design.   A—$75

Pitt River bag, triangular design. It has the highest quality loomed bead work and of the type done only by Indians on the Pitt River, Oregon. Specimen has an amber background with blue and white geometric designs, with beaded handle. Piece is 10 in. by 10 in. and ca. 1930.   G—$175

Beaded bag, blue background with Nez Perce woman beaded as design. Well-done piece, 11 in. by 12 in., and scarce pictorial bag. Excellent condition.   G—$240

Beaded tobacco bag, average condition.   D—$250

Beaded bag, Woodland floral patterns, 6½ in. long. Beaded front and back on black trade-cloth velvet. Good condition, and collected in the Great Lakes area.   C—$245

Beaded bag, Iroquois, beaded both sides on velveteen with red cloth binding. Piece is 6½ in. by 7½ in. and a good specimen. Ca. 1920.   G—$160

Strike-a-light bag, Sioux, for flint and steel. Beaded one side, with carrying strap; piece is 3½ in. by 6¼ in. in good condition.   C—$235

Beaded bag, Apache, buckskin with typical bead fringe and geometric designs.   G—$145

Plateau bag, fully beaded using glass beads. Floral design; bag is 11 in. high and 9 in. wide.　　　　　　　　　　　　G—$185

Carry-all bag, Woodlands Indian, rounded bottom and lower edge of closing flap. Piece is 11 in. high and 11½ in. wide. Beadwork design on black velvet. Had carrying strap, now missing. Very good condition, very few beads gone.　　　　　　　　　　　C—$315

Beaded bag, Caddo, fully beaded including flap and handle. Buckskin with cloth lining, and 5½ in. by 6 in. Piece has an unusual looped bead fringe. Ca. 1890.　　　　　　　　　　　G—$175

Beaded belt pouch, Plateau area.　　　　　　　　　　A—$65

Strike-a-light bag, beaded in Plains Indian style.　　　D—$145

Beaded bag, 9 in. by 10 in., zipper top with handles. Beads used to make bag are 40 to 50 years old. Gray background with stylized floral designs; excellent condition.　　　　　　　　　　G—$170

Medicine bag, Plains Indian, worn around the neck. Rare item, and ca. 1880.　　　　　　　　　　　　　　　　　　　D—$100

Tobacco bag, bead designs of standing Indian, and American flag. Slight damage.　　　　　　　　　　　　　　　　　G—$235

Beaded container, Apache, 8 in. wide and 5 in. high, black on buff designs.　　　　　　　　　　　　　　　　　　　C—$185

BEADED BOTTLES

Beaded bottle, done by the Paiute Indians after they ceased doing basket bottled. Extra-large specimen, and 28 in. tall. White background with variety of geometric designs. Perfect condition.
　　　　　　　　　　　　　　　　　　　　　　　G—$535

Beaded bottle, very small 2¼ in. high and ¾ in. wide. With top, specimen is done on yellow beaded background with black and green geometric designs. Perfect.　　　　　　　　　G—$60

Beaded bottle, 18 in. high. It has a zigzag pattern done in red, white, blue and black beads, very attractive.　　　　　G—$325

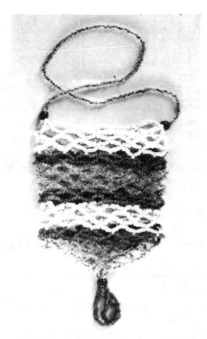

BEADED PURSE, 5 in. long, not counting strap. Tourist item, Southwestern states and possibly Apache work. Ca. 1950. *C—$45*

Private collection.

Winnebago BEADED BANDOLIER BAG, 36 in. long and 18 in. wide, beaded floral motifs. Note the superb condition of this excellent example of Indian art, ca. 1880. *D—$995*

Photo courtesy Winona Trading Post, Santa Fe—Pierre & Sylvia Bovis.

Small Delaware BEADED PURSE, 6 in. in diameter, with nicely balanced floral design on front. About 100 years old, it is ca. 1870-80. *D—$225*

Photo courtesy Winona Trading Post, Santa Fe—Pierre & Sylvia Bovis.

Beaded bottle, 5 in. high. Beaded over small perfume bottle. Fully beaded including bottom with early crystal beads with red and blue geometric designs. G—$95

Plains Indian fetish, 6½ in. long, lizard form, but more nearly resembles a horned toad. Beaded design on top, beaded strip around edges, limbs and tail. C—$385

Beaded turtle umbilical fetish, for twins; two turtles are fastened together. Sioux Indian and extremely rare. G—$665

Lizard fetish, 6 in. long and 2 in. wide. A Sioux piece, it has blue beads on greasy-yellow background and two horsehair dangles on each end. One seam coming apart but easily repared. Excellent condition and ca. 1890. G—$285

Turtle fetish, 4 in. by 2½ in. Multi-colored beadwork on commercial leather, done on reservation in the 1920's. A few beads missing but in excellent condition. G—$80

Turtle umbilical fetish, a Sioux beaded piece, old and in good condition. G—$255

MISCELLANEOUS BEADED AND QUILLED PIECES

Chippewa beaded panel, floral designs done on velvet and possibly originally a pillow cover. Old and fine condition. G—$175

Crow beaded panel, red trade cloth and 12 in. by 12 in. Floral motif; considerable moth damage and some beads missing. G—$55

Beaded necklace, probably Ottawa. Piece is 18 in. long, ¾ in. wide at sides and back, 2 in. wide at lower portion. Small beads in red, green and yellow, the whole very well done and unusual. C—$250

Beaded cigarette case, Chippewa, and contemporary. D—$15

Sioux cuffs, fully beaded, and 5 in. by 10 in. Piece has light blue background with red, blue and yellow geometric designs. Excellent condition, and 4 in. fringes on edges. Ca. 1930's. G—$125 the pair

Beaded blanket strip, Northern Cheyenne, and flag designs.

A—$650

Crow belt, standard Crow stitch and colors in lavender, blue, yellow and red. Belt is 39 in. long and 2¾ in. wide. It is on harness leather and has brass tacks. Some beadwork is loose and some missing but in generally good condition. Pre-1890.   G—$175

Athabascan beaded hair ties.   A—$12

Beaded watch fob, Plains Indian and ca. 1920.   D—$22

Beaded belt, fully beaded and Sioux. Piece is 28 in. long and 2 in. wide, fine condition.   G—$255

Beaded sash, Woodland loom-beaded specimen.   D—$95

Contour beadwork, four fine and old pieces, sold as one lot.

A—$70

Choker, made by blackfoot Indians sometime prior to 1930 when it was collected. Choker fully beaded and 14 in. long and ¾ in. wide. An original scalp may be hanging from this choker, making it a very rare piece.   G—$225

Arm bands, full beadwork over rawhide on these Sioux items.

D—$100

Beaded cuffs, pair, Yakima.   A—$65

Beaded strip, Cheyenne, and 25 in. long and 1¾ in. wide. Sinew-sewn beadwork in excellent condition. Ca. 1900.   G—$175

Beaded head band, Sioux, 20 in. long with beads sewn on buckskin. Ends have ties.   G—$40

Beaded bag front, rest of bag gone. Beadwork is excellent and complete. Piece is 5 in. by 5½ in. and done in old cut-glass beads, depicting bird motif. A good basis for a new pipe bag.   G—$35

Beaded dress yoke, Apache.   A—$28

Beaded arm bands, pair, Ponca, fully beaded on trade cloth and ca. 1890.   D—$125

APACHE BEADED BAG, 7½ in. long. Piece has tin cone jangles, and is ca. 1880.
G—$450
Photo and item courtesy Fenn Galleries, Ltd., Santa Fe, New Mexico.

Bugle bead vest, very old.   A—$425

Baby bonnet, Sioux, fully beaded and nice condition.   G—$395

Beaded belt, 33 in. long and 2¾ in. wide. Fully beaded with overlaid stitch — not loomed. White background, geometric designs in red, yellow, blue and green beads, backed with cloth. Not too old but in excellent condition.   G—$175

Loom-beaded belt, Northern Plateau area.   A—$40

Beaded strip or belt, 46 in. long and 3 in. wide. Sinew sewn on buckskin in yellow, blue and red.   G—$235

Sioux KNIFE AND SHEATH, 11 in. tall, fully beaded on side, and ca. 1880.   *D—$295*
Photo courtesy Winona Trading Post, Santa Fe—Pierre & Sylvia Bovis.

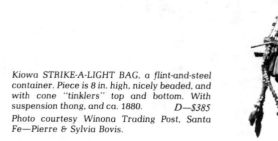

Kiowa STRIKE-A-LIGHT BAG, a flint-and-steel container. Piece is 8 in. high, nicely beaded, and with cone "tinklers" top and bottom. With suspension thong, and ca. 1880.   *D—$385*
Photo courtesy Winona Trading Post, Santa Fe—Pierre & Sylvia Bovis.

Wrist cuffs, beaded pair, Plains Indian.   D—$80

Frame of seed beads, 8 in. by 12 in. and with multi-colored seed beads in floral motif, on trade cloth.   D—$40

Beaded pillow, Chippewa, 6½ in. square. Has floral beadwork designs with beaded edging in seven colors. Quite unusual.
                                                    D—$65

Beaded armbands, Flathead Indian.   A—$28

Beaded headband, Sioux, beads on buckskin and ca. 1900.
                                                    D—$45

Armbands, Blackfoot, 10½ in. long and 1 in. wide quilled dangles. Collected in Montana in 1932, but are much older. Pair.   G—$110

Beaded headband, loom-beaded Cree, ca. 1885.   D—$45

Fine Sioux BEADED SADDLE BLANKET, leather and 25 in. wide, 46 in. long. Excellent designs, well-balanced piece, ca. 1880.
                                    D—$1600
Photo courtesy Winona Trading Post, Santa Fe—Pierre & Sylvia Bovis.

Pin cushion, Chippewa, 8 in. long. Piece has floral design in very small (18/0) beads, red, dark green, blue, pink and yellow.

G—$75

Headband, Sioux, beaded with string hair-drops.   D—$85

Beaded belt, Indian group unknown, 30 in. long and 3 in. wide. Loomed work; white background with seven deer woven into the design.   G—$175

Suggested Reading

Whiteford, Andrew H.; *North American Indian Arts*, Golden Press, New York, 1970

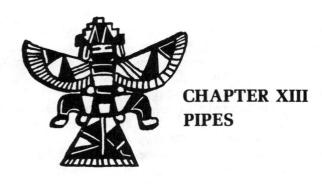

CHAPTER XIII
PIPES

Pipe forms began in the Archaic time-frame, and various types were made throughout North America. Generally pipes were made from a select material, a hardstone that was both compact and colorful.

The form, in principle, is simple. A pipe has an enclosed area that contains the smoking material — tobacco as we know it was not used widely until historic times — and a smaller, intersecting hole through which the smoke was drawn. Pipes range from large to small, effigy to plain, with workstyle from passable to superb.

Pipes are classified according to shape — tube, elbow, elongated, platform, and so forth. Some are mere bowls, while others are complete with stems and incised decorations. Earlier pipes tend to be simple; later forms more elaborate. Many specimens took a great deal of time and skill to make and are avidly sought by collectors today.

For this discussion, pipes can be divided into two large collecting fields. As with many other Amerind collectibles, these are before (prehistoric) and after, White-contact times (historic period). Prehistoric pipes tend to be the most varied in form, the most geographically divergent.

Historic Plains Indian style pipes are much more similar for the times. There is a certain sameness of size, design and material, with Minnesota red pipestone (also called Catlinite) the common stone. Such pipes were also popular in the Great Lakes area and other regions.

Value considerations for prehistoric pipes include material from which the pipe is made, with harder substances ranked higher than loose-grained stone. Polish is important, as are size and workstyle. All drilling should be complete and well-done. Some tube-type pipes combine the two in a single elongated hole.

Effigy pipes usually command higher prices than ordinary pipes, and depictions of the human figure are especially valued. The rare

Hopewellian effigy pipes — often mini-sculptures of birds or animals — can be worth in excess of $2000.

Historic times had many White-made pipes. They ranged from the rare Russian lead stem-and-bowl pipe of the far Northwest to numerous baked-clay and porcelain pipes of White mold-manufacture. The pipe-tomahawks of Eastern regions (covered elsewhere) are yet another example. The big collector item, however, is the Indian-made Plains-style pipe.

The typical Plains Indian Catlinite smoking instrument had a high, rounded bowl and a stem-receptacle of similar proportions. In profile, the two form either an "L"-shape or an inverted "T"-shape. Some pipe forms were two-piece, with stem connecting the receptacle. And the stem, in turn, was either of wood or Catlinite.

Better pipes were stored and transported in the beaded and/or quilled pipe-bags, and were used on special occasions. The current value range for Plains-style pipes is $300 to $600, and more for extra-fine specimens. Most pipe heads are about the same size, so this is not usually a big value factor.

Overall workmanship is important, plus surface polish and completed and accurate drilling. Twisted-wood or paneled-wood stems are more desired than plain wooden stems, and Catlinite stems are very much sought-after. Pipes that can definitely be associated with an actual (and famous) Indian leader are definiately in the minority, and should be thoroughly documented.

It is pointed out that contemporary Catlinite pipes are being made by American Indians at the Pipestone National Monument in Minnesota. These are modern reproductions that much resemble Plains-style historic specimens; they sell in a range of $20-$50, and, with wood stem, are from 12 in. to 30 in. in length.

PREHISTORIC STONE PIPES

Sandstone tube pipe, 4½ in. long and 1¼ in. in diameter. A well-made piece, fully drilled the length.   A—$75

Caddo long-stem pipe, 9 in. long. Piece, from Arkansas, has minor stem breaks, but repaired; no bowl damage. Nice item.   G—$195

CLAY PIPE, 4 in. long and 2½ in. high, from Brant County, Ontario, Canada. This is a strudy and well-made piece, late prehistoric or early historic.   C—$40-$50

Photo courtesy Robert Calvert, London, Ontario, Canada.

STONE EFFIGY PIPE, platform type, 3 in. high and 1¼ in. wide. Probably Woodland; pipe bowl top made in image of a turtle in its shell a common Midwestern Hopewellian motif. From Canada, Lake Huron reegion. (Condition uncertain.)   C—$300-$600

Photo courtesy Robert C. Calvert, London, Ontario, Canada.

BROWN CLAY PIPE, 6¼ in. long and 2-5/8 in high. Piece is from Ontario, Canada and may be Huron in origin. Note the graceful shape and punctate marks for decoration.   C—$55-$70

Photo courtesy Robert C. Calvert, London, Ontario, Canada.

Hardstone tube pipe, 10¼ in. long, 1¼ in. in diameter near center. Made of black compact stone, highly polished on surface. Larger end evidences some battering, but nothing major.   D—$495

Bowl-type pipe, 1½ in. long, 1½ in. high, and made of Ohio pipestone.   A—$55

Round bowl-type pipe, made of a compact light sandstone. Large hole ½ in. in diameter with smaller hole for stem. Pipe, with rounded bottom, is 1¾ in. high.   C—$45

STONE PIPE, made of banded slate, and an unfinished item. Pipe is 2¼ in. long and is drilled at both bowl and stem ends. Bowl top has a curious set of 4 lines around bowl, which could have been a centering guide for drilling, or just decoration, or a symbol representing the four directions.   C—$45-$65

Photo courtesy Robert C. Calvert, London, Ontario, Canada.

Diegueno Indian **soapstone tube pipe,** 5 in. long and 1 in. across at smoking end. Drilled entire length, small to larger hole, no damage.   C—$295

Cylindrical banded-slate pipe bowl, flat bottomed. Bowl is 2-1/8 in. high, exterior highly polished, good banding.   D—$125

Wine-glass type pipe, Washington state, 4½ in. long and 7/8 in. wide at end. Polished stone resembling steatite, well-carved, perfect condition.   D—$345

Sandstone effigy pipe, 4 in. high and 3¼ in. wide. A crane-like bird is depicted, with beak touching ground, and bowl on back. Restored.   A—$295

Prehistoric CERAMIC EFFIGY PIPE, found in Canada, and 6¼ in. long. Color is dark brown, and surface has a nice sheen.　　　　　　　　　　　　　　　　　　　　　　　　*C—$115*

Photo courtesy Howard Popkie, Arnprior, Canada.

Green soapstone or **steatite pipe**, from Virginia, bowl at one end of a flat base. Piece is 5-3/8 in. long. Some damage to expanded rim of bowl, now expertly restored.　　　　　　　　　　　　C—$355

Platform-type pipe, steatite, 4 in. long and 1½ in. high, nicely polished.　　　　　　　　　　　　　　　　　　　　　　　　A—$135

Raised-bowl pipe, with flat stem extending for 3¾ in. Height, 1½ in. Stem is just over 1 in. wide, with raised ridge along top center.　　　　　　　　　　　　　　　　　　　　　　　　A—$445

Effigy platform pipe, pipestone, 3 in. long and 1¾ in. high, depicting a bird. Piece done in Hopewellian fashion. Head is restored.　　　　　　　　　　　　　　　　　　　　　　　　A—$285

Steatite elbow-type pipe, 2½ in. long and 1½ in. high, very well polished.　　　　　　　　　　　　　　　　　　　　　　　　A—$120

Sandstone effigy pipe, 3 in. high and 2 in. long, depicting a human figure with arms around the bowl. Piece is broken but not seriously.　　　　　　　　　　　　　　　　　　　　　　　　A—$215

Steatite pipe, large bowl 4¼ in. high and with smaller stem about 2¾ in. long. Highly polished.　　　　　　　　　　　　　　D—$325

EFFIGY CLAY PIPE, 5 in. long and 3¼ in. high at top of effigy head. Effigy types of artifacts tend to be more valued than plain types; this is a Canadian piece.   *C—$80-$95*
Photo courtesy Robert C. Calvert, London, Ontario, Canada.

Tubular pipe, pipestone, 7 in. long and 1¼ in. wide, with fully drilled, tapering hole. A very well-made piece, though broken and restored.   A—$525

Granite effigy pipe, 3½ in. high, 1½ in. wide. Bird figure with bowl on the back.   A—$255

Sandstone pipe made to represent a sitting frog or toad. Pipe has large smoking hole in middle of the back, stands 2 in. high. Good condition, and a well-made piece. Intensive wear around top of bowl.   C—$160

Hopewellian **platform-type pipe,** sandstone, very nicely carved and proportioned, 4¾ in. long. Piece is unfinished, having never been drilled for bowl or stem.   C—$195

Steatite pipe, tubular form, 1¼ in. in diameter and 3½ in. long. Ends lightly scarred, all minor, surface highly polished.   D—$85

Sandstone pipe, barrel type. 2¼ in. high. Late prehistoric, Midwest. Some damage to top of bowl.   C—$65

Slate pipe, tubular form, 4¼ in. long and 1-1/8 in. in diameter. Good banded material, high polish, drilled completely through, no damage.   C—$205

Stone pipe, elbow type, 3½ in. long and 1-7/8 in. high. Squared edges, rather heavy in appearance, well-polished surface. One chip from mouthpiece area, but minor. 　　　　　　　C—$175

Pipe, Northwest Coast "wineglass" tubular variety. Pipe is 2-7/8 in. long, 7/8 in. in diameter at larger end, hole drilled the length. Smaller "bottom"-mouthpiece end had hole drilled in corner, possibly for securing thong. 　　　　　　　D—$315

STONE ELBOW PIPE, excavated from a Texas Panhandle Pueblo site nar Spearman. It is made from a material that is very fine-grained; a charred smoking substance is still inside the bowl. Bowl top has incised markings; pipe is 2 in. in length, and probably dates AD 900—1300. C—$135 Photo courtesy Wayne Parker, Texas.

Steatite bird-effigy pipe, with sitting bird facing pipe bowl; 4¼ in. long. Small scratches on surface, none deep. Unusual; unknown time period, but prehistoric. Effigy well-carved. 　　　C—$825

Sandstone pipe, elbow-type, 2¾ in. long, 1¼ in. high. Plain, but well-made. From Oklahoma, and prehistoric. Surface still rough. 　　　　　　　　　　　　　　　　　　D—$55

Pipestone pipe, platform type, concave platform base, plain bowl. Piece is 4-1/8 in. long, perfect condition, highly polished.　C—$1295

"L"-shaped pipe of greenish pipestone, 2-1/8 in. high and 2 in. long. Bowl has two incised lines around top near rim. 　　　C—$125

CLAY PIPE, 3-1/8 in. long and 1¾ in. high, and 1½ in. diagonally across pipe bowl. This is a Canadian piece and may be Neutral or Attawandoron in origin.   C—$30-$45

Photo courtesy Robert Calvert, London, Ontario, Canada.

STONE PIPE, prehistoric, unusual squared and elongated form. Larger end has pipe bowl, with connecting hole for stem in center of bottom side. Smaller end has two drill-holes connecting in "L" configuration. Smaller end is additionally grooved, and there are several deep grooves on topside—which would have been pipe front when in use. Unusual, and tally-notched. Piece is 2½ in. long.   C—$225-$275

Photo courtesy Robert C. Calvert, London, Ontario, Canada.

Platform-type pipe of limestone, 3½ in. long and 1¾ in. high.

A—$125

Disc-bowl pipe, Illinois, made of gray-white material. Has a short rounded stem and is 1¾ in. high, 2½ in. long.   C—$265

Effigy pipe of sandstone, 5 in. long and 3 in. high, possibly representing a sitting bird with squat body and raised head.

A—$650

Iroquois pipe, pipetone, 5 in. long and 2 in. high. Bowl and stem form a right angle; top of bowl has a widened, flat rim. The piece has been restored.   A—$135

Elbow-type pipe, North Carolina, expanded bowl set at right angles to squared base. Material a yellowish compact stone. Piece is 3 in. long.   C—$315

Large **platform-type pipe**, 4-7/8 in. long, 3¼ in. high. Made of a polished dark brown stone, no damage. Well-polished; bowl fully drilled and stem partially drilled. C—$530

Granite elbow-type pipe, 4 in. long and 2½ in. high. A—$110

Iroquois pipe, long-stem type, 4½ in. long and 2 in. high. Round bowl, tubular stem, made of pipestone. This piece has restoration. A—$125

Tubular pipe, state of Washington, of a type called "wineglass". One end flares abruptly, other end tapers to rounded and expanded mouthpiece. Piece is 5-1/8 in. long, of a compact black stone. Slight damage to rim of smoking bowl, but minor. C—$415

Elbow-type stone pipe, made of a fine-grain yellowish siltstone, and 3½ in. long, 1¾ in. high. Well-made and with good polish. C—$300

Quartzite barrel-type pipe, 2 in. high and 1¾ in. in diameter, with hole for stem in center which connects with smoking compartment. A—$160

CLAY PIPE, 3½ in. long and 2¼ in. high and found near Hyde Park, London, Ontario, Canada. A well-shaped and sturdy late-prehistoric or early historic pipe. C—$40-$55
Photo courtesy Robert Calvert, London, Ontario, Canada.

INDIAN-MADE HISTORIC PIPES

Red pipestone pipe, made in the form of a pipe-tomahawk, 19½ in. long. Plains Indian and probably late 1800's.   C—$385

T-shape Catlinite pipe, bowl 3¼ in. high and overall length 22½ in. Round stem with carved and painted design.   G—$420

Catlinite pipe head, Plains Indian, with redstone head 4¼ in. high and 6 in. long. Well-carved and nicely polished. Probably late 1800's.   C—$275

Catlinite pipe, old, with stem of pipestone also.   A—$265

Red pipestone pipe, head 7 in. long and with 18½ in. wood stem.
                                                                D—$435

Catlinite pipe and stem, early period, both showing great age and use.   G—$325

Pipe, Catlinite, 9 in. long and 4 in. high, a classic specimen of the Plains Indian style. Carved and polished; Northern Plains region, and mid-1800's.   G—$330

FRENCH TRADE PIPE, historic, from Ontario, Canada. Piece is 2 in. high and 2 in. long, quite well made and in fine condition.   *C—$35*
Photo courtesy Robert C. Calvert, London, Ontario, Canada.

Pipe, with original pipe bag; Sioux, and pre-1900.　　　A—$725

Tube pipe, historic Chumash Indian, of green steatite.　　A—$125

Pipe bowl, 4 in. long, 3½ in. high. Ornately sculpted Catlinite pipe bowl in unusually elaborate design. Surface worn to a fine patina. Northern Plains and mid-1800's.　　　G—$430

Eskimo pipe, with Siberian influence. Carved from wood, with inlayed pewter decorations.　　　A—$750

Pipe bowl, 10 in. long and 4 in. high. Large Catlinite pipe bag, with pierced-design "fin" between end and bowl. Cheyenne, and ca. 1900.　　　G—$325

Catlinite pipe and stem, with early spiral-carved stem. Top quality piece and in very nice condition.　　　G—$435

Sioux Catlinite pipe, with head 3 in. high and 8 in. long, with carved snake. The twisted wood stem is 15 in. in length. Piece is ca. 1920.　　　G—$325

Sioux Catlinite pipe, 3 in. high and 7 in. long. Carved squirrel facing the bowl. Wooden stem is 17 in. long. This piece is ca. 1920.　　　G—$295

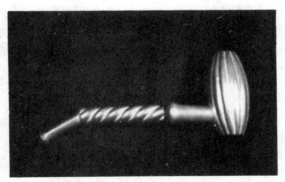

Red Catlinite "SQUAW PIPE," with an intricately carved stem and bowl, each a separate piece. Pipe is about 7 in. long, including the spiral-carved stem.　　　*D—$325*
Photo courtesy Crazy Crow Trading Post, Denison, Texas.

Blackfoot pipe, Reservation-collected in the early 1900's. Bowl is black and carved in Blackfoot design; wooden stem, with old collection number. Excellent condition.   G—$375

L-shaped Catlinite pipe, with short wooden stem. Head is 1¼ in. high and wooden stem is 6 in. long. Old label reads "Kowa, from Missouri River".   G—$195

Catlinite Sioux pipe, finest workmanship and condition. Pipe bowl and lower portions are inlayed with lead or pewter.   C—$795

Sioux Catlinite pipe, bowl 6 in. long and 3 in. high, in the form of an eagle claw with cone. Wooden stem is 17 in. long. Ca. 1920.
                                                                  G—$375

Sioux Catlinite pipe with quilled stem. Collected prior to 1900 and formerly in a major collection, Oklahoma. An early and fine piece.
                                                                  G—$675

Sioux Catlinite pipe, bowl 4 in. high and 8 in. long, with solid Catlinite stem 17 in. long. Ca. 1880.   G—$425

Hupa **soapstone tube pipe,** California, ca. 1890.   D—$55

Catlinite pipe, Western Plains Indian, bowl 3 in. high and 5 in. overall, with wood stem and additional 17¾ in. Bowl is cracked at base, but is barely visible.   D—$415

Suggested Reading

Bierer, Bert W., *Indian Artifacts in the Southeast: A Sketchbook*; Privately published, Columbia, South Carolina, 1977

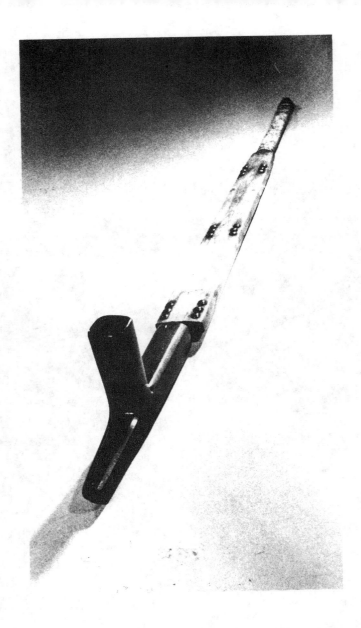

PIPE, 31 in. long. Catlinite pipe bowl and wood stem ornamented with brass tacks and wrapped
with plaited quilling. Northern Plains area, and pre-1900.   G—$1225
Photo courtesy Kenneth R. Canfield, Plains Indian Art, Kansas City, Missouri.

Paiute Indians, on the Kaibab Plateau, near the Grand Canyon of the Colorado, in northern Arizona. Photo by John K. Hillers, Powell Expedition, 1871-1875. The Indians here are playing the game of "Ni-aung-pi-kai", or "Kill the Bone".

Photo courtesy Utah State Historical Society, Collection of Smithsonian Institution.

CHAPTER XIV

CLOTHING, MOCCASINS AND LEATHERWORK

As with all natural and rendered materials to be worked, historic and recent Amerinds excelled in clothing and footwear. The leather was well-tanned and supple. Any decorations — beads, quills, paint — was put on with innate taste and practiced skill.

The sums being paid for such items, as evidenced by this chapter, are one indication of the esteem in which such work is now held. Faked pieces have thus far not been much of a problem, due to the complexity of matching both materials and artistic designs. Stone, in some cases, is easier to market than leather.

Articles most in demand appear to be complete and decorated dresses, skirts, vests and leggings, hopefully with documentation, usually without. If old and good, these are museum-quality items. Designs should be pleasing, the leather whole, and almost all beads and quills in place. Paint should still be somewhat bold, designs still visible. Leather fringes should be mostly intact and the item itself of some size.

For moccasins, Eastern examples tend to be soft-soled and floral-decorated. Moccasins can show some wear, but should not be holed on the bottoms or ripped badly.

Sides and top should be in good condition, with most bead and quill designs intact. Generally, the more beads or quills the greater the value, whether the piece is historic or recent. And note that items collected before about 1950 tend to be premium-priced.

WOMEN'S CLOTHING

Small girl's dress, 15 in. wide and 20 in. long, in Plains Indian design. Base is blue cloth with leather fringe and cowrie shell design; excellent condition and dresses this small are unusual. A pre-1900 piece. G—$255

Buckskin dress, medium-size, Plains Indian, fawn color and fringed. Some bead decorations. D—$575

Woman's dress, made of satin in bright purple color and with hundreds of metal dangles hanging from dress. Excellent condition and a Plateau piece. Ca. 1940's. G—$185

Woman's dress, for tall person, shoulder sections well-beaded, and overall made of doeskin. Superb condition and probably late 1880's; beading excellent, all fringes present. Typical Plains Indian beadwork designs in red, white and blue. D—$1750

Woman's dress, single unit, dark brown and 41 in. long. Beadwork strips, in good condition. D—$565

Woman-size Apache LEATHER DRESS, ca. 1900. Nicely tassled overall, and yoke at top has beaded fringe and fine designs, on shoulders.
D—$4500

Photo courtesy Winona Trading Post, Santa Fe—Pierre & Sylvia Bovis.

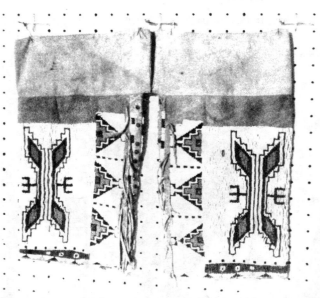

WOMEN'S LEGGINGS, 9½ in. wide and 16 in. long. They have cloth tops, geometric full-beaded on both sides, with fringes and brass tacks. Collected in South Dakota and in excellent condition. Sioux, and ca. 1890.   C—$1090
Photo courtesy Bill Post Collection.

Woman's dress, small size and Nez Perce. On green cloth, yoke is nicely beaded with blue, black and red beads. Many cowrie shell decorations. Excellent condition, and probably from the 1920's.
G—$465

Woman's dress, Navajo, skirt and blouse, red and blue designs in weave; combined length of pair 53 in. long. Worn but good condition.   D—$415

Leather vest, woman's size, geometric beadwork designs, some damage to back but beadwork in good condition.   C—$275

Woman's vest, light-colored thin leather, beads and quillwork, old but in good condition.   A—$280

Woman's leggins, 7 in. by 12 in., fully beaded with yellow, red, green and purple beads. Very decorative set; Plateau origin and ca. 1930's.   G—$225

Woman's leggings, Plains Indian, good beadwork in good condition.
D—$355

Woman's leggings, Sioux, beautiful designs and colors. Sinew-sewn on buckskin and in excellent condition. Tag indicates they belonged to the wife of a famous Lower Brule Sioux chief. G—$665

PLAINS BEADED VEST, 20½ in. long. Vest has the same design front and back. Circa 1890.
G—$960

Photo and item courtesy Fenn Galleries, Ltd., Santa Fe, New Mexico.

MEN'S CLOTHING

Man's outfit, quilled, and Blackfoot. Set includes a war shirt, pair of gauntlets, rifle case and knife sheath. Quills are red, yellow, green, purple and natural, woven on hide. Outstanding and like-new condition. Ca. 1910-20.   G—$4000

Woodlands jacket, 26 in. long, of leather; piece has beaded cuffs, front, and design on back. Fringes along underside of sleeves, and probably ca. 1930's.   A—$415

"War shirt", probably Sioux, beaded front and back, but poor to fair condition overall. Piece was badly stored for a number of years and sections of beadwork are lost. About 75% of beadwork remains. Back design better than front.   C—$295

Boy's jacket, Crow, floral beadwork and outlined. Jacket is lined, and made of buckskin with very fine beadwork. Good condition and ca. 1880.   G—$575

Leather vest, sleeveless, 18¼ in. from top to bottom. Beaded in floral designs at bottom and middle of front flaps. Piece was collected in northeastern Pennsylvania and is ca. 1920's.   D—$445

MAN-SIZE KIOWA LEGGINGS, ca. 1880, and with small beadwork circles and figures.   D—$850
Photo courtesy Winona Trading Post, Santa Fe—Pierre & Sylvia Bovis.

Man's vest done on commercial leather and lined in old cloth. Arrows and circles beaded front and back, in orange, yellow and bright blue colors. Medium-size, and ca. 1920-30's.   G—$190

Leggings, beaded on old blanket material. Beaded panels at bottom and measuring 7 in. by 12 in. Old blanket shows ribbon work on edges and slight moth damage; beadwork nearly perfect. Crow Indian, and ca. 1885.   G—$645

Man's leggings and vest, matched outfit, Plains Indian style. Well beaded the both, and ca. late 1880's.   D—$1275

Leggings, 24 in. long, 7 in. wide, with short fringes on outer sides. Cheyenne.   A—$250

Leggings, Ponca or Oto Indian. They are of black trade cloth with tan cloth trim on bottom. All trim is outlined in light blue beads with many white stars beaded on cloth. Beautiful fine yellow fringe on edge of leggings. Ca. 1910.   G—$535

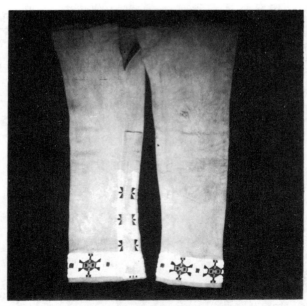

ARAPAHO LEGGINGS, man-size, on leather and with well-beaded sections around bottom, and with beaded strips up inside of leg region. Colors are white, red, yellow and black; excellent condition, and probably late-1800's.   *D—$565*

Photo courtesy Crazy Crow Trading Post, Denison, Texas.

MAN-SIZE SIOUX LEGGINGS, ca. 1880, and with fine beadwork designs.   *D—$695*
Photo courtesy Winona Trading Post, Santa Fe—Pierre & Sylvia Bovis.

GAUNTLETS

Moose hide gauntlets, Nez Perce Indian, 7 in. long. Decorated with cut-glass beads and with beaded floral-design panels on backs. Large, excellent condition and ca. 1930's.   G—$240

Gauntlets, pair, woman's size. Partially beaded on cuffs, of Indian-tanned leather and cloth-lined.   G—$85

Gauntlets, pair, 17 in. overall length with 6 in. fringe. Blackfoot, early, and man-size. Stylized floral designs beaded on cuffs; fingers have deteriorated and pair should be set behind glass to preserve the pieces.   G—$125

Gauntlets, pair, Indian-tanned leather. Simple horseshoe designs beaded on cuff. Medium-size, in excellent condition.   G—$85

Gauntlets, large and beautiful pair from Northern Plains region. Pair lined with fur-trade cloth, ca. 1870.   D—$125

RELATED INDIAN APPAREL

Man's belt, of thick black commercial leather. Plains Indian, 35 in. long, with geometric designs in beadwork. Collected in Montana and in excellent condition. Possibly ca. 1900. C—$215

Two Sioux **arm bands,** both different, sold as one lot. A—$55

Very rare **wolf skin medicine cap,** and piece was in a University collection. Hair mostly present but some deterioration from age. An original Blackfoot item, ca. 1800. G—$200

Hair roach, done with porcupine guard hairs and red-dyed horsehair. Piece has a yarn and leather base; old and symmetrical. G—$195

Man's belt, 42 in. long and 2½ in. wide. Beadwork on one side, geometric designs, fair condition and Blackfoot in origin. D—$180

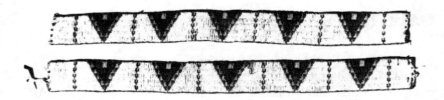

Sioux man's BEADED LEGGING STRIPS. 29 in. long and 3 in. wide, and in excellent condition. Ca. 1880. *D—$575*
Photo courtesy Winona Trading Post, Santa Fe—Pierre & Sylvia Bovis.

Nez Perce **dance apron.** A—$13

Rectangular cape, red and blue cloth, 36 in. long and 19 in. wide. Piece has two loom-beaded strips 1¼ in. wide and 10 in. long. Attached are hawk bells, small mirrors and brass cone jingles. Very unusual item. G—$100

Sioux **cuffs,** pair, good condition and workstyle. D—$135

Dew claw medicine piece, made from the hide of a deer leg. Museum quality, decorated with mirrors and brass tacks. Sioux, and very early. G—$315

Man's hair drop, beaded, Plains Indian style. D—$195

Woman's **beaded collar,** worn around neck and across shoulders. Shell beads cover the outside; done in several designs in glass beads. Fringed. D—$175

Woodlands **apron,** deerskin on velvet backing; tree and flowering plants done in beadwork. C—$300

Headband, beaded Plains Indian type, 1-1/8 in. wide and in good condition. D—$115

Penobscot **fur hat,** ca. 1900. D—$25

Infant's **cap,** northern Plains region, possibly antelope hide; completely covered on outside with tiny seed beads. Piece is 4½ in. in diameter, in good condition; an unusual item. D—$415

MOCCASINS-Adult Size

Cree moccasins, 8 in. long, with quillwork on hide. Simple floral design and in excellent condition; ca. 1900. G—$140

CEREMONIAL MOCCASINS, fully beaded including soles and sometime called "Burial moccasins". Geometric beading in red, green and white with blue thread around tongue. Moccasins are 7½ in. long and hide shows age; beading in excellent condition. Crow Indian, and collected in Canada. C—$625

Photo courtesy Bill Post Collection.

Quilled and beaded **Sioux moccasins,** man's size. D—$290

Plains Indian beaded **moccasins,** beaded tops, rawhide bottoms. Very old and in good condition. A—$130

Sioux "**burial moccasins**", entirely beaded in geometric designs including soles. Adult size, good condition, almost all beadwork intact. C—$525

Fully beaded **Sioux moccasins,** good early designs, and sinew-sewn on buckskin with rawhide soles. C—$195

Cheyenne moccasins, very nicely beaded. D—$225

Taos Pueblo moccasins, beadwork on toes, originally painted in yellow ochre. D—$215

Arapaho moccasins, fully beaded, and 10½ in. long. Extremely fine condition with beaded cuffs; have "trail dusters" and red cloth bindings, sinew-sewn and beaded. Ca. 1910. G—$230

Quilled **moccasins,** fine early designs, very old. A—$360

Pair of Nez Perce BEADED MAN'S MOCCASINS, ca. 1880, excellent condition and with fine beadwork overall. *D—$325*
Photo courtesy Winona Trading Post, Santa Fe—Pierre & Sylvia Bovis.

Deerskin **moccasins,** Woodlands Indian, upper parts covered with fine beadwork. Overall reddish leather, and ca. late 1880's.

D—$250

Blackfoot moccasins, man-size, partially beaded in blue, lavender and amber beads, classic style for this group. Collected on the Blackfoot reservation in the 1930's. G—$180

Sioux beaded moccasins, good design. A—$170

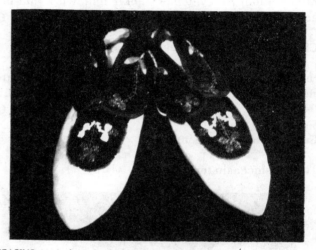

Huron MOCCASINS, 9½ in. long. Smoked buckskin with black cloth flaps and toe panels, beaded floral designs. Like-new condition, and ca. 1890. D—$215
Photo courtesy Crazy Crow Trading Post, Denison, Texas.

Sioux moccasins, man-size, light blue background with green and yellow designs. Excellent condition, and ca. 1910. G—$195

MOCCASINS-Child's Size

Baby moccasins, 5 in. overall length and 2 in. wide. Toes partially beaded; Indian-tanned leather. C—$34

Plains Indian **baby moccasin,** single specimen, 4¼ in. long. Top area beaded, bottom worn through; very nice beadwork design and that section in good condition. C—$24-30

Blackfoot baby moccasins, beaded pair. A—$25

RELATED INDIAN FOOTGEAR

Apache boots, pair, 27½ in. long. They have beaded crosses on the toes with small beaded band on tops. 　　　　　　　G—$250

Three Plains Indian **beaded moccasins,** left foot only, and in man, woman and child sizes. Possibly, and for reasons unknown, three pairs were divided and marketed. Early 1900's fine beadwork, and excellent condition. All evidence similar handwork and may have been made by same person. 　　　　　　　C—$225

Pair of **Cheyenne moccasins,** beaded. 　　　　　　　A—$85

Southern Cheyenne or Kiowa boots, 15 in. high. Decorated with seed beads in strips, on yellow ochred hide. Excellent condition and ca. 1870-80. 　　　　　　　G—$935

Pair of **Cree beaded moccasins.** 　　　　　　　A—$40

Pair of Tlinget **moccasin tops.** 　　　　　　　A—$15

Oglalla Sioux WOMENS BOOTS, sinew sewn and fully beaded front and sides. The high tops make this pair a distinctive collector item; ca. 1920-25. 　　　　　　*D—$275*
Photo courtesy Crazy Crow Trading Post, Denison, Texas.

LEATHERWORK COLLECTIBLES

Plains Indian saddle bags, matched pair, made of rawhide and fringed. C—$1775

Small **parfleche envelope,** 5 in. by 9 in. in standard design and excellent condition. Marked "Pendleton, Oregon" and dated 1930.
G—$80

Leather **carrying bag,** Plains Indian and early. D—$350

Southern Plains pipe bag, 27 in. long, nicely glass-beaded, leather fringes, late 1880's. D—$515

Apache **carrying pouch** of shaped hide, 7 in. long. D—$135

Plains Indian lariat or lasso, with eye or slip-loop at one end, knotted at other. Still coiled and rawhide is hard. Estimated length is 23 feet. Very slight mouse-nibble damage, barely noticable. Lariat averages 3/8 in. in diameter. Private collector values the piece at $10 per foot. Braided. C—$345

Matching pair of painted parfleche envelopes, 12 in. high and 26 in. long. Very nice designs painted; in excellent condition. Pairs are hard to obtain; good art pieces and very collectible. G—$675

Carrying bag, partially decorated front and back in geometric beadwork, late 1800's. Bag is 3 in. by 13 in. by 15 in., worn but good condition. Leather. D—$210

Strike-a-light bag, 5 in. by 3½ in. wide, northern Plains region. Leather with beadwork designs on one side. C—$195

Hair roach of deerhide and porcupine quills, very well preserved and an attractive piece. Ca. early 1900's. D—$95

Parfleche box, 6 in. by 9 in. by 14 in. All painted designs, early reservation period, nice condition. G—$235

Set of Plains Indian **leather dance bell straps,** which attached to outer sides of legs. Early 1900's, good bells. D—$90

SADDLEBAGS, 10 in. wide and unfolded length 62 in. Set of classic Apache saddlebags with rawhide cutouts over red tradecloth. This set is ca. 1890.   G—$525

Photo courtesy Kenneth R. Canfield, Plains Indian Art, Kansas City, Missouri.

Parfleche envelope, 8 in. by 7 in., with flexible leather wrap that closed front. Faint painted design. Plains Indian. A—$75

Dew claw necklace as used by the Sioux and many other tribes. All carved dew claws with trade beads, and pre-1900. G—$265

Chippewa shoulder bag, 12 in. by 15 in. and with 2½ in. wide carrying strap. Floral designs done in red, green and white beads, and bag with beaded tassles. G—$1035

Awl case, leather with beadwork, some beads missing. Piece is 9 in. long. D—$65

Miniature pipe bag, probably late 1800's. Deerskin, beaded designs on side, nicely fringed, and 10½ in. long. D—$145

Parfleche knife sheath with painted designs and tacks. Sioux, and old. G—$135

Dew claw bag, made from the leg skin of an elk. Old piece and in very good condition. G—$295

BUCKSKIN SHIRT, 39 in. in length. Fringed shirt, partly machine-stitched, of the type affected by cavalry officers in the field; note perforations in shoulders, possibly caused by attachment of insignia shoulder-boards. Beadwork cuffs added by subsequent Indian owner, and made from old Sioux woman's leggings. An old tag attached to the shirt reads: "Buckskin shirt picked up on Wounded Knee, S. D., battelfield Dec. 29, 1890. Sioux, and pre-1890. G—$2100

Photo courtesy Kenneth R. Canfield, Plains Indian Art, Kansas City, Missouri.

Flint and steel or **strike-a-light bag,** possibly Apache, with small hawk bells. Size, 3½ in. by 6¼ in. and likely late 1800's.   C—$245

The listings that follow have been selected because they are highly unusual or significantly different to warrant presentation. All were selected from Kenneth R. Canfield's Plains Indian Art Catalogues Nos. 1 and 2.

Following is an excerpt from Catalogue No. 1, written by Mr. Canfield. It allows a fleeting glimpse of artistic inspiration in the Plains Indian past. Used with permission.

"The American Great Plains is an awesome sweep of land and sky bounded by mountains and long sinuous rivers. The Northern Plains were dominated by the tribes of the Teton (or western) Sioux, who called themselves collectively the Dakota, and to a lesser degree by the Blackfeet, Crow, Gros Ventre, Assiniboin and Plains Cree. In the south were Kiowa and Comanche. Cheyenne, Arapaho and Pawnee ranged along the western margins of the grasslands. On the east lived Osage, Iowa, Oto, Mesquakie and Mandan.

"They differed widely by tribe — linguistically and ethnically — but they had much in common socially and culturally. The Northern Cheyenne and Sioux lived in such proximity that their artistic production overlaps.

"The plains tribes shared a way of life imposed upon them by the vast, harsh world in which they lived, a landscape of dazzling color and light, of violent contrast and great distance. Theirs was an environment of blinding white snow, of depths of blue sky, of the carmine red of lifeblood, of the endless green seas of grass of ochre plains.

"Death was always at hand, but they lived serenely at one with the universe. It seems hardly surprising that a sense of vivid intensity and wonder and magic should communicate itself to the view through the still living art of the Plains Indians."

PLAINS INDIAN ART (Courtesy Kenneth R. Canfield)

Whetstone case, 5 in. long. Hide container ornamented with blue and white beadwork front and back. Sioux, from South Dakota, and pre-1890.

G—$35

PLAINS SHIELD, with paper-stuffed heron head tied on. The top half is painted in rainbow designs of red, black, green and yellow. Item is Northern Plains and pre-1880.   *G—$3250*
Photo and item courtesy Fenn Galleries, Ltd., Santa Fe, New Mexico.

Man's warshirt, 38 in. long. Painted buckskin with beaded strips on shoulders and sleeves and beaded rosettes front and back. Ten winter-pelt weasel skins attached. Beaded geometric designs in orange, black and pale blue on a white background. Collected in Canada; Blackfeet (Piegan), from Alberta. Piece is ca. 1910.

G—$2600

Carved wooden flute, 21½ in. long. Cedar flute incised in a spiral pattern. Lead soundplate surmounted by a wooden sound block carved in the shape of a horse and stained with red ochre. Paper tag affixed to sound block. Eastern Sioux, from the Northern Plains area, and mid-1880's.   G—$495

Quillwork pipe bag, 28 in. long with fringes. Deerskin tobacco bag embroidered with red and yellow dyed porcupine quills, front and back. Quilled suspensions with tin cone and feather attachments. Old tag attached reads "Quilled pipe bag 1875". Northern Plains, and mid-1880's.   G—$1560

Woman's boots, 25 in. long. Hard-soled boots of soft yellow dyed deerskin, with fringing at the tops. Narrow lines of beadwork in white, red and blue encircle the tops and ankles and frame the front flaps, which are studded with double rows of german silver buttons. Kiowa, Southern Plains area, ca. 1875.   G—$780

Ration ticket pouch, 4 in. long. Beaded bag with triangular figures of brown, yellow and light blue on a lavender field; flap and thong drawstring. Carry-strap of woven pale blue beadwork. Southern Plains region, and pre-1900.   G—$155

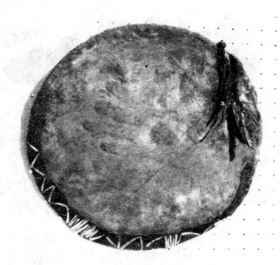

BUFFALO HIDE SHIELD, ¼ in. thick and 16½ in. in diameter. Green hand painted on center of shield with red dot in the hand. A Plains Indian piece, some Plains tribes pictured hand on shield, war shirt or pony to denote an enemy killed in combat. old red cloth sewn around the bottom edge and decorated with dentalium shells, old ribbed type, all sinew-sewn. Remains of bird sinew sewn on edge, probably the owner's good luck charm or fetish. Ca. 1880.   *C—$1115*
Photo courtesy Bill Post Collection.

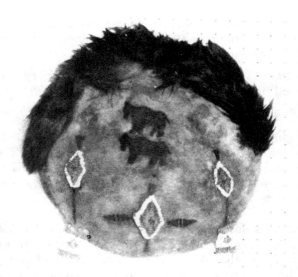

BEAR CULT SHIELD, 16 in. in diameter. Probably Cheyenne or Assiniboin, Montana. Piece has arm straps, 2 bears painted in black with humps, probably grizzley. Has 2 beaded diamonds and beaded tabs. Made of hide shrunk by heat process to ¼ in. to 5/16 in. thick. Bear hair trim across top of shield. Ca. 1860-70.   C—$1125
Photo courtesy Bill Post Collection.

Tepee liner, with entire canvas 85 in. by 142 in. and area of ornamentation 55 in. by 92 in. Heavy canvas tepee liner ornamented in the traditional linear pattern with predominantly orange bands of beadwork, interspersed with red yarn tufts. Along the top are 14 beaded medallions to which are attached cornhusk-wrapped suspensions, each terminating in a loop and deer-hoofs. Collected by Reese Kincaid about 1900 from the Nightwalker family. Cheyenne, from Oklahoma, and ca. 1900.   G—$3500

Cornhusk belt, 37 in. long and 6 in. wide. "Cornhusk" — actually woven hemp fibers—on leather, with geometric designs imbricated in yarn. Three brass buckles, lined with calico. Nez Perce, Plateau area, and pre-1900.   G — $625

Quilled breastplate, 10 in. wide and 16 in. long. Ornate breastplate of hide strips wrapped in predominantly bright red quillwork in a geometric pattern. Ribbon, feather and tin-cone attachments. Sioux, Northern Plains region, and ca. 1890's.   G—$1750

Pipe, 29 in. in length. Catlinite pipe bowl with wooden stem, wound with braided quilling and feathers. Provenance: Lawson Collection,

Philbrook Art Center, Tulsa. Collected by Roberta Lawson, acquired by the museum in 1946. Deaccessioned in a trade in 1976. Sioux, Northern Plains area, and mid-1800's.   G—$885

Pipe tamper, 11 in. long. Wooden pipe tamper carved of ash, the end shaped like a human foot, wrapped in braided red and white quillwork. Northern Plains region, and ca. 1910.   G—$140

Baby leggings, 6 in. wide and 9 in. high. Diminutive pair of buckskin leggings, outlined with a band of geometric beaded figures on a blue field, edges trimmed with faceted metallic beads. An old tag attached reads "Paul Good Bear, Cheyenne". Cheyenne, Plains region, and ca. 1900.   G—$145

Pair of child's dolls, large doll 13 in. high, smaller doll 11½ in. high. Pair of dolls made of buckskin and trade cloth, animal hair and yarn. Decorated with beading and blue and red paint. The smaller doll is painted with an eagle front and back on its buckskin shirt. The large doll has a crescent moon front and back, and a cross and falling star pattern under the shirt flaps. The painted images are similar to those found on ghost dance costumes of the period. Northern Plains area, and ca. 1895.   G—$440 pair

Toy canoe, 42 in. long and 10 in. wide. Child's toy canoe, a detailed replica of full-size craft. Birchbark sealed with pitch, cedar planking, pine thwarts, tied with cedar root and fastened with wood pegs. (Compare no. 33 in Norman Feder's catalogue of the Jarvis collection of Eastern Plains Indian art in the Brooklyn Museum.) Ojibwa, and pre-1900.   G—$325

Mide bag, 46 in. long. Otter skin medicine bag of the Mide society, used to hold sacred objects for curing rites. Beaded panels of ribbon-edged velvet. The otter retains its claws, skull and teeth, and has one coat-button eye. Red-dyed feathers have been inserted into the nose. An old brass thimble is attached to one claw. Great Lakes area, and ca. 1870.   G—$825

Ghose dance vest, 21 in. long. Man's vest beaded in pictographic style using blue, green, greasy yellow and transparent red beads. Front and back are four Ghose Dance-style crows executed in dark blue faceted beads. On the back are three zoomorphic forms with forked tails, perhaps lizards or dragonflies. On the front are geometric figures, composed of stepped triangles, and eight crosses. Sioux, ca. 1890.   G—$1950

CHILD'S MOCCASINS, 6½ in. long. Orange quillwork bands and an outline strip of pale blue beadwork. Northern Plains area, ca. 1880.   G—$340

Photo courtesy Kenneth R. Canfield, Plains Indian Art, Kansas City, Missouri.

Hairbrush, 12 in. long. Porcupine tail hair brush, with buckskin-wrapped and fringed handle. Bead detailing in transparent red, dark blue and lavender. A strip of quill-wrapped rawhide runs the length of the brush. Sioux (?), ca. 1890.   G—$295

Peyote rattle, 15 in. long, not including fringe. Gourd rattle on a wooden shaft, stitched with multicolored beadwork. Extensive use of small, faceted beads. Feather tip and cord fringe. Oklahoma, ca. 1930.   G—$210

Dance wand, 18 in. long. Quirt-style dance piece, red painted handle with brass tacks, braided rawhide suspension. Sioux, and ca. 1910.   G—$165

Loop necklace, of mandrel-wound white tradebeads, strung on thongs between rawhide strips. Six red beads, one at center of each strand; top strand broken and retied. Attachments include a cluster of deer-hoof janglers, a medicine bag of rough cloth stained dark and a long tassel of red-dyed horsehair partly wrapped in hide and with a wrapping of seed beads. Crow (?), and early 1880's.

G—$775

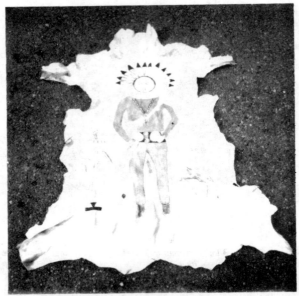

Painted, tanned deer hide; Navajo Indian of Arizona. Depicting the Yei Bi Chai dance leader, ceremonial corn symbol, and Yei figure dancing with a fox hide in hand. Only deer which had been killed by suffocation could be used to allow the spirit to go to the heavens.

Hide is 49 in. long and 41 in. wide, and ca. 1920. G—$1100

Photo courtesy W. J. Crawford, The Americana Galleries, Phoenix, Arizona.

Peyote bag, 5½ in. long. Metallic faceted beads around edge and at center of four-point star. Southern Plains region, ca. 1900.

G—$145

Breastplate, 21 in. in length. Large man's breastplate composed of bone hairpipes, brass beads, rawhide spacers and thongs. Provenance: Abourezk collection, Mission, S.D. Sioux, and from the 1890's. G—$1000

Tab bag, 12 in. long. Yellow-painted buckskin bag with beaded patterns of stepped triangles on a white background. Pendant from the bag is a long hide tab with two narrow strips of diagonal black and white beading. Soutern Plains area, ca. 1900. G—$255

BRAIDED SCALP-TANNED SKIN on beaded leather back; this is a leather medicine bag. The two feathers are from the golden eagle. Circa 1870. G—$495

Photo and item courtesy Fenn Galleries, Ltd., Santa Fe, New Mexico.

Awl case, 39 in. long with trailers, Large, elaborate woman's awl case with long beaded trailers. Tin-cone and breath-feather attachments. Southern Plains region, and ca. 1900.   G—$525

Cape or yoke, 37 in. wide. Fringed buckskin edged in cowrie shells and trade beads. (Beaded in geometric patters as described by Father Peter J. Powell in the Chicago Art Institute catalogue. The Native American Heritage.) Beaded in rose, blue, green and greasy yellow on a deep blue field. Sioux (?), and ca. 1880.   G—$1450

Bag, 5 in. long. Partly beaded with tiny faceted glass and brass beads. Lined with cotton cloth. Santee (?), and ca. 1895.   G—$140

Suggested Reading

(By the Editors), *The American Heritage Book of Indians,*
McGraw Hill Book Company dist.; American Heritage Publishing Co., Inc. 1961

Koch, Ronald P., *Dress Clothing of the Plains Indians,* University of Oklahoma

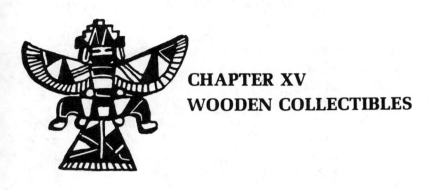

CHAPTER XV
WOODEN COLLECTIBLES

The great number of hafted stone woodworking tools from forested and coastal regions of prehistoric North America suggest wooden art and artifacts were once common. Certainly specialized chipped artifacts were also employed to carve wood into useful and pleasing objects. Almost all of such objects have been lost to time, bacteria — and the present.

The average person, asked to name early American Indian wood items, might mention some well-known examples. These might be prehistoric bows and arrows, or historic Northwest Coast totem poles or Iroquois false-face masks, or a few other memorable examples. With the exception of wood preserved by arid conditions in the Southwest and by permafrost in the far North, very few of such cultural creations survive.

One interesting and exceptional sidelight is that at least nine prehistoric or very early historic dugout canoes or watercraft have been found in North America. For whatever reason, they are not widely known, and the information is presented here for the first time in summary form, and to a general readership.

Further explanation of the chart: "Unknown" is abgreviated. Entry 4. was not verified by follow-up information, but the first report indicates a very old wooden dugout was indeed found. Wood used for some of the dugouts was identified as oak and pine. In Eastern North America, the finds were mainly preserved underwater, except in the New York case.

EARLY AMERICAN INDIAN DUGOUT DISCOVERIES

Case	Location	Date Found	Dimensions	Estimated Age
1. & 2.	Ontario, Canada (Lakes?) *Two* dugouts	Unk.	Unk.	2000 years
3.	Northwestern Ohio (Lake)	Late 1976	22½ ft. Long, 3¼ ft. wide	2000-3000 years
4.	Southwestern state (River)	1970 (?)	Not large	Unk.
5.	Manhattan, New York (Landfill)	1906	Broken half of dugout was 7 ft. long, 3 ft. wide	Unk.
6.	Tennessee (River)	1797(?)	Unk.	Pre-1797
7.	Michigan (Lake)	1971	17 ft. in length	300 years old; possibly earlier
8.	Georgia (River)	Early 1977	24 ft. long	250 years
9.	Florida (Lake)	1977/78 (?)	19 ft. long	200 years (sides burned)

Leaving the prehistoric and unknown regions, there are many wood collectibles from historic and recent times. The more desirable items have age as well as beauty, and are mainly from the 1700's into the early 1900's.

The wood should preferably be a heavy hardwood, with some surface patina due to age. Marks of manufacture, generally from White-supplied iron and steel tools, can be visible but not prominant to the point of distraction. Splitting and splintering should be at the absolute minimum, and wood rot or decay is a serious value negative. Some stain is permitted, especially with items like pemmican-pounders, for these are use-signs.

Many wood artifacts were further decorated with quilling (early) or beading (later), brass tacks or paint. This chapter consists of all-wood collectibles or Indian items that have a major part made of wood.

PREHISTORIC WOOD ITEMS

Southwestern **wooden rabbit-stick,** a slightly flat and curved stick about 23 in. long. These were thrown to bring down small game; sticks did not return, like the boomerang, but were retrieved on foot.   C—$125

Oregon **Atl-atl,** 16¾ in. long and recovered from a dry cave. One end is thicker for handgrip, opposite end has antler or ivory hook for lance-butt and a shallow groove for the shaft connects the two. Pale evidence of paint remains. Piece is in fair condition. Rare.
                                                    C—$365

Wood **digging stick,** Montana, 39 in. long and with lower end heavier and sharpened to a point. It may have been fire-hardened. Bark peeled from entire length; used for grubbing out roots.
                                                    C—$27

Section of arrowshaft, 9 in. long, and a portion somewhere between missing front and back. Flint tools used for shaft smoothing, and marks still show on surface.   C—$25

HISTORIC WOOD ITEMS

Central California **cradleboard,** full size, and decorated with sun shade with yarn ties.   G—$355

Papago **carved wood club,** potato-masher type, and 1800's. D—$65

Carved wood Northwest Coast **Salish-shaker power stick,** with deer toes and cover. This piece was made when the Shaker church was influential in the area.   A—$1200

Ree Indian **wood-handled crooked knife,** 8¼ in. long, from a site in northern South Dakota. Handle has a small knife blade set at lower end, with working edge 1-3/8 in. long. Not a common item, and old.
                                                    C—$145

Cedar **canoe baler**, Northwest Coastal group.   A—$30

Late historic Chippewa **wooden food container** or trencher, old and unusual. Rectangular, 5 in. deep, 13¼ in. long and 7 in. wide. Carved from hardwood, possibly maple. Wood sides and bottom average 5/8 in. thick, with some small age-cracks at ends. Smaller ends have a thickened projection to serve as handles.   C—$355

Plains Indian **dance wand,** 19½ in. long, wood; top has tied feathers, base is hide-wrapped. Appears very old.   D—$130

Sioux cane or **dance stick,** a natural wood formation carved and painted in the shape of a smiling snake. Colorful and a primitive art piece of exceptional note.   G—$435

Cherokee **stick-ball racket,** 27 in. long, wood with rawhide lace.
          G—$55

Haida (NW Coast) **foot trencher,** rectangular form, 15 in. long, 9½ in. wide. Ends up-curved, sides down-curved, and piece well-made of spruce (?) wood. Exterior once painted; an old item.   C—$935

Northwest Coast **spoon,** Kwakuitl, 14 in. long, curved wood.
          A—$75

Canoe paddle, possibly middle-1800's, Eastern Woodlands group. All wood, with even, flowing lines, well-carved. Upper handle region has some light incising in a simple pattern. Fine condition and not a common piece.   C—$450

Navajo wood **battan weaving tool,** ca. 1880.   D—$25

Lacross stick, probably Canadian Indian, just over 35 in. long. Hitting end has a laced rawhide flattish cup, handle end has thong-wrapped section for non-slip use. Excellent condition.   C—$180

Sioux **beamer** or hide-scraping tool, 14½ in. long. It has a two-handed wood handle with metal blade insert. Wood is beautifully grained.   G—$120

Central California **cradleboard,** full-size, with yarn decorated design on the sun shade. Piece has doeskin straps.   G—$235

Ball-headed wood club, Woodland region, from Great Lakes area. It is carved from a single piece of wood, possibly oak burl, and is 22½ in. long. Plain, business-like piece.   C—$755

Eastern Sioux **fertility wooden statue,** 14 in. high. Good condition and rare; piece could be older than ca. 1900.   G—$1550

Sioux cradleboard, original wood frame and 24 in. long. Leather over wood, with beadwork designs.   C—$550

Ball-headed war club, turn of the Century period; head has stone inset. Cross-hatching decoration on the handle, and good condition.   G—$785

Pair of rather plain **wood stirrups,** both with portions of original rawhide fastenings at top. Northern Plains region, simply carved, nicely matched.   C—$195

Plains style **fleshing tool,** with metal blade edge; from Taos Pueblo and probably from the 1800's.   D—$65

Wooden bowl, made from hardwood log, 7 in. wide and 20½ in. long. Good condition. Undecorated.   C—$235

Blackfoot **fleshing tool,** wooden handle with sinew-wrapped metal blade, unusual shape to handle. Piece is 15 in. long.   G—$125

Wood **stirring spoon,** California, 14 in. long, with well-carved handle. Early historic and from one of the interior desert groups.   C—$100

Sioux, **willow back rest,** zone-painted, with incised tripod legs.   G—$625

Sioux **fleshing tool,** wood with metal side blade, ca. 1850.   D—$65

Ball-type wooden club, 20 in. long, with diameter of ball 4¼ in. May be Chippewa, but uncertain. Some incised lines on handle; and old and good piece.   D—$565

Wood and leather **cradleboard,** 21 in. high, and a basic wood-slat frame. Whole is somewhat deteriorated due to lack of attention in the past; a late 1800's item, and some beadwork remaining on leather portions, which is brittle.   C—$310

Four **Northwest Coast carvings:** Rattle, Adz, Potlatch bowl, and Shaman's spirit bent-box with lid. All are finely carved.   C—$1000, the four

RECENT WOOD ITEMS (1900-1970)

Canadian Indian **meat drying rack,** unusual item. It consist of 8 peeled-bark wands secured to 3 crosspieces; the former are 40 in. long, the latter about 35 in. and thicker. Collected years ago North of Lake Erie and probably early 1900's. May have been used to dry or smoke freshwater fish. C—$95

Northwest Coast **wood totem,** Raven effigy, old. D—$80

Northwest Coast **war club.** A—$80

Tlinget (NW Coast) **paddle-spoon,** shaped like a miniature dugout canoe paddle, and 14½ in. long. (The more ornate forms were undoubtedly reserved for special occasions. Paddle-spoons were used to eat a Northwest Coast delicacy called "sopalalli" or "soapberry", a mixture of berries and cold water frothed with oil from the olachen or candlefish). Very good condition; relief carving on straight wide lower portion may represent a mountain goat. C—$285

Wooden bow, 46½ in. long, narrowed and thicker at center. Believed to be from Plateau area, perfect, painted in faint black and red designs. This Century, early, probably pre-tourist times. Well done piece. C—$175

Left: MIDE WATER DRUM WITH BEATER STICK, drum 8 in. wide and 10 in. high, made from an old wooden keg. Ends are hide-covered and painted with symbolic figures; hole is for adding water. Collected in Minnesota, ca. 1910. Drum with bent drumstick. C—$325

Center: BIRCH BARK RATTLE WITH STICK HANDLE, 5 in. in diameter with 10 in. handle. A ceremonial piece, but undecorated. Collected in Minnesota, ca. 1910. C—$165

Right: CARVED WOODEN SPOON, 5 in. in diameter, with a 5 in. handle. Carved handle in the shape of three hearts with bird head on end; piece was collected at Crawling Stone Lake, northern Wisconsin, ca. 1915-20. C—$165

Photo courtesy Bill Post Collection.

WOODEN KWAKIUTL PORTRAIT MASK, Northwest Coast carving, 9 in. high. This is a recent piece, and face is painted in black and red. Made by Calvin Hunt, ca. 1965. C—$225-$250
Photo courtesy R. M. Weatherford, Columbus, Ohio.

Northwest Coast **paddle-spoon,** undecorated, 13¾ in. long. Fair condition with cracking. C—$95

Northwest Coast **miniature canoe,** a copy of the high-prowed sea-going dugouts; piece is 3¾ in. wide and 19 in. long. Well-constructed of thin wood strips and held together with sinew through small holes. C—$235

Paiute **cradle board,** made of wicker and covered with partially beaded hide. Large and well-designed; some wicker missing. Made in the 1930's or 40's. G—$550

Wooden **Iroquois mask,** False-Face society, about life-size or larger and with long horsetail hair. Shell eyes, red feathers and with black details. Not older than 1900; may be considerably later. C—$435

IROQUOIS FETISH BOX, two views. Piece is 6½ in. high and 10 in. long, from Wayne County, New York. From historic times, this is a very old piece and very rare. While other Indian groups had fetish containers, it is quite unusual for one to be found in a collection or at auction. The rectangular hole in one side was used for ceremonial feeding of the fetishes within. Item has been authenticated by the curator of a major museum in New Mexico.

C — Museum quality; no value listed.

William Sosa photo; Marguerite Kernaghan Collection.

Dance wand, Plains Indian, about 16 in. long. Knob head end has false scalp-lock of long hair, possibly bison beard, and with faded painted lines along shaft. Unusual.

C—$155

Chippewa **maple sugar spoon.**

A—$25

Pair of Northwest Coast **carved miniature paddles,** 18 in. long. They have good stylized carving and are ca. 1930.

G—$165

Iroquois **wooden mask,** about 12 in. high and with exaggerated and twisted features. Ca. 1900.

C—$495

Eastern Woodlands Indian **lidded birchbark sugar box,** probably used for maple sugar storage. It is 9¼ in. by 11 in. and 7 in. high. Ca. 1930's.

C—$100

Plains Indian **wooden-frame loom,** late period, probably for weaving of sashes. Piece is about 1½ ft. long, and 5 in. wide, with some original thread ties remaining.

C—$125

Northwest Coast **raven rattle,** 14 in. long by 4½ in. in diameter. Piece is ca. 1930.

G—$1550

CHIPPEWA COURTING FLUTE, 1½ in. in diameter and 15 in. long. This is a courting object and has double chamber, carved bird head on end, and traced of red and green paint. Decorated with old hide and fringe; piece is 1890.

C—$325

Photo courtesy Bill Post Collection.

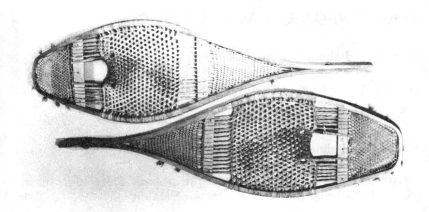

SNOWSHOES, 22 in. long; hardwood frames laced with sinew or hide, with tufts of red yarn around the frame. Ojibwa (?), and ca. 1880.   *G—$400*
Photo courtesy Kenneth R. Canfield, Plains Indian Art, Kansas City, Missouri.

THREADING SNOWSHOES, Mackenzie River, North West Territories, ca. 1920's.
Photo courtesy National Photography Collection, Neg. # C-38174, Public Archives of Canada.

CONTEMPORARY WOOD ITEMS

Navajo **cradleboard,** 36 in. long. G—$85

Northwest Coast **carved halibut hook,** done by Tsungani. A—$125

Signed Northwest Coast **wood houseboard.** A—$70

Apache **cradleboard,** 36 in. long. G—$140

Northwest Coast **carved paddle,** 15½ in. long. Piece has painted killer-whale design, signed, John Bennall, Haida. G—$95

CHAPTER XVI
KACHINAS, DOLLS, TOYS, AND MUSICAL ITEMS

Hopi Kachinas are difficult to explain easily, for they are much more than doll-like forms. Kachinas depict Kachina dancers, which in turn represent spirits and forces important to the traditional and modern Hopi lifeway. Even inanimate objects may have such powers.

The Kachina dolls — and there are about 300 different characters that appear regularly and some 200 that appear occasionally — served to instruct Hopi children. Often superbly carved from cottonwood, Kachinas of the late 1880's and early 1900's soon became collector items.

Eventually original supplies were depleted, but demand continued and a new collecting field developed. Today no assemblage of Southwestern Indian works is considered representative without a Kachina or two.

Kachina figures vary in size from a few inches to several feet. Value factors include size and material, with hand-carved wood — some with moveable arms and legs — a favorite. Modern copies are made by non-Indians in plaster and plastic and ceramics. For Indian made Kachinas, the skill of the maker counts for a great deal, and usually the more handwork the higher the value. Beyond the basic figure, Kachinas may be painted, and clothed and wear various ornaments, carry different symbols.

Two important sub-areas for collecting are the old, pre-tourist Kachinas and those made by well-known contemporary Indian artists. The best way to get a good Kachina at a good price is to know your source.

WARRIOR KACHINA or Ewiro Kachina (Hopi name), 22 in. high and width front to back 12½ on.
Unsigned.   G—$575
Photo courtesy William Scoble, The Ansel Adams Gallery, Yosemite National Park, California.

KACHINAS

Kachina doll, 9 in. high and ca. 1940's.   G—$100

Hopi "Owl" Kachina, 7 in. high.   G—$80

"Hummingbird" Kachina, 8½ in. high and ca. 1940's.   G—$220

Two old Kachinas, ca. 1920, sold as one lot.   A—$95

Hopi "Ogre" Kachina, 7 in. high.   G—$85

Kachina doll, 16 in. high, in the form of a wolf with bow and arrow,
in "Strongbow" form. Made by Fred Kubota; well-painted.

G—$275

Kachina doll, 8 in. high, and ca. 1940's.   G—$95

Kachina doll, 9½ in. high, ca. 1940's.   G—$110

Hopi "Mouse Warrior" Kachina, 14 in. high and well carved. Signed "N. Seltewa".   G—$265

Kachina doll, 7 in. high and ca. 1940's.   G—$95

"Mana" Kachina doll, 9 in. high and ca. 1940's.   G—$110

"Mud-head" Kachinas, set of four on a base.   A—$125

"Mouse Warrier" Kachina, 8 in. high and signed, "S. Jackson".   G—$105

"Black Ogre" KACHINA, excellent condition, Hopi Indian, from northeast Arizona. Figure is 29 in. tall, craftsman unknown, ca. 1965.   *G—$825*

Photo courtesy W. J. Crawford, The Americana Galleries, Phoenix, Arizona.

WHITE BUFFALO DANCER, 21½ in. high 12½ in. wide. Hopi piece, from the Gallup area, and done by Larry Hobbs.   *G—$800*

Photo courtesy William Scoble, The Ansel Adams Gallery, Yosemite National Park, California.

NON-KACHINA DOLLS

"Koshare" doll, with figure holding baby. Piece is 15 in. high and signed, "Regina Naha".   G—$335

Cochiti "Storyteller" doll, with nine babies. Doll is 8 in. high and ca. 1960.   G—$415

Iemez "Storyteller" doll, and six babies. Piece is 7 in. high, and signed, "Toledo".   G—$195

For fine contemporary Kachinas and non-Kachina dolls, a prime source is the Hopi Arts and Crafts Guild, Second Mesa, Arizona. Here is a sampling of items and prices.

Flat Kachinas dolls, 8 in. high.   List — $30

Non-Kachinas, like Koshare and the Buffalo Dancer:
    9 in. high   List—$110
    12 in. high   List—$85-350

Non-action Kachinas (other sizes available)
    7 in. high   List—$45-55
    11 in. high   List—$135

Action Kachinas (other sizes available)
    8 in high   List—$25-75
    12 in. high   List—$50-235
    16 in. high   List—$70-320
    20 in. high   List—$95-525

INDIAN DOLLS

Indian doll, 13 in. high and from Western U.S., dressed in fringed moccasins, leather skirt. Wood face, non-moveable arms and legs, good condition. Ca. 1930's.   D—$125

Contemporary **Navajo dolls,** pair, man 8 in. high and woman 7½ in. high. Modern items done by Navajos and dressed in authentic costumes; all handmade.   G—$24 each

Old **Indian doll,** 11 in. high, with beaded hair. Face made of old paper or corn husk; figure wrapped in part of an old blanket.
    G—$195

Doll moccasins, fully beaded and just over 1 in. long. Pair.   C—$40

Old Pacific Plateau **beaded doll.**   A—$45

Navajo doll, probably Indian child's "companion", depicting woman in ceremonial dress. Doll is 10½ in. high and ca. 1910.

C—$145

Sioux pair of **man and woman dolls,** matched set 11 in. high. The dolls have human hair and are ca. 1900.   C—$575

Plains Indian doll, 9 in. high and with wood base. This was made for the old tourist trade; hide face with yarn hair and hide dress that is nicely beaded. Piece has partially beaded cradle on back, with child.

G—$55

Apache gun-dance dolls, averaging 10 in. high. The set of five is hand-carved.

G—$385

Commanche beaded doll with Plains bonnet and ca. 1880-90.

D—$65

Doll moccasins, pair of Sioux fully beaded items, old and of good quality.

G—$95

Snohomish **basketry dolls,** man and woman, both 8 in. high.

A—$110

Child's play or **toy cradleboard,** late 1800's, and 11 in. high. Leather, partially beaded on wood frame. Good condition and rather scarce item.

C—$230

Miniature cradleboard with doll, 14 in. long and 5½ in. wide. Of old tan buckskin, piece has a fully beaded top section 5 in. wide and 6 in. long.

G—$375

Sioux **pair of buckskin dolls,** both 11 in. high. Female has buckskin face and male has black face made of dried apple. Clothing has beaded decorations; good condition, and ca. 1920.   G—$285

Doll, Canadian Indian made, contemporary, carved from wood with a thin leather dress. Painted features, and 9 in. high.   C—$55

Iroquois corn husk doll, 8 in. high and 3½ in. wide. From false face society; good early tourist piece and with some beadwork; well-carved on a wood base.

G—$85

INDIAN DOLL, about 24 in. in height. It was hand made by Kay Bennett, whose Indian name is Kaibah, and she is a full-blooded Navajo Indian. Simulated turquoise nuggets and jocula are around the doll's neck, and dress and top are velvet. Silver style conchas are on the belt. Excellent workstyle and condition. Doll was made arount 1973.   G—$250-$350

Courtesy Hugo Poisson, photographer; Edmunds of Yarmouth, Inc: West Yarmouth, Massachusetts.

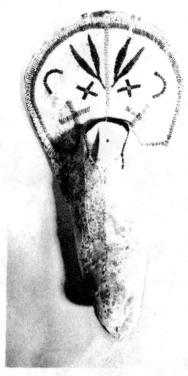

DOLL AND CRADLE, 20 in. long. Child's doll in buckskin-covered Plateau-style cradle. Doll has cloth body and human hair with large blue tradebeads for eyes. Cradle beaded in multicolored geometric designs, with extensive use of faceted metallic beads. Plateau region, ca. 1885.

G—$550

Photo courtesy Kenneth R. Canfield, Plains Indian Art, Kansas City, Missouri.

Seneca doll, collected in Eastern Canada, and probably from the 1940's. Corn husk body with thin cotton dress stained brown. Piece is about 10 in. high. C—$45

Sioux child's tipi, old, with pictograph drawings and tin cone dangles. Much faded and shows considerable age; completely assembled with poles. G—$300

Fraser River **miniature cradle,** 5½ in. by 13 in. A—$125

Carved doll in cradle, item 18 in. high and 7½ in. wide. Cradleboard in authentic style; doll has well-carved wood face. Done by LaLooska. G—$375

TOYS AND GAMES

Kiowa toy cradle with slat, 15 in. high. Made up of stained hide and partial beading.   C—$545

Beaded buckskin **toy tipi,** Santee Sioux, an old item and in good condition.   G—$465

Miniature travois, 17 in. long, Plains Indian and old. Two poles and small hide platform; unusual item.   C—$95

Miniature Hupa cradle, 3¾ in. by 8½ in.   A—$25

Miniature cardlel, Paiute style, 14 in. long and 5 in. wide. Has wicker base, covered with hide and partially beaded. Piece is ca. 1930.   G—$65

Child's toy travois, Sioux, in very fine condition.   G—$100

Two **miniature Hupa cradles,** sold as one lot.   A—$40

MUSICAL ITEMS—DRUMS

Drum, double-headed, painted with buffalo and eagle; a Pueblo piece and ca. 1890.   D—$220

Plains-type drum, 14 in. in diameter, made of hide stretched on wood. Painted figure on hide. Old.   G—$225

Cree single-head drum, painted head, ca. 1920.   D—$100

Drum, California Indian type, 6 in. high and 7 in. in diameter. Hide stretched over wood, both ends covered and wood is painted. Good condition.   G—$125

Sioux drum, done on square box and 14 in. square. Painted with deer on one side and star on the other; stretched hide covers ends. Good sound and comes with early beater.   G—$145

Sioux drum, rawhide covered and laced wood drum, painted designs on ends, with beater.   G—$175

Sioux hoop drum, 13 in. in diameter, hide covered single face, and piece has some age.   D—$100

Tourist-type drum, 10 in. in diameter, hide stretched over wood frame. Figure painted on hide, trimmed with feathers, and ca. 1940's.   G—$95

Indian drum, 11½ in. in diameter, some age.   A—$35

Sioux hand-held drum, wood hoop type and hide covered. Drum is 11 in. in diameter.   G—$65

Plains-type drum, 16 in. in diameter and 3 in. thick, with beater. Hide stretched on wooden hoop; no design but pleasing tone.
                                                               G—$125

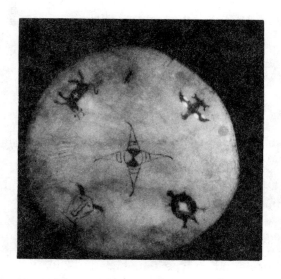

Cree Indian HAND DRUM, 16 in. in diameter. It has a very old hand-hewn wooden frame, and with painted zoomorphic designs on drumhead. Leather has a very small slit; a more modern drum-beater is included.   *D—$195*
Photo courtesy Crazy Crow Trading Post, Denison, Texas.

Left, larger CEREMONIAL RATTLE, companion piece to item on right. It is 5 in. in diameter with overall length 15 in. Pictured on rattle face is the Mide-related supernatural character Misshipeshu, otherwise known as the Underwater Panther with a supernatural bird. Ca. 1895. *C—$235*

Photo courtesy Bill Post Collection.

Right, small CEREMONIAL RATTLE, Midewiwin Grand Medicine Society, Chippewa (Ojibway), 4 in. in diameter and 14 in. long. From Leech Lake, Minnesota; 5 small green turtles on rattle face and edged in red color. All hide including sinew-sewn handle. Ca. 1895.

C—$235

RATTLES

Hopi gourd rattle, painted black on white and with swastika symbol. D—$85

Peyote gourd rattle, recent, with red, white and blue beadwork; ebony handle has a buckskin figure. D—$65

Medicine rattle, type sold by Northern Cheyenne Indians in Montana. Has a small leather ball on the end with horsehair; handle wrapped in rawhide. Made by Marion King. G—$28

Plains rattle, 10 in. long and 3½ in. wide, and done with hide that has been made into the entire rattle. Has some light green painted design; 19th Century. G—$140

Medicine rattle, Southwest type, a black leather hoop 4½ in. in diameter, with attached handle. Authentic. G—$95

311

Commanche rawhide rattle with horsetail decoration. Ca. 1890.

D—$80

Elk hoof rattle, part of medicine bundle, extra-fine condition.

G—$195

Bird-bone rasp, 9 in. long, from New Mexico.   D—$50

Peyote fan, Peyote style with gourd rattle. Seed bead design on wooden handle. Dyed hair on one end and woven leather fringe on the other.   G—$225

Plains Indian "bullroarer", a 9¾ in. flattened section of wood with hole in smaller end. Item was whirled around the user on a cord, making a humming roar. Painted, but faded.   C—$40

FLUTES & WHISTLES

Sioux love flute, 21 in. long, well carved and decorated, in good condition. Ca. 1920.   G—$120

Small **Sioux flute,** sinew wrapped.   G—$110

Bone flute, Plains Indian.   A—$90

Sioux Grass Dance whistle, fine early piece with carved openmouthed bird head.   G—$240

Mogollon bird-whistle, red pottery, New Mexico.   D—$50

CHAPTER XVII
WEAVINGS: BLANKETS
AND RUGS

American Indian weavings are probably the warmest-looking and most useful of Amerind contemporary arts and crafts to live with. You can look at them, walk on them, sleep under them. Most of the older blankets are quite valuable as collector items, but modern rugs of good quality can be obtained at reasonable prices.

Weaving in North America has ranged from Northwest Coast spruce root mats to Plains robes made of rabbitskin strips. Today, the Navajo weavings are best known. They are certainly one of the Big Four of contemporary Amerind collectibles: Baskets, Blankets & Rugs, Jewelry and Pottery.

For the record, Pueblo blankets were made for centuries, but the Hopi Indians (here, the men often weave) now do most of the work. The Navajo Indians used natural cotton but then began to raise sheep for the wool.

The wool is chipped, cleaned and carded before it is spun on a whirling, handheld wooden spindle. Weft thread may be spun twice, while warp thread, which must be tight and strong, may be spun three times. If the wool is to be dyed, this step takes place; the dry wool is then rolled into balls, ready for the weaver.

The Navajo woman, the weaver, generally dyes only enough wool for the intended rug. This is for economy, but also so that any one dye color will match in the same rug and not be a different shade. Rugs, and the blankets before them, are woven on an upright loom which the Navajos may have developed and refined themselves. The warp threads (except for some historic Chief's blankets, where it is opposite) run up and down on the loom, or the length of the rug when it is completed.

Warp yarn is important, and experts say a wool warp is generally better than a cotton warp. It is more durable, making an all-wool rug, and the two age nicely together.

The weft threads run horizontally on the verticle loom, or the width of the finished rug. These are the design elements, formed by different weft colors. Any pattern will then be formed by the weft yarn. Without getting into a discussion of the actual weaving and tools used, it is enough to say that a good rug takes many hundred hours to make, and considerable degrees of experience of skill.

There are three colors of wool that might be in any one rug or late blanket, and they are sometimes combined to form different colors in the same rug.

1. **Natural:** Whitish, brown, gray and reddish black. Blackish wool is often dyed to make a solid black.
2. **Vegetal:** Dyed wool, the dye made from plant stems, roots, bark, etc. There are currently some 135 slightly different vegetal-dye colors. The best of these rugs are said to come from the Klagetoh region.
3. **Commercial:** (synthetic) Called "aniline" dyes, these were widely used in the last quarter of the 1800's and are still popular today.

Here are some of the historic Navajo blanket types, mostly from the 1850-1900 period. It is good to understand that these blankets were made for the Navajo's own wearing use and for trade.

The Chief's blanket was "exported" to other tribes and were so well-made that only an important person was said to be able to afford them. The best Navajo blankets — especially the complex double-faced blanket with different patterns on both sides using two distinct wefts — could hold water for awhile without seepage.

Shoulder blankets—ca. 1850 and later, men and women's sizes, simple stripes.

Striped blankets—Wearing blankets common among the Navajos until 1900's.

Banded blankets—"Fancier" striped varieties with additional designs between stripes.

Chief's blankets—Three varieties or "Phases" recognized, ca. 1850-1895.

1st Phase: Stripes of blackish color, red, white and blue

2nd Phase: Some red stripes divided into blocks; some blocks no longer joined by red. Greens sometimes used; deisgns within blocks

3rd Phase: Some stripes have large diamond patterns, with the diamonds on the corners, the four sides, plus one in the center, nine in all. Multi-colored. Diamonds later became larger square crosses in some cases. Original 1st Phase stripes now only a small part of background.

Serape/Poncho-style blankets—Early and late periods, ca. 1860's-1880's. Diamond patterns, natural dyes. Some had a slit woven at center to go over the head.

Eye-Dazzler blankets—Ca. 1880-1910. Aniline or commercial dyes used. Blankets had a multitude of designs, especially zigzag lines and smaller, "busy" patterns. Examples had as many as nine different colors.

Other important blankets include **pictorial, wedge-weave, child's blankets,** and the smaller **saddle throws. Bayeta blankets** were woven, when flannel-like red English blankets were unraveled and the yarn used in Navajo blankets. The period ca. 1850-1870 is considered to be the Classic Period, the golden age of Navajo blankets.

The last major Navajo blanket made a genuine break from the past. It is the **transitional blanket,** made in many eccentric patterns, some very well done. Ca. 1885-1900, some resembled earlier forms, others reverted to natural and vegetal colors. One significance is that these weavings are the last of the Navajo blankets before the changeover to rugs.

Before the turn of this century, quality White-made machine-woven blankets faltered and the White Indian traders decided to try something different.

With the completion of the railroads and many Eastern travelers in Navajo lands, a new demand arose for blankets. But it was for blankets used as rugs and tapestries, or floor coverings and wall hangings.

The Indians were encouraged to weave with heavier yarns, and in new sizes with new designs. Except for experiences like the "pound" rungs — when traders bought weavings according to weight, not quality — the enterprises have been highly successful.

Today, there are a dozen or so major Navajo weaving areas, each of which produces distinctive rug styles. The early blankets are commonly classed according to pattern. Today's rugs, except for the Yei rug or blanket and pictorials were named after the regions where they have been for many years. But there has been so much departure from traditional and blending of patterns that these identify more rug style than a place style.

Here are some of the better-known contemporary Navajo blanket types.

Burntwater—Central panel in geometric style and a broad geometric border. Vegetal dyes.

Crystal—Simple and elegant patterns, vegetal dyes; these rugs have a certain "modern" look that is quite pleasing.

Ganado—Four-colored rugs; two natural (white, gray) and two aniline (red and enhanced black) colors are used.

Pictorial—Rugs woven with patterns of identifiable objects, people, animals, plants, feathers, etc.

Pine Springs—Designs are similar to Wide Ruins, but more vivid and with constrasting colors; earth tones.

Storm pattern—Symbolic dark geometric forms at the four corners, separated by broad white lightening designs.

Teec Nos Pos—Geometric designs in multi-colored shades, boldly outlined. Aniline dyes.

Two Grey Hills—Geometric basic designs, natural wools used; they are combined, also, to produce buff and gray.

Wide Ruins—Patterns closely follow those of late-Classic wearing blankets; horizontal bands, geometric designs with some bands.

Yei weavings—Yei figures copied from scared sand-paintings (part of healing ceremonies). Light in weight compared with other contemporary rugs. These are often hung.

OLDER BLANKETS

Navajo saddle blanket, 3 ft. 5 in. by 5 ft. 11 in., diamond patterns in red, natural-wool tufts as fringes. Several small burn holes in this specimen. D—$400

Wearing blanket, 4 ft. 10 in. by 6 ft. 4 in., diagonal cut line. Homespun yarns, vegetal dye, good condition. Blanket is ca. 1885. G—$1400

Serape-style blanket, Navajo, commercial (aniline) dyes, 4 ft. 3 in. by 6 ft. 1 in. Blanket made in four colors, in extra-good condition. Ca. 1880's. C—$1995

Eye-dazzler blanket, size unknown, cotton warp. Large blanket with damage that is repairable. Ca. 1890. G—$675

Serape-style blanket, 6 ft. 3 in. by 4 ft. 3 in., striped designs. Condition fair, with normal wear that shows. Late 1800's. C—$1275

Transitional blanket, 50½ in. by 63½ in. A—$95

PUEBLO PATTERN WOMAN'S DRESS, Navajo women, in excellent condition. Colors are red, gray and black. Dress is 27½ in. by 48½ in.; ca. 1900. C—$700
Photo courtesy Rob Swan Townshende, California.

CHILD'S BLANKET of Merino sheep wool, which is like Angora. Rare, and condition excellent. Blanket, red, gray, white and black, is 30 in. by 50½ in. Ca. 1875-90. C—$1300
Photo courtesy Rob Swan Townshende, California.

Classic *DIAMOND PATTERN CHIEF'S BLANKET, in colors black, buff, red and white. In excellent condition, blanket is 49 in. by 64 in., and is ca. 1880-95.* C—$1950

Photo courtesy Rob Swan Townshende, California.

Early *COARSE-WEAVE CHILD'S BLANKET, 36 in. by 59½ in., and in colors black, brown, buff and white. There is minor fraying; ca. 1890-1900.* C—$495

Photo courtesy Rob Swan Townshende, California.

Navajo blanket with red and rust designs, fawn-colored background. Minor moth damage; piece is 3 ft. 1 in. by 5 ft. 7 in.

C—$495

Transitional blanket, 4 ft. 6 in. by 7 ft. Design is serrated diamond showing heavy wear. Piece is ca. 1890.

G—$885

Navajo blanket, handspun wool with commercial dyes. Size is 5 ft. by 6 ft. 5 in. Excellent condition as blanket was stored for years.Wedge-weave pattern.

C—$1295

Zuni blanket, man's shawl style, 3 ft. 8 in. by 7 ft. 1 in. Multi-colored vegetal dyes; woven by men only, a rare piece in good condition. Blanket is pre-1920.

G—$2950

DIAMOND PATTERN BLANKET, medium-coarse weave, in colors red, white, black and gray. Excellent condition, and ca. 1895-1910.   *C—$600*

Photo courtesy Rob Swan Townshende, California.

Rare GERMANTOWN SERAPE-STYLE CHIMAYO BLANKET, in excellent condition. Colors are white, red, blue and yellow. Blanket measures 39½ in. by 74½ in., and is ca. 1875-90.   *C—$1250*

Photo courtesy Rob Swan Townshende, California.

Chimayo blanket measuring 4 ft. 4 in. by 6 ft. 10 in.   A—$210

Saddle blanket, Navajo, 2 ft. 3½ in. by 3 ft. 1 in. Small size, good condition.   A—$150

Indian **blanket fragment,** section cut from old handwoven blanket. Red background, black designs. Piece is 19 in. long, 13 in. wide, with edges sewn to keep from fraying. All four sides decorated with horsehair. Unusual piece, unknown work.   C—$80

Classis CHEVRON/TERRACE CHIEF'S BLANKET, black, orange, pink and gray. Has eye-dazzler center, and is very soft. Excellent condition, and 54½ in. by 77½ in. It is ca. 1875-85.   C—$2350

Photo courtesy Rob Swan Townshende, California.

SERAPE-STYLE WOMAN'S BLANKET, early coarse weave. Black-bordered orange stripes on a cream background. It is 43½ in. by 63½ in., in very good condition. About Bosque Redondo.   C—$1275

Photo courtesy Rob Swan Townshende, California.

Classic DIAMOND PATTERN BLANKET, in colors red diamonds in white background and white diamonds in red background, brown borders. Eye-dazzler patterns, and excellent condition. Blanket is 39½ in. by 81½ in. It is ca. 1885-90.   C—$1950

Photo courtesy Rob Swan Townshende, California.

TANSITIONAL DIAMOND PATTERN BLANKET, tight weave, in white orangeish, and brown. Fair condition, and 47 in. by 62 in. Ca. 1890-1900.   C—$770

Photo courtesy Rob Swan Townshende, California.

Indian on horseback, pulling crossed-stick travois with traveling bundle; photo taken in Montana, unknown date, prob. late 1800's.

Photographer Roland Reed; Courtesy Photography Collection, Suzzallo Library, University of Washington.

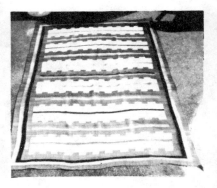

Navajo **saddle blanket,** 3 ft. 7 in. by 4 ft. 8 in., gray and black designs. Natural wool, fair condition.   D—$285

Navajo **serape blanket,** unknown size, but large. Zigzag alternate bands of white, blue, red, green and blue against red background. Small black crosses with white tips against red. Very attractive piece and ca. 1870. Offered NYC/NY.   G—$6500

RECENT AND CONTEMPORARY RUGS

Teec Nos Pos rug, 50 in. by 90 in. Pristine condition, vibrant colors, and a rare piece. Ca. 1920.   C—$4000

Navajo rug, diamond designs in many colors, 3½ ft. by about 6 ft., rust-red background with zigzag bands.   C—$875

Throw rug,. Gallup (?), 17 in. by 39 in. Patterns in black, gray and white, excellent condition.   G—$35

Pictorial rug, 48 in. by 66 in., and all natural wool colors. Weave is medium, and twenty feathers are woven into patterns. Item has a few minor stains and is about 1920's or 30's.   G—$575

Yei rug, 52 in. by 72 in. Pattern is five yeis surrounded by Rainbow God. Rug has "lazy lines" and comes with appraisal papers. Piece is about 50 years old.   C—$1350

Navajo rug, 43 in by 67 in., in good but worn condition.   C—$850

Navajo rug, moderated Klegetoh pattern, 5 ft by 7 ft. Contemporary, and medium weave.   G—$1225

Two Grey Hills rug, 30 in by 35 in. Standard pattern, colors in tan, brown, black, gray and white. Rug has a tight weave and intricate pattern.   G—$525

Navajo **Tree of Life tapestry weaving,** from Shiprock, New Mexico. This rug type copies sandpainting designs.   A—$650

Navajo rug, Yeibichai dancers and head man. Rug is superfine, and 4 ft. 8 in by 6 ft. Very tightly woven and in fine condition. Ca. early 1900.   G—$1950

Two Grey Hills rug, 39 in by 47 in. Colors gray, white, brown and black, and in good condition. Ca. 1950.   G—$810

Early **Navajo rug,** 33 in. by 58 in., with fine, tight weave. Good colors and designs; rug has slight stains on one side.   G—$245

Wide Ruins rug, tapestry weaving style, 33 in. by 39 in., all natural wools and vegetal dyes.   A—$165

Navajo Sandpainting rug, 48 in. by 51 in., with very fine weave and in excellent condition. Ca. 1950's.   G—$1300

Yei rug, 3 ft. by 5 ft., white background with five Yei figures. Good condition and ca. 1940.   C—$660

Early **Navajo rug,** small size, good weave.   A—$215

Germantown rug, 24 in. by 31 in. Red with multi-color Eye-Dazzler pattern. Fringe on bottom intact; excellent condition. Ca. 1900.
G—$545

Very old **Navajo rug,** 36 in. by 60 in. A high quality rug, but dirty and in need of repair. Poor condition.   G—$45

Navajo rug, 3 ft. by 5½ ft., double-diamond pattern with geometric border. Medium-good condition, ca. 1930. G—$275

Small **Germantown rug,** 22 in. square. pattern in green and white on red background. Nice condition and ca. 1900. G—$200

Yei rug, 35 in. by 53 in., multi-colored with brown background. Ca. 1950. G—$675

Pine Springs rug, 34 in. by 39½ in., natural wools and vegetal dyes. A—$85

Teec Nos Pos rug, 42 in. by 64 in. Deep red predominates, with black, gray, white and orange colors. Very good design and in excellent condition. Ca. 1910-20. G—$625

Two Grey Hills rug, 49 in. by 73 in., colors are gray, white and black. Good condition, and ca. 1910. G—$1000

Banded rug, 3 ft. 9 in. by 6 ft. 5 in., natural grays and whites, aniline reds and greens. Pattern may be derived from old wearing blankets. Contemporary. D—$875

Navajo rug, 31 in. by 56 in., vegetal dyed. Pattern is double-diamond with outlined design. Nice weave, and contemporary. G—$380

Tapestry rug, Sandpainting designs, 53 in. by 72 in., and multi-colored. Gray background, extremely fine weave, a rare piece. Ca. 1960. G—$5200

Navajo rug, 5 ft. wide and 7 ft. long, diamond pattern in gray, white, red and black. Good condition. G—$1100

Teec Nos Pos rug, 41 in. by 68 in., diamond pattern. Colors are red, black and gray and rug has a good, tight weave. Item is 40 to 50 years old. G—$825

Navajo rug, 58 in. by 83 in., very large and colorful with red and white swastikas. In good, sound usable condition. G—$675

Navajo rug, Klagetoh area, sunrise pattern with bows and arrows. Rug is 45 in. by 80½ in. A—$680

Ganado rug, 32 in. by 61 in., in good condition. Rug made by Daisy Mano, colors red, white and gray. Ca. 1920.   G—$560

Navajo rug, Klagetoh area, measuring 38 in. by 57 in.   A—$150

Navajo rug, small, 20 in. by 40 in. Natural wool colors in gray, black and tan. Nice condition.   G—$185

Storm pattern rug, 4 ft. by 6 ft., in excellent condition. Ca. 1940.   G—$950

Yei rug, 4½ ft. by 6½ ft., with colors beige, brown, orange, vegetal-red, rust and blue. There are five central figures surrounded by Rainbow figure. Rug is ca. 1910.   C—$1075

Two Grey Hills rug, measuring 40 in. by 70 in.   A—$625

Navajo rug, 2½ ft. by 5 ft. Pattern is double-diamonds with geometric border.   G—$175

Pine Springs rug, 30 in. by 56 in., colors tan, gray with white. Nice design and perfect condition. Made in 1976 by Florence James. Burnwater Post tag still attached.   G—$610

NAVAJO RUG, 24 in. by 46 in., in seven colors. From the Shiprock area, contemporary, and tagged.   *D—$185*

Photo courtesy of American Indian World, Ltd., Denver, Colorado.

YEI/YEBECHAI RUG, about 60 in. by 8 feet, plus. Tight weave, and very good condition: colors predominantly black, white, burnt-orange and red. Ca. 1920.   C—$1750

Photo courtesy of Bob Swan Townshende, California.

Eye-Dazzler rug, 43 in. by 64 in., natural wool colors and red aniline dye. Handspun wool, and ca. 1920.   C—$850

Mr. Al R. Packard does business as Packard's Indian Trading Company, of Santa Fe, New Mexico. He is a third generation Indian trader, in Santa Fe since 1929. The writer was referred to Mr. Packard as being one of the most knowledgeable persons in the country on the subject of American Indian weavings, old and new.

Mr. Packard kindly consented to offer six tips on buying a Navajo rug, with two additional observations. These involve esthetic values and where to buy. Used with permission.

A PERSON BUYING A NAVAJO RUG SHOULD LOOK FOR THE FOLLOWING:

1) *Symmetry:* Place the rug on a floor without any background design. This way one can tell whether the edges and design are straight or crooked. If there is not an unobstructed area to throw the rug on, then fold the rug in half (warp end to warp end) and see if the width at each end is close to the same.

If there is a two inch or more difference on a 6 foot long rug, then it will look crooked on the floor. Two inches would not matter on a twelve foot rug but even on inch would matter on a 3 foot rug.

2) *Stains:* Although nearly all Navajo rugs have identical designs on both sides, the buyer must be sure to examine both sides. Occasionally there will be a rust, grease, ink, coffee, urine, etc. stain on one side but won't show through. An unethical dealer or weaver would throw the rug down with the unstained side showing.

3) *Cotton vs. wool warp:* Since the warp in a Navajo rug is completely hidden the buyer must pull the weft apart to tell whether the warp is cotton or wool. Wool warp is preferred and generally only an expert can tell the difference. However, wool is never quite as white as cotton, and cotton warp really looks and is cotton string.

4) *Weft packing:* For a long lasting rug, be sure that the weft is packed tightly together.

5) *Weft thickness:* The finer the weft threads are spun the sharper the design will be. Also, the finer the weft the more expensive the rug.

6) *Design:* The "one of a kind" designs in Navajo rugs offer endless patterns and colors. Peoples tastes differ also, so choose a rug of your own liking.

Do not look for absolute perfection when buying a Navajo rug. Using a primitive loom combined with natural human error cannot result in a perfect product. This is what makes Navajo weaving a true work of art. Buy it for what it is and treat it and enjoy it as you would a painting on your wall.

Buy at a reliable store, preferably an Indian Arts and Crafts Association member. Mexican imitations are saturating the market and although they don't compare with a true Navajo rug they can fool the uninformed buyer.

(A. R. P.)

The following at-auction results have been used courtesy of Garth's Auctions, Inc., Stratford Road, Delaware Ohio. Five recent individual sales are covered.

INDIAN RUGS AT AUCTION

Indian rug, Wide Ruins style, 38 in. by 57 in. Subdued colors in gray, yellow, white and sand, in wide and narrow stripes. Center stripe has thunderbird, two stars and an arrow. A—$125

Indian rug, Yei style, 35 in. by 52 in. Yei figures on white background, with red, blue, yellow, orange, green and black colors. A—$265

Indian rug, 40 in. by 60 in. Finely woven, with heavy yarn; colors, gray, white, orange, scarlet and black. This is a Navajo piece. A—$325

Indian rug, 33½ in. by 56 in. Early Ganada style, with colors in black, gray, white and scarlet. A—$210

Indian rug, 45 in. by 70 in. Red and black border with gray ground. Animal and geometric figures alternate in white, brown and orange. End borders are frayed. A—$650

Indian rug, Two Grey Hills style, 5 ft. by 11 ft. 3 in. Colors, dark brown, gray and white. One end faded, and rug has several holes. Large for type. A—$225

Indian rug, 40½ in. by 62 in. Medium weight, dark brown, gray white and red. Cross designs in from edges, with large diamonds in center. A—$210

Indian rug, Yei style, 51½ by 77 in. Corn stalk central motif, with colors yellow, red, black, gray and white. Weather rug with "sugar"; minor wear to rug. A—$325

Indian rug, Chinle style, 57 in. by 61 in. Striped in tan, brown, white, brick red and wine red. Tagged; made in 1931. A—$100

Indian rug, Two Grey Hills style, 5 ft. 8 in. wide, 9 ft. 3 in. long. Designs near long sides of diamonds, with stepped pyramids on inner bands. Probably recent. A—$925

Indian rug, Four Corners area, colors in gray, white, tan and dark brown. Rug measures 50 in. by 77 in.   A—$295

Indian rug, Early Ganada style, 41 in by 66 in. Stepped pyramids around outer sides, "eye-dazzler" pattern toward center.

     A—$315

Indian rug, 40 in. by 58 in. White and gray colors with interlocking zigzags of orange, black, red and white. Rug ends are frayed.

     A—$125

Indian rug, 56 in. by 101 in. Tan background with white and dark brown border with a red zigzag; large crosses at each end. Item has two holes and urine stains.   A—$265

Suggested Reading

James, George Wharton, *Indian Blankets and Their Makers;* Dover Publications, Inc., New York NY 1974 (Reprint)

Kahlenberg, Mary H. and Berlant, Anthony, *The Navajo Blanket;* Praeger Publications, Inc., in association with the Los Angeles County Museum of Art, 1972

Amsden, Charles Avery, *Navajo Weaving;* Rio Grande Classic edition, Southwest Museum, Los Angeles, CA 1974

Arizona Highways magazine, July 1974 issue

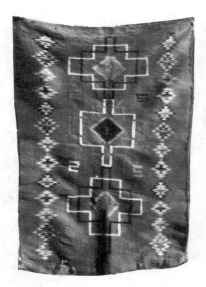

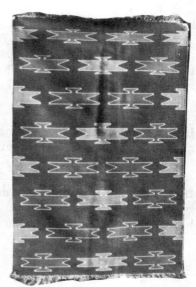

GERMANTOWN RUG OR BLANKET, black,
white blue and green designs on red ground.
In poor condition, ca. 1890.   C—$1200
Photo courtesy Jack Barry.

GERMANTOWN RUG OR BLANKET, blue
and green designs outlined in white against
red ground. Ca. 1890, good condition.
Photo courtesy Jack Barry.   C—$1850

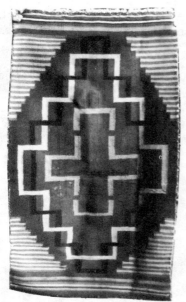

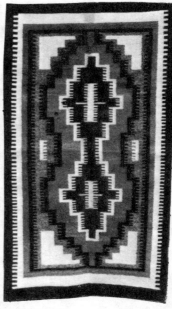

GERMANTOWN RUG OR BLANKET, green
striping, white, black and blue designs
against red ground. In good condition, ca.
1890.   C—$1450
Photo courtesy Jack Barry.

TWO GREY HILLS RUG, design in two shades
of brown plug grey, black and white, black
border. Ca. 1973.   C—$1050
Photo courtesy Jack Barry.

Left: YEI RUG, figures in white, buff and grey against rich brown ground, border in black. Ca. 1973.   C—$400

Photo courtesy Jack Barry.

Right: YEI RUG, figures in red, yellow, white and blue-grey against grey ground. Ca. 1973.   C—$425

Photo courtesy Jack Barry.

Left: RUG, natural & vegetal dyes, ca. 1973.   C—$450

Photo courtesy Jack Barry.

Right: PICTORIAL RUG, natural and vegetal colors, ca. 1973.   C—$575

Photo courtesy Jack Barry.

Cheyenne woman making tipi cover from bison hides. Meat is drying on racks in background. Photo probably early 1900's.

Photo courtesy South Dakota State Historical Society.

CHAPTER XVIII
SILVER AND
TURQUOISE JEWELRY

Probably no other category of contemporary Amerind art forms has so captured the attention of the general purchasing public as has jewelry. Silver and turquoise necklaces and bracelets and rings went for surprising sums in the early AD 1970's. Few buyers cared, or cared to check, whether the items were either well-made or authentic American Indian-made.

Behind the in-fashion publicity and money came the sharpsters. They proved, if nothing more, that Taiwan has some excellent crafts-people and that modern plastics can be made to resemble the shapes and colors of natural turquoise. More than one disenchanted buyer proudly called in an insurance agent to cover a $650 squash-blossom, and found that the acquisition was indeed a good item—at one twentieth the price.

A few years have passed and three major changes have occurred. Many of the offending merchandisers have gone out of business, and consumer-protection agencies have gained some clout. Collectors and buyers have become more street-wise, educated, in the ways and means of purchasing good items.

And the Amerind artisans have themselves come to understand that craft quality in design and manufacture provide both a livelihood and a continuation of buyer/collector demand. It is the general opinion of dealers in contemporary jewelry that very good pieces are still available at reasonable prices; in other words, the investment aspect has not been lost.

Following is information pertaining to a special class of older Indian jewelry known as "Old Pawn". The background story of Old Pawn is fascinating; this, and the description of Old Pawn pieces, along with prices, is courtesy Don C. Tanner's Indian Gallery, 7007—5th Avenue, Scottsdale, Arizona. Reprinted by permission.

OLD PAWN—THE REAL INDIAN JEWELRY

"Old Pawn", when correctly used in conjunction with Indian jewelry, means a piece made by an Indian craftsman, acquired, worn, treasured and finally pawned by an Indian and sold by the trader when it becomes "dead". The term "old pawn" has a romantic appeal. It represents native ideals, craftsmanship, tradition, and intrinsic worth.

The pawn system today is still used as it was back in the late 1800's. However, the number of traders has diminished markedly due to increased legislative controls and the use of the monetary system. The pawn system began with the Reservation traders and became an integral part of the Reservation economics. Since most business was transacted by barter and exchange, money per se meant very little. Silver coins could be hammered, melted and cast into jewlery that could be worn, exchanged, or used as collateral for a loan. Guns, saddles, blankets, buckskins, baskets, and robes could be pawned also, but jewelry was most common.

The Southwest Indians used the pawn system regularly, primarily as collateral for a loan to get them by between sheep shearing seasons, lamb crops, pay checks, etc. In addition they would pawn their jewelry in order to keep it safe when they didn't need it. It also served as the Indian's visible bank account, displaying his worth. During the summer months there were the ceremonials and to appear at their best they made every effort to redeem their pawn, even though custom allows the Indian to take out their ornaments without redeeming them, after which they were conscientiously returned.

The Indian's personal jewelry is generally of the best quality. However, some will try and pawn their least valuable jewelry first. The pawn dealers usually have their own set of standards of what they will or will not accept. The pawn dealers then gain a reputation among the Indians by which they know what they can or cannot pawn.

There are some characteristics of "old pawn" Indian jewelry that one can recognize and should be familiar with.

The early jewelry was made out of hammered coins or by casting. In the 1940's most silversmiths were using sheet silver which didn't have to be melted or hammered. The older pieces tend to be heavier and massive compared to the newer jewelry. Old jewelry that has been worn should have a patina or light to dark gray coloration caused by the skin acids, etc. This can be done chemically so again one must exercise caution in their selection.

Some bracelets were originally made as plain silver bands and then the stones were set afterwards. Wire bracelets were made by hammering the wire to the desired size. This can be seen by the different thicknesses and twists of the wire.

Old jewelry was made by designing the bezel to fit the stone. Newer jewelry is the opposite. Some stones were used first as earrings and pendants, then reset in bracelets or rings. Consequently, small holes can sometimes be seen in the reused stones.

The real "old pawn" is becoming a scarce item. However, it is still available in limited quantity through reliable dealers. We see "old pawn" jewelry as an intimate relic of a people and a culture which is slowly and inevitably disappearing into history. This fact alone makes legitimate "old pawn" jewelry valuable in today's market place.

Old Pawn (Courtesy Don C. Tanner's Indian Gallery, Scottsdale, AZ)

Old pawn necklace, with red coral cylindrical beads with small drilled and polished turquoise nuggets. Jaclas suspended, each of graduated-size turquoise beads and with five shell beads at bottom centers.   G—$975

Old pawn silver bracelet, with petitpoint turquoise settings. Eleven medium-size oval stones in center row; twenty-two teardrop smaller stones in two edge rows. Beaded silver designs on bracelet edges between settings.   G—$1400

Old pawn silver finger ring, set with six small turquoise stones, two rows of three each.   G—$85

Old pawn silver bracelet, sandcast and set with single large turquoise stone.   G—$125

Old pawn squash-blossom type necklace on double strand of large silver beads. Eight cluster-settings per side, each with seven turquoise stones. Large and elaborate naja has 47 individually set turquoise stones.
G—$1950

Old pawn necklace, highly polished red coral beads with a few flat turquoise drilled stones; jaclas attached, of graduated-size turquoise beads, with five white-shell beads at bottom centers.
G—$1550

Old pawn jaclas, (originally worn as earrings), with coral and turquoise beads. Red coral beads at top, graduated-size turquoise beads along strands, shell and coral beads at bottom centers.
G—$325

Old pawn all-turquoise necklace, long strand, with flat turquoise nuggets, small turquoise spacers.
G—$1200

Old pawn concha belt, large ovate conchas with butterfly spacers and conchas with single turquoise stone; large and well-made buckle.
G—$1900

Old pawn all-silver squash-blossom necklace, strand of large silver beads to which are attached 24 elongated "blossoms", 12 per side. Unusual and well-shaped sandcast naja.
G—$450

Old pawn necklace, made up of eight long strands of heishe-type beads, all pink coral with a few same-size beads of turquoise. Uniform diameters and highly polished.
G—$1350

Old pawn squash-blossom necklace, double strand of round silver beads, five turquoise clusters per side with "blossoms", each cluster containing 10 turquoise stones. Ornate naja has 41 individually set turquoise stones.
G—$1220

Old pawn necklace, consisting of small white shell beads and flat turquoise nuggets. Jaclas are of graduate-size turquoise beads, with a single red coral bead at both ends of each strand, four in all. Turquoise highly polished.
G—$650

The information that follows—Indian Silversmithing; Navajo, Zuni and Hopi Silverwork; Santo Domingo Beadwork—has been reprinted with the kind cooperation and permission of Mr. Armand Ortega, owner of the Indian Ruins Trading Post at Sanders, Arizona.

Armand Ortega is a well-known and respected Indian trader, the product of four generations of life among the Indians of the Southwest. His expertise in the field of native American arts and crafts stems from this life-long experience, during which he learned the intricacies of turquoise, became fluent in the Spanish and Navajo languages, and developed a deep understanding and respect for Indian culture.

INDIAN SILVERSMITHING

Silversmithing is a relatively recent Indian craft which began its development in the late 1850's. The Navajo, the first to engage in silversmithing, used the silver ornaments of the Spanish explorers as a basis for many of their designs. Conchas, originally from the bridles of Spanish horses, influenced the familiar concha belt. The squash blossom is an elongated version of the Spaniards' pomegranate ornament.

The Zunis began their silversmithing in the 1870's with most of the other Pueblos learning the art by 1890. Each tribe, influenced differently, developed its own special style. The Zunis worked initially as stone cutters and became well-known for their expertise and skill.

Much of the jewelry was originally made by the Indians for their own adornment, and the amount worn signified personal wealth. As the White traders close to the Indians began to see and appreciate the jewelry, they encouraged the craft and supplied turquoise, silver, and finer tools in order to refine the designs and increase quality. The Indians have never mined silver and only mined small quantities of turquoise. White traders today continue to supply them with the materials for their craft.

The first Indian jewelry marketing venture was initiated by the Fred Harvey Company in 1899, selling Indian jewelry on Santa Fe trains and at railroad station shops. Harvey provided silver and turquoise to the area trading posts and paid local silversmiths for finished work. This introductin of Indian jewelry to tourists from across the nation was a contributing factor in the popularity of handmade jewelry which has grown over the years.

With more silversmiths than ever improving designs and workmanship, it is easy to see how the once crude craft has developed into the art it is today.

Indian women in Nebraska jerking or preserving beef by drying in the sun. The meat was cut into thin, flat strips and hung over poles; sections were propped open with sticks so that no part would spoil.

Photo courtesy of John A. Anderson Collection, Nebraska State Historical Society.

NAVAJO SILVERWORK

The work of the Navajos is generally massive and simple in design. The Navajos are expert silversmiths and enhance their silver work with turquoise stones. Along with their silversmithing, the art of sandcasting silver was begun long ago by the Navajo tribe. Recently they have started overlay silver-work with the inlay of chips of turquoise and coral in contemporary designs.

ZUNI SILVERWORK

The emphasis of the stones rather than the silver characterizes Zuni craftsmanship. The Zunis are expert in cutting and setting stones in clusters, delicate needlepoint, and inlays of turquoise, coral, jet and shell. Setting and cutting stones was well-known to the Zunis long before they began working with silver.

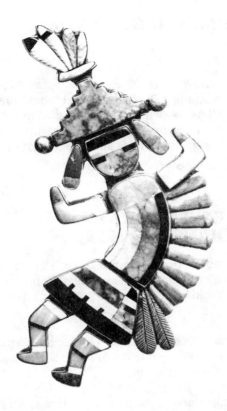

HOPI SILVERWORK

The overlay technique of the Hopi was developed in the 1930's. The Hopi had previously copied many of the Navajo and Zuni styles. With encouragement from the Museum of Northern Arizona, they developed their own overlay technique. Using many of their distinctive pottery designs, Hopi overlay is executed by cutting out a design in silver and attaching it to another layer of oxidized silver, allowing the design to stand out.

SANTO DOMINGO BEADWORK

Santo Domingo bead work is an ancient art which originally made use of handmade tools and original techniques. Turquoise and coral as well as assorted shells are used in their bead making. The material is drilled and the stones are then strung on cord and rolled or ground to the shape and size of bead strands desired.

OLD AND RECENT SILVER
AND TURQUOISE JEWELRY

Southwestern Indian **turquoise necklace,** 19½ in. long, consisting of raw stones and finished beads which alternate along the length. Blue turquoise, and very old piece, probably from early historic times.   C—$625

Single oblong **turquoise pendant,** 1½ in. long, drilled at smaller and thinner end. From a prehistoric Southwestern site, and accompanied by other bone artifacts.   C—$85

Navajo chunk necklace, 1900 or before. Jaclas attached, and with handmade heishi; all turquoise is a natural green. One sing attached. Rare piece; necklace has both age and quality.   G—$1650

Heavy Navajo man's old SILVER SQUASH BLOSSOM NECKLACE, made with U.S. and Canadian dimes. No sets; fastened. necklace is 15 in. long and Naja is 4 in. wide. Has abalone piece tied to top. Sandcast Naja. This is a pawn piece from Teec Nos Pos Trading Post, Navajo reservation and ca. 1915.   *C—$850*

S. W. Kernaghan photo; Marguerite Kernaghan Collection.

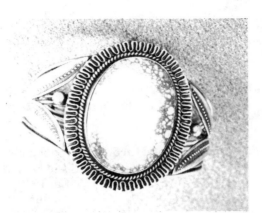

OLD NAVAJO SILVER AND TURQUOISE BRACELET, with circumference of bracelet 6¼ in. and stone measures 1¾ in. thick, 1¼ in. wide. A very fancy silver setting surrounds the turquoise, the stone along the edges give an appearance of being spotted, with dark blue and a lighter blue. At bottom of bracelet back are etched two words, "Joann" and Becent". Outstanding workstyle and in excellent condition, the piece is ca. 1920's. G—$875

Courtesy Hugo Poisson, photographer; Edmunds of Yarmouth, Inc: West Yarmouth, Massachusetts.

Navajo man's pawn belt, with six conchas, each 3 in. by 3½ in. Buckle and conchas set with turquoise; belt also has seven butterflies and is ca. 1930's. G—$1275

Silver necklace, Navajo, about 25 in. long, with beads hammered from old silver dimes. Central pendant of silver-mounted turquoise. Ca. 1950's. D—$625

Old Navajo bracelet, 2¼ in. at widest point. It contains 49 pieces of good turquoise set in silver; beautiful blue stone, excellent condition. G—$495

Sheet-silver bracelet, 1½ in. wide and set with turquoise nuggets. This is an old piece. G—$375

Tlingit **silver bracelet,** by Leo Jacobs of Haines. A—$115

Solid silver cockroach, 3 in. long and 2 in. wide. Item has eyes of inlayed turquoise, and is quite old and unusual. G—$95

Silver wrist **bowguard,** recent Zuni, stamped silver on leather. Large carved central plate, well done. D—$245

Pawn silver, **Navajo concha belt;** piece has five conchas, five butterflies and buckle. All inlayed with turquoise and with original leather backing; early period.   G—$850

Squash blossom necklace, Navajo, all silver with naja, and blossoms on each side. Necklace has a double row of beads, and is ca. 1950.   G—$375

Assorted Indian silverwork and turquoise: Concha belt,   C—$850
                                              Concha belt,   C—$450
                                              (Ca. 1940)
                                              Cluster bracelet,
                                                               C—$650

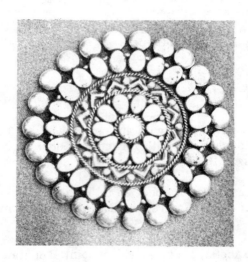

ZUNI CLUSTER PIN, measuring approximately 3 in. by 3 in. The turquoise stones are from the Lone Mountain mine; pin is signed on back in print, "Zuni" and in script, "Lee Mary". There are 23 tear-shaped stones on outer rim of the cluster, 10 on inner cluster, with one stone set in the center.

Lee Mary's work has been pictured in the Collectors Edition of ARIZONA HIGHWAYS and in several other Indian jewelry books. Workstyle is outstanding and pin is in excellent condition. Pin was made in the late 1950's.   G—$900

Courtesy Hugo Poisson, Photographer; Edmunds of Yarmouth, Inc: West Yarmouth, Massachusetts.

Navajo **Concha belt,** with six hand-stamped silver conchas on leather, with turquoise. Seven hand-stamped butterflies with single stones. Belt has multi-stoned buckle, and piece is ca. 1930.
                                                               G—$1600

Bolo tie fastener, Navajo, with pawn ticket attached. Fastener has two turquoise stones and is dated 1970.   G—$125

Sunburst cluster bracelet, Zuni, very nice piece and ca. 1940.
                                                        G—$650

Navajo concha belt, with eight hand-stamped conchas and buckle.
                                                        G—$1225

CONTEMPORARY JEWELRY

Silver necklace, contemporary Navajo, double beaded. Turquoise inlay of flying birds, crescent naja or pendant, also with chip inlay.
                                                        D—$675

Navajo pawn belt, woman's size, conchas 1½ in. in diameter. Buckle and conchas inlayed with turquoise; recent work.   G—$510

Concha belt, 32 in. in length, made of nine finely worked thin silver conchas and a rectangular belt buckle. No stones.   G—$335

Silver concha belt, made by Monroe Ashley, with thirteen conchas each 1½ in. by 2 in., plus buckle.   C—$400

Silver concha belt, disc-type conchas about 3 in. in diameter, with rectangular silver spacers. All with blue turquoise centers; contemporary Navajo.   D—$1200

Concha belt, made of nine sandcast silver conchas. Circular pieces, no stones, with belt buckle sandcast and in rectangular shape. Recent or contemporary item.   G—$335

Silver bracelet, narrow, turquoise chip inlay, contemporary Navajo.   D—$45

Silver bracelet, ¾ in. wide, handmade and contemporary Hopi Indian.   D—$135

Silver bracelet, contemporary Navajo, with turquoise chip inlays.
                                                        D—$85

Silver bracelet, rope-twist style, contemporary Navajo.   D—$39

Silver bracelet, wide, man's size, contemporary Navajo. Piece has turquoise chip inlay, traditional designs.   D—$165

Finger ring, handmade silver with two blue turquoise stones.   D—$48

Finger ring, 5/8 in. interior diameter, contemporary Navajo and handmade. Set with turquoise chips.   D—$70

Silver earrings, contemporary Navajo, handmade.   D—$25

Silver earrings, contemporary Hopi, simple design in silver overlay.   D—$55

Silver pendant, 1-7/8 in. long, contemporary Hopi handmade, with natural turquoise stone.   D—$95

Contemporary silver letter-opener, probably Navajo, and 8½ in. long. Handle is set with one large turquoise stone and one small stone. Very well-done work.   D—$55

Silver belt buckle, 2¼ in. by 3-1/8 in., probably Hopi, entirely handmade.   D—$185

Silver bolo tie fastener, die-stamped silver, set with turquoise and red coral. Contemporary Navajo.   D—$175

CAST-SILVER BRACELET, 6½ in. in circumference, with a magnificent Blue Gem mine turquoise stone. Stone is 2 in. long. Bracelet was made in the early 1950's and the craftperson did an outstanding job. Three silver bands support the sonte and bands have been etched.
On the back of the turquoise is a silver plate ¾ in. by 1¼ in. and on which has been worked an intricate design. Bracelet is in excellent condition.   G—$1400-$1700
Courtesy Hugo Poisson, Photographer; Edmunds of Yarmouth, Inc: West Yarmouth, Massachusetts.

Silver pendant, large size, contemporary Navajo. Traditional inlay designs; chip inlays of turquoise and red coral.   D—$200

Silver belt buckle, contemporary Navajo, with design in turquoise chip inlays.   D—$125

Solid silver Navajo cross, 3¼ in. wide and 5¼ in. high. Nice inlayed turquoise center; this is a well-done sandcast piece.   G—$95

Silver pin, 3 in. long and sandcast; contemporary Navajo.   D—$45

Silver cross-form pendant, 2 in. high, recent Navajo in origin. Piece set with several small turquoise stones.   D—$75

Bolo tie fastener, sandcast silver, 2¾ in. high, and with elongated natural turquoise stone. Solid silver front, with tool-marked designs.   D—$200

Silver brooch, 1¾ in. in diameter, set with natural turquoise stones; contemporary Hopi.   D—$125

Silver hat band, contemporary Navajo, with a dozen and a half miniature concha plates on leather strip.   D—$95

Bolo tie fastener, contemporary Hopi, large, all silver.   D—$125

Sandcast silver belt buckle, 3 in. long, contemporary Navajo; double-naja motif, and graceful lines.   D—$120

ADVANCED COLLECTOR PIECES

Open bird fetish necklace, by Leekya Desyee and reported to be last one made. Necklace has nine birds, with small 1 in. wide and large birds 2 in. wide. Very fine heishi and birds made of mother-of-pearl.
G—$1350

Concha belt and bolo tie set, Navajo sandcast pieces. Superbly cast and inlayed by Zuni with Fox Mine light blue turquoise. There are eight conchas and a buckle; bolo has tips and shirt clip.   G—$1700

Concha belt and set, done by Lambert Homer, Jr. There are seven conchas, one buckle to the belt. Also two bolos, two bracelets and eight inlayed butterflies. The butterflies, one bolo and one bracelet are done in four-seasons pattern. The conchas, the buckle, one bolo and one bracelet are done in the Knife Wing Dancer design. Inlays are mother-of-pearl, turquoise and coral. A rare set, and one virtually impossible to replace.
G—$7800

Concha belt and bolo, done by Lambert Homer, Senior, with Roger Skeet silverwork. There are seven conchas and one buckle, inlayed with mother-of-pearl and depicting different Kachinas. There is one bolo with tips, all different, and silver inlayed with turquoise, coral and jet. An exquisite outfit for the collector who desires the best.
G—$7950

Navajo man's SQUASH BLOSSOM NECKLACE, made of copper and Indianhead pennies. The Naja is set with one variscite stone. This is a pawn piece from the Sanastee Trading Post, Navajo Reservation; it is 16 in. long, when fastened, and 4 in. wide at Naja. Ca. 1907
C—$1200
S. W. Kernaghan photo; Marguerite Kernaghan Collection.

Pieces From The Armand Ortega Collection: Reprinted by permission:

Santo Domingo necklace, made of nuggets of stabilized turquoise strung on olive-shell heishi.   C—$68

Santo Domingo choker necklace, graduated-size disc beads made of mother-of-pearl, jet, turquoise and red pipestone.
                                                        C—$79

Santo Domingo necklace, strung with high-grade Lone Mountain spiderweb turquoise.   C—$650

Silver bracelet, with multi-stone inlays.   C—$950

Silver concha belt, ten conchas and buckle, all in Devil Dancer design with turquoise clusters. Belt made by Leonard and Edith Lonjose.   C—$7500
                          Matching necklace,   C—$4700

Silver and turquoise set, five pieces, concha belt, necklace, earrings, finger ring and bracelet. Design is Devil Dancer in inlay, with surrounding turquoise clusters. Concha belt buckle alone has 177 individual turquoise stones in separate sets. Signed, "VMB".   C—$16,000

Five-piece silver and turquoise matching set, squash-type contemporary necklace, earrings, finger ring, bracelet and concha belt. Stone is highest-grade Bisbee Blue turquoise; rare set, and made by Navajo silversmith Coolidge Begay.   C—$28,000

BEARCLAY NECKLACE, silver and turquoise, with four suspensions and centerpiece. Suspensions each have two bear claws, turquoise stone and silver feather motif.   D—$650
Photo courtesy Howard Shaw, Casa Kakiki, Sunland Park, New Mexico.

Here are three examples of Indian-owned and operated arts and crafts businesses. All carry a selection of silver and turquoise jewelry.

Hopi Arts &
  Crafts Guild
PO Box 37
Second Mesa, Arizona 86043

Navajo Arts &
  Crafts Enterprise
PO Drawer A
Window Rock, Arizona 86515

Zuni Craftsmen
  Cooperative Association
Indian Pueblo Cultural
  Center
2401-12th N.W.
Albuquerque, New Mexico 87102

The following information on turquoise is courtesy of Mr. Armand Ortega, owner of the Indian Ruins Trading Post, Sanders, Arizona, and reprinted by permission.

TURQUOISE—THE SKY STONE

To the Indians, turquoise has the life-giving power of sky and water and is held in high esteem. This beautiful blue gem that the earth has given is their sign of wealth as well as a symbol of protection from the forces of evil.

The "sky-stone" has been part of Indian cultures for centuries. The oldest well-documented record of the use of turquoise was the discovery of two turquoise ornaments at southeastern Arizona's Snaketown ruin estimated to have been made before 300 A.D. Turquoise deposits found in the West have shown evidence of prehistoric mining. It is said that turquoise mining predates any other kind of mining in the United States.

Technically, turquoise is a mineral belonging to the copper group and is found in arid regions of the Southwestern United States and parts of Asia. It is formed by the action of water which deposits it in veins in existing rock. This mother rock creates the markings or matrix which appear in the turquoise as thin black lines, brown or black blotches, iron pyrite or bits of quartz, and gives each stone its own natural beauty.

The color of turquoise varies from light blue to deep blue and green. As well as color variations, turquoise has many grades. Of each mine producing turquoise, only a small percentange is of high-grade gem quality. High-grade stones are those with greatest density, hardest consistency and deepest color, as well as those with the finest matrix pattern or "spiderwebbing" as it is commonly called. Turquoise is sold by carat weight with high-grade stones costing considerably more per carat because of their quality and scarcity.

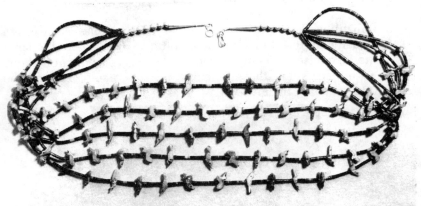

FINE TURQUOISE AND TORTOISE SHELL NECKLACE, length 32 in. end to end. Fetishes of turquoise are in the form of birds, turtles and bears. Hand-carved by Juanite Chapella, with stone from the Kingman mine. There are 100 fetishes on the necklace, workstyle is outstanding and condition is excellent.

Juanite Chapella had Atsidi Chon (Ugly Smith) of the Standing House Clan as an ancient grandfather. Atsidi Chon was one of the teachers of Slender-Maker-of-Silver.   G—$3200-$3700

Courtesy Hugo Poisson. Photographer; Edmunds of Yarmouth, Inc: West Yarmouth, Massachusetts.

As turquoise grades go downward, the hardness decreases accordingly and the color seems to get lighter. These medium-to lower-grades of turquoise are more abundant than the high-grade stones and most often stabilized to increase durability and deepen the color of the stones. Naturally, stabilized turquoise is less expensive than the higher grades but commands a greater price than unstabilized stones of the same grade.

Much confusion exists as to the merits of stabilized turquoise. Many people are under the impression that stabilization alters the true stone. covers faults, and makes it less valuable. On the contrary, proper stabilization of turquoise enhances the color and durability of the stone so that it will resist cracking and retain its sky-blue color through the years.

People are suddenly becoming suspicious of stabilized turquoise, when for many years turquoise and most other precious and semi-precious stones have been treated in similar and equally advantageous ways.

Turquoise is a relatively soft mineral and stabilizing does just what it implies—strengthens the stone. This added durability makes the turquoise easier for silversmiths to work with and assures the consumer that daily encounters with water, oils and moisture will no longer turn the stone a dull green.

Stabilization is scientifically done while turquoise is in rough form using material of a resinous nature which seals the pores of the turquoise while in a vacuum. No foreign or unnatural color is added, since the stabilizing process itself deepens the natural color of the stone.

SILVER AND TURQOUISE NECKLACE, with one large and three smaller stones. All silver, contemporary styling.   *D—$495*

Photo courtesy Howard Shaw, Casa Kakili, Sunland Park, New Mexico.

BEARCLAW NECKLACE, silver and turquoise, with two bear claw inclusions.   D—$215
Photo courtesy Howard Shaw, Casa Kakiki, Sunland Park, New Mexico.

There is a very old turquoise mine at Cerrillos, southwest of Santa Fe in New Mexico. The material was traded in prehistoric times even into present-day Mexico. Mining there began sometime in the early A.D. centuries.

Other well-known turquoise mines are: Castle Dome, Kingman, Number Eight, Carrico Lake, Fox, Villa Grove, Valley Blue, Battle Mountain, Globe, Lander Blue, Lone Mountain, Morenci, Bisbee, Blue Gem, Poe and Stormy Ridge.

The following provides additional accurate information about turquoise, including several little-known aspects of this attractive gemstone. This material has been provided by Edmunds of Yarmouth, Inc., of West Yarmouth, Massachusetts, and is reprinted by permission.

A SHORT STORY OF TURQUOISE

By Edmunds of Yarmouth, Inc.

"Turquoise" comes from the French word meaning Turkish, indicating the origin (Middle East) of the stones. Turquoise is said to bring success in love and money. It is also the birthstone for December. Turquoise has not only found popularity in this country, but goes back to the early civilizations of foreign lands. Queen Zer of the first Egyptian Dynasty owned turquoise jewelry.

Turquoise is found in many locations all over the world. Most of the southwestern states (Nevada, Arizona, New Mexico, Colorado) produce turquoise ranging in quality from low grade to gem. The mines around Nishapur, in Iran, yeild the high guality stones known to us as Persian turquoise. Low to medium grade turquoise is also found in Africa, Australia, China and Tibet. The Indians of the Southwest were mining turquoise centuries before the White man came to the area. Now the White man mines the stones and the Indians buy from the traders.

Turquoise is cut usually in dome shape. The stones are usually cut so that the finished gem includes some of the matrix in which the turquoise is found. The matrix can be brown, black, yellow, red or even white in color. Many people judge a stone by how much matrix is in the stone. However some people find the matrix more attractive. One form of matrix which is very popular today is that known as "spiderweb". In this type of turquoise, the matrix is formed in very fine lines which show patterns similar to life-like spider webs.

Turquoise, especially the lighter blue stone, is a porous stone. Therefore we recommend removing a turquoise ring before washing dishes, bathing, or washing hands, as the soaps and oils may change the color of the stone. Many Indian rings, especially Zuni inlay pieces, can have their stones loosened by prolonged exposure to water. Zuni rings are almost impossible to size, as heat in sizing the ring would harm the stone.

In the past few years turquoise has become very popular. We see the stars wearing it on television, and people from all walks of life wearing it on the street. The jewelry comes in many forms. It can be bought for babies; as silver spoons, diaper pins, bibpins. It can be bought for grandmother; as bowls and flatware as well as the more common earrings, rings, bracelets, and necklaces. The men haven't been forgotten either, as bolas and belt buckles, tie tacs, rings, bracelets, watchbands, money clips, and cigarette cases are being made.

Like anything else where there is money to be made, people will try to sell anything. There are White men making jewelry that looks like Indian jewelry, and many have even signed the pieces. This is unfortunate, so be sure the person you are dealing with can guarantee that what you have purchased is American Indian made. Beware of plastic sold as turquoise, or inferior turquiose mixed with plastic, or dyed turquoise sold as genuine turquoise. Be sure the person you are dealing with will stand behind the merchandise. Matrix can be faked as well as the stone itself, by using iodine and also shoe polish.

To prove that so much of the Indian jewelry that is on the market today is not Indian made, this is a fact: The Indians only realize one to two percent of their income from making jewelry; the rest of it comes from sheep herding and harvesting their crops.

-O. BODINGTON -

ZUNI INLAY NECKLACE AND EARRINGS, with total necklace length about 21 in. Jewelry is set with turquoise, jet, coral and mother-of-pearl. On the back of the larger half-moon is scratche the name of the maker, "Margaret Chico."

A limited edition of hand silk-screened tiles were made from its outstanding piece in 1975. Workstyle is exceptional and condition is excellent.   G—$2300

Courtesy Hugo Poisson, Photographer; Edmunds of Yarmouth, Inc; West Yarmouth, Massachusetts.

TURQUOISE JEWELRY

Heishe turquoise choker necklace, contemporary Santo Domingo Pueblo, and 13 in. long, looped. Made of graduated-size natural turquoise beads. D—$140

Navajo nugget necklace, with treated turquoise; nuggets strung with white heishe. G—$545

Turquoise nugget necklace, strung with shell heishe, with coral bead spacers and bear claw capped with silver and turquoise and set as pendant. Contemporary Southwestern. G—$75

Navajo nugget necklace, turquoise strung with gray heishe; nuggets machine-drilled. G—$750

Turquoise nugget necklace, 14½ in. long, fastened. Graduated-size natural stone, deep blue. Machine-drilled, hand-shaped and polished. D—$1350

Navajo turquoise necklace, two strands of nuggets and strung on gray heishe. G—$580

Navajo turquoise necklace, single strand natural stone strung with white heishe. G—$525

ABOUT CONTEMPORARY JEWELRY

G.S. Khalsa, of Albuquerque, New Mexico, is an experienced and perceptive dealer in fine contemporary Indian jewelry. Mr. Khalsa consented to offer some tips on buying contemporary silver and turquoise jewelry. Used with permission.

"In recent years, American Indian jewelry has become the focal point of American Indian art and crafts. Since its emergence in the eighteen hundreds, Indian jewelry has been sought after and collected.

"The great demand for Indian jewelry was at its peak in the early 1970's. The market subsequently became flooded with cheap imports, mass-produced styles and junk turquoise, including plastic imitations.

"Because of the growing skepticism as to authenticity, the fever for American Indian pieces subsided as the decade wore on. At present, the market is stabilizing and once again growing in popularity woldwide.

"The average buyer or collector who wants to buy quality American Indian jewelry (whether it costs $5 or $5000) has the responsibility to discriminate between authentic, handmade American Indian jewelry and contemporary Southwestern-style jewelry.

"Southwestern-style is usually machine-made, cast jewelry made by non-Indians. For those who are unsure about how to pick authentic, handmade American Indian jewelry, here are some simple guide-lines and information.

14-K GOLD BRACELET, 5¾ in. in circumference and ¾ in. wide. This piece was handmade by Roland Begay, and cutout design depicts the Navajo way of life. This is a contemporary piece.
G—$850

Courtesy Hugo Poisson, Photographer; Edmunds of Yarmouth, Inc: West Yarmouth, Massachusetts.

"The three major silversmithing tribes are Navajos, Zunis and Hopis. Navajo jewelry is easily distinguishable because it features a more elaborate silver work, incorporating a leaf or feather motif. Sometimes their work does not include stones, such as sandcast jewelry. Sandcast jewelry is made by pouring hot molten silver into a mold carved out of volcanic rock.

"The Zunis, on the other hand, are expert lapidaries. Stone-on-stone inlay, needlepoint, and cluster work usually predominate their silver work. It should be noted that some Zunis are doing a Navajo style, as, too, Navajos are doing more and more inlay and cluster work. Nevertheless, the work is authentic.

"Hopi silver overlay is an altogether different style. The Hopi craftsman uses two layers of silver. The bottom layer is oxidized black. On the top layer, a design is drawn and cut out, then overlayed on the bottom. The final texture to the oxidized layer is achieved by etching lines into the black.

"The finished jewelry has a satin-brushed look quite different from Navajo or Zuni style. Stones are rarely incorporated into the design. Although Hopi jewelry is frequently imitated by the Navajos, the imitation may be inferior in quality and lower in price.

"The most important aspect to consider in buying American Indian jewelry is your choice of retail dealer. Your dealer must be reputable, honest, and willing to guarantee in writing the authenticity of each piece of jewelry. Large in-store inventories or memberships in jewelry associations do not necessarily guarantee the dealer's integrity.

"A bona-fide dealer has the responsibility to know and share with the customer all pertinent information about his merchandise: Who is the silversmith? Where is the stone from? What quality of stone is it? It is no longer valid to simply name the tribe. Be aware that phrases such as 'Zuni-style' or 'Indian-style' do not guarantee that the piece is authentic or handmade. Well buffed and nicely displayed jewelry is a good indication of how much the dealer respects what is being sold.

"When making a purchase, be sure the jewelry is 'clean'. The silver work should be neat, bezels around the stones ought to be seamless, and the soldering carefully done. There should be no sharp edges on the silver work. Insist on natural turquoise stones that are cut and polished, but not treated.

"The term 'natural' means genuine. Genuine stones may be real turquoise, but it may be that the stone is of very poor quality and treated to look better. It is considered acceptable that Zuni inlay jewelry and Santo Domingo heishe use stabilized turquoise, which provides the hardness needed for the delicate lapidary work involved. In Navajo silversmithing, insist on natural stones.

"Some simple rules of thumb to determine the relative quality of natural turquoise are hardness, intensity of natural color (either blue or green), hardness of the matrix (does it chip out with your fingernail?), and the ratio of turquoise to matrix.

"In Zuni channel work, a clean piece will not have filler to gap the distance between poorly cut stones and the silver. The surface of the entire inlay should be very smooth with a brilliant sheen to it. When looking at needlepoint or cluster work, the uniformity of shape and color of the stones determines quality.

"To appreciate American Indian jewelry is to become a part of the rich heritage and culture of the American Indians. The 'complex simplicity' of their lifestyle is expressed in their artifacts, sophisticated in design and workmanship, yet reflecting perfectly the individualism and undying spirit of Native Americans. So many of us long for such simplicity of spirit, and for the intimate communion with Nature from which it is spawned.

"The charm and desirability of authentic American Indian jewelry is that it looks and feels like it is made from a perfect mixture of the Southwestern landscape and a human spirit, overflowing with the joy of life."

(G. S. K.)

Suggested Reading

Arizona Highways, issue of August, 1974

Arizona Highways, issue of March, 1975

Bahti, Mark, *A Consumer's Guide To Southwestern Indian Arts and Crafts*; Indian Pueblo Cultural Center, Alburquerque, New Mexico

Gillespie, Alva H., *How To Invest In Indian Jewelry*, Diamond Press Albuquerque, New Mexico

Rosnek, Carl and Stacey, Joseph, *Skystone And Silver-The Collector's Book of Southwest Indian Jewelry*, 423 Chestnut Ridge Road, Woodcliff Lake, New Jersey 07675

Original caption reads "Indian Camp—cooking by the Rosebud Creek. Picture probably from early 1900's due to presence of White-made goods, bucket, coffee pot, handbag, harness and wagons, and burlap bags.

Photo courtesy of South Dakota State Historical Society.

Indian tending salmon trap in the state of Washington, probably early 1900's.
Photographer, B. C. Collier; courtesy Photography Collection, Suzzallo Library, University of Washington.

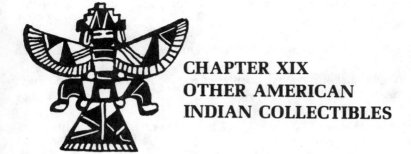

CHAPTER XIX
OTHER AMERICAN
INDIAN COLLECTIBLES

The material in this chapter is a wonderful assemblage of authentic Amerind items. They are listed in no particular order and without regard to materials, regions or age. The listings either did not fit conveniently into other chapters or the information arrived after individual chapters were closed. Many are one-of-a-kind.

Probably only the Plains-style war club has enough entries for a separate heading. So it is practically impossible to locate a particular item for price-comparison, at least on first reading.

This section is probably treated best as a broad survey of Amerind creations for casual reading and general knowledge.

Certainly of special interest will be the last portion of the chapter, which covers auction results of the well-known and important Allard Collection.

AMERIND COLLECTIBLES

Osage **hand-woven wool sash,** 54 in. long including fringe. Colors are red, white and blue, and in nice condition. D—$50

Old **Indian powder horn,** 6½ in. long, with rawhide carrying thong. Wooden end-plug set with large brass tacks which added decoration. Plains Indian, probably mid-1800's. A—$115

Sioux war club, with rawhide-wrapped handle; fine example. A—$195

High quality **beaded saddle blanket,** with bells, fringed, and in excellent condition. Sioux. D—$1975

Chippewa martingale, on cloth with beaded panels. Piece is 26 in. by 44 in., with patterns in floral design. Excellent condition.

G—$925

Apache rawhide **quiver and assorted arrows.** A—$325

Paiute buckskin covered **cradleboard,** moderately beaded. Yarn decorated sun shade.

G—$445

Wool blanket with beaded strip 2 in. wide and 80 in. long, and with four large colorful rosettes.

G—$190

Saddle blanket, possibly Crow Indian, and needs repair. A—$135

Club with beaded handle, stone head with one chip missing; handle is thin and 12 in. long, fully quilled. Piece has four cone dangles.

G—$240

Indian Wars weapon, 1873 Springfield carbine, tack-decorated stock.

A—$325

Leather awl case, Apache, 12½ in. long. Piece has rows of small tin bells on yellow leather, with yellow and blue beadwork. A—$100

Santee Sioux **horse bridle,** with red and navy trade cloth; canvas-backed, with nice floral designs.

G—$315

Crow bridle with German silver bit; engraved and inlayed German silver with flat headstall. Beaded in typical Crow designs; leather formerly dyed red. Rare piece, excellent condition.

G—$675

Kiowa **war club,** rawhide wrapped; hide cracking. Ex-museum piece and quite old.

G—$100

Sioux bow with two bone-tipped arrows.

G—$155

Sioux **dog travois** sticks and rawhide laced platform. Fine display or museum piece, high quality.

G—$175

Beaded **horseman's gauntlets,** Plains Indian and probably Nez Perce, with very small designs in beads on back. Fair condition andca. 1890.

D—$255

From left to right:
CHERT WAR CLUB OR AXE, with a modern elkhorn handle. Blade was found on an Archaic
period site in state of Georgia. C—$115
WAR CLUB made by the Comanche Indians near Anadarko, Oklahoma, ca. 1890—1900. Weapon
has a granite stone head with wooden handle wrapped in rawhide and stitched with rawhide
thongs. Wrap aroung stone head is all sinew sewn. C—$415
CELTILFORM axe or war club, with a modern wood and rawhide handle. Celt head came from a
cave site in Missouri. C—$115
Photos courtesy Wayne Parker collection.

Northwest Coast **silver salad fork and spoon,** both 9½ in. long. Native-incised handles. G—$235

Sioux **war club** with rawhide wrapped handle, stone head; an old and good piece. G—$215

Sioux beaded **cradleboard cover,** with trade cloth sinew sewn. Geometric design on white back. Colors of beads are red, blue, green and yellow. G—$465

Peyote fan, pheasant feathers with finely beaded handle. G—$55

Buckskin **knife and awl case,** 8 in. long and 2 in. wide. Small knife and awl included, both with carved handles in shape of bear's head. Tin cone dangles on tassles. G—$105

Northwest Coast **painted hide** with effigy figure painted on it in brilliant blacks and reds. Very decorative and fine art work. G—$1550

Northwest Coast **carved halibut hook,** 10 in. long. G—$155

Dance wand, may be Ghost Dance period; 15 in. overall length. Top is comprised of two small horns and handle decorated with beaded horse hair. G—$235

Tepee bag, probably made from cradle cover. Designs are Sioux, Cheyenne and Crow motifs. Piece is 15 in. by 23 in. Fully beaded on front and in excellent condition. G—$615

Haida **argillite carving,** depicting miniature totem pole. Item is 13 in. high and shows mythical creatures. Ca. 1930 (?). C—$675

Quilled contemporary breastplate, 12 in. by 20 in. Done in Blackfoot design and excellent work. G—$515

Taos Pueblo **complete bow set,** with bow case and quiver, painted cedar bow that is sinew strung. Painted war arrows without feathers. Items are ca. 1860-70. D—$850

Cheyenne buffalo hair **medicine case,** ca. 1900. D—$95

Apache **arrow quiver,** 15½ in. long, made of soft leather and about 3½ in. wide. Unusual, and good condition. C—$195

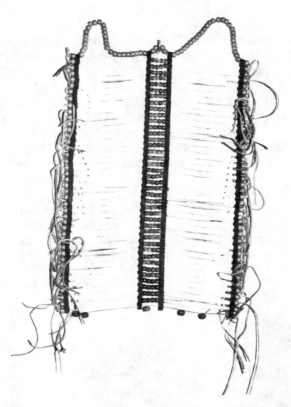

Sioux man's BREASTPLATE, of leather thongs, bone tubes and large beads. Piece is 20 in high and 12 in. wide, ca. 1900. D—$1200

Photo courtesy Winona Trading Post, Santa Fe—Pierre & Sylvia Bovis.

Gueverra **long bow** with four cane arrows with fancy foreshafts. Set is ca. 1870. D—$140

Beaded case, 3 in. by 4 in., with geometric designs in green and white, with blue, yellow and pink. One beaded fringe missing; Sioux. A—$35

Fish effigy made of yellow-gray shale, drilled at dorsal fin region, from Virginia. Piece is 2-1/8 in. long, good condition. C—$28

Sioux **bow and quiver case** with bow and arrow. Made of moose hide, and has beaded edge with fringe and strap. Good condition. Piece is ca. 1920. G—$240

Martingale, Blackfoot, and loom-beaded. Has red, white and blue ribbons, hawk bells and tin cone danglers. Fine condition. G—$230

Apache saddle bags with intricate cutout designs backed with red trade cloth. Made of rawhide and with long fringe. Such items are seldom encountered.   G—$1825

Cheyenne **baby cradle** with fully beaded hood, and with bottom part made of calfskin. Good condition, and ca. 1880.   G—$530

Old Russell Green River **trade knife,** complete with leather sheath. Rare piece, with a polished antler handle; knife is 9 in. in length.
G—$150

Leather partially beaded **case for rifle,** probably an early flintlock or percussion weapon. Case is 4 ft. 1 in. long, and may have been used by a Mountain Man trapper, though certainly Indian-made. Old tag states that piece was collected in Idaho in 1907.
C—$675

Pair of WOVEN FIBER SANDALS, from a cave shelter in New Mexico. Twelve pair came from this particular site, on privately owned land. Material is yucca plant fibers, and sandals are Anasazi culture. Ancient corncobs also shown.   *C—$135-$185*
Photo courtesy Wayne Parker, Texas.

MEDICINE BAG, Cheyenne, 6 in. wide and 14 in. long, with fringes. It is of unlined hide, sinew-sewn, and bead design indicate the owner might have belonged to the Cheyenne Warrior Society because of the four (black bead) horseheads with red arrow emerging from their mouths. (Sacred arrows?) Other designs are geometric; hide strap across bag top. Piece is ca. 1880. C—$625

Photo courtesy Bill Post Collection.

War club, stone head, hide-wrapped handle, good condition.
D—$195

Sioux painted **parfleche box,** 11 in. by 9 in. by 7 in. G—$75

Painted pottery tile, 4¼ in. wide and 5¼ in. high, with painted Kachina face on front. A—$50

Plains Indian **knife and sheath,** the sheath 9½ in. long, the knife blade 5¼ in. long, with bone handle. Sheath well-beaded and nicely fringed; alone, $155. Knife White-made and used, possibly hide-skinner's tool, blade well-worn. Knife alone, $55. Presented as a set, but knife and sheath obviously mismatched.
C — uncertain value

Sioux **saddle blanket,** with 6 in. beaded panels, and with bells and heavy fringe. Excellent condition. G—$1850

Plains Indian **parfleche container,** 6¼ in. by 9½ in., painted at one time. Good condition. D—$110

Indian **carrying net,** collected in California, over 20 in. long. Woven with wide spaces, each about 2 in. square. Used for transporting unwieldy loads; natural fiber. C—$100

WOODEN-HORSE STICK, 24 in. in length. Plains Indian, and ca. 1880. *G—$975*
Photo and item courtesy Fenn Galleries, Ltd., Santa Fe, New Mexico.

Bison hide, painted with various designs; very fine work and may show a "count" of years and events. Condition average. D—$720

Bow and arrows, old set, bow 3 ft. 4 in. long, and with five arrows. Condition not good; feathers missing from arrows, and string from bow; arrows iron-tipped. Set found in old house and had been exposed to elements for many years. C—$185

Parfleche container, nicely decorated, medium size. A—$160

Flesher, from Taos Pueblo, 15 in. long. Piece has wooden handle, inset metal blade, and in fine condition. Ca. 1890. G—$115

Nez Perce **corn husk pouch.** A—$50

Plains **"egg-head" skull-cracker club,** good condition. D—$185

Sioux **saddle blanket,** fully beaded on hide, and 36 in. by 80 in. Piece has canvas center and yellow fringe; beads are on blue background with fine geometric designs and four different colored horses. Perfect condition and ca. 1910. G—$1850

Plains Indian **knife sheath** about 12 in. long, and about late 1800's. Small beadwork designs, geometric pattern, one side.   D—$125

Beaded **knife sheath,** fringed and some beadwork missing; leather is parfleche, good condition.   C—$95

Pair of beaded **horseman's gauntlets,** wide-cuffed.   A—$140

Bolo tie fastener, 2 in. high; shell inlayed with jet, turquoise and coral in the form of a quail. Exquisite work by Eliot Quelo, and signed.   G—$960

Columbia River **basalt carving,** 23 in. tall.   A—$225

Large and fine Plains Indian woman's **hair-pipe breastplate,** many beads, all with beautiful patina. Ca. 1880.   C—$1600

Nez Perce **"sally-bag",** 7 in. by 10¾ in.   A—$215

Cherokee **plaited mat,** made of river cane.   A—$15

Old Sioux **quill and deer hair roach;** good condition.   D—$115

Sioux Indian man performs in the Sun Dance in the Black Hills. Dancer may be blowing on bone whistle or flute.
Photo courtesy South Dakota State Historical Society.

367

Four YEI BI CHAI MASKS: The Navajo medicine man is extremely important during ceremonies. The Yei Bi Chai dance is held during the winter months as a major curing ceremony. The Yei Bi Chai dancers appear during the last two nights of the nine day ceremony. The Yei represent supernatural beings who have great powers.

The Yei masks are made of buckskin from deer which have been suffocated with sacred meal. The full masks are worn by male dancers. These masks are approximately 18 in. long and 14 in. wide; ca. 1920.   C—$1950 each

Photos courtesy W. J. Crawford, The Americana Galleries, Phoenix, Arizona.

Five STONE FIGURES OF MEN; prehistoric Kiva pieces of the Mimbres culture from south-western New Mexico. They range from 20 in. to 30 in. in length, and are ca. AD 500.

In the prehistoric cultures, a Kiva was a large pit, usually round but sometimes square in shape, which the Indian peoples used as a religious temple for their priests and honored guests. Rarely was a non-Indian allowed to enter the Kiva. A bench on the four walls provided seating space for selected members of certain clans who were permitted to enter the Kiva. In the center of the Kiva, a depressed area was the primary focus in that the most sacred rituals were performed there.

The five stone figures were found standing upright, in a circle, in this depressed area and were obviously very highly regarded as part of a ritual. The large carved figure depiceted with his hands secured behind his back is presumed to represent a captive who was to be offered in sacrifice. The other four carved stone figures are presumed to represent the population who would benefit from the sacrifice.

Kivas have been used continuously by the Indian peoples from prehistoric times to present. The Hopi, Zuni, Acoma and Taos Indians today are some of the Indians who still use Kivas in their rituals. These are probably the only stone Kiva pieces in existence, singly or otherwise.   G—$90,000

Photos courtesy W. J. Crawford, The Americana Galleries, Phoenix, Arizona.

Original **lance with point,** California desert region; lance is 52 in. long, with obsidian point about 3 in. long, still secured with original lashings. Unknown age, but old. D—$315

Squaw axe, trade iron, 5 in. high. Excellent condition, and blade has flower-like stamping. A—$50

Wood comb, 9 in. long, with 13 long wooden teeth. Piece has early chip-carving and abalone shell inlays. Northwest Coast. A—$30

Tubular pipe, of a reddish-yellow quality stone, 3-3/8 in. long, just less than 1 in. in middle diameter. Highly polished in the vague effigy of an unknown animal. Probably a late B.C. piece, from Archaic and Woodland site in the Midwest. C—$515

Silver and turquoise concho belt, 34 in. long. Conchos elongated, with much stampwork and well-set with turquoise. Spacers in butterfly shape; ornate buckle, eleven worked silver pieces in all. Good overall tooling. A—$470

Birchbark basket, rectangular, 7¼ in. long and 3-3/8 in. wide, with floral designs in dyed quills. Historic, Great Lakes area. Probably Canadian Indian. D—$115

Beaded belt, 30½ in. long, beaded on leather and with tying thongs. Geometric designs done on blue field, with colors red, yellow and black. A—$55

Silver and turquoise squashblossom necklace, large, all beads made from liberty dimes. Naja with 7 large stones and 10 "blossoms", each with 2 stones. Well-made piece. A—$450

Carved bullet, 45-70 cartridge, unfired, with lead bullet portion carved to represent human face. Believed to be Indian work; shell casing of brass has heavy patina. From Kansas, estimated to be late-1800's. C—$30

Trade-silver cross, 2½ in. high, with back touchmarked "Montreal", and front hand-stamped. Suspended on necklace consisting of black beads with silver beads at intervals. A—$115

Kachina doll, 8¾ in. high, painted wood, and recent. D—$50

Silver ketoh or wrist bowguard, leather, with turquoise stone in silver attached. Silver plate measures 2½ in. by 3½ in.   A—$120

Trade-iron arrowhead, 2-7/8 in. long with squared stem serrated on edge for lashings.   C—$15

Shell necklace, 18 in. long, made of thin disc-beads of clamshell. Necklace somewhat resembles puka shell; well-made.

A—$39

Apache bow and two arrows; arrows without points. Bow was once painted and is 42 in. long. Documented; pre-1901.   A—$145

Two Pomo arrows, cane shafts with wooden tips; each, 36 in. long, and in very good condition.   G—$38 ea.

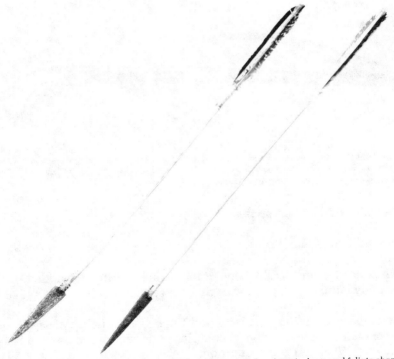

TWO PLAINS INDIAN ARROWS; example to left has an iron head 2¼ in. long, and foliate-shaped head has beveled edges and squared shoulders. Mid to late 1800's, and Sioux Indian from North Dakota.
C—$50-$75 each
Photo courtesy Sheridan P. Barnard, Franklin, Massachusetts.

Rawhide quirt, intricately braided, and contemporary.   G—$35

Bridle and reins, bridle with some beadwork and lined with trade cloth (on leather); rawhide reins 3½ ft. long.   C—$345

Medicine weasel, pelt stuffed with sweetgrass; piece has beaded eyes and nose.   G—$210

Sioux **war club** with large stone head and ca. 1900.   D—$85

Cheyenne **knife sheath,** fully beaded with five colors of beads; piece is 2¾ in. wide and 7 in. long. Sinew-sewn rawhide and buckskin, and ca. 1910.   G—$175

Sioux **"skull-cracker" war club,** wooden handle covered with rawhide, with stone head. Piece is 17 in. long, in good condition, and ca. 1900.   G—$195

BUFFALO-HORN "SKULL-CRACKER", 17¾ in. long. Piece had been brought to Springfield, Oregon in the 1930's by a family who came from South Dakota, purchased by them on the Pine Ridge reservation. This would be a Sioux item.   C—$325
S. W. Kernaghan photo; Marguerite Kernaghan Collection.

Fine old Haida **silver spoon.**   A—$285

Umatilla **"sally-bag".**   A—$55

Sioux **cradle cover,** fully beaded top triangle with later added Hudson Bay blanket wrap. Good early colors; high quality.   G—$400

Birch-bark container, Canada and Upper Great Lakes area. Made from folded sections of bark; container has reinforced top and is 14 in. long. Worn but good condition.   C—$95

Parfleche knife case, probably Sioux, painted and old; knife goes with case.   D—$110

Large **frame of Basket-Maker** artifacts—projectile point flakers, cordage, yucca strings, rope, and so forth. Shelter finds from New Mexico. D—$95

Plains Indian **bow-drill outfit,** pump-style with short bow, cord and wooden drillstick. Probably late 1800's. C—$170

Rawhide **knife sheath,** Western Plains, 6½ in. long and made of very heavy leather. Well-done, authentic, old. D—$100

Hopi **painted bow,** sinew-strung and with four small game arrows. Items are ca. 1890. D—$185

Crow Indian **beaded knife sheath,** 7¾ in. long, not in good condition. Many beads are missing; design uncertain. C—$45

Columbia River region **stone club,** 13½ in. long, about 3 in. wide, with a polished handgrip. Purpose unknown, but may be related to the "slave killer" monolithic axes. May be an unfinished piece as it is rather thick in proportion to length. C—$225

Pair of Cheyenne **beaded saddle blanket strips.** A—$330

Pair of **hair ties,** braided and quilled, good condition. D—$85

Sioux **pemmican hammer,** rawhide covered handle with granite stone for base; item shows much age and use. G—$170

Horse **martingale,** Blackfoot, 12 in. by 48 in., and fringed with 4 in. of basket beads with hawk bells at ends. Piece collected in the 1930's. G—$410

Kiowa **war club,** bound with rawhide; old piece. D—$135

Plains-type **war club,** 1800's. Stone fully encased in rawhide with rawhide-wrapped handle. Some beaded decoration, but probably added later. G—$230

Northern Sioux **saddle bags,** buffalo hide with large beaded panels and a heavy fringe; piece has connecting beaded strips and is ca. late-1800's. Scarce, and quality item. G—$1800

Tsimshian **basketry hair receiver.** A—$50

Corn husk bag, 11½ in. long by 13½ in., with geometric designs on one side only. Nicely woven and sturdy, and probably ca. 1950.

C—$75

Cheyenne **baby carrier,** fully quilled hood and partially quilled sides. Full size, and ca. 1870.

G—$2350

Parfleche container, envelope-type, with triangular red and green designs. Piece is 17 in. long, 12¼ in. high, and with wraparound thong fastener.

C—$365

Crow **saddle blanket,** made of old tepee canvas as base with beaded strip of cloth. Good condition, and ca. 1880.

G—$660

Nez Perce **corn-husk container,** probably for small personal items; unrolled length 17 in. Unusual wool embroidery on sides, and a recent piece.

C—$260

Pomo **cane arrows,** California, with hardwood foreshaft that is sinew-tied. Ca. 1880.

D—$40, ea.

Plains Indian bow with three iron-tipped and feather-vaned arrows, all good condition.

C—$235

Sioux **umbilical fetish.**

A—$110

Unusual Catlinite **napkin ring,** 2 in. in diameter, said to have been traded on an Army post in mid-1800's. Probably once part of a set. Carving on outside depicts a Western Army post.

C—$85

Old Sioux **tobacco cutting board** in the shape of a turtle or possibly a beaver pelt; piece has brass tack eyes.

G—$70

Zuni **bear-hunting fetish,** made of fur, feathers and beads. A rare item and ca. 1870.

D—$75

Plains Indian **fan,** probably Prairie hen feathers (several missing), handle of sinew and some beadwork.

D—$45

Pair of beaded **guantlet gloves,** possibly Crow, with slight damage.

G—$175

Mojave **painted bow** with one painted arrow; ca. 1870-80.

D—$180

Gila River effigy, 4 in. wide and 8 in. long, good condition with some restoration. G—$675

Warm Springs **beaded leggings.** A—$80

Skokomish **slate spear,** 12 in. long; a ceremonial item and ca. 1860. D—$80

Salish **woven tumpline,** Columbia River area, wide leather band and braided rawhide straps. About 20 in. long, fastened. C—$115

Nez Perce **corn-husk martingale,** 18 in. wide and 31 in. long; Rare, and in good condition. Ca. 1900. G—$675

Sioux **umbilical lizard,** worn but in good condition. G—$160

Pair of **hair ties** with beadwork and feather down; small brass dangles or tinklers. D—$50

Sioux **miniature tepee,** 14½ in. high, with nine thin lodge poles. Leather covering for the structure has the remnants of fringe at bottom, so may have been taken from a worn-out shirt or dress. Unusual, fine condition. C—$255

Mono **cradleboard,** with woven red and green sash straps and a decorated hood. G—$370

Horse bridle, trade cloth, with good designs, beadwork in Plains Indian style. A—$290

Cheyenne **beaded sheath and knife,** buckskin. Knife is trade-steel, edge well-worn, and with antler or bone handle. D—$155

Old **Navajo shirt,** with approximately 400 hand-made silver buttons. G—$660

Old **dance sash,** 44 in. long and 12½ in. wide, with trade beads the length. Fine condition. G—$290

Colonel Doug Allard, a Flathead Indian, has long been associated with extra-high quality Amerind artworks of many types. In this important auction, 1200 pieces went on the block, and Col. Allard served as auctioneer. Of these, 86 new objects are listed here.

In-depth coverage is accorded these objects for several reasons. One is the high quality of the items, most being in the advanced-collector category. Another is the great range of the artifacts, from many different tribes, geographic regions and time periods. This provides a broad-spectrum look at Amerind works.

Criteria used to select objects for inclusion here included: Types collectors will likely encounter, unusual pieces, or those which, due to rarity, are not covered elsewhere in the book.

My thanks to Col. Allard for special permission to reprint the auction descriptions and results. All included here of course would carry an "A" designation. A special feature for this edition is the inclusion of a number of photographs from the Allard auction, illustrating the range of items sold. It was held in Scottsdale, Arizona.

CHAPTER XX
ESKIMO, ALEUT
& ALASKAN INDIAN
ITEMS

Today two main but related groups—with roots stretching far back into prehistory with the Umnak people—inhabit the Alaskan region. They are the Aleuts, who inhabit the Aleutian Islands, and the Eskimos. The word "Eskimo" was a non-complimentary term applied by a Northcentral Amerind group, and it meant something like "Eaters of raw fish".

Eskimos on the coastal areas called themselves "Inuit", while more inland Eskimos were the "Nunamuit". Technicalities aside, all groups were almost totally dependent on fish, birds and animals.

There are two other Alaskan-area Indian peoples who still make traditional arts and crafts. There are the Athabascan Indians (of inland and coastal areas) and the Tlingit-Haida (southern coastal parts).

Some contemporary painting and sculpting is done, but the emphasis is on items made of ivory, bone, soapstone and woodworking, plus some basketry and clothing. Much work is characterized by combining simplicity and clean, almost stark, but dramatic lines in the best artistic fashions. Some nephrite (jade) is mined northeast of Kotzebue, Alaska, and is made into small objects.

At Little Diomede Island, near the International Date Line and not far from the USSR's Siberian coast, a pair of walrus tusks is valued at about $200. However, if the native carvers make the ivory into small art objects, the same ivory can eventually return nearly $2000.

Not many people, compared with other Amerind items, as yet collect Alaskan-area and Eskimo artifacts and artworks. It would appear to be a very good area to explore. The most valued material is ivory, which usually comes from walrus tusks; sometimes whale teeth are used, more rarely the single tusk of the narwhale. Included here is some very interesting information about walrus ivory, which will aid in identifying the type used in making certain collectibles.

Special thanks are due Mary Lou Lindahl, General Manager of Alaskan Native Arts & Crafts, INC., for permission to reprint these facts on ivory, plus other material as noted.

For a catalog, write (and enclose a couple of stamps) to: Alaskan Native Arts & Crafts, 425 D Street, Anchorage, Alaska 99501. The Co-op employs only native craftspeople, and their Trademark is "ANAC".

WALRUS IVORY

Alaskan ivory comes from the walrus that inhabit the Arctic Ocean and Bering Sea areas. Walrus herds generally migrate north in the spring and at that time villages along the coast harvest the animal for a variety of uses. Although the walrus provides the main meat supply for many villages the year round, it is a renewable resource, in the same sense that cattle are, and the impact of the Alaskan Native on the walrus herds is far below the herd growth level. The walrus is in no danger of becoming extinct.

The ivory tusk of the walrus protrudes downward from the upper jaw, extending as much as three feet. The tusk has three layers: an inner core of light tan, dark tan and white; a second layer of soft white, and an outer shell that, when properly worked, can be polished to a brilliant sheen.

The ivory is found in three basic forms, identifiable by color ation.

1. New ivory—that which has been recently harvested, is the gleaming white color described above.
2. Old ivory—like that commonly found along beaches, is usually tan or brown from exposure to the elements.
3. Fossilized ivory—is often very dark from having been buried in the permafrost for many years.

The Alaskan native peoples, in comparison with better-known Amerind groups, have a significantly smaller output of traditional arts and crafts. However the art forms are so unusual that there is usually little difficulty in assigning an Eskimo, or far northern, origin.

OLD ESKIMO & ALEUT ITEMS

Small ivory **Eskimo bear fetish** or toggle, 1 3/8 in. long. Ivory is a rich amber color; small hole drilled in shoulder region for cord. Perfect condition, and very old. C—$100

Steatite (soapstone) Eskimo **bowl oil lamp,** oblong, 13 in. long and 9 in. wide, 3¼ in. deep. One small end has a groove which held a twist of moss for a wick. Bottom almost perfectly flat. C—$180

Rounded **fish lure,** Eskimo, carved from bone or ivory, and 4 in. long. Curved iron hook set into body; hole drilled at front end, both to represent eyes and to hold fishing line. C—$85

Eskimo **lidded basket,** 13 in. in diameter and 9 in. high. Good condition, and ca. 1900. G—$195

Portion of Eskimo **compound harpoon,** carved from bone. Piece is 4-3/8 in. long, has socketed base, drill hole for cord, and cut-out notch in tip for harpoon head section. Plain, but very well made and good lines. Old. C—$65

Eskimo **tobacco container,** nicely beaded, and ca. 1900. G—$140

Small **bone Eskimo comb,** very old, 2¾ in. wide and 1¾ in. high. Few teeth are broken, but very well made. C—$45

Small **ivory effigy,** or decorative toggle, Eskimo. Piece is just over 1 in. long, cylindrical, and in the shape of the upper portion of a walrus. C—$80

Eskimo basket, 5 in. high by 10 in. and 12½ in. A—$30

Bone meat hook, Alaska, 14½ in. long and with a sharply angled ivory inset to form holding barb. Used to catch and strip blubber when butchering large sea mammals. C—$275

Eskimo **chipped bear point,** made from material resembling chert, 3¾ in. long. Stemmed, shoulders rounded, edges show extensive wear so may have also been a working blade. C—$40

Eskimo **baleen basket,** made from the fibrous material in the mouth of some whales, used to screen plankton. Piece is 4½ in. in diameter and 4-1/8 in. high. Several small ivory animals on lid; all in good condition. G—$245

Carved-ivory snow goggles, from an early group. About 4½ in. wide and 1½ in. high, with drill-holes at ends for fastening cords. Eye-slits are straight lines; very unusual and well-carved item. Prehistoric. C—$520

Old pre-Eskimo **whalebone mask,** from northern Alaska. It has typical inset eyes with vision slits, protruding and elongated nose and mouth opening. Piece is 8¾ in. high, and in average good condition. C—$625

Eskimo **walrus ivory hunter's tally.** A—$175

Eskimo or Aleut **ivory chisel,** with ground-down orca or killer whale tooth set in bone handle. Very rare item. C—$240

Eskimo **wooden point scabbard,** a hollowed holster-like device used to protect sharp harpoon tips when stored. Piece is 4 in. long, 1¾ in. wide at base; may have been carved from driftwood. Good condition. C—$40

Walrus-tusk adz-blade, from very early Alaskan coastal site, without handle. Tusk section is 8¼ in. long. C—$165

Eskimo **wooden fire-making set,** with curved fire-bow, pointed and worn drill-stick, and fire-base with drilled holes for friction starts. Unusual items, and in good condition. C—$85

Eskimo **ulu** or woman's knife, with bone handle. A—$20

Eskimo **ulu,** with walrus design carved on handle. A—$35

Eskimo ivory **hairpin or perforator,** 4-1/8 in. long and polished from use. Incised-line decorations. C—$35

Ivory bow **wristguard,** attached to inside of lower arm holding bow to protect against bowstring slap. Piece is 4½ in. long and drilled front and rear for fastening. C—$150

Pre-Eskimo **microlith blade**, 1-3/8 in. long, evidencing ultra-fine chipping, nearly 20 flakes to the inch. Very thin tip; may have served as a barb for harpoon, but actual use unknown.   C—$25

Ivory harpoon tip, Alaska, from Dorset site, 3¼ in. long. Double barbs on each side, and in good condition.   C—$135

Eskimo doll, of carved wood, about 5 in. high. May be from early 1900's; miniature skin parka, probably made of seal-gut.   C—$120

Eskimo **snow shovel**, bone blade and about 48 in. in length. Good condition and ca. 1900.   G—$195

RECENT ESKIMO & ALEUT ITEMS

Eskimo **baleen "wolf-scarer"**, a long, flat object attached to thong and swung in a circle; makes a vibrating, whistling roar.   A—$25

Eskimo **lidded basket**, 4 in. in diameter, 3¾ in. high. Coil-weave, natural plant fibers.   C—$145

Eskimo **fossilized ivory bracelet**.   A—$50

Pair of Eskimo **leather mittens**, 14½ in. long with extension for thumb. Coastal Alaska, in fair condition.   C—$120

Pair of Eskimo **sealskin boots**, thigh-length and man-size, with waterproofed seam stitching. Good condition, and unusual.   C—$400

Miniature skin mukluks, footgear, from St. Lawrence Island.   A—$30

Eskimo **fur doll**, from Yukon Delta.   A—$40

Aleut basket, Alaskan islands, of braided grass 11 in. in diameter. Has braided carrying strap, and is probably a light-weight collecting basket.   C—$280

Walrus **ivory carving**, depicting a snowy owl.   A—$40

Eskimo **miniature skin kayak**.   A—$35

Miniature umiak or woman's boat, actually used by families to hunt and travel, 17 in. long, and gut-covered wooden frame. There are four tiny paddles, each about 5 in. long. C—$280

Scrimshaw **walrus ivory box.** A—$65

Eskimo **walrus-tusk etching,** soot-impregnated thin incised lines, illustrating wintertime activities. Tusk section is just over 13 in. long, decorated both sides. Not signed, and probably ca. 1930's. From Point Hope, Alaska. C—$650

Carved seal, of fossilized ivory, set on base. A—$60

Walrus **ivory cribbage board,** Eskimo, and ca. 1930. A—$120

Walrus tusk **ivory cribbage board,** 13½ in. long and lacking game pegs. Fine condition, ivory a golden tan brown. C—$170

Attu **lidded basket,** miniature style, with fine weave. A—$570

Eskimo **lidded basket,** 11 in. in diameter and 12 in. high; basket has a swirling stairstep design, and is in good condition. G—$230

MINIATURE TWO-MAN KAYAK, 35½ in. (93 cm) long. Kayak is gut over wood frame, with gut garments on wooden carved dolls. One is painted black-face. There are miniature paddles, bow and lance, made of wood, ivory and sinew. From Nushigak area, ca. 1935-38. G — Not listed. *Photo and item courtesy Walrus Gallery, Kennebunkport, Maine.*

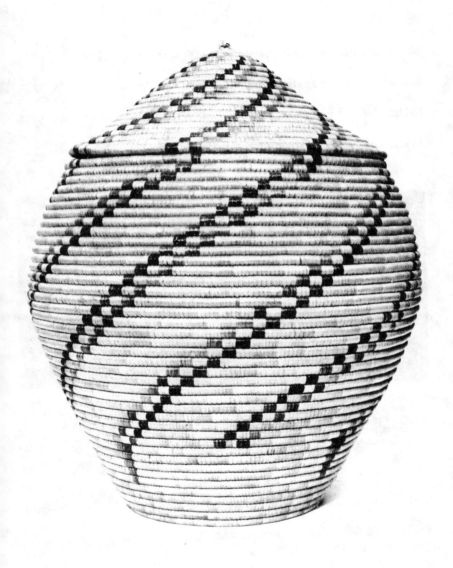

ESKIMO LAP GRASS BASKET WITH COVER, 15½ in. (39.5 cm) high and 12¼ in. (31 cm) in diameter. Done in spiral design. From Nelson Island, ca. 1936.   G — Not listed.
Photo and item courtesy Walrus Gallery, Kennebunkport, Maine.

Eskimo basket, measuring 5½ in. by 13 in. A—$40

Small **Eskimo doll,** with carved-ivory face. A—$45

Eskimo **carved soapstone fish,** done by Tom Mayac. A—$50

Eskimo **baleen basket,** with ivory seal and bear. A—$195

Eskimo carving of a drummer, done on walrus jawbone. A—$115

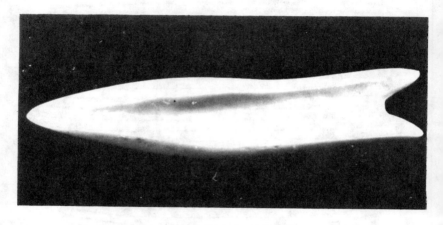

Very fine and highly polished ESKIMO BONE POINT or blade. Artifact is 4½ in. in length. It is a type that can be found around Spence Bay in the Arctic. There, from frozen ground conditions (perma-frost) help to preserve organic materials almost indefinitely. C—$28
Photo courtesy Howard Popkie, Arnpior, Ontario, Canada.

Eskimo yo-yo, braided sealskin with a baleen handle. A—$30

Eskimo **lidded basket,** polychrome geometric design, 4½ in. in diameter and 4½ in. high. G—$100

Two walrus **ivory carved seals,** set on soapstone base; done by Tom Mayac. A—$30

Eskimo basket, 4½ in. in diameter and 3 in. high. Basket has geometric designs, and is in good condition. G—$65

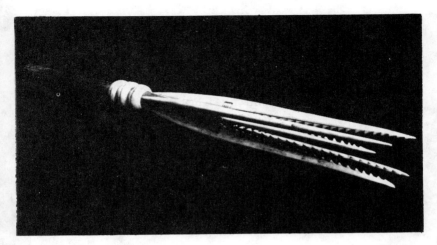

IVORY SPEAR POINT, Eskimo, 9¾ in. (25 cm) long.   G — Not listed.
Photo and item courtesy Walrus Gallery, Kennebunkport, Maine.

The following are recent auction results, all concerning Eskimo items. The material is courtesy Rod Sauvageau, Trade Winds West Auction Gallery, Vancouver, Washington. Used with permission.

Eskimo skin parka.   A—$235

Eskimo basket, large, 13½ in. by 15½ in.   A—$75

Eskimo whalebone mask, by Alex Frankson of Point Hope, Alaska. Piece has ivory teeth and eyes, with baleen pupils and jade labrets.
     A—$125

Eskimo bracelet, ivory on fossilized ivory; a fine carving with gold nugget.   A—$170

Eskimo adz, long-handled and with stone blade and oogruk lashing.
     A—$80

Ivory carving, unusual, of Eskimo man hunting walrus with a gun. Polychrome, and ca. 1890.   A—$400

Eskimo caribou hunter's belt, with teeth, beads, and cartridge case suspensions. Belt has 248 sets of caribou front teeth.   A—$1450

Eskimo bracelet of fossilized ivory, with finely carved relief of polar bears. A—$135

Eskimo storyboard, with many carved figures attached. A—$975

Two Eskimo harpoons and an ivory harpoon point. One lot. A—$180

Walrus ivory cribbage board, by Joe Ignatius. A—$260

Eskimo bolas, set of 14, used for hunting birds. A—$35

Eskimo miniature sled, made of caribou jaw, with baleen bottom. A—$40

Eskimo applique skin mat, 38 in. in diameter, and an exceptional piece. A—$850

Eskimo tom cod jigging outfit, complete with baleen line, ivory weight and lure. A—$45

Eskimo whalebone snow shovel. A—$115

Eskimo carver's box, filled with items relating to carving. A—$225

Eskimo fish net and line made of hide. A—$180

Eskimo skin boots, very old. A—$80

Eskimo kayak paddle, full size. A—$70

Eskimo cup, made from the jaw of a walrus. A—$80

Eskimo small-game harpoon, fine piece. A—$75

Two Eskimo bow-drills. A—$160

Eskimo doll, fur and wood, from the Kuskokwim River Delta. A—$25

Eskimo baleen woven box, with ivory lid and bottom. A—$240

CONTEMPORARY ESKIMO & ALEUT ITEMS

The material that follows is a selection of typical and authentic artifacts and artworks from the Alaskan region. All examples are from the current Alaska Native Arts & Crafts catalog; used by permission.

Game sled, weight two pounds, with walrus ivory sled on base made of fossilized ivory. G—$170

Ivory birds, from 1½ in. to 4½ in. in length. Artists include works by Peter Mayac and by Kokuluk. Birds have wings etched in india ink and colored beaks and feet; ivory birds can be purchased with or without bases.

Smaller birds, G—$110
Larger birds, G—$165

Whalebone mask, from Point Hope, Alaska, 9 in. high and 6 in. wide. Use of bone shows that very few parts of the whale go to waste. G—$115
(Price range on plain to elaborate masks is $80—$135.)

Masks, made of caribou skin, with wolf or fox trim; these are made in the community of Anaktuvuk Pass in the Brooks Mountain Range. Size is 9 in. high and 5 in. wide. The masks began as a Halloween prank many years ago, but have since become art objects to the trade. G—$45—$95

"Strong Man" mask, by Willie Marks of Hoonah. Mask depicts an ancient legend in which a youth is strong enough to save his village from sea demons. Item, 9 in. high and 7 in. wide. G—$135

Ivory pendant, of fossilized ivory, constructed and etched by Lincoln Nayapuk of Shishmaref. Pendant is a cross-section of fossil ivory, 2½ in. across. Pendant has gold chain. G—$69

Medium coil grass basket, from Kuskokwim Delta village of Kipnuk, showing use of both dried grass and seal gut. This membrane is very thin and strong; it is woven as an overlay to the grass. Quality depends on how well the seal gut is tied back into the grass. G—$142

Miniature harpoon, by Eric Tetpon of Shaktoolik, and 14 in. long. The detachable ivory head is tied to the wooden shaft with sinew.

G—$40

Ivory owl, by Keith Oozeva, from recently harvested walrus ivory. All three layers of walrus ivory tusk can be seen. Owl's eyes are darkened with india ink and wing outlines are etched and countersunk.

G—$52

Dyed grass and seal gut basket, 11 in. in diameter and 10 in. high. Basket handcrafted from marsh grasses collected in the summer months; patterns are whipped into the basketry by using dyed grass and sometimes dyed seal gut. Made by Mrs. Milton Mandigo of Chefornak.

G—$195

Soapstone carvings on various themes, all hand-carved:

Soapstone bird, 6 in. long, by Levi Tetpon,   G—$22
Soapstone kayak, 5 in. long, by Walton Tetpon,   G—$42
Soapstone bear, 10 in. high, by Robert Tevuk,   G—$230

MUSK OX PRODUCTS

For contemporary fashion-clothing items made from the soft, brown underwool of the musk ox, write:

Musk Ox Producers'
  Cooperative
604—H Street
Anchorage, Alaska 99501

Suggested Reading

(By the Editors), *Indians of the Americas,* The National Geographic Society, 1955

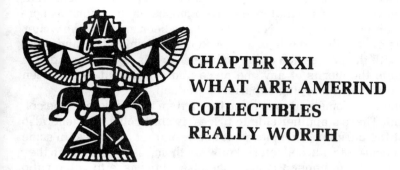

CHAPTER XXI
WHAT ARE AMERIND
COLLECTIBLES
REALLY WORTH

Here is a look at the four major sources for prices used in this Guidebook. They are each, in their special way, valid interpretations of value.

A, or auction, puts down an actual, recent, high bid. Since bidders are often present for a pre-viewing, many catalogs do not fully describe the piece sold, or the small details that can make a big difference in bids. Regional and human factors also are important.

An East Coast object may be auctioned on the West Coast at a lower price than in the "home territory", and vice-versa. Or, an item may go much higher than usual because of keen competition evidenced by spirited and high bidding. The auction may cover a large and respected collection, in which case the prices are likely to be higher than usual.

Or, bad weather may keep important out-of-state collectors away, with bids then somewhat lethargic. On the whole, auction prices should "average out", and be a fairly close indication of item values.

C, or collector prices, would seem to be the most accurate, because the owner has had time to study objects and make comparisons. Contributors were in all cases asked to set a "fair market value", and most did. The collector, in his or her collecting field(s), tends to keep abreast of "going rates". While the collector attempts to purchase and evaluate realistically, other angles can be considered.

People and interests change. In a few cases, collectors got into Amerind objects and then, for whatever reasons, kept the collection but did not continue active collecting. In such cases, the "C" listings were below current market rates and were either dropped from the book or, with the collector's permission, were corrected to reflect current set prices and ranges.

Correspondingly—and the psychology of pricing enters strongly here—several collectors sent photos and descriptions of items that may have been somewhat over-valued, based on the nebulous concept of fair market price. No changes have been made by the writer in this area unless the figure seemed outlandishly high, and then, only with the permission of the collector. So it is up to the reader to evaluate the merits of any one piece and relate that to the given figure—quite a learning experience in itself.

Collectors sometimes pay more for an item to complete a type collection. There's another side to prices, in that collectors tend also to get the bargains, fine pieces at below market averages. In some instances—and all collectors know of them, especially that they always seem to happen to someone else—purchase to value ratio would be a few cents on the dollar. Such windfalls are probably reflected occasionally in the Guidebook, being lower priced, but examples would not be common.

D, or dealer, is a good source of study, for in most cases dealers are in the field of Amerind collectibles for both love and money. Love, because that is how they choose to spend a great deal of time and effort. Money, because to exist as dealers they must average a certain profit to continue the business.

Further, dealers, probably more than any other source-category, must be aware of what collectors want, and how much they are willing to pay for items, common-grade to select. Many dealers offer a wide range of good pieces. Most concentrate in one of the three major Amerind collecting time-spans, prehistoric, historic or contemporary.

G, or gallery, is a special classification, and the writer defines a gallery as a business which is concentrated in a limited Amerind collecting field. That area is irrelevant, and a characteristic is high-quality, authentic pieces. The owner or manager may also be very knowledgable in his or her own right, and tends to deal with advanced collectors.

For the beginner—and not referring necessarily to classifications of A, C, D, or G—it would be wise to pay nearly as much attention to the seller as to the desired object itself. To be a good purchase, the item must offer both authenticity and high quality, both of which should also be reflected by the seller.

For example, America is loosening up a bit, getting away from traditional antiques shops, dealers and second-hand stores in pursuit of collectibles. All and more have been combined in the great buy-sell-trade arenas called flea markets.

True, tremendous bargains can be obtained when the wise collector spots a good Amerind piece at a giveaway price. Sometimes a tremendous buy turns out to be "hot stuff", stolen goods. Then the collector is left with an item that cannot be displayed or sold, or even admired with an easy mind.

In all categories of Amerind collectibles, but especially those from prehistoric and historic times, there is a chance that damage has occurred. Very minor damage can merely be taken as a sign of authenticity, depending on the type; however, major damage detracts from value. Sometimes, major damage has been concealed by a veriety of methods. This may not have been done to deceive, and the seller may not even know that a piece has been restored.

No matter how the item came to be restored and no matter how well the work has been done, the piece is still not as valuable as a complete and original specimen. And it should not be sold as such or paid for as such. Check out the various methods that have been used in any area you are interested in collecting, for restoration can be quite subtle.

Regarding Amerind collectibles as a whole, a friend has some interesting observations: "The goal is to get a superb piece in excellent condition, and at a good price. Steady buying in the $1—$10 range, the purchases are just a hobby. In the $10—$100 range, it is still a hobby, but a serious one. And in the $100—$1000-and-above range, the buyer is involved with fine art—or had well better be!"

Attribution can be tricky. In buying an historic Amerind item that is said to have been owned by a known historic figure—or a contemporary object made by a "name" craftsperson—be sure all documentation is in order. Be sure the documentation is also authentic.

Be equally certain that if the item is being sold as having been in a long-time collection, that that is factually the case. Many large collections are sold at public auction by specialized auctioneers. Buying from them, you can be sure of the source, and you are also buying, at competitive prices, directly from that collection.

Collector demand in a specific area can send prices nearly beyond the financial reach of average collectors. The high prices of good pieces are partly the result of competition, plus some inflation. Also add to this the fast-growing awareness that genuine Amerind items of prehistoric, historic and recent times are limited in number, while collector demand increases.

Only in the area of recent and contemporary jewelry—silver, turquoise and other valuable metals and stones—does the material itself make up a significant part of the value. Otherwise, and with a few exceptions, the actual material is of limited worth.

What, really, is the value of several pounds of deer hide, the quills from a few porcupines and the sinew from a bison? And yet, all worked into a Plains Indian dress, the current owner has quite a treasure.

The real worth of the majority of Amerind items is a different sort of worth, and has to do with a number of factors. One of the things that definitely intrigues collectors is that everyday materials were treated in unique ways. They were made into items quite different from those known to our prevailing culture.

Beyond the importance of the basic form, decoration of almost any kind, if harmonious with the form, adds to value. In short, and a repetition of what the whole Guidebook is about, collecting good Amerind pieces is collecting good art. A Picasso, for instance, is not valued at ten dollars worth of paint and canvas.

As the value of the basic material increases, this contributes to overall value today. Ivory is generally more valuable than bone and gem-quality flint more valuable than listless, drab chert. Even in White-made goods, an iron and steel-bladed pipe-tomahawk is more valuable than an all-iron head. The better the material the higher the price.

For the book, price ranges are helpful in that they give an idea of upper and lower price structures. The actual price is even more useful, in that there is no doubt what the piece sold for or is currently valued at. As to terms used, the words "piece", "specimen", "item" and so on are used interchangeably throughout the Guidebook.

People in the field of Amerind collectibles, with only a few collecting area exceptions (old baskets), tend to be vocally aware of the problem of fakes. The writer acknowledges similar feelings, but there is a danger that people who are just starting collecting may feel that every other piece is nonauthentic, questionable, etc. Sweeping statements have been made regarding the supposed percentage of fakes in certain collecting areas, and each expert has a different expert opinion.

Several things need to be said. The problem of spurious specimens, bad pieces, is not confined to the field of Amerind collectibles, nor will it be. Artifacts and artworks "in the style of" earlier periods, and for which a market demand exists, have been around for thousands of years. This is so from coins and stamps to furniture and glass and paintings.

Unless one has many years of in-depth experience, an encyclopedia-like knowledge of all other collecting areas, and a computer's capacity and speed of summation, few accurate comparisons can be made. All collecting fields of things that are worth collecting will have the problem. But—the chances of a person being "taken" decrease in direct proportion to that person's knowledge of what is being collected.

Keeping in mind several key characteristics of Amerind-made collectibles—that they are and were largely created in unique forms and styles, and with a great deal of time spent in that making — what might be some good collecting areas for the future?

In the prehistoric field, chipped artifacts predominate. Prices tend to be high for large blades and those of exceptional materials. Often overlooked are the mundane tools like scrapers, which may evidence both excellent materials and workstyles.

Some hardstone tools are probably under-priced, but the type varies with the locality. Good axes are now high and will certainly go higher. Slate forms, especially the less dramatic specimens, are probably a good bet. Items like effigy slates will one day approach the prices of average birdstones.

In the historic Amerind fields, there are of course two types of collectibles, those made by Whites and those made by Amerinds. Both have appreciated greatly in the last decade, with collector focus on items used for war or hunting, in the trade iron field. Strike-a-lights might be good, plus any trade objects entirely or partly made of copper or brass.

Smaller historic Amerind pieces of good beadwork ought to be solid buys, if only because more collectors will be able to afford them in the future. Some plainer containers, basketry and pottery, are still priced at reasonable levels. Often pieces made for the early 1900's tourist trade have excellent quality.

In the contemporary collectibles field, jewelry is still very much in demand. There are so many aspects to this field that only very general guidelines can be given. First, learn as much as possible about good silver, turquoise and shell. If the contemplated object is a poor-grade piece, it is not a bargain no matter how many times it has been sale-discounted.

Also, buy only what appeals to you personally, jewelry you can live with easily and proudly. Last—and even the experts repeat this time and again—buy only from a reputable source. This above all is your guarantee of quality at a fair price.

There are two fields of contemporary collectibles that the writer feels have been somewhat overlooked. One is good baskets by non-famous makers; the other is good weavings by competent makers.

The amount of time—exclusive of gathering and preparing the materials—that goes into a 6 in. diameter basket is amazing. Faye Stouff, Chetimacha Indian basket weaver of Route 2, Jeanerette, Louisiana, advised the writer that at least three days are required to make one of her smaller pine-needle coiled and split-stitch lidded baskets. In the opinion of the writer, the work of this crafts-lady—and many similar Indian artisans—will triple in value in the next few years.

Weavings, in terms of time/price, are much the same on a larger scale, with the average non-famous weaver working at something like half the national minimum-wage rate. Reading between the lines of statements made by a number of authorities, here are some things that are happening in the basketry and weaving areas.

The Indian craftspeople have recognized they are spending a great deal of time on work that yields very little monetary return; almost anything else, workwise, pays much better. Contrary to some popular beliefs, most Indians in this country do not make a living with arts and crafts. Probably fewer than five percent are so-involved.

In a number of cases, only a few skilled older people are still at work, and their productions will not be found in the market-place in quantity. That's now, and in the future. It would probably not be a bad idea to concentrate on collecting items made by the smaller Amerind groups. This not only helps support such craftspeople, but their work is often superior to more publicized creations.

Good-quality jewelry, by all signs, is still a good buy, whether from the standpoint of use or investment. In fact, when the U.S. dollar sinks drastically on the international currency market, there are a number of people who place excess funds in quality Indian jewelry.

Pieces purchased are often in the $500-$1000 range, and so do not diminish the supply for the typical collector or casual buyer, or unduly elevate prices. For top-quality pieces, it has always been a seller's market, always in demand.

There was some concern when the Guidebook was being put together that auction (A) values would predominate. There is a feeling among some collectors that auction prices tend to be higher than average. "After all", a collecting friend said, "Don't forget that the winning bid is one 'raise' above what every other bidder thought the item was worth".

Perhaps so, but auctions still, on average, do not noticably price items beyond a fair market value. In fact, the writer is aware of non-publicized, single-item sales between advanced collectors, or dealers and collectors, that are well above several type categories listed.

As to what American Indian items are really worth, there is a stock reply that insists any one piece is worth whatever the seller can get for it. Not really, because both seller and buyer may have reached monetary (or trade material) agreement on a value, but that may still be high or low for the type.

It is, the writer suggests, the medium figure (of many such similar-item exchanges) that can give a resonable idea of fair market value. And the collector goes on from there.

Inscription House Ruin, one of the three largest and most elaborate of known cliff dwellings. The other two are Betatakin and Keet Steel.

Photo courtesy of U.S. Department of the Interior, National Park Service.

Prehistoric dwellings and storage areas constructed in natural dry and shallow caves. Note human, left center, for proportion. Gila Cliff Dwellings National Monument, New Mexico.

Photo courtesy of U.S. Department of the Interior, National Park Service.

CHAPTER XXII
HELPFUL AGENCIES

The average person interested in contemporary and traditional American Indian materials might like to know something about two very relevant agencies. One is professional, the other governmental.

The trade organization is the Indian Arts and Crafts Association, commonly referred to as I.A.C.A. or IACA. The United States government agency is the Indian Arts and Crafts Board of the U. S. Department of the Interior. Both have kindly given permission for use of pertinent facts. IACA is discussed first.

INDIAN ARTS AND CRAFTS ASSOCIATION

The Indian Arts and Crafts Association is a national non-profit association of traders, museums, collectors, individual Indian craftspeople, tribal co-ops and guilds.

Its primary purposes include the promotion of Indian arts and crafts, development of a worldwide security system to reduce theft of Indian arts, and maintenance of high ethical standards.

An important part of the IACA security program is a marking system which makes use of the National Crime Information Computer for faster, more efficient and wider coverage than any previous state of local program.

The IACA is active in introducing and supporting legislation that provides stiff penalties for misrepresentation of Indian arts and crafts.

Members are pledged to guarantee honest representation of any and all items they sell. Any member who, after a complete investigation of both sides, is found to be in violation of the IACA

Code of Ethics, is ejected from the IACA. The information gathered is turned over to the appropriate authorities if there has been possible violation of federal, state or local law. All complaints are handled on a confidential basis for the protection of both parties.

Finally, the IACA acts as a clearing house for information that individuals, organizations or firms may request on Indian arts and crafts.

In short, if a business displays the IACA seal of membership, that means the personnel will honestly and correctly represent its merchandise as to nature and origin. The IACA additionally sponsors regular seminars by Indian craftspeople and other recognized experts on both Indian arts and crafts and cultures.

Following, reprinted in full, is the IACA Code of Ethics. All members of the Indian Arts and Crafts Association agree to adhere to these principles.

IACA CODE OF ETHICS

1. To honestly represent American Indian arts and crafts as to nature and origin within the realm of their control and to offer return privileges for articles found by the Indian Arts and Crafts Association to have been misrepresented.

2. To abide by all Federal, state, and local, and tribal laws pertaining to Indian arts and crafts, artifacts, and natural resources.

3. To abide by ethical business conduct regarding advertising, appraising, pricing, and guarantees offered.

4. To respect and support ethical business activities of all Indian Arts and Crafts Association members.

5. To encourage consumer confidence in the authenticity of articles identified with the IACA seal.

6. To cooperate with law enforcement agencies and the IACA in the investigation of crimes involving Indian arts and crafts and to promote proper identification of Indian arts and crafts.

Anyone may obtain a free Directory of Members simply by writing and requesting same.

Write to: Indian Arts and Crafts Association
             2401—12th Street N.W.
             Albuquerque, New Mexico 87102

As another example of IACA work, the Association has recently drawn up Guidelines for ethical appraisal practices. The recommended guidelines section alone has twelve key parts, while eleven containments are suggested for the actual appraisal report.

The purpose of the IACA Ethical Appraisal Guidelines is ". . . to provide a needed service to our clients and to encourage public trust in the objectivity and competence of appraisals performed by IACA members".

Finally, in its role of introducing and supporting legislation, the IACA has been instrumental in amending New Mexico's Indian Arts and Crafts Sales Act, which is considered by many to be one of the few state legal Indian arts and crafts acts with "teeth". It is Chapter 334, 1977 Laws, 1st Session of the 33rd Legislature, State of New Mexico.

According to Jean E. Herzegh, IACA Executive Director (personal communication): "This is now one of the better laws in the U.S. This can and is being used as 'model legislation' in other states which need to up-date and improve existing statutes, and to guide introduction of legislation in other states with no laws."

The Act includes a legal definition of terms commonly used (Indian handcrafted; natural turquoise), required duties of arts and crafts dealers, unlawful acts (mainly, misrepresentation), and possible penalties for such unlawful acts.

Included is possible action by the state attorney general (". . . civil penalties not to exceed five thousand dollars per violation . . ."), as well as a private right of action. This last means the damaged party can sue for damages in district court.

Legislation of the sort just mentioned will, both in short-term and long-range, help assure the buyer that he or she is getting exactly what the item is supposed to be. Such legislation offers three-way protection, to the authentic Indian-made goods and the Indian craftspeople, the reputable dealers, and the buyer.

Another helpful agency is **THE INDIAN ARTS AND CRAFTS BOARD OF THE U.S. DEPARTMENT OF THE INTERIOR.** Established in 1935, the Board promotes the development of Native American arts and crafts—the creative work of Indian, Eskimo, and Aleut peoples.

The Indian Arts and Crafts Board concentrated on stimulating what Indian arts and crafts existed, and engaged in aiding production, in marketing and public awareness. Eventually, advisory groups—such as the Navajo Arts and Crafts Guild, and the Alaska Native Arts and Crafts—were soundly established.

A demand for authenticity and quality increased, and training programs were set up. These concentrated on individual craftspeople, with teaching by example. The reason is well-expressed in this extraction from the Board's recent Fact Sheet:

"This is because, in any art of any culture in history, it has always been impossible to separate absolutely the influence of the whole culture from the unique influence of the individual. An artist expresses both background and a special view of it in the work, and an individual whose work is good inspires and stimulates many others in the immediate community and beyond."

The Board actively assists artists and craftspeople to develope co-operative marketing organizations and to advance professional careers. A special emphasis has been placed on helping Native leaders regarding the preservation and evolution of Native culture in the years ahead.

The Board's Advisory Staff has played a major role in helping Native craftspeople and organizations counteract a wave of misrepresentation of imitation Indian-type crafts products that occurred as part of a fashion craze for things Indian. The Board served as a clearinghouse for information, and successfully gained the co-operation of state and local consumer protection officials, various Federal agencies, newspapers—all to heighten consumer awareness to discriminate between genuine and imitation products.

As a result of these efforts, major distributors began to show a much greater sensitivity to honest representation in their marketing. The staff's continuing effort is to help Native people to register trademarks in the U.S. Patent and Trademark Office, so that their work can receive full legal protection when it is marketed.

The Board's Museums, Exhibitions and Publications Staff administers three Indian art museums. These were founded in the 1930's and 1940's by the U.S. Department of the Interior's Bureau of Indian Affairs, with advisory assistance from the Indian Arts and Crafts Board.

Each of these museums operates in a similar way. There is a permanent exhibition of historic tribal arts of the immediate region, plus a series of changing displays devoted to works by outstanding

Native American artists and craftspeople. Sales shops offer the customer some of the finest contemporary artworks to be found.

The museums operate year-round, and there is no admission charge. They are:

MUSEUM OF THE PLAINS INDIAN
P.O. Box E
Browning, Montana 59417

SOUTHERN PLAINS INDIAN MUSEUM
Highway 62 East
Anadarko, Oklahoma 73005

SIOUX INDIAN MUSEUM
P.O. Box 1542
Rapid City, South Dakota 57701

The sales shops at the museums are operated, respectively, by the Northern Plains Indian Crafts Association, the Oklahoma Indian Arts and Crafts Cooperative, and the Tipi Shop, Inc. These highly successful Native American arts businesses are independently operated, provide their own management and handle their own affairs. They buy works directly from the artists and craftspeople. The works are then offered to the public, either at the individual museum, or through mail order.

The Indian Arts and Crafts Board's Washington, D. C., office helps the buyer of Indian art in several ways. The Board periodically publishes, and updates, a Source Directory dealing with American Indian crafts organizations and individual workers. This lists only Native American owned and operated arts businesses throughout the United States.

Copies of the Source Directory can be obtained on request, by writing:

General Manager
U. S. Department of the Interior
Indian Arts and Crafts Board
Washington, D. C. 20240

In addition, the Washington office also issues a Bibliography listing major books on contemporary Indian arts titles. Single copies of the Bibliography will be sent, again, free, on request. Write the General Manager of the Board at the Washington address.

The writer recommends that the person interested in contemporary Indian arts and crafts obtain both the IACA Directory of Members and the Board's Source Directory. And books listed in the Bibliography can be found either in a library (another fine source of Amerind information) or at a bookstore.

The writer also recommends the Indian Craft Shop in Washington, D. C. This retail-only, no mail-order business (operated by Government Services, Inc.) has Indian and Eskimo arts and crafts, these obtained from cooperatives and artists and craftspeople. Hours are 8:30 AM - 4 PM, Monday through Friday. The address is:

Indian Craft Shop
Main Interior Building
18th/19th Streets on C/E Streets, N. W.
Washington, D. C. 20240

The **U. S. Department of the Interior's Bureau of Indian Affairs** also deserves mention here. The Bureau, in 1962, established the Institute of American Indian Arts. The purpose, as recommended by the Board, was to provide heritage-centered instruction to Indian youths with artistic talent.

Today, the Institute has achieved an international reputation for creative and innovative education. Now chartered as a junior college, many of the Institute's graduates are in the assertive vanguard of Indian artists and craftspeople.

The Institute has two public exhibits called Student Sales Shows, with a gallery of sales items priced by the students. The exhibits are held in May and December, both in the second week of the month. The Institute of American Indian Arts is located on Cerrillos Road in Santa Fe, New Mexico.

The Institute of American Indian Arts is also responsible for the Traveling Exhibit, called "One With The Earth". The Exhibit consists of fine contemporary Indian art, as well as historic pieces from the Institute's Honors Collection. The Exhibit includes pottery, sculpture, painting, beadwork, weaving, basketry and other creative works.

In the 1960's, fine Indian works of many kinds began to decorate the offices of the U. S. Department of the Interior. Appreciation spread until even U. S. embassies abroad used Indian art in their decor.

The Traveling Exhibits have toured Europe, the Far East, and South America. And now, full circle, the Exhibits are being shown in Native American communities.

The buyer/collector, it can be seen, has some valuable and powerful agencies which are extremely interested in seeing that American Indian arts and crafts are fairly and accurately represented at all times. Beginner and advanced collectors alike are advised to make use of the available information.

Very early photograph, taken in 1871. Scene is in a Pawnee village at Loup Fork, Nebraska, near Genoa. There are a number of very large earth-covered dwellings. Assemblage here may be of spectators to a dance or ceremony.

Photo courtesy of John A. Anderson Collection, Nebraska State Historical Society.

An exotic Indian meal: Sioux women singeing hair from just-killed dogs before they are roasted. Dogs were a favorite dish for some feasts.

Photo courtesy South Kakota State Historical Society.

CHAPTER XXIII
DIRECTORY

The Directory is intended as a guide to both selected businesses and further sources of information.

The criteria for inclusion of a shop, dealer or gallery in this section is that each has, in some important fashion, contributed to putting this book together. Each has been instrumental in providing factual data, photographs, necessary permission for use of material, or all three.

Some of the enterprises are long-established, others are relatively recent. Some keep regular business hours, others are by chance or appointment. As a further help, a brief notation is given regarding the main line of American Indian collectibles for that business. Besides those listed, other items are usually carried as well.

Before making a long trip, it would be best to call ahead and determine hours, current stock, special collectibles you might want to see, and so forth. A few businesses are mainly wholesale dealers to the trade, and will be so-noted. You would need to be a dealer to purchase there; however, your favorite shop can handle your order as intermediary.

The Directory to businesses handling American Indian material has been set up on a state basis, alphabetically.

DIRECTORY

THE AMERICANA GALLERIES
3901 East Anne Street
Phoenix, Arizona 85016
(602) 268-3477

Ancient and
Primitive Art

INDIAN RUINS TRADING POST
P.O. Box 46
Sanders, Arizona 86512
(602) 688-2787

Contemporary Silver & Turquoise

DON C. TANNER'S INDIAN GALLERY
7007—5th Avenue
Scottsdale, Arizone 85251
(602) 945-5416

Old Pawn Jewelry;
Other varieties

CADDO TRADING COMPANY AND GALLERY
Rt. 2, Box 669
Murfreesboro, Arkansas 71958
(501) 542-3652 / 524-6563

Moundbuilder Art

INDIAN ROCK GALLERY
P.O. Box 583
Davis, California 95616
(916) 758-2561

Old and Contemporary Pottery

WHISPERING PINES GALLERY
8243 La Mesa Boulevard
Le Mesa, California 92041
(714) 460-3096

Historic and
Other Material

THE ANSEL ADAMS GALLERY
Village Mall / Box 455
Yosemite National Park,
   California 95389
(209) 372-4211

Contemporary
Selections

AMERICAN INDIAN WORLD, LTD.
451 E. 58th Avenue, Room 1740
Denver, Colorada 80216
(303) 629-7208

Wholesale; wide
selection, Contemporary

TOH-ATIN TRADING COMPANY
145 West 9th Street
Durango, Colorado 81301
(303) 247-1252 / 247-8277

Wholesale; Old and
Contemporary

JAY EVETTS
Yoder, Colorado 80864
(303) 478-2248

Navajo blankets,
Early rugs, historic
pottery

THE WALRUS GALLERY
10 Ocean Avenue
Kennebunkport, Maine 04046
(207) 967-2264

Indian and
Eskimo Art

KHALSA Trading Company
1423 Carlisle N.E.
Albuquerque, New Mexico 87110
(505) 255-8278

Contemporary
Jewelry

EDMUNDS OF YARMOUTH, INC.
P.O. Box 788
West Yarmouth, Massachusetts 02673
(617) 775-9303

Contemporary
Indian material

Indian Room
FORT MILLE LACS VILLAGE
Onamia, Minnesota 56359
(612) 532-3651

Old and Contem-
porary Arts &
Crafts

PLAINS INDIAN ART
609 Greenway Terrace
Kansas City, Missouri 64113
(816) 361-1599

Plains Indian
Items, many types

HYDE'S
P.O. Box 2304
Santa Fe, New Mexico 87501
(505) 983-2096

Historic; Plains
Indian

PACKARD'S CHAPARRAL TRADING POST
61 Old Santa Fe Trail
Santa Fe, New Mexico 87501
(505) 983-9241

Old and Contem-
porary Items

FENN GALLERIES LTD.
1075 Paseo de Peralta
Sante Fe, New Mexico 87501
(505) 982-4631

Plains Indian
Materials

CASA KAKIKI
P.O. Box 111
Sunland Park, New Mexico
(915) 584-0195

Contemporary
Jewelry;

WINONA INDIAN TRADING POST
211 - 213 Galisteo Street
Santa Fe, New Mexico 87501
(505) 988-4811

Plains, Southwest,
Northwest, Eskimo

SUMMERS REDICK
35 West Riverglen Drive
Worthington, Ohio 43085
(614) 885-0665

Prehistoric
Artifacts

JAMES O. APLAN
HC 80 / Box 793-25
Piedmont, South Dakota 57769
(605) 347-5016

Plains Indian
Items

CRAZY CROW TRADING POST
107 North Fannin
Denison, Texas 75020
(214) 341-7715

Plains and
Historic Items

MANITOU GALLERY
1718 Capitol Avenue
Cheyenne, Wyoming 82001
(307) 635-0019

Original Indian
Materials

Another good source for authentic Amerind material is:

KACHINA SHOP
Denver Museum of Natural History
City Park
Denver, Colorado 80205
(303) 297-3813

One of the fine pleasures of collecting American Indian items of any kind is learning more about them and the people who made them. Books are an important source of information; following is a sourcelist of seven booksellers who carry a selection of books on Indian-related subjects.

BOOKS, INDIAN-RELATED:

COLLECTOR BOOKS
P.O. Box 3009
Paducah, Kentucky 42001

BOOKS AMERICANA
P.O. Box 2326
Florence, AL 35630

GEM GUIDE BOOKS
315 Cloverleaf Dr.
Suite F
Baldwin Park, CA 91706

GOLDEN AGE ARMS CO.
West Winter St.
Delaware, Ohio 43015

HOTCHKISS HOUSE
18 Hearthstone Road
Pittsford, New York 14534

INDIAN HILLS TRADING
COMPANY
P.O. Box 546
Petoskey, Michigan 49770

IROQRAFTS, LTD.
RR #2, Oshweken
Ontario, Canada
NOA IMO

Hothem House
P.O. Box 458
Lancaster, Ohio 43130

PUBLISHER'S CENTRAL
BUREAU
1 Champion Avenue
Avenel, New Jersey 07131

THE REFERENCE RACK
P.O. Box 445
Orefield, Pennsylvania 18069

R. M. WEATHERFORD-Books
10902 Woods Creek Rd.
Monroe, WA 98272

WALLACE-HOMESTEAD
BOOK CO.
One Chilton Way
Radnor, PA 19089

AMERICAN INDIAN BOOKS
9911 Torigney
St. Louis, Missouri 63126

MACRAE'S INDIAN BOOK
DISTRIBUTORS
P.O. Box 652
Enumclaw, Washington 98022

Auctions are one very good way to obtain exceptional American Indian items, and here are three that have such sales on a regular basis. Write for information on Indian-item mailing lists.

AUCTION HOUSES

TRADE WINDS WEST AUCTION GALLERY
P.O. Box 4306
Vancouver, Washington 98662

GARTH'S AUCTIONS, INC.
2690 Stratford Road
Delaware, Ohio 43015

SOTHEBY, PARKE BERNET, INC.
980 Madison Avenue
New York City, 10021

PAINTER CREEK AUCTION SERVICE
10040 S.R. 224 West
Findley, Ohio 45840

AMATEUR ARCHEOLOGICAL ORGANIZATIONS

The archeological societies are excellent for learning more about American Indians and their cultures, especially the earlier peoples. The cost of belonging is nominal; while many have regional names, membership is nationwide.

These non-profit organizations concentrate on education, and the dissemination of facts about prehistoric lifeways. Each of the societies puts out a quarterly journal, and these alone are reason enough to become a member.

Most states and regions have such archeological groups. Six of the major organizations are listed here, from East to West, and some areas between the two. You may write, at no obligation, to the society that interests you. Thus you can easily learn what the society is and does, and how to become a member.

THE CENTRAL STATES ARCHAELOGICAL SOCIETIES
6118 Scott
Davenport, IA 52806

EASTERN STATES ARCHAEOLOGICAL FEDERATION
RD #2, Box 166
Dover, Delaware 19901

GENUINE INDIAN RELIC SOCIETY, INC.
3416 Lucas-Hunt Road
St. Louis, Missouri 63121

OHIO ARCHAEOLOGICAL SOCIETY
5210 Coonpath Road
Pleasantville, Ohio 43148

OKLAHOMA ANTHROPOLO-
GICAL SOCIETY
1000 Horn Street
Muskogee, Oklahoma 74401

OREGON ARCHAEOLOGICAL SOCIETY
P.O. Box 13293
Portland, Oregon 97213

COLLECTOR'S WHO'S WHO

Your attention is directed to a hardcover book series called *Who's Who In Indian Relics*. (Early editors were Hubert C. Wachtel, Dayton, Ohio and more recently, Cameron W. Parks, Garrett, Indiana; recent editor is Ben W. Thompson, Kirkwood, Missouri.) In the writer's opinion, these books are invaluable in collecting fields for the prehistoric and historic time-spans.

Each book (with No. 8 underway; Nos. 1-6 are collectors' items in themselves) is a North American guide, with biographical data, to hundreds of major collectors. Amerind items range from the early prehistoric to contemporary goods. Many thousand fine artifacts and artworks are shown.

For further information, write:

Janie Weidner
Who's Who Editor
P.O. Box 88
Sunbury, OH 43074

PUBLICATIONS

There are three publications in the field of American Indian items that the writer does not hesitate to recommend. These periodicals cover artifacts, handicrafts and artworks of many kinds. You may write directly to the publications, as listed below, for subscription information.

Editor
THE INDIAN TRADER
P.O. Box 1421
Gallup, New Mexico 87305

Pamela Forbes McLane
Managing Editor
AMERICAN INDIAN ART Magazine
7045 Third Avenue
Scottsdale, Arizona 85251

Editor
INDIAN-ARTIFACT Magazine
RD No. 1, Box 240
Turbotville, Pennsylvania 17772

SOME FINAL NOTES . . .

To remain faithful to materials sent by contributors, and to demonstrate the variety in words, spelling of key terms has not been standardized. In fact, there is often no single "correct" version.

A good example is "heishe" which appears in half a dozen slightly different ways. The guideline has been that such words must resemble one another only to the extent that there is no confusion as to the intended meaning.

If anyone who contributed to the book was not thanked in the Acknowledgment section or listed in the Directory or credited with photographs that were published, you have the writer's apology in advance. Any such oversight will be corrected in subsequent editions.

Any reader who feels an important area of American Indian collectibles was either not recognized or was insufficiently covered may contact the writer, in care of the publisher. If quality photographs and authoritative information are available, the requirements for possible future contributions can be discussed.

GLOSSARY
POINT AND BLADE TYPES

⅓ Approximate size

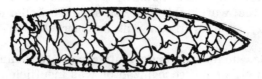

Dovetail (St. Charles) Blade

Fluted-base points

Folsom
(Paleo)

Triangular
Arrowhead
(unnotched)

Clovis-type

Woodland Period

Hopewell point or blade
(notched)

Adena point or blade
(stemmed)

Triangular
blade
(no notches or stem)

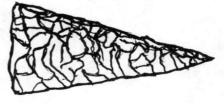

Archaic E-notch
beveled blade

Late-Paleo
stemmed & shouldered blade

Leaf shaped
Adena cache blade

Serrated edge
point or blade

Bifurcated-base
point or blade
(Archaic)

Late Arrowhead
Triangular, notched

Northwest Coast
Gempoint

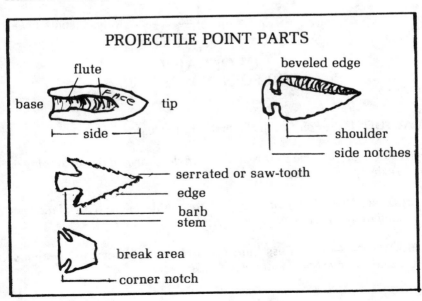

PROJECTILE POINT PARTS

415

COMMON AXE TYPES
Scale: 1/6

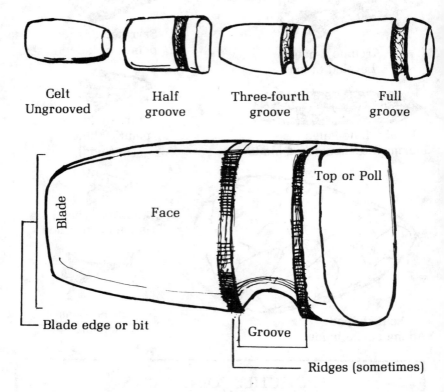

| Celt
Ungrooved | Half
groove | Three-fourth
groove | Full
groove |

GLOSSARY
FOR POINTS & BLADES

AUTHENTIC—*Point actually made in prehistoric times*

BEVEL—*Blade edge that is sharply angled, formed by rechipping or resharpening edge*

BIRFURCATE—*Point base split into double lobes with identation similar to notches on sides*

BIRDPOINT—*Small (less than 1 inch) late prehistoric arrowheads, either stemmed or notched at base*

BLANK—Otherwise finished point or blade but without base notches or stem put in

CACHE BLADE—Quantities of points or blades found together in an undergound depository or in a mound. Adena cache blades (large, leaf-shaped) are common in the Midwest

DUO-NOTCH—Point with double set of notches, but rare. A few duo-tipped points also exist

FAKE—Modern-made point passed off as authentic and old

FLUTE—Channel-chip taken from both faces of a Paleo point, extending towards tip. Shaft end fitted grooves and allowed deep penetration in target animal

FRACTURE-BASED—Special chipping techinque that knocked off long thin slivers of flint from point edges. Usually done on base bottom, occasionally on lower shoulders. May have been a chipping "short-cut"

GEMPOINT—Smallish points made of very high grade (colorful and/ or translucent flints), commonly found in the Pacific Northwest

GLOSSY—Flint with high surface sheen, usually denoting quality

GRINDING—Base of point or blade with sharp edges ground off and smoothed. Evidently done so binding thongs were not cut

HAFT—Means a method of fastening to shaft or handle, generally notches or stem. A "hafted shaft scraper" once had a handle

NOTCHES—Matching indentations in point base area, may be in base, at point corners or sides

OBSIDIAN—Common in western regions, this natural volcanic glass exists in shades of red, brown and black

PATINA—Surface coloration or thin deposits from soil chemicals; in short, how point exterior differs from interior fling

PERCUSSION FLAKING—Large flakes removed by direct or indirect blows from flaking hammer

POT-LID MARKS—*Conical depressions in flint that prove the item was once in a fire. Heat caused moisture in tiny hollows to expand and blow out a section of flint*

PRESSURE FLAKING—*Controlled flaking that used finger pressure to create delicate work, edge retouch, deep notches, etc.*

QUESTIONABLE—*Point or blade is probably not "good", ie., is a fake*

REPRODUCTION—*Modern point made without intent to deceive, as exercise in chipping skill*

SERRATIONS—*Saw-tooth projections on blade or point edges*

STEM—*Hafting method at base where flint extends in a central column*

TIP-BASE—*The top and bottom of point or blade*

TRANSLUCENT—*Chipped material that transmits a certain amount of light; usually means high quality*

WARPOINT—*Small, late prehistoric arrowheads with triangular configuration, without notches or stem*